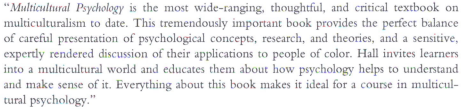

"*Multicultural Psychology* is the most wide-ranging, thoughtful, and critical textbook on multiculturalism to date. This tremendously important book provides the perfect balance of careful presentation of psychological concepts, research, and theories, and a sensitive, expertly rendered discussion of their applications to people of color. Hall invites learners into a multicultural world and educates them about how psychology helps to understand and make sense of it. Everything about this book makes it ideal for a course in multicultural psychology."

James M. Jones, *University of Delaware, USA*

"*Multicultural Psychology* presents a comprehensive and in-depth analysis of this important topic. This new edition provides up-to-date research on multicultural psychology's growing literature to introduce students to the centrality of multiculturalism in our life. *Multicultural Psychology* is a must read for all psychology students as well for everyone interested in multiculturalism."

Lillian Comas-Diaz, *George Washington University, USA*

Multicultural Psychology

Multicultural Psychology introduces students to the myriad ways in which multicultural issues affect our understanding of, and research in, a wide range of domains, including biological, developmental, social, and clinical psychological science. It provides in-depth coverage of the largest groups of color in the United States: African Americans, Latinx Americans, Asian Pacific Americans, and Native Americans. Students will gain an understanding of how race, ethnicity, and culture shape their own behavior, beliefs, interactions, and expectations, and those of the people around them.

New to this edition:

- New chapters on Clinical Psychology and Racial/Ethnic Identity and Acculturation
- Greater coverage of intersectional identities
- Incorporates up-to-date research from a rapidly growing literature
- Expanded coverage of qualitative research methods
- Companion Website where instructors will find PowerPoint slides and discussion questions, and students will find review questions and resource links

Gordon C. Nagayama Hall is a Professor of Psychology at the University of Oregon. His research interests are in culture and mental health with a particular interest in Asian Americans.

Multicultural Psychology

Third Edition

Gordon C. Nagayama Hall

Routledge
Taylor & Francis Group

NEW YORK AND LONDON

Third edition published 2018
by Routledge
711 Third Avenue, New York, NY 10017

and by Routledge
2 Park Square, Milton Park, Abingdon, Oxon, OX14 4RN

Routledge is an imprint of the Taylor & Francis Group, an informa business

© 2018 Taylor & Francis

First edition published by Pearson Education, Inc. 2002

Second edition published by Pearson Education, Inc. 2010

Library of Congress Cataloging in Publication Data
Names: Hall, Gordon C. Nagayama, author.
Title: Multicultural psychology / Gordon C. Nagayama Hall.
Description: Third edition. | New York, NY : Routledge, 2018. | Includes bibliographical references and index.
Identifiers: LCCN 2017035347| ISBN 9781138659773 (hb : alk. paper) | ISBN 9781138659797 (pb : alk. paper) | ISBN 9781315537092 (eb : alk. paper)
Subjects: LCSH: Ethnopsychology–United States. | Minorities–United States–Psychology.
Classification: LCC GN502 .H335 2017 | DDC 155.8/20973–dc23
LC record available at https://lccn.loc.gov/2017035347

ISBN: 978-1-138-65977-3 (hbk)
ISBN: 978-1-138-65979-7 (pbk)
ISBN: 978-1-315-53709-2 (ebk)

Typeset in Bembo
by Wearset Ltd, Boldon, Tyne and Wear
Visit the companion website: www.routledge.com/cw/hall

To my children and college students Jackie, Kashi, and Koko

Contents

Preface

When I was writing the first edition of this textbook 16 years ago, I did not think I would live long enough to see a non-White President of the United States. Eight years ago, when I wrote the second edition of this textbook, Barack Obama had been elected. At that time, I was hopeful that the United States would never again take a large step backwards with respect to the civil rights of people of color. The election of Donald Trump proved me wrong again.

Although Trump's election is seen by many as a major setback for people of color and other minority groups, the number of people of color in the United States is large and constantly growing. Psychology operates at its own peril if it overlooks people of color. Relegating multicultural psychology to a single course or, worse yet, to a single week of a course will not adequately prepare students to live and work in a country and world that already is multicultural. The material in this textbook is an introduction to the study of multicultural issues that should be addressed in all psychology courses. As can be seen in this textbook, multicultural psychology is relevant to all areas of psychology.

This is the third edition of *Multicultural Psychology*. The literature in this area has grown rapidly since the previous two editions. There are now multiple meta-analytic studies on populations of color, from which stronger conclusions can be drawn than from individual studies or narrative literature reviews. There is also more research on intersectional identities than before. Race/ethnicity, gender, and sexuality intersect in their influence on a person's identity.

I have retained the basic structure of the previous editions. After each chapter, I provide links to amplify the material from my *Psychology Today* blog, "Life in the Intersection: A Multicultural Psychology Approach." I also provide links to relevant videos.

The first section of the book is an Introduction to Multicultural Psychology. In Chapter 1, I have tried to make the material more accessible to readers who do not have a personal or academic background in multicultural psychology. I have used attitudes toward climate change, a topic that many are familiar with, as an analogy of people's attitudes toward cultural diversity. Chapter 2 on Racial/Ethnic Identity and Acculturation is a new chapter to this edition. The literatures in these areas have developed rapidly since the first two editions and now warrant a full chapter rather than being part of the introductory chapter. Chapter 3 is on Multicultural Research Methods, with more depth on qualitative methods than in the previous editions.

The second section is on Multicultural Issues in the Context of Psychology. Chapters 4 through 7 cover Biological Psychology, Developmental Psychology, Social Psychology, and Clinical Psychology. The Clinical Psychology chapter is new to this edition. In each chapter, I have selected three major issues in each field that impact people of color. The major issues in Biological Psychology are: (a) genetic psychology; (b) the emerging field of cultural neuroscience; and (c) health disparities. In Developmental Psychology, the issues are: (a) parents and families; (b) racial and ethnic identity; and (c) intersectional identities. The major issues in Social Psychology are: (a) current forms of discrimination; (b) stereotype threat; and (c) intergroup relations. In Clinical Psychology, the major issues are: (a) psychopathology; (b) underutilization of mental health services; and (c) culturally-adapted interventions.

The third section is on Psychology in the Context of Multicultural Issues. Chapters 8 through 11 provide more depth on African Americans, Asian Pacific Americans, Latinx Americans, and Native Americans. There is more empirical research on these groups than on other groups of color. Each chapter has three sections: (a) history; (b) gender roles; and (c) a prominent issue for each group based on its coverage in the literature. For each group, I address the intersections of racial/ethnic, gender, and sexual identities. The prominent issue for African Americans is religious and spiritual identity, for Asian Pacific Americans is the model minority myth, for Latinx Americans is *familismo*, and for Native Americans is historical trauma.

The groups of color that are missing from this textbook are notable. In the second edition of this book, I included a chapter on the emerging literature on multiracial Americans. This group continues to grow. However, the growth in the population has outpaced the research in this area. There are too few studies to consider the intersections of racial/ethnic, gender, and sexual identities among multiracial Americans (Charmaraman, Woo, Quach, & Erkut, 2014), as I have done with the other groups of color that I have covered. Similarly, the literature on Arab Americans is limited but growing. The recent *Handbook of Arab American Psychology* (Amer & Awad, 2016) offers excellent coverage of the literature that exists on this group.

If you are a person of color, this textbook is for you. I hope that you will see yourself reflected in this textbook in a way that is missing from most other psychology textbooks. If you aren't a person of color, this textbook is also for you. Multicultural issues are important for everyone in a multicultural world.

I thank Valerie Tsai for reviewing previous drafts of the book. I also thank my University of Oregon Writing Circle for giving me the motivation and accountability to complete the book. The Writing Circle included Jacques Abelman, Yvette Alex-Assensoh, Kemi Balogun, Ben Clark, Kathie Carpenter, Diane Del Guercio, Rachel DiNitto, Maria Escallon, Leigh Johnson, Dyana Mason, Sarah Stapleton, and Roxi Thoren. I also thank my wife, Jeanne Nagayama Hall, for her continuing encouragement throughout all three editions of this book.

Gordon C. Nagayama Hall
University of Oregon

Introduction to Multicultural Psychology

CHAPTER 1

WHAT IS MULTICULTURAL PSYCHOLOGY?

Joe is a 20-year-old European American man who is a college junior and is taking a multicultural psychology course to fulfill his university's multicultural education requirement. College is the most ethnically diverse setting that he has ever experienced. He likes psychology courses because they help him understand people. He has been taught by his parents and in school to be "color blind" and he feels that he treats everyone equally regardless of their background. His psychology courses so far have focused on people's similarities and there has been almost no attention to cultural differences. Joe considers himself open-minded but wonders why the emphasis in this course is on how people differ from one another.

Maria is a 19-year-old Mexican American woman who is a college sophomore and is excited about taking a multicultural psychology course because it is an opportunity to study her own cultural group. Maria grew up in a predominantly Mexican American community. College has been the first time in her life that she has felt like a minority.

She is pleased that the whole course is devoted to culturally diverse groups, unlike most of her psychology courses in which there is limited attention to diversity. In her other psychology courses, Maria has noticed that the research has primarily involved European Americans and she has wondered if these findings apply to other groups.

Joe and Maria have very different reasons for taking a course in multicultural psychology. For Joe, the course is something of an obligation and he is a bit skeptical. Conversely, Maria is enthusiastic about the focus on diversity. Joe may have been more comfortable in his other psychology courses because the focus on European Americans was an opportunity for him to study his own group. For Maria, the multicultural psychology course is one of her first opportunities in psychology to study Latina Americans. Your reasons for studying multicultural psychology may be similar to Joe's or Maria's or somewhere in between.

The United States consists of multiple groups with diverse and rich cultural backgrounds. Understanding this cultural diversity is critical to life in the United States.

Because the cultural groups in the United States have roots from around the world, understanding cultural diversity in the United States can also inform one's knowledge about global society. Yet, as Joe and Maria have accurately observed, most psychology courses do not focus on cultural diversity nor does most of the literature in psychology.

Joe likes psychology because it helps him understand people. However, a psychology without attention to cultural diversity does not adequately provide a current or future understanding of people. Nearly half of people in the United States under the age of 18 are not White (U.S. Bureau of the Census, 2015). Census data project that within 30 years the majority of both adults and children in the United States will not be White. Although 30 years may seem like a long way off, this population shift is already underway and the presence of non-White groups in the United States will become increasingly prominent. Personal, educational, and work experiences that include only European Americans are a thing of the past. In many large cities in the United States, people of color already are the majority, which was Maria's experience.

In this chapter, we will consider why, in a multicultural society, cultural diversity has been neglected in psychology. Definitions of multicultural psychology, race, ethnicity, culture, and minority status will be presented. The influence of social class on groups of color and the influences of multiple identities, known as intersectionality, are discussed. Consideration of multicultural issues leads to a better understanding of human behavior than when these issues are overlooked.

DEFINITIONS

It is useful to define some terms before we delve too deeply into the issues. *Culture* has traditionally been defined as involving attitudes, beliefs, norms, roles, and self-definitions shared and practiced by particular ethnic groups (Betancourt & López, 1993). Maria is likely aware of her Mexican American family's cultural practices (e.g., language, food, family responsibilities) whereas Joe may not frame his experiences in terms of culture and sees himself as an individual who is not heavily influenced by others. Yet, not framing one's experiences in terms of culture and perceiving oneself as unique is a culture (Oyserman, Coon, & Kemmelmeier, 2002). *Cultural diversity* is defined as the cultural differences within and between cultures of ethnic groups. The differences between Maria's and Joe's cultures may be more obvious than differences within their cultures. One source of difference within Maria's Mexican American culture is acculturation, with the immigrant generation being less acculturated to mainstream United States culture than generations born in the United States. There is also variability within Joe's European American culture. Not all European Americans are equally individualistic nor do all share the same political views.

Multicultural means multiple ways of knowing or multiple worldviews. Joe's worldview appears to be that his own experiences apply broadly to others, which is similar to the mainstream psychology worldview that research with European Americans is generalizable to other groups. Maria's worldview appears to be that one size does not fit all and that there are many differences across groups. *Multicultural psychology* is the study of the influences of multiple cultures in a single social context on human behavior (G. Hall & Barongan, 2002). A social context in which a group that shares the same culture interacts with other groups is known as a *sociocultural* context. Maria and Joe both are part of

Picture 1.1
Source: shutterstock.

the United States and their cultural backgrounds and the interactions of their cultural groups with other groups help shape the culture of the United States.

An *ethnic group* has a unique cultural/social heritage and practices (G. Hall, 2010). Japanese Americans and Mexican Americans are examples of ethnic groups. A *race* is a group of people with origins in a single geographic area who are more closely related than are members of groups who live greater distances apart (Wang & Sue, 2005). Phenotypic characteristics (e.g., skin color, facial features) are often one basis of perceptions of race. Racial differences in psychological characteristics are often presumed to be biologically based, but attributions of racial differences do not directly correspond with genetic variation (Wang & Sue, 2005). Although race may not be particularly useful as an actual biological entity, race is a *social construct*. This means that perceptions of race are used as a marker to determine which groups have access to resources in society, such as education, health care, and political power, and which groups do not (Smedley & Smedley, 2005).

When two or more groups are in a single sociocultural context, their interactions affect behavior. One effect of cultural group interaction is *bicultural orientation* in which a person may internalize more than one culture, such as learning two languages (Nguyen & Benet-Martinez, 2013). The group in the majority is more influential than groups in the minority, so minority groups may find it more necessary to become bicultural (e.g., learn English) than majority groups (e.g., learn Spanish).

There can also be negative effects of intergroup contact. *Prejudice* is a negative view of minority groups that may be experienced as anger, disgust, or fear (Earnshaw, Bogart, Dovidio, & Williams, 2013). A *stereotype* is an attribution of particular characteristics to a whole group of people, such as impulsivity, low intelligence, or even high intelligence.

Stereotypes are inaccurate because not all members of a group are the same. Nigerian novelist Chimamanda Adichie, in her popular 2009 TED talk, the *Danger of a Single Story* (www.ted.com/talks/chimamanda_adichie_the_danger_of_a_single_story), observed that "the problem with stereotypes is not that they are untrue, but that they are incomplete." Prejudice and stereotypes are often difficult to change even if a person who holds biased beliefs is exposed to people who are counter-stereotypical. People who are counter-stereotypical (e.g., African American astrophysicist Neil deGrasse Tyson) may be viewed as exceptions to the rule.

Discrimination is unfair behavior based on prejudice or stereotypes. For example, a math department at a university may have a poor record of hiring European American women or people of color because of prejudice against or stereotypes about the excellence of members of these groups. Prejudice and stereotypes do not have to be overt or blatant to influence behavior. A person could justify discrimination on grounds that are apparently unrelated to prejudice or stereotypes, such as where a person went to school or how they would fit in a department. Although anyone can engage in prejudice, stereotyping, and discrimination, those in the majority often have more power to exclude others (e.g., hiring) than those in the minority.

Some may believe or contend that the United States is a post-racial society since the election of Barack Obama as President in 2008. Yet, ethnically- and racially-based discrimination persists. An online survey of over 3000 adults in the United States (American Psychological Association, 2016) indicated that over 70% of people of color vs. 61% of all adults experienced everyday discrimination as defined by the following events:

- You are treated with less courtesy or respect than other people.
- You receive poorer service than other people at restaurants or stores.
- People act as if they think you are not smart.
- People act as if they are afraid of you.
- You are threatened or harassed.

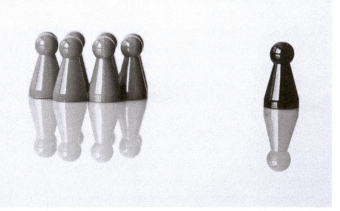

Picture 1.2
Source: courtesy of Pixabay.

The percentages of people in the United States by ethnic group who have experienced everyday discrimination are presented in Figure 1.1. European Americans, who are included in the "all adults" category, experience discrimination but less so than people of color. In addition, 39% of African American men (vs. 19% of all men) reported that police had unfairly stopped, searched, questioned, physically threatened, or abused them. More than a third of Asian American men reported being unfairly denied a work promotion (vs. 24% of all men).

In addition to being bicultural, people's identities are intersectional. *Intersectionality* involves the simultaneous consideration of multiple categories of identity, such as gender, race, class, and sexual orientation (E. Cole, 2009). Any identity (e.g., gender) cannot be fully understood in isolation. A bicultural Latina American is a woman who may also be middle class and lesbian. This intersectionality provides both similarities to and differences from others. For example, she may be similar to other Latina American women but dissimilar to Latina American heterosexual women. Her identity as a woman may make her similar to European American women but her middle class identity may make her dissimilar to lower socioeconomic status European American women. The data previously reported from the national survey suggest that being an African American man is associated with risk for police profiling more than being African American or being a man (American Psychological Association, 2016). Thus, any single identity exists in the context of other identities. Identities are characteristics of the individual as well as

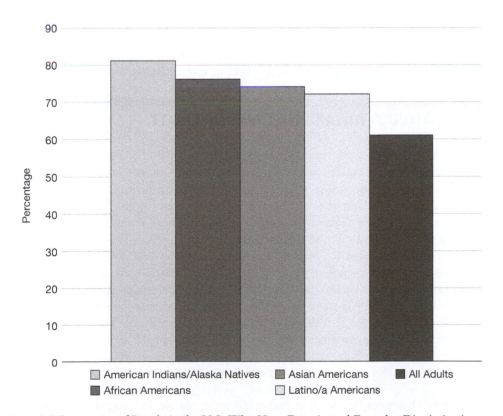

Figure 1.1 Percentage of People in the U.S. Who Have Experienced Everyday Discrimination.
Source: APA, 2016.

characteristics of the social context (Else-Quest & Hyde, 2016). For example, an Asian American's lesbian identity may have strong personal relevance and this identity may or may not be validated and conditioned by those in the communities that she participates in, such as lesbians, Asian Americans, women, or communities in which these identities intersect.

Inequality and power are also embedded within intersectional identities (Else-Quest & Hyde, 2016). For example, women of color have not always been accepted or included by European American women. Despite African American women's participation in gaining women's right to vote, some European American women, particularly in the South, attempted to restrict African American women's voting rights (National Women's History Museum, 2007). Moreover, women of color have often been marginalized by men of color in the civil rights movement.

Intersectional identities create the potential for multiple forms of discrimination. For example, people with multiple devalued identities (e.g., race, gender, sexual orientation, weight) report more types of discrimination (Grollman, 2014). In addition, more types of discrimination were associated with poorer mental and physical health. Socioeconomic status and race/ethnicity also form intersectional identities. However, higher socioeconomic status does not necessarily protect one against discrimination. Higher socioeconomic status African Americans have been found to experience greater discrimination than lower socioeconomic status African Americans because of broader social contacts and more opportunities for higher socioeconomic status African Americans (Dailey, Kasl, Holford, Lewis, & Jones, 2010).

With the definitions in this section, we can begin to consider how cultural diversity affects people. Some embrace it, others ignore it, still others may fear it. Regardless of one's attitudes toward cultural diversity, it is here to stay and is increasing.

THREE ATTITUDES TOWARD CULTURAL DIVERSITY

People's attitudes toward the rapid demographic and cultural changes that are occurring in the United States are analogous to their attitudes toward climate change, which also is already underway and occurring relatively rapidly. Global climate change and cultural climate change in the United States both involve social and political implications that elicit a range of attitudes from skepticism to activism. Three groups of persons with a range of attitudes toward cultural diversity have been identified: *Dissenters*, *Passive Supporters*, and *Active Supporters* (G. Hall, Martinez, Tuan, McMahon, & Chain, 2011). Dissenters are a skeptical group, critical of attention to cultural diversity because it is considered a violation of meritocracy. Passive Supporters understand the value of cultural diversity but are relatively inactive or apathetic. Active Supporters believe in and support cultural diversity. Each group is described in more detail below with comparisons to attitudes toward global climate change prevention. As you read the descriptions, you may find that your own beliefs are similar to one or more of these groups. Keep in mind that none of these attitudes are wrong but are different reactions to and beliefs about cultural diversity.

Dissenters. Dissenters believe that individual merit should be judged independent of race, ethnicity, or culture and consider themselves to be "color-blind." It is possible that Joe's beliefs fit in the Dissenter category. This group is analogous to those who are skeptical that the climate is changing or that human behavior can influence climate change. Although climate change skeptics tend to be politically conservative (Jacques, 2009), Dissenters may include political conservatives as well as liberals who believe in egalitarianism (Dovidio & Gaertner, 2000). Similarly, climate change skeptics tend to be European American men (Leiserowitz & Akerlof, 2010), as do Dissenters. However, some people of color who value assimilation and emphasize the similarities of all people may also be Dissenters, although Dissenters of color are a very small group (G. Hall, Martinez et al., 2011). Those who are dismissive of climate change range from 7–11% of the U.S. population (Maibach, Roser-Renouf, & Leiserowitz, 2008).

BOX 1.1 COLOR-BLIND RACIAL IDEOLOGY (NEVILLE, AWAD, BROOKS, FLORES, & BLUEMEL, 2013)

People who claim to be color blind tend to have certain common characteristics. They tend to deny: (a) race; (b) blatant forms of racism; (c) institutional racism; or (d) White privilege. Those who deny race attempt to reject notions of White superiority by claiming that everyone is the same. Denial of racism involves the claim that blatant racism (e.g., racial slurs) is a relic of the past and no longer occurs. Those who deny institutional racism may claim reverse racism – that institutional policies (e.g., college admissions) unfairly benefit racial and ethnic minorities. Denial of White privilege is the argument that European American people do not have certain advantages because of the color of their skin. All four forms of denial justify the racial status quo of inequality. Color blindness can occur among both European Americans and people of color.

Discussion

1   Can you think of alternative perspectives to each of these forms of denial?
2   Why might some people of color attempt to be color blind?

In order to estimate the percentage of Dissenters, Passive Supporters, and Active Supporters of cultural diversity in the population, G. Hall (2014) administered a brief measure of attitudes toward and actions involving cultural diversity to 647 psychology undergraduates (65% women; 73% European Americans, 14% Asian Americans, 5% Latinx Americans, 2% African Americans) at a Pacific Northwest university. Measure items were:

1   Diversity issues are not one of my priorities.
2   I have not taken action to support the university in its mission to increase diversity and multicultural competence.
3   Achieving diversity is something I would advocate for, even if no one else was.
4   Achieving a diverse group of people in my program/department is worth fighting for.
5   The inclusion of underrepresented individuals creates a more enriching work/learning environment.

Dissenters would tend to agree with #1 and #2 and disagree with #3, #4, and #5. Active Supporters would have the opposite pattern of agreement/disagreement and Passive Supporters would be somewhere in between Dissenters and Active Supporters. The data revealed that 18% were Dissenters, 63% were Passive Supporters, and 19% were Active Supporters. As can be seen in Figure 1.2, the percentage of Dissenters with respect to cultural diversity is somewhat larger than the percentage of Dissenters (skeptics) with respect to climate change prevention. This may be because the merits of cultural diversity may be considered somewhat more disputable than the reality of climate change.

Similar to those who deny that climate change is occurring, some Dissenters may want to deny that the U.S. is changing demographically. Demographic change is documented and indisputable and might appear more difficult to deny than climate change, which is a more complex phenomenon. Yet, being in a non-diverse setting may contribute to the denial of demographic change because personal experiences are easily generalized (Weber & Stern, 2011). Even in diverse settings, people tend to gravitate toward their own group and may have limited contact with outgroup members. Such limited contact with diverse others may create a perception of cultural homogeneity. Those who personally experience their world as culturally homogeneous may expect their homogeneous world to persist into the future.

Members of dominant groups may fear the possibility of change that is posed by increases in size and possible power of non-dominant groups. When the prospect of a majority-minority nation is presented to European Americans, they endorse conservative policy positions, including opposition to affirmative action and immigration (Craig & Richeson, 2014). Indeed, the threat of increasing national diversity motivated many European Americans to vote for Donald Trump, particularly those who were highly

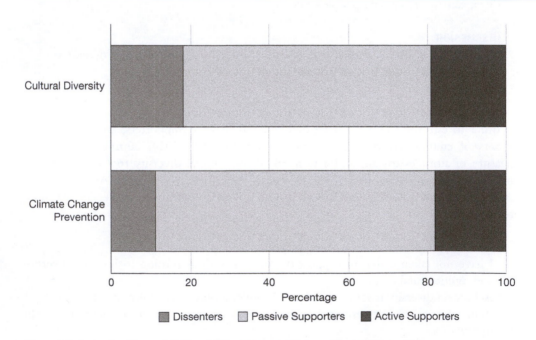

Figure 1.2 Attitudes Toward Cultural Diversity and Climate Change Prevention.

Source: G. Hall, 2014; Maibach et al., 2008.

identified with being White (Major, Blodorn, & Blascovich, 2016). Because assimilation is the societal philosophy that dominant groups are most familiar with and prefer, they may fear being assimilated if another group becomes the majority (Hehman et al., 2012). Thus, Dissenters may actively resist efforts to allow additional privileges for minority groups, such as contending that affirmative action constitutes reverse racism.

An escapist approach by Dissenters who feel threatened by cultural diversification might involve associating only with people like themselves. An analogous reaction to the anxiety of climate change is continued or increased material acquisition and consumption (Maiteny, 2002). Efforts to prevent or escape cultural diversification may be intentional or apparently unintentional and may occur under the guise of some other principle. Few would want to be viewed as having racist motivations. For example, those who oppose immigration may claim that they are protecting employment opportunities for Americans.

Some members of dominant groups may believe that their worldview is benevolent with respect to culturally diverse minority groups. A meritocracy that is blind to race, ethnicity, and culture may be seen as unbiased. However, the proponents of such beliefs are typically not culturally diverse (G. Hall, Martinez et al., 2011). Rather than allowing culturally diverse groups to speak for themselves, non-diverse dominant groups may believe that they have the requisite knowledge to prescribe what is best for others. In a climate change context, some deniers may believe that not imposing behavioral changes to slow climate change is benevolent because it creates fewer impositions (e.g., higher cost of environmentally friendly actions such as buying an electric vehicle), particularly on those who cannot easily afford to make needed behavioral changes.

Passive Supporters. Some Passive Supporters may have fatalistic views about cultural diversification, not knowing how to react to it or not believing that their actions will have an impact. These views are similar to the views of some with respect to climate change (Gifford, 2011; Langford, 2002; Norgaard, 2011). Climate change may be believed to be occurring gradually, which does not necessitate immediate action (Gifford, 2011; Reser & Swim, 2011; Weber & Stern, 2011). Similar to those who have become habituated to warnings about climate change (Moser, 2007) or do not perceive immediate personal difficulties (Gifford, 2011), some Passive Supporters do not have a sense of urgency concerning the effects of cultural diversification. Cultural diversity is but one priority among many (G. Hall, Martinez et al., 2011). A majority of the U.S. population is interested in climate change, although this does not necessarily translate into action (Maibach et al., 2008). Similarly, 63% of students in a college sample were Passive Supporters with respect to cultural diversity (G. Hall, 2014).

Other Passive Supporters may be willing to support cultural diversification efforts that are relatively low cost (e.g., talk to high school students of color who are visiting a university campus) but may be less willing to support efforts that are relatively high cost (e.g., support protests by African American students concerning discrimination). This is analogous to those who understand that climate change is occurring but who have either not engaged in behavioral change to prevent it or have engaged in low-cost changes (e.g., recycling to lower waste bills). Such a "green consumer" response involves concern for the environment without major lifestyle changes (Maiteny, 2002). Passive Supporters may believe that they have done their share for cultural diversity or preventing climate change with these low-cost activities.

Passive Supporters are characterized by passivity. Although they may believe discrimination is wrong and would not actively discriminate against a person from a culturally diverse background, they would not make an extra effort to help that person succeed, fearing that such behavior would be a form of discrimination. They also may not be inclined to intervene if they witness discrimination against another person. In a climate change context, a Passive Supporter might personally try to limit their carbon footprint (e.g., drive less) but would not criticize the driving habits of others, much less the manufacture of large gas-guzzling cars. Shallow commitment may reflect shallow knowledge of the benefits of cultural diversity or of preventing climate change. Passive Supporters sometimes can be swayed by arguments of Dissenters or Active Supporters.

Offsetting is an approach to assuaging guilt among Passive Supporters. Offsetting involves doing good in one area to offset bad behavior in another. For example, buying a carbon offset compensates for emission of carbon dioxide (e.g., air travel) by supporting projects or organizations that reduce the emission of carbon dioxide (e.g., via renewable energy). In the diversity realm, a person might believe that they are compensating for the lack of diversity in their organization by signing an online petition that promotes diversity (e.g., a petition against racial profiling by police). However, the effects of offsetting can also be temporary if commitment to the offset wanes (Gifford, 2011). For example, an organization might successfully hire a single person in an effort to bring cultural diversity to an organization and may believe that the presence of this single person nullifies any obligation to hire additional culturally diverse colleagues. In other words, the organization may feel that they have "checked the diversity box" off the list of things to do. Moreover, some offsets are token efforts (Gifford, 2011). Offsetting in the form of hiring a person who demographically represents diversity (e.g., racially) but has status quo beliefs is unlikely to change an organization's diversity climate or to attract other persons who might diversify the climate.

Active Supporters. This is probably the category that Maria fits in. This group regards cultural diversity as a top priority that benefits all and believes that it should be a top priority for others. The more cultural diversity the better. Active Supporters also believe that wholesale change (e.g., changing the goals and climate of an organization) is necessary and that surface diversity (e.g., demographic diversification) is inadequate without corresponding change at deeper levels. For example, a university can recruit underrepresented students to change their image but corresponding efforts to include these students in campus life and leadership are necessary for such recruitment to be successful and more than window dressing. Active Supporters may believe that society is capable of effectively responding to cultural diversification, similar to those who believe that communities can effectively work together to reduce climate change (Langford, 2002). This group is analogous to climate change activists who take major steps to slow climate change consequences by reducing their carbon footprint (e.g., buying an electric car, growing and producing their own food, engaging in civic action to achieve policy changes).

Only 18% of the U.S. population is convinced of the reality and danger of climate change (Maibach et al., 2008). Similarly, 19% of undergraduates were found to be Active Supporters of cultural diversity (G. Hall, 2014). Persons of color, women, and younger people are more likely to be activists with respect to cultural diversity than those in other groups (Hurtado, 2001; Maruyama & Moreno, 2000; Mayhew & Grunwald, 2006).

The goals of Dissenters and Active Supporters appear to be at odds and it is easy to envision an adversarial relationship between the two groups. However, it may be possible for the groups to benefit one another (G. Hall, Martinez et al., 2011). Dissenters' criticisms of cultural diversity could help Active Supporters develop a stronger rationale for their positions and more persuasive arguments. For example, Dissenters' criticisms of the financial costs of cultural diversity on a university campus can be countered with arguments of the benefits of cultural diversity, such as the empirically-demonstrated increases in critical thinking and learning that cultural diversity brings for all students, including European Americans (Hurtado, 2001). Politically liberal Dissenters who believe in equality might realize that color-blind admissions policies have not diversified the student population and might be persuaded by Active Supporters that some effort to recruit students from culturally diverse backgrounds is necessary for all citizens to have an equal chance of benefitting from a college education.

Let me reiterate that none of the attitudes in these three groups is wrong. However, assessing your own attitudes relative to these three categories of attitudes may help you determine how open you are to multicultural psychology and what kinds of issues you will consider as you read this book. Regardless of your attitude toward cultural diversity, I encourage you to be open to the material in this book because it might help you more fully appreciate and benefit from our multicultural society.

Summary

In summary, there are three types of attitudes toward cultural diversity that mirror attitudes toward climate change. Dissenters are skeptical of cultural change and resist it. Passive Supporters typically do not resist cultural change but are not actively engaged with it. Active Supporters "lead the charge" of cultural change. Dissenters and Active Supporters are relatively small groups, with Passive Supporters as a large group.

THREE RESEARCH APPROACHES TO RACE, ETHNICITY, AND CULTURE

Similar to the three types of attitudes toward cultural diversity, there are also three major research approaches to psychology, known as *generalizability research*, *group differences research*, and *multicultural psychology* (G. Hall, Yip, & Zárate, 2016). These three research approaches correspond to some degree to the three types of attitudes toward cultural diversity. Generalizability research expects to find similarities and universalities across diverse groups. The assumption is that race, ethnicity, and culture are not influential. Therefore, many researchers who espouse the generalizability approach may be Dissenters with respect to cultural diversity.

The second approach, group differences research, examines how cultural contexts might influence generalizability. One might expect those interested in group differences based on culture would be Active Supporters of cultural diversity. However, many group differences researchers are more interested in the cultures of other countries than the cultural diversity within the United States. So, group differences researchers do not fit neatly into any of the three attitudes toward diversity category. Nevertheless, some group differences researchers might be opposed to an emphasis on domestic rather than international diversity because they view this emphasis as too narrow, and would be

Dissenters. Other group differences researchers are not opposed to attention to cultural diversity in the United States but this also is not their priority, which would make them Passive Supporters. Most group differences researchers may be Passive Supporters. Some group differences researchers, particularly those who study group differences in the United States, could be Active Supporters.

Multicultural psychology, the third approach, focuses on cultural influences on behavior in ethnocultural groups underrepresented in research, including people of color in the United States. These groups are valued for their own merits and not in terms of how they compare to other groups, which is the group differences approach. Most multicultural psychology researchers are Active Supporters of cultural diversity.

Generalizability research. Generalizability approaches are *etic*, in that they apply constructs from one cultural group to another. The generalizability approach is rooted in the natural sciences, in which phenomena are assumed to have universal properties or apply to the whole species. For example, brain functions are assumed to be the same for all humans. However, as we will learn in Chapter 4, brain functions can be conditioned by culture.

Joe and Maria observed limited attention to people of color in their psychology courses, which may be a reflection of the dominance of generalizability research. A common (but often untested) assumption in psychological research is that findings obtained with European Americans apply to other groups. If psychological phenomena are considered to be universal and it is convenient to study European Americans such as college undergraduates, then the study of diverse groups is considered unnecessary. Many European American psychology researchers may not consider themselves a part of an ethnic group (e.g., White Americans) and also may not view membership in an ethnic group as an important quality of the people that they study. Because only 15% of psychology faculty members across the United States are non-White (Kohout, Pate, & Maton, 2014), psychology faculty members whose social network is primarily other European Americans may be oblivious to cultural diversity.

An advantage of the generalizability approach is its breadth. It identifies commonalities among humans and does not require a new theory for each new geographic or cultural context. The breadth of universality is emphasized over the depth of cultural specificity. An example of a research finding with European Americans that seems to apply universally is the Five Factor personality model. The dimensions of extraversion, agreeableness, conscientiousness, emotional stability, and openness to experience have been identified among cultural groups worldwide (Ehrhart, Roesch, Ehrhart, & Kilian, 2008).

Group differences, such as those based on culture, tend to be overlooked or treated superficially in the generalizability approach (G. Hall, Yip, & Zárate, 2016). Researchers invested in generalizability often fail to report the ethnic composition of their samples. For example, 60% of studies in social psychology research were found not to report sample ethnicity (Arnett, 2008).

When group characteristics are considered in psychological research, a method of minimizing variability to demonstrate generalizability is to approach group characteristics as a demographic category, such as nationality or ethnic group. A common method of demonstrating the generalizability of a finding is to compare European Americans with a combined group of ethnic minorities in a sample. Ethnic minorities are often combined because they constitute a small proportion of the sample. However, ethnic minorities may be from multiple groups (e.g., African Americans, Asian Americans, Latinx

Americans) and differ from one another. So, if research examines group differences between European Americans and a combined group of minorities on anxiety, there will be people who will be highly anxious, moderately anxious, mildly anxious, and not anxious in both groups. Because of this within-group variability, the differences between European Americans and minorities are likely to be minimal.

Although broad groupings can have meaning (e.g., African Americans generally experience more race-based discrimination than European Americans), such broad groupings are heterogeneous. For example, an older African American woman who is a leader of a non-profit civil rights organization in a large city may be quite different from a teenage African American woman high school student living in a predominantly European American suburb with no contact with African Americans other than her own family. Yet, the demographic approach would categorize them both as African Americans. You may wonder why these broad ethnic groupings are used in this book. These broad groupings are a source of identity for many people. But the chapters go beyond the broad groupings to address intersectional identities within each group. The purpose is not comparison but to explore nuances within each group.

An additional limitation of the demographic approach is that when a group difference is detected (usually inadvertently when the purpose of research is generalizability), the basis of the difference is unknown. For example, finding that Asian Americans differ from European Americans on anxiety does not reveal if this is culturally-based or is based on something else, such as minority status or history of trauma. This is why it is important not simply to infer the sources of difference but to actually measure them. For example, measuring loss of face could reveal whether concern about how one's behavior affects others influences one's own anxiety levels. In other words, people who are concerned about their impact on others may be more anxious than those who are less concerned about their impact. Loss of face is a prominent cultural value among Asian American groups that may explain why Asian Americans are anxious and might also explain why other groups are anxious.

Group differences research. The group differences approach starts by attempting to determine if a theory is generalizable, as well as the limits of generalizability, by comparing two or more groups. The standard in this approach is European Americans or other Western samples with Western European origins (e.g., England, France, Germany). If group differences are revealed, the second stage of the group differences approach is to determine the potential cultural reasons for these differences (Heine & Norenzayan, 2006). The advantage of this approach is attempting to understand why groups differ by carefully identifying cultural variables that might distinguish groups.

An example of a cultural variable that differs across groups and is commonly studied by cultural psychologists is individualism/collectivism, also known as independent/interdependent self-construals. Independent self-construals involve a view of the self as unique apart from others and are common in Europeans and European Americans. Independent persons focus on expressing and promoting their own ideas and taking care of themselves (Markus & Kitayama, 1991). On the other hand, interdependent self-construals involve a view of the self in relation to others (e.g., daughter, student, partner) and are common in East Asia and perhaps as much as two-thirds of the world. The focus among interdependent people is on getting along with others and social responsibilities (Markus & Kitayama, 1991).

Figure 1.3 shows data on how individualistic and collectivistic Asian Americans, Latinx Americans, and African Americans are relative to European Americans based on a

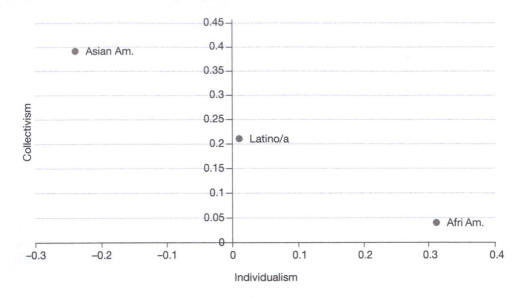

Figure 1.3 Effect Sizes for Asian American, Latino/a American, and African American Individualism and Collectivism Relative to European Americans.

meta-analysis by Oyserman and colleagues (2002). A meta-analysis is a quantitative summary of the effects of multiple studies and determines an average effect across all studies. The effect size is expressed in standard deviation units (e.g., an effect size of $1 = 1$ SD above the mean). In the Oyserman et al. (2002) study depicted in Figure 1.3, differences from zero indicate differences from European Americans. It can be seen that Asian Americans are less individualistic and more collectivistic than European Americans. Latinx Americans are also somewhat more collectivistic than European Americans but approximately the same on individualism. African Americans are more individualistic than European Americans but slightly more collectivistic.

The finding on relatively high individualism among African Americans may seem counterintuitive. Many African Americans are highly identified with their group. However, African American individualism may serve a different purpose than European American individualism. Individualism for many African Americans has been a way of coping against racism, which treats African Americans as if they are all alike (Whaley, 2003). Moreover, African American individualism occurs in the context of other African Americans (J. Jones, 2003). For example, improvisation is personal creative expressiveness that other African Americans appreciate because it enhances African American culture. Rather than separating individuals from others, the purpose of African American individualism is to serve the group.

Of course, independent/interdependent is a broad dichotomy. Independence and interdependence may be very different from group to group. The previous example of African American individualism demonstrates variation in independence. Interdependence and the welfare of the group are so strong in Japan that very few people have access to guns. Although most people in the United States are not willing to give up gun rights, interdependence might be expressed in terms of recycling to reduce the amount of waste in a community. Moreover, all cultures include people who vary on independence and interdependence. For example, European Americans may be interdependent when they focus on family responsibilities and Asians may be independent in creative expression, such as art.

Using the previous anxiety example in which the basis of group differences was unknown, group differences researchers would attempt to explain differences between Asian Americans and European Americans in anxiety. Concern about loss of face is one possible cultural reason for greater anxiety regardless of group membership. So, European Americans who are concerned about loss of face would be more anxious than European Americans who are less concerned about loss of face. And European Americans concerned about loss of face would be more anxious than Asian Americans who are less concerned about loss of face. So it is not simply group membership that determines how anxious one is. Nevertheless, the emphasis on group differences may obscure the reasons for the group differences. Because relatively few European Americans may be concerned about loss of face, the take home message for many may be the group difference – Asian Americans are more anxious than European Americans.

The group differences approach is inherently evaluative. If European Americans are the standard of comparison then it is difficult not to view differences from this standard as deviant. Higher anxiety in a group other than one's own may be viewed as excessive. Lower anxiety in a group other than one's own may be viewed as insensitivity to the environment. Of course, these interpretations are arbitrary. Higher or lower levels of anxiety may be appropriate depending on the expectations of one's context. In contexts in which it is important to be part of a group or team (e.g., a business), anxiety about one's impact on others may be warranted. In other more individualistic contexts where one's success is less dependent on others (e.g., mechanic), anxiety about one's impact on others may be less important. However, the emphasis on comparing one group to another in the group differences approach may cause many to overlook such nuanced interpretation of the mechanisms of group differences.

Those who conduct group differences research tend to have an outsider perspective. The group differences approach is common in cultural psychology, in which the primary focus is on culture but not on multicultural issues, such as majority or minority cultural status in a single nation or society in which there are multiple cultural groups. The most prominent cultural psychology researchers are European or European Americans who are studying cultural groups other than their own (G. Hall & Maramba, 2001). There can be advantages to an outsider's perspective, such as objectivity. As an example in another context, therapists have an outsider perspective that can be valuable. On the other hand, outsiders may filter what is actually happening in a cultural community. Outsiders may not understand and communicate what is most important to the community itself.

Another potential limitation of the outsider perspective is that culture can be treated as a commodity (D. Groot, personal communication, January 2016). In this sense, a cultural psychologist is analogous to a foreign tour guide who profits from making a culture accessible for other foreigners. Nevertheless, cultures and the people who practice them do not exist for the sole purpose of being visited or studied by outsiders.

Group differences cannot be examined if a characteristic exists in one group but not in another. For example, Black identity, which involves the importance and meaning of being Black, is important to many African Americans (Sellers, Rowley, Chavous, Shelton, & Smith, 1997). Black identity is salient for many African Americans but is generally non-existent among European Americans. A European American might identify with Black culture because of experiences with it, but the person is not Black. Some European Americans might have a White identity, but experiences of being Black and being White are quite different and do not lend themselves to direct comparisons (G. Hall, Yip, & Zárate, 2016). For example, most African Americans are aware of being Black and Black identity may provide a sense of connection and community. On the other hand, many European Americans do not think of themselves as being White or similar to other European Americans unless they are in the minority, which is atypical in the United States. White identity also often has negative connotations, such as White supremacy. A European American who associates White identity with White supremacy might also believe that Black identity is equivalent to Black supremacy. Although one form of Black identity involves being separate from other groups, Black identity is a source of well-being for many African Americans and generally is not intended to denigrate other groups (Sellers et al., 1997). These issues illustrate the difficulty in attempting to compare characteristics that exist in one group but not in another.

Multicultural psychology research. The third approach, multicultural psychology, examines the unique and nuanced characteristics of one or more groups and does not necessarily propose that characteristics in one group exist in others. Such group-specific characteristics are known as *emic*. However, existing theories from other groups can be applied to a new group, which is the *etic* approach, and the existing theories can be augmented or challenged by the data from the new group. For example, the Five Factor Model of personality was developed among European Americans with the assumption that these five factors are consistent across social contexts. The Five Factor Model can be evaluated among Asian Americans not primarily to examine its generalizability but to identify what specific characteristics of Asian Americans might affect the model's fit. The Five Factor Model has been demonstrated not to fit well among Asian Americans who are concerned about loss of face (Eap et al., 2008). Loss of face concerns cause a person to be sensitive to and adjust their behavior to the social context and to be less likely to act consistently across social contexts, which is the assumption of the Five Factor Model.

Unlike the generalizability and group differences approaches, multicultural psychology explicitly focuses on giving a voice to populations that are underrepresented in research (e.g., minority populations) and is rooted in social justice traditions (David, Okazaki, & Giroux, 2014). The insider's perspective is valued over the outsider's perspective. People from an ethnic or racial community, including researchers, are the experts on the community and those from outside the community, including researchers, are seen as less knowledgeable. It is possible for outsiders to become knowledgeable about a community but only in close collaboration with community insiders (G. Hall, Yip, & Zárate, 2016).

Samples in generalizability research are selected more for convenience (e.g., college students) than for their particular characteristics, whereas sample selection in multicultural psychology research is deliberate and seeks samples that have unique characteristics (e.g., immigrant Latinx Americans). Whereas samples in the generalizability approach are easily accessed via psychology department subject pools, accessing samples in multicultural psychology research is challenging, often requiring culturally competent outreach, direct involvement with communities, and demonstration that research will benefit the communities (Castro, Rios, & Montoya, 2006). A racial or ethnic group's unique characteristics may include language use, preference, and proficiency; social affiliation; daily living habits; cultural traditions, values, knowledge, beliefs, identification, pride, and acceptance; communication styles; perceived prejudice and discrimination; and family socialization

(Zane & Mak, 2003). This approach differs from the group differences approach that assumes that members of a group are similar to each other. Although multicultural psychology can be criticized as being limited in scope because of its focus on underrepresented groups, these groups are rapidly growing in the United States and have cultural roots with the majority of the world's population.

An advantage of the multicultural approach is its depth of understanding particular cultural groups free from the constraints of comparison to other groups (G. Hall, Yip, & Zárate, 2016). For example, if one is studying Black identity in African Americans, it is not necessary for Black identity to exist in other groups for comparison purposes. The focus is not on a particular ethnic, racial, or cultural group in isolation but on the group in the sociocultural context of other groups. Black identity, for example, is conditioned not only by cultural background but also by experiences with other groups, such as minority status, discrimination, and a bicultural orientation involving the ability to function within two or more interacting groups (e.g., African Americans and European Americans).

For many students from underrepresented groups, such as Maria, their first experience in psychology to focus on their own group is in a multicultural psychology course. The focus on one's own group creates inherent interest, which is typically the experience of European American students in most psychology courses. The experience of students of color in a multicultural psychology course is quite different than that of many European American students, who may feel somewhat uncomfortable in a multicultural psychology course in which the focus is not on themselves.

An example of multicultural psychology research is work on ethnic and racial identity. Ethnic and racial identity develop because of connections and common experiences based on cultural or ethnic ancestry (Umaña-Taylor, Wong, Gonzales, & Dumka, 2012). Ethnically- or racially-based discrimination makes one's ethnic or racial identity more salient (Greene, Way, & Pahl, 2006). The characteristics of ethnic and racial identity vary from group to group among people of color, which makes it important to focus on the unique aspects of ethnic and racial identity shared by a group (e.g., African Americans, Latinx Americans, Asian Americans, Native Americans). Figure 1.4 shows that racial/ethnic

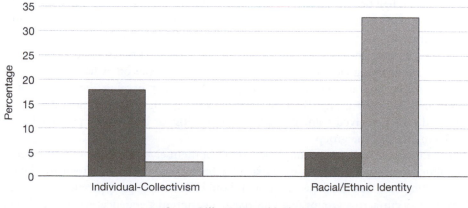

Figure 1.4 Percent of Articles on Individualism–Collectivism and Racial/Ethnic Identity in Group Differences vs. Multicultural Research Journals.

identity is the topic of one-third of the articles published in the leading multicultural journal, *Cultural Diversity and Ethnic Minority Psychology*, but is the topic of only 5% of the articles in the leading group differences journal, *Journal of Cross-Cultural Psychology*. In constrast, individualism–collectivism is the topic of 18% of the articles published in the *Journal of Cross-Cultural Psychology* but is the topic of only 3% of the articles published in *Cultural Diversity and Ethnic Minority Psychology* (G. Hall, Yip, & Zárate, 2016). Thus, group differences and multicultural psychology research are different fields because they focus on different topics.

The primary purpose of multicultural psychology research is not group comparison. However, a phenomenon identified within one group can be studied in other groups. For example, concern about loss of face has been found to deter private (self-reported) and public aggression (showing someone something they don't want to see) among Asian Americans (G. Hall, DeGarmo, Eap, Teten, & Sue, 2006). The pattern was different among European Americans, with loss of face not influencing private aggression but deterring public aggression. Thus, loss of face, a behavior that has a pervasive influence in Asian cultural groups, appears to have a situation-specific influence in European Americans. This is the converse of the Five Factor Model that has a pervasive, cross-situational influence among European Americans but is less influential among Asian Americans, particularly those concerned about loss of face (Eap et al., 2008). These examples demonstrate that phenomena may be culture-specific and that it cannot always be assumed that influential phenomena in one culture will be equally influential in another. And in some cases, phenomena in one culture may not exist in another culture, such as Black identity, as discussed previously.

Unlike the generalizability and group differences approaches to anxiety discussed previously, the multicultural approach would focus on unique nuances of anxiety in a particular group. As discussed in the group differences section, anxiety among Asian Americans might be associated with concern about loss of face. Going beyond this general explanation, the way in which anxiety is expressed and might be associated with loss of face would be investigated. An Asian American individual disclosing anxious thoughts to others might cause others to lose face because the others may appear blameworthy for not adequately taking care of the individual. Therefore, anxiety might be expressed as a physical illness via symptoms such as indigestion or skin conditions that would be seen as within the individual and not someone else's fault. Another important aspect to understanding anxiety from a multicultural perspective is the social context in which the anxiety occurs. An Asian American may not feel anxiety among European Americans because she understands that they are less concerned about losing face than Asian Americans are. On the other hand, another Asian American might feel anxious among European Americans because she stands out as a member of a minority group. Similarly, anxiety among other Asian Americans might be heightened by a perceived cultural emphasis on face loss or lessened by perceived acceptance as a member of the group.

Some European Americans who do not think of themselves as White may wonder why multicultural psychology focuses on racial or ethnic groups. Some cultural psychologists have also suggested that the focus of research should not be groups of people but patterns of culture that occur across groups (e.g., independence-interdependence; Markus & Hamedani, 2007). However, racial/ethnic identity is a source of meaning for many people of color and is associated with physical and psychological health (Rivas-Drake et al., 2014). Thus, a focus on racial or ethnic group membership may contribute to the well-being of people of color. The generalizability and group differences approaches in which Europeans/European Americans are the standard would overlook this source of meaning and health because racial/ethnic identity is largely absent among Europeans/European Americans.

People from individualist backgrounds, including many psychologists, may view group identification, including identification with racial/ethnic groups, as less influential than an individual's influence. Even when group influences are acknowledged, individuals are considered to be as influential on the group as the group is on the individual (Markus & Hamedani, 2007; Shweder, 1990). However, for many who identify with racial or ethnic groups, group identification is stronger than individual identification. As discussed previously, identification with a racial or ethnic group has positive consequences. Of course, there are also disadvantages of collectivism and individualism. For example, unquestioning loyalty to a group can have negative consequences, such as when obligations to one group (e.g., a sorority or fraternity) outweigh other obligations (e.g., schoolwork, personal safety). Conversely, extreme individualism can lead to isolation. We will consider racial and ethnic identity in depth in Chapter 2.

Summary

Similar to the three types of attitudes toward cultural diversity, there are three main approaches to research. Generalizability research seeks to establish universal principles and is the most common research approach. The group differences approach examines culture but in comparison to a reference group, which is typically European Americans. Multicultural psychology research focuses on the unique cultural contexts of ethnic and racial groups.

CONCLUSION

Multicultural psychology is the study of the influences of multiple cultures in a single social context on human behavior. People's attitudes toward the rapid demographic and cultural changes that are occurring in the United States range from dissent to support. Most people in the United States are not opposed to these changes but may not know how to react to them. Research approaches to cultural diversity also range from dissent to support. Some researchers view the effects of culture as minimal. Others are interested in comparing how patterns found in one culture may vary in others. Multicultural psychology researchers focus on the unique and nuanced characteristics of groups, giving a voice to populations that are underrepresented in research.

RESOURCES

Blog:
If You've Seen One, You've Seen Them All? Variety is the Spice of Life www.psycho logytoday.com/blog/life-in-the-intersection/201702/if-you-ve-seen-one-you-ve-seen-them-all.

Videos:

The Danger of a Single Story, Chimamanda Ngozi Adichie www.ted.com/talks/chimamanda_adichie_the_danger_of_a_single_story.

The Science Behind Why People Think Stereotypes Are True www.colorlines.com/articles/watch-science-behind-why-people-think-stereotypes-are-true.

A Conversation With White People on Race www.nytimes.com/2015/07/01/opinion/a-conversation-with-white-people-on-race.html.

White Privilege www.youtube.com/watch?v=_zjj1PmJcRM.

CHAPTER 2

Racial/Ethnic Identity and Acculturation

Carmen is a 19-year-old African American woman who is a freshman at a state university that is predominantly White. Her grandparents were involved in the civil rights movement. Carmen's parents are both teachers and are leaders in their African American church where she is a member. She has a strong sense of her identity as an African American woman and plans to major in African American Studies. For the first time in her life, she feels like a minority in the state university setting and she is aware that some other students wonder if she is on campus because of affirmative action.

Dyan is a 20-year-old African American woman who is a sophomore at a private liberal arts college for women. This college is similar to her suburban neighborhood that was predominantly White. Her mother is a computer systems analyst and her father is an information technology manager. She has no close African American friends and the only African Americans that she associates with are her family members. Dyan is an English major. She does not feel that others treat her differently because she is Black and feels that she has much in common with the other women at her college.

Carmen and Dyan are both African American women and are about the same age. However, their experiences are quite different. Carmen has a strong connection to the African American community and has a strong identity as an African American woman. Dyan, on the other hand, is not connected with African Americans or an African American identity. She identifies more as a woman than as an African American. These two African American women vary in their racial identity.

In this chapter, we begin with a consideration of models of racial/ethnic identity. Some are group specific (i.e., African Americans, Whites) and others address multiple groups. The second part of the chapter is a consideration of models of acculturation. These models apply to multiple immigrant groups of color.

MODELS OF RACIAL/ETHNIC IDENTITY

Identities based on race, ethnicity, culture, and minority status will serve as the framework for this book. *Racial identity* focuses on the meaning and importance of race, and responses to racism (Helms, 2007). *Racism* assumes that group differences are biologically-based, that one's own race is superior, and that practices that formalize the domination of one racial group over another are justifiable (J. Jones, 1997). *Ethnic identity* involves the strength of identification with one's ethnic group (Phinney, 1996). Components of ethnic identity include self-labeling, a sense of belonging, positive evaluation, preference for the group, ethnic interest and knowledge, and involvement in activities associated with the group. The distinction between racial and ethnic identity is often arbitrary depending on which groups are studied (e.g., African Americans, multiple ethnic groups) and which measures of racial or ethnic identity are used (Yip, Douglass, & Sellers, 2014). A person is not born with a fully formed racial or ethnic identity. Racial identity develops and changes over time (Umaña-Taylor et al., 2014).

The Kenneth and Mamie Clark (1947) doll studies were some of the earliest and most influential work on the identity of people of color in the United States. The Clarks found that when presented with white and brown dolls, most African American three- to seven-year-old children preferred to play with the white doll and considered it to be nice, and regarded the brown doll to be bad. These studies were the behavioral science basis for the United States Supreme Court's 1954 decision to end school segregation in Brown v. Board of Education.

BOX 2.1 KENNETH AND MAMIE CLARK'S ADVOCACY FOR SCHOOL INTEGRATION

During the 1940s, Kenneth and Mamie Clark conducted the famous "doll test" to examine the effects of school segregation on African American children. The test involved the presentation of a white doll and a brown doll, and asking children the race of the dolls and which one they preferred to play with. Most African American and European American children preferred the white doll and regarded the brown doll as bad. The Clarks found some of the children's responses to the doll tests disturbing. Some African American children refused to answer the question or cried and ran out of the room. An African American boy in the rural South pointed to the brown doll and indicated, "That's a n—. I'm a n—" (Severo, 2005).

Results of the doll test were used to demonstrate the harmful effects of school segregation in the Brown v. Board of Education (1954) Supreme Court ruling. Racially segregated schools had been legal since the 1896 Plessy v. Ferguson case that held that racially segregated public facilities were constitutional as long as they were equal to each other. Oliver Brown was an African American who filed a class action suit against the Topeka, Kansas Board of Education because his child had been denied access to Topeka's White public schools. The Supreme Court unanimously decided that the racial segregation of children in public schools violated the Equal Protection Clause of the Fourteenth Amendment. The Supreme Court did not acknowledge one of the Clarks' other research conclusions that segregated schools also inhibited the development of White children (NAACP Legal Defense Fund, 2014).

The Clarks experienced several "firsts" for African Americans. Kenneth was the first African American to earn a PhD degree at Columbia University and Mamie was the second. Kenneth was the first African American tenured professor at the City University of New York and the first person of color to serve as President of the American Psychological Association in 1971.

Both Drs. Clark worked with New York City and the state of New York to racially integrate schools. Their advocacy for integration was met with opposition not only from White supremacists but also from African American separatists who believed that African Americans should not cooperate with the oppressive majority (Severo, 2005). Although they worked to improve Harlem schools, the Clarks moved their family from Harlem to Westchester County for their own children's education.

Discussion

1   What do you think the results would be if the doll test was given to children today?
2   Although school segregation is illegal, how and why might it still occur?

Yip et al. (2014) have traced the roots of racial/ethnic identity research to ego identity and social identity theories in psychology. *Ego identity* theory is a developmental approach proposed by Erik Erikson (1968). Adolescents and young adults begin an internal process that involves stages of exploration, crisis, and resolution that lasts for a lifetime and moves toward a coherent sense of identity. The Cross (1971, 1991; Cross & Vandiver, 2001) Model of Racial Identity, the Helms (1990) Model of White Racial Identity, the Phinney (1989) Model of Ethnic Identity, and the Poston (1990) Biracial Identity Development Model, which each involve stages of identity development and are discussed below, are in the ego identity tradition.

In contrast to the internal struggle of the ego identity approach, the social environment is more influential in the *social identity* approach (Tajfel, 1981; Tajfel & Turner, 1986). Social identity theory posits that individuals desire positive self-evaluations, social group membership involves self-evaluations via ingroup and outgroup comparisons, and positive self-evaluations result from favoring the ingroup over the outgroup (Yip et al., 2014). When one's social group is devalued by society, the meaning of membership in that social group is reinterpreted to maintain positive self-evaluations. The Sellers, Smith, Shelton, Rowley, and Chavous (1998) Multidimensional Model of Racial Identity, discussed below, is influenced by social identity theory. In this section, I will highlight influential models of racial and ethnic identity.

Cross (1971, 1991; Cross & Vandiver, 2001) Nigrescence Theory

One of the earliest models of racial/ethnic identity that has influenced subsequent models was the nigrescence theory developed by William Cross (1971). Nigrescence is a French term that means "the process of becoming Black" (Yip et al., 2014). Cross's (1971, 1991) model initially was developed with African American college students during the civil rights era, but this model has implications for life-span development and for other ethnic groups. Although the model was developed during the civil rights era, attention to race and ethnicity was extremely limited in psychology, which makes the development of this model remarkable. Cross conceptualized racial identity as a process involving four stages: pre-encounter, encounter, immersion/emersion, and internalization.

In the *pre-encounter* stage, African Americans view the world as non-Black or anti-Black. Because African Americans in this stage view European Americans as superior to African Americans, the goal is assimilation into European American society. African American identity is devalued. Such an assimilationist identity might be likely among African Americans who grow up isolated from other African Americans. Dyan, who is described at the beginning of the chapter, may be in the pre-encounter stage. Cross's (Cross & Vandiver, 2001) revised model includes three identity clusters in the pre-encounter stage. *Pre-encounter assimilation* identity involves a low salience of race and a strong identification with being American. *Pre-encounter miseducation* identity involves internalization of negative stereotypes of African Americans (e.g., lazy, criminal). *Pre-encounter self-hatred* identity involves negative views about African Americans and oneself. An example of an African American in the pre-encounter stage would be someone in a primarily European American organization who does not identify as African American and believes that they can fit in and succeed as well as anyone else. Such a person may not perceive any barriers to fitting in or to success as a result of their race or discrimination.

In the *encounter* stage, African Americans become aware of what it means to be African American, and begin to validate themselves in terms of that ethnic identity. Movement into this stage is often precipitated by some encounter with discrimination. For example, an African American who is attempting to succeed in a corporation realizes that there are no African Americans in upper management. Moreover, they may see themselves passed over for an upper management position by a European American with the same credentials and seniority. Because the person cannot escape that their status as an African American makes them different from others, they actively search for new and different interpretations of their identity.

African Americans in the *immersion-emersion* stage immerse themselves in African American culture and may reject all values that are not African American. Rejection of European American values may be viewed as necessary to prove that one is African American. Such a person on a college campus might be an activist in African American student organizations and be considered a "radical" or a "militant." A person emerges from this stage with a strong African American identity. Cross's (Cross & Vandiver, 2001) revised model includes two immersion–emersion identities. *Immersion-emersion intense Black involvement* identity views everything African American or Afrocentric as good. *Immersion-emersion anti-White* identity views everything European American or Eurocentric as bad. Carmen, described at the beginning of the chapter, could be in the immersion–emersion stage or the internalization stage.

Picture 2.1
Source: shutterstock.

In the final *internalization* stage, African Americans develop a self-confident and secure African American identity and are also comfortable expressing interests and preferences for experiences from other cultures. Anti-European American feelings decline. Persons in the internalization stage identify with the oppression of all people and often become involved in social activism. Malcolm X moved from the immersion–emersion stage to the internalization stage when he became a Muslim and began to accept and become involved in the struggles of persons of multiple ethnic backgrounds. Cross (Cross & Van-diver, 2001) proposed two internalization identities in his revised model. *Black nationalism* involves an Afrocentric identity that is not reactionary to other identities. *Multiculturalist inclusive* involves an African American identity as well as at least two other identities (e.g., gender, sexual identities).

Racial identity may intersect with other identities. The pre-encounter and encounter stages were associated with traditional attitudes toward women among African American women in New York City (Martin & Hall, 1992). Although the immersion–emersion stage was not associated with attitudes toward women, the internalization stage was associated with feminist attitudes.

Models similar to the Cross model have been developed for White racial identity, African American racial identity, ethnic identity, and biracial identity. These models are reviewed below. Table 2.1 compares the stages of these other models to the Cross model.

Table 2.1 Comparison of the Cross Model of Racial Identity to Other Models

Cross	Pre-Encounter	Encounter	Immersion-Emersion	Internalization
Helms	Contact	Disintegration	Reintegration, immersion/emersion	Autonomy
Sellers	Assimilationist, humanist	Oppressed minority	Nationalist, oppressed minority	Humanist
Phinney	Diffusion	Foreclosure	Moratorium	Achievement
Poston	Personal identity	Choice of group categorization	Enmeshment/denial, appreciation	Integration

A strength of the Cross theory is that it was one of the first to account for the diversity of African Americans' racial identity. A limitation is that, like all stage models, the implication is that a person cannot be in more than one stage at a time. However, the Cross Racial Identity Scale (Cross & Vandiver, 2001) measures all stages of the theory and allows the possibility of having characteristics of more than one stage. Another limitation of stage models is that some stages appear implicitly more advanced developmentally (e.g., internalization) than others (e.g., pre-encounter) and it is easy to value the advanced stages and devalue the less advanced stages. Another implication of the model is that each person experiences each stage of the model, although racial identity development is not necessarily a linear process. A person may remain in a single stage or may skip stages.

Helms (1990) Model of White Racial Identity

Do European Americans develop a racial identity? European Americans are typically taught, implicitly or explicitly, to ignore or minimize the meaning of their racial group membership (Ponterotto, Utsey, & Pedersen, 2006; D. Sue, 2004). Nevertheless, some European Americans do develop an identity in terms of their race or ethnicity. Helms (1990) has developed a model of White racial identity that is analogous to the Cross (1971) model. As with the Cross model, there are a series of stages. The White Racial Identity Attitude Scale (Helms & Carter, 1990) is based on the Helms (1990) model of White racial identity.

The *contact* stage in the Helms (1990) model is one in which race is not a distinguishing factor in psychological development. A person in this stage sees all people as having much in common. This stage is analogous to the Cross (1971, 1991) pre-encounter stage.

The second stage in the Helms (1990) model is *disintegration*, and involves a confusion and perplexity about being White. A European American in this stage may face moral dilemmas about what it means to be White in a society that denigrates persons who are not White. The disintegration stage is analogous to the Cross (1971, 1991) encounter stage. The encounter for European Americans involves a recognition that European Americans perpetrate discrimination. This differs from the encounter stage for African Americans in which they recognize that they are the targets of discrimination.

The third stage in the Helms (1990) model, *reintegration*, is an attempt to deal with the sense of disintegration by asserting racial superiority. For persons in this stage, African Americans and other minorities are viewed as inferior. The reintegration stage is similar to immersion in the Cross (1971, 1991) immersion-emersion stage.

Pseudo-independence is the fourth stage of the Helms (1990) model, in which a person gains a broader understanding of the impact of race, ethnicity, and culture on psychological development. However, race issues become important only during interactions with persons of color. A person in the pseudo-independence stage may develop generalized, sometimes stereotypical, assumptions about various ethnic groups.

The next stage, *immersion/emersion*, is an attempt to develop a personal and moral definition of Whiteness. A person in this stage may also encourage other Whites to redefine Whiteness. The immersion/emersion stage is similar to emersion in the Cross (1971, 1991) immersion-emersion stage. This person realizes that European Americans have a culture that differs from that of other groups.

The final stage of the Helms (1990) model, *autonomy*, involves the development of a non-racist White identity. A person in this stage gains an awareness of both the strengths and the weaknesses of European American cultures. This stage is analogous to the Cross (1971, 1991) internalization stage. This person is comfortable with their own identity as well as with the identities of others who are not European Americans.

A strength of this model is that it defines and delineates White racial identity in a manner that corresponds to some extent with models of African American identity. Many European Americans have not thought about having an identity based on race. A limitation of the concept of White racial identity is whether a healthy White racial identity can exist (Roediger, 1999). It is difficult to disentangle Whiteness from societal privilege.

Sellers et al. (1998) Multidimensional Model of Racial Identity

A model of racial identity influenced by social identity theory is the Multidimensional Model of Racial Identity (Sellers et al., 1998). Sellers and colleagues (1998) contended that mainstream perspectives emphasized the stigma of belonging to a racial minority group, whereas the underground perspective emphasized the unique experiences of African Americans in a sociohistorical context. The purpose of the Multidimensional Model of Racial Identity was to reconcile the mainstream and underground perspectives. Unlike the Cross (1971, 1991) model in which an individual is placed in sequential stages, the significance and meaning of racial identity in the Sellers et al. (1998) model may vary across time and situations. The Multidimensional Model of Racial Identity is assessed with the Multidimensional Inventory of Black Identity (Sellers et al., 1997), which has been used in studies discussed in other chapters of this book. Although the Multidimensional Model of Racial Identity focuses on race and was developed for African Americans, many aspects of the model are relevant to other ethnic groups (Phinney & Ong, 2007).

Racial identity in the Multidimensional Model of Racial Identity (Sellers et al., 1998) involves: (1) the importance of race in the individual's perception of self; and (2) the meaning of being a member of a racial group. Race is considered one of many important identities, such as gender and occupational identity. Sellers and colleagues proposed four dimensions of racial identity: racial salience; the centrality of the identity; the regard in which the person holds the group associated with the identity; and the ideology associated with the identity.

Racial *salience* involves the relevance of race as part of one's self-concept in a particular situation. For example, race might become salient if one is the only member of a race in a social setting. Race has become salient for Carmen in the predominantly White university where for the first time in her life she feels like a minority. It also might become salient if one experiences racist comments or behavior. Although being a minority is not different from Dyan's previous experiences and does not make her race salient, a racist incident, such as a blackface party at a sorority, might. There are likely to be individual differences in salience within the same situation based on past experiences. In the case of being the only member of a race in a social setting, race might be less salient for a person if they have commonly been the only member of their race in a setting than for a person who is not used to having solo status. Racial salience is more relevant to people of color in North America than to European Americans, insofar as European Americans typically are the majority and race issues are not salient unless they are in situations in which they are the minority.

Racial *centrality* is the extent to which persons normatively identify themselves with race. Unlike racial salience, racial centrality is relatively stable across situations. Racial centrality also involves the importance of race relative to other identities, such as gender. Race would be the most important identity for someone for whom race is central. However, race is not the central identity for all members of a group. Thus, upon meeting an African American, it cannot be assumed that the person is strongly identified with their race. Race is a central identity for Carmen but not for Dyan. They also may have other identities that are more central, such as gender, sexual identity, or occupational status. Dyan's identity as a woman is more central than her identity as an African American.

Regard involves the positive and negative feelings a person has about their race. *Private regard* involves positive or negative feelings about one's race and positive or negative feelings about being a member of the racial group. *Public regard* involves perceptions of the positive or negative feelings of others in society toward African Americans. Private and public regard are not necessarily positively correlated. One could have positive private regard about one's race despite perceptions of negative public regard and vice versa. Carmen has positive private regard about being an African American but perceives the negative public regard some of her fellow students hold about African Americans' academic abilities. Dyan's public and private regard concerning African Americans is unclear.

Private and public regard interact with body dissatisfaction and self-esteem among African American men and women (Oney, Cole, & Sellers, 2011). High private regard and low body dissatisfaction boosts self-esteem, whereas low public regard and high body dissatisfaction lowers it. Figure 2.1 shows that African Americans with low private regard had relatively low self-esteem whether they had low or high body dissatisfaction. Having high private regard and low body dissatisfaction boosted self-esteem, but African

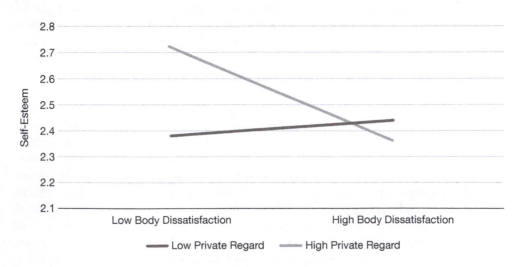

Figure 2.1 Body Dissatisfaction, Private Regard, and Self-Esteem.
Source: Oney et al., 2011.

Americans with high private regard and high body dissatisfaction had self-esteem as low as African Americans with low private regard.

Figure 2.2 shows that for African Americans who believed that others in society view African Americans positively (i.e., high public regard), low or high body dissatisfaction did not influence self-esteem (Oney et al., 2011). Having high public regard and high body dissatisfaction was associated with low self-esteem but high public regard and low body dissatisfaction was not associated with low self-esteem. Thus, perceptions of one's body that are consistent with one's private feelings (low body dissatisfaction, high private regard) or with the way one perceives society (high body dissatisfaction, low public regard) are the conditions that boost or lower self-esteem.

Ideology involves a person's beliefs about the way African Americans should live and interact with society. A *nationalist* ideology emphasizes that African Americans should control their own destiny with minimal input from other groups. An *oppressed minority* ideology emphasizes the similarities between oppression faced by African Americans and oppression faced by other minority groups. Carmen's views probably fit into the nationalist or oppressed minority ideologies. The *assimilationist* ideology emphasizes similarities between African Americans and the rest of American society, particularly the mainstream, with a goal of becoming an indistinguishable part of American society. The *humanist* ideology is more global than the assimilationist ideology and emphasizes similarities among all humans, de-emphasizing the importance of race and other distinguishing characteristics such as gender. Dyan's views probably fit into the assimiliationist or humanist ideologies.

These ideologies correspond to the Cross (1971, 1991) stages. A nationalist ideology is similar to the immersion-emersion stage. The oppressed minority ideology has similarities to the encounter and immersion-emersion stages. The assimilationist ideology corresponds to the pre-encounter stage. The humanist ideology is similar to the internalization stage, but is also similar to the pre-encounter stage insofar as race is de-emphasized.

A strength of the Sellers et al. (1998) Multidimensional Model of Racial Identity is that it captures the complexity and nuances of racial identity by simultaneously

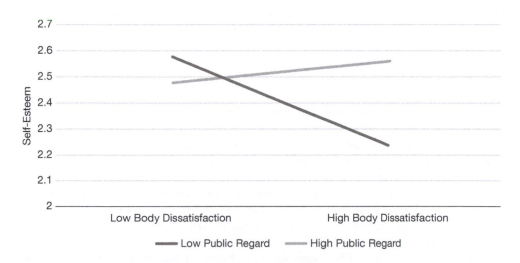

Figure 2.2 Body Dissatisfaction, Public Regard, and Self-Esteem.

Source: Oney et al., 2011.

considering multiple dimensions. The focus has been on African Americans but components of the model, such as salience and centrality, are applicable to other groups. A limitation is that the model focuses on racial discrimination and less on cultural heritage, which is an important component of racial identity (Phinney & Ong, 2007).

Phinney (1989) Model of Ethnic Identity

Models of racial identity have primarily focused on African Americans and to some degree on European Americans. Models of ethnic identity have focused on multiple ethnic groups. Phinney's (1989) influential model of ethnic identity is based on Marcia's (1980) model of personal identity, which did not focus on ethnic identity. Marcia (1980) conceptualized identity formation as involving: (1) exploration of identity issues; and (2) commitment, or a sense of belonging. Unlike personal identity, ethnic identity involves a shared sense of identity with others in one's ethnic group and is less determined by individual choice (Phinney & Ong, 2007). For example, one's appearance may cause others to associate them with an ethnic group even if the individual does not strongly identify with the group. Phinney (1993) was more interested in the process by which individuals come to understand the implications of their ethnicity and make decisions about its role in their lives than the behaviors and attitudes associated with being a member of an ethnic group. The development of ethnic identity moves from ethnic identity *diffusion* (low exploration and low commitment), to either *foreclosure* (commitment without exploration) or *moratorium* (exploration without commitment) to ethnic identity *achievement*, which involves a clear understanding of ethnicity based on exploration and commitment (Marcia, 1980; Phinney, 1989). The Phinney (1989) model spawned the Multigroup Ethnic Identity Measure (Phinney, 1992), the most widely used measure of ethnic identity.

The beginning and end points of the Phinney (1989) model are analogous to Cross's (1971, 1991) pre-encounter and internalization stages. Foreclosure is somewhat similar to the encounter stage, although the encounter stage is characterized by exploration. Moratorium is also somewhat similar to the immersion/emersion stage, although the immersion/emersion stage is characterized by commitment. In a study of African American adolescents and adults using the Marcia (1980) and Sellers et al. (1998) identity models, Yip, Seaton, and Sellers (2006) found that racial centrality scores were higher for persons having achievement status than for persons having other statuses. Moratorium and foreclosed individuals also had higher scores on racial centrality than did diffused individuals. Achievement individuals had higher private regard than did moratorium and foreclosed individuals, who had higher private regard than did diffused individuals.

A strength of the Phinney (1989) Model of Ethnic Identity is that the ethnic identities of multiple groups can be directly compared. However, there are unique aspects of individual ethnic groups that are not addressed by this general model (Phinney & Ong, 2007). Moreover, the use of the terms diffusion, foreclosure, and moratorium in the Marcia (1980) and Phinney (1989) models is somewhat counterintuitive. Diffusion typically means that pieces of something are dispersed or scattered, whereas diffusion in the Marcia (1980) and Phinney (1989) models means that identity is not yet developed. Foreclosure and moratorium typically mean inactivity, but in the Marcia (1980) and Phinney (1989) models, these stages involve activity with respect to identity.

Poston (1990) Biracial Identity Development Model

The preceding models have focused on individuals of a single race or ethnicity. They do not account for the possibility of identifying with multiple racial or ethnic groups (Poston, 1990). However, there is much less empirical research on multiracial identity than there is on the monoracial models discussed above.

Poston (1990) proposed a stage model of biracial identity development to address identification with multiple groups. The *personal identity* stage involves a sense of self that is independent of racial or ethnic background, involving such factors as self-esteem or self-worth. Persons in this stage are often very young. The personal identity stage is analogous to the Cross (1971, 1991) pre-encounter stage.

Choice of group categorization is the second stage in which individuals usually choose one ethnic group (Poston, 1990). This choice is sometimes forced and influenced by the status of the ethnic groups to which one belongs, social support for acceptance and participation in a culture, and other factors, such as physical appearance and cultural knowledge. A choice of a multiethnic identity is unusual at this stage because it requires knowledge of multiple cultures and acceptance of multiple identities within a single individual. Choice of group categorization has some similarities to the Cross (1971, 1991) encounter stage.

The third stage of the Poston (1990) model is *enmeshment/denial*. This stage involves confusion and guilt over choosing one identity over the other. Inherent in this stage is a sense of disloyalty and guilt over rejecting the identity of one parent. There may also be perceptions of a lack of acceptance from other groups. Enmeshment/denial is similar to the immersion/emersion stage of the Cross (1971, 1991) model.

The *appreciation* stage is when individuals begin to appreciate their multiple identities and to explore these identities (Poston, 1990). However, they still tend to identify with one group. Appreciation has some similarities to Cross's (1971, 1991) immersion/emersion stage.

In the *integration* stage, biracial persons recognize and value all their ethnic identities. Their identity is secure and integrated. This stage is similar to the Cross (1971, 1991) internalization stage.

A strength of the Poston (1990) Biracial Identity Development Model is that it incorporates aspects of other stage models for application with biracial persons. Unlike the other models, however, this model has not stimulated much research interest. Much of the work on biracial identity is theoretical or qualitative.

Summary

In summary, racial identity focuses on the meaning and importance of race, and responses to racism, and ethnic identity involves the strength of identification with one's ethnic group. Identity development is an internal process, as proposed by ego identity theory, that develops in a social context, as proposed by social identity theory. Racial/ethnic identity develops over time and may be expressed at a particular time point (Yip et al., 2014). The Cross model of racial identity, which includes pre-encounter, encounter, immersion-emersion, and internalization stages, was pioneering and is reflected in subsequent models of racial and ethnic identity. Identity models have been developed for European Americans, African Americans, multiple ethnic groups, and biracial persons.

MODELS OF ACCULTURATION

Elena is 21 years old and is a junior at a state university. She, her parents, and younger sister moved to California from Mexico for her parents' work to manage a landscaping company when she was in high school. Elena is fluent in Spanish and first learned English when she was in Mexico. Her parents have taught her Mexican cultural traditions and she was raised Catholic. Her community in California was about half Latinx and half European American and she has good friends in both groups. Elena has done well academically in high school and in college.

Ajay is 20 years old and is a sophomore at an Ivy League university. Both his parents are physicians and he came with them and his sister to Texas from India for his parents' medical residency training when he was five years old. His parents wanted their children to assimilate to the United States. The family has no religious traditions. He considers himself to be an American and associates Indian traditions with his parents' generation. Although there were a few Asian Indian Americans in his community, most of his friends are European Americans. Ajay has excelled academically in high school and college.

The previous models of racial and ethnic identity address issues of persons who presumably already live in a single context in which there are multiple ethnic, racial, and cultural groups. Accessing and developing one's racial or ethnic identity may be challenging if one is removed from it by generations (e.g., one's family has been in the U.S. for several generations) or geography (e.g., living in an area where there are not others with the same racial or ethnic background). In contrast, models of acculturation address movement from one culture to another and involve immigrants who come to the United States from other countries, as well as their children. The balance between the culture of origin and the host culture is central to the identity of immigrants and their children. Contact between a cultural group and a host culture that changes either or both groups is known as *acculturation* (Berry, 2003). Acculturation affects cultural values and behaviors, media use, language use and preferences, ethnic identity, and family obligations (Telzer, 2010). The host culture usually has more power than other cultural groups and exerts this power to change the other cultural groups. For example, there is strong pressure for immigrant groups in the United States to learn English, and some Americans want English to be the official language of the United States.

Immigrant adults are considered to be the first generation and their children born in the United States are considered the second generation. Children who come to the United States with their parents, as Elena and Ajay did, are considered *1.5-generation* immigrants (Portes & Rumbaut, 1996). Learning a new culture and language is more challenging for first generation immigrants than for their children (Birman & Simon, 2014). The challenge for the second generation is to integrate or choose between their culture of origin and mainstream United States culture. Differing rates of acculturation may also create conflicts between immigrant parents and their children. For example, different choices between parents and children in language, food, and ethnicities of friends may spur conflict.

Acculturation is not necessarily a linear process in which a person smoothly transitions from one culture to another. Indeed, the acculturation process may be stressful (Berry, 2003; C. Williams & Berry, 1991). There are different strategies that individuals adopt in the process of acculturation.

Picture 2.2
Source: shutterstock.

Berry (1974) Model of Acculturation

Berry (1974) proposed *assimilation*, *separation*, *integration*, and *marginalization* as modes of acculturation that involve attitudes and behaviors in intercultural encounters. When a cultural group does not wish to maintain its cultural identity, it may seek to assimilate. This is the "melting pot" model of acculturation. The *assimilation* model may be more relevant for European immigrants, whose race and cultures are more similar to those of European Americans, than for immigrants of color. Moreover, some persons of color may seek to assimilate into the European American mainstream, but may be prevented by the mainstream from doing so. For example, because of their appearance, many Asian Americans may be viewed as foreigners regardless of how many generations they have been in the United States (Tuan, 1998). Although Ajay wants to assimilate, in some settings people will see him and assume that he is not an American. Because of language barriers or discrimination in the United States that may bar immigrants from the jobs or positions that they had in their countries of origin (e.g., teacher), "downward assimilation" to a lower social class may occur (Portes & Rumbaut, 1996). In an international study of over 5000 adolescent immigrants from 26 cultural backgrounds who immigrated into 13 White majority countries (U.S., Canada, Australia, New Zealand, European countries, Israel), less than one-fifth of the sample had an assimilation profile, in which identity with the host nation (national identity) was strong and ethnic identity weak (Berry, Phinney, Sam, & Vedder, 2006). Assimilation corresponds to the pre-encounter stage in the Cross (1971, 1991) model of racial identity and to the assimilationist ideology of the Sellers et al. (1998) model.

Separation occurs when a group wishes to maintain its culture and does not wish to interact with others in the host culture. For example, transnationalists who travel back to and from their country of origin (Vertovec, 1999) or sojourners who intend to return to their culture of origin may not wish to adopt the customs of the host country. Other separatists may believe that the host culture's values are detrimental or may be reacting to rejection by the host culture. Separatists are often segregated from the host culture, voluntarily (e.g., choosing to live in a particular community, such as Little Saigon) or involuntarily (e.g., exclusion from a particular community). A separatist group would need to be relatively large and powerful to successfully maintain an identity. In the international study of adolescent immigration, about one-fourth of the respondents had a strong ethnic identification and weak national identification, which could be considered a separatist orientation (Berry et al., 2006). Separation generally corresponds to the Cross (1971, 1991) immersion-emersion stage and the Sellers et al. (1998) oppressed minority ideology.

The *integration* strategy involves maintaining one's culture while interacting with the host culture. Elena's relationships with two cultures characterize the integration strategy. Integrationists seek to participate in the host culture as members of their culture of origin. Integration can occur only when the dominant group is open to and inclusive of diverse groups. Such a multicultural society in which power is shared and in which integration is possible is difficult to achieve in practice (LaFromboise, Coleman, & Gerton, 1993). The U.S. has been characterized as relatively assimilationist and Canada as relatively integrationist (Berry, 2003). However, in both countries, persons of European ancestry are in power and there is limited evidence of willingness to share power at all levels of society. For example, until 2008, all the chief political leaders of both countries had been men of European ancestry. In the international study of adolescent immigrants, ethnic identity and identity with the host country were positively associated among about one-third of the respondents (Berry et al., 2006). This was considered an integration strategy, but it is unclear how strongly the members of the host countries identified these immigrants as part of their country and culture. Integration corresponds to Cross's (1971, 1991) internalization stage and the Sellers et al. (1998) humanist ideology.

Marginalization involves not being interested in maintaining one's culture of origin or in interacting with the host culture. As with separation, marginalization may be voluntary or involuntary. Those having low ethnic and national identities were the smallest group in the international adolescent immigration study (Berry et al., 2006). Marginalization does not exactly correspond with any of the Cross (1971, 1991) stages or Sellers et al. (1998) ideologies, although a person in the encounter and immersion-emersion stages or having an oppressed minority ideology could feel marginalized.

In reading about these four acculturation strategies, you are probably thinking that they affect a person's adjustment and mental health. Yoon and colleagues (2013) studied the effects of these acculturation strategies on mental health in a meta-analysis (see definition in Chapter 1) that included 325 studies and 72,013 participants. Mental health outcomes were negative and positive mental health. Negative mental health included depression, anxiety, psychological distress, and negative affect. Positive mental health included self-esteem, satisfaction with life, and positive affect. As can be seen in Figure 2.3, the integration strategy was negatively correlated with negative mental health symptoms (meaning that the integration strategy was associated with fewer negative symptoms) and was positively correlated with positive mental health symptoms. Marginalization was positively correlated with negative mental health symptoms (meaning that it was associated with more negative mental health symptoms) but the correlation between marginalization and positive mental health symptoms was near zero. The other acculturation strategies were weakly correlated with negative and positive mental health symptoms.

The results of the Yoon et al. (2013) study suggest that integration is the most adaptive strategy and marginalization the least in terms of mental health. Integration may be adaptive because the individual can access cultural resources from two cultures. For example, the support of a cohesive family and racial/ethnic community is offered by the culture of origin, which is less emphasized in the host culture. At the same time, seeking help for mental health problems may be viewed with less stigma in the host culture than in the culture of origin.

A strength of the Berry Model of Acculturation is that it accounts for the possibility of maintaining a culture of origin while adapting to a new culture. Missing from the model is the new identity that immigrants may develop in a new culture that is unlike their culture of origin or the new culture. For example, most immigrant adolescents from China and Mexico in a study in Los Angeles considered themselves to be Chinese Americans and Mexican Americans rather than Chinese, Mexican, or American (Fuligni,

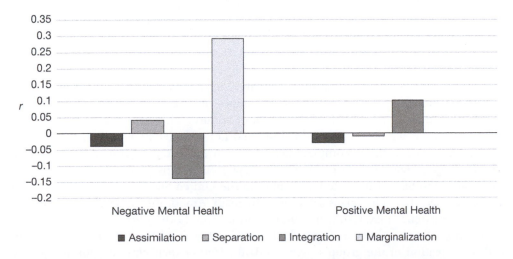

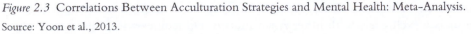

Figure 2.3 Correlations Between Acculturation Strategies and Mental Health: Meta-Analysis.
Source: Yoon et al., 2013.

Witkow, & Garcia, 2005). Berry's integration model involves alternating between two cultures rather than fusing them as many immigrants, particularly children, do. Moreover, similar to other acculturation models, Berry's model does not fully address the experiences of the children of immigrants.

LaFromboise, Coleman, and Gerton (1993) Models of Acculturation

LaFromboise and her colleagues (LaFromboise et al., 1993) have proposed models of acculturation that are applicable to North American ethnic minority groups and offer alternatives in addition to the four acculturation strategies proposed by Berry (2003). The LaFromboise model describes five models of acculturation: assimilation, acculturation, fusion, alternation, and multicultural. *Assimilation* involves absorption into the dominant or more desirable culture. Immigrants who voluntarily come to the United States are more likely to desire to assimilate than those who have been forced to immigrate (e.g., slaves, refugees; Ogbu, 1986). Similarly, you are more likely to identify with a college that you are attending if you have chosen it than if your parents have chosen for you. In a sense, you are an "involuntary immigrant" if your choice of college is restricted for economic or geographic reasons, whereas you are a "voluntary immigrant" if you are able to attend the college of your choice. However, not all who desire to assimilate into a culture are able to assimilate.

The cultural distance between one's culture of origin and the second culture may affect one's ability to assimilate (C. Williams & Berry, 1991). For example, an Asian Indian who is Hindu will probably have a more difficult time assimilating into mainstream American culture than a person from England who is a Christian. There is relatively little cultural distance between Ajay's family and the mainstream United States culture insofar as his parents are physicians without a religious background that might be at odds with religious traditions in the United States. The dangers of assimilation involve loss of one's original cultural identity and rejection by the members of one's culture of origin (LaFromboise et al., 1993). Each ethnic group has its pejorative terms for persons of color who are trying to assimilate or are "White on the inside" but not on the outside. These include "oreo" (African Americans), "coconut" (Latinx), "banana" (Asian Americans), and "apple" (American Indians). The assimilation model is analogous to Berry's (2003) assimilation strategy.

A second model of acculturation is actually known as *acculturation* (LaFromboise et al., 1993). This involves a person who is competent in a second culture, but always will be identified as a member of the minority culture. This person may be relegated to a lower status within the second culture and not completely accepted. Such bicultural competence without complete acceptance in mainstream United States culture might be Ajay's fate because of his physical appearance. His parents are Asian Indian physicians who have had residency training in the United States and are competent in medicine. Yet, these physicians are viewed by many Americans as somehow "foreign." Such an experience may result in marginalization from both cultures. One reaction to such marginalization is separatism, which involves the formation of one's own group with the creation of the group's own standards. Rather than compete for acceptance in mainstream American culture, Asian Indian physicians might form their own group and associate exclusively with other Asian Indians. Difficulties with separatism are that some interaction with other groups is usually necessary unless one is in a large community of others similar to oneself (e.g., Chinatown). Another difficulty is that the mainstream can more easily ignore a separatist group than a group that attempts to interact with the mainstream. The acculturation model incorporates aspects of Berry's (2003) separation and marginalization strategies.

Another model of acculturation is *fusion* (LaFromboise et al., 1993). Fusion involves cultures sharing an economic, political, or geographic space fusing together until they are indistinguishable and form a new culture. The fusion model differs from the assimilation model because aspects of multiple cultures are integrated into the new culture. It differs from the multicultural model because cultures of origin are not distinctively maintained. An example of fusion cuisine in sushi is the California roll. Sushi in Japan typically includes Japanese rice, seaweed (*nori*), vegetables, and seafood. The California roll includes Japanese rice and nori plus vegetables (avocado) and seafood (crab) from California. Thus, Japanese and American cuisines are fused to create something new. However, what typically occurs when multiple cultures share the same space is that the cultural minority groups become absorbed into the majority group at the price of their cultural identity (LaFromboise et al., 1993). Fusion is not clearly represented in Berry's (2003) model.

A fourth model of acculturation is *alternation*, which involves competence in two cultures (LaFromboise et al., 1993). The two cultures are regarded as equal, and a person maintains positive relationships with both cultures without having to choose between them. The biculturally competent individual alters their behavior to fit a particular sociocultural context. For example, if one's cultural background values restraint, one is restrained in contexts where restraint is valued. In other settings where free expression is valued, such as in many European American settings, a biculturally competent person is able to shift to a more expressive mode. Alternation is regarded as an optimal mode of functioning by LaFromboise and her colleagues (1993). However, American society does not equally value all cultures, and alternation may be difficult to maintain in practice. A truly biculturally competent person may have to overemphasize the non-European American culture in order to balance the emphasis of European American culture in society. In other words, an overemphasis on a minority culture may be required to actually regard the minority culture as equal to European culture and to achieve positive relationships with both cultures. Alternation incorporates aspects of Berry's (2003) integration strategy.

The *multicultural* model of acculturation involves distinct cultural identities that are maintained while cultures are tied together within a single multicultural social structure (LaFromboise et al., 1993). Individuals from one culture cooperate with those of other cultures to serve common needs. An example of this might be ethnic communities that have intergroup contact but at the same time maintain their culture of origin. A city might have Little Tokyo, Little Saigon, and Little Italy neighborhoods that are in geographic proximity and work cooperatively as part of the larger city structure. However, in real-life situations, separation of cultural groups is more common than interaction and cooperation. When there is interaction, there also tends to be mutual influence and cultures of origins tend not to be distinctly maintained. Thus, the multicultural model is difficult to achieve in practice (LaFromboise et al., 1993). The multicultural model is analogous to Berry's (2003) multicultural strategy.

Summary

In summary, acculturation involves contact between a cultural group and a host culture that changes either or both groups. Berry's classic model proposed assimilation, separation, integration, and marginalization as modes of acculturation. This model has parallels with racial identity models. LaFromboise and colleagues' theory of acculturation describes five models of acculturation: assimilation, acculturation, fusion, alternation, and multicultural. These models are alternatives to Berry's model.

CONCLUSION

There is much diversity within racial and ethnic groups. No two members of a group are exactly alike. Individual group members vary on how much they identify with their group, how they feel about their group, and how much experience they have had with their group and its culture. Similarly, members of racial and ethnic groups vary on their levels of acculturation. Although two people from the same group may look similar, a person whose family has been in the United States for multiple generations will likely differ on acculturation from a person who is an immigrant. Despite this within-group diversity, however, racial/ethnic identity and acculturation are shared experiences for people of color. Racial/ethnic identity and acculturation provide a framework to understand these common experiences.

RESOURCES

Blogs:
Be True to Your School(s): Integrating Identities www.psychologytoday.com/blog/life-in-the-intersection/201705/be-true-your-schools.
Never Home for the Holidays: The Unbearable Otherness of Being Biracial www.1.com/blog/life-in-the-intersection/201612/never-home-the-holidays.

Video:
Immigrant Voices Make Democracy Stronger – Sayu Bhojwani www.ted.com/talks/sayu_bhojwani_how_immigrant_voices_make_democracy_stronger.

CHAPTER 3

Multicultural Research Methods

Audrey is a 20-year-old Mexican American sophomore at a research university. She is majoring in psychology and is planning to apply to graduate school in clinical psychology. Audrey appreciates the fact that psychological research can quantify people's experiences, making them less subjective. She is interested in clinical psychology because it is an evidence-based approach to helping people. Audrey feels that the public perception of psychology is "anything goes" and she wants to counter this perception by pursuing quantitative approaches to human experience.

James is a 20-year-old Chinese American sophomore at a private college. He is majoring in psychology and is planning to apply to graduate school in counseling psychology. James appreciates psychology because of its flexibility in including both quantitative and qualitative approaches. James feels that existing personality tests impose someone else's reality on others. He believes that people should be able to describe their unique perspectives. Counseling psychology is an opportunity for him to learn to help people understand their own experiences.

Most psychology research does not focus on unique cultural contexts of behavior. As discussed in Chapter 1, generalizability research minimizes differences and group differences research examines differences relative to a reference group, usually European Americans. In contrast, multicultural research focuses on the unique characteristics of understudied groups. It is possible that many psychology researchers are invested in their generalizability or group differences approach and are not interested in unique cultural characteristics or do not want to take the time and effort required to study them. However, it is also possible that many psychology researchers do not know how to study the unique cultural aspects of groups.

The purpose of this chapter is to review research design issues relevant to multicultural psychology. A consideration of these issues will allow you to critique the research of others and to conduct culturally competent research of your own. Unfortunately, much psychological research addresses few, if any, of these issues. No single study can address all the issues raised in this chapter. However, the more issues that are addressed, the more culturally competent the study will be.

This chapter begins with a discussion of issues in quantitative research. Most research in psychology, including multicultural psychology, is quantitative. Quantitative methods are what interest Audrey, mentioned at the beginning of this chapter, the most. The second section of the chapter is on qualitative research, which is particularly relevant when there are not existing theories or research on phenomena. James, mentioned at the beginning of the chapter, appreciates the flexibility of psychology to include qualitative approaches.

QUANTITATIVE RESEARCH METHODS

The Scientific Method

Similar to other sciences, research in psychology is guided by the scientific method. The scientific method has four steps:

1   Observing phenomena.
2   Formulating a hypothesis.
3   Using the hypothesis to make a prediction.
4   Testing the prediction with an experiment.

An example would be that you observe that many Asian Americans are concerned about the impact of their behavior on others, particularly those in their own group. You formulate a hypothesis that Asian Americans are concerned about the impact of their behavior on others because they are also concerned about loss of face and loss of face is more likely and important in one's own group than outside the group. Your prediction is that in a group discussion Asian Americans will be more concerned about face loss when they are part of a group than when they are not part of a group. You test this hypothesis in the following experiment: You randomly assign Asian American college students to one of two groups of mixed ethnic composition in which: (a) the group works together to create a mutually agreed upon alternative to raising tuition; or (b) individuals are expected to create their own alternatives to raising tuition and then discuss their alternatives with the group. The mixed ethnic composition of the two groups is to prevent Asian Americans from feeling connections with other group members solely based on ethnicity (i.e., seeing other Asian Americans as part of their group). After the Asian American participants create the alternative to raising tuition, you give them a measure of concerns about loss of face. Asian American participants expressing greater concern about loss of face in the first group in which a mutual solution is developed than in the second group in which individual solutions are developed would be support for the hypothesis. Loss of face should be more prominent when an Asian American is part of a group than when they are not. If there are no group differences or if Asian Americans in the individual solution group express greater concern about loss of face, then the hypothesis would not be supported.

The participants in the alternatives to raising tuition study are all college students. However, college students differ from other Asian Americans in terms of many variables, including age, education, and socioeconomic status. Yet, most psychology experiments involve college students, particularly European American ones, in laboratory settings (Arnett, 2008). In the example, the discussion about raising tuition occurs in a laboratory setting, which is contrived and does not necessarily resemble behavior outside the laboratory. Psychology experiments are conducted with college students in controlled laboratory settings to maximize experimental control and *internal validity*, which allow the identification of cause–effect relationships. However, Stanley Sue (1999) has contended that psychological science has overemphasized internal validity and underemphasized *external validity*, which is the extent to which results can be generalized to populations and settings of interest. An externally valid example of face loss research could be concern about losing face for one's family preventing Asian Americans from seeking mental health services. Not seeking mental health services is much more consequential than a contrived laboratory experiment on alternatives to tuition increases, which may not have much real-world impact when the experiment is over. This book's primary focus is on externally valid research.

Theory-Guided Research

A scientific theory is a set of statements that is *explanatory* and *predictive*. A theory explains why a phenomenon occurs. This explanatory function involves the basis or mechanism of a phenomenon. For example, the Multidimensional Model of Racial Identity (Sellers et al., 1998) discussed in Chapter 2 explains how race affects self-perception. If race is salient in a particular situation and central to a person's identity, the person has positive regard for their racial group, and they have a nationalist identity, then they are likely to have a positive self-perception.

A second function of a theory is prediction. Rather than simply describing a current phenomenon, a theory makes predictions concerning the future. Using the Multidimensional Model of Racial Identity as an example, the model would predict that a person with the characteristics described above would be politically active in causes that support the rights of African Americans to form their own identity and make their own decisions.

A good theory will lead to testable hypotheses and will guide the selection of measures, data analyses, and interpretation of data. A carefully designed study can provide support or lack of support for a particular theory. A single study does not prove or disprove a theory, but may offer support or lack of support for the theory. However, a series of studies can provide evidence for the accuracy of a theory's predictions or may provide clues on how the theory should be modified.

As an example of how a theory can guide research, Smalls, White, Chavous, and Sellers (2007) used the Multidimensional Model of Racial Identity (MMRI) as a theoretical framework to predict academic engagement among African American adolescents. The theoretical model predicted that African American youth who endorsed an assimilationist ideology, emphasizing their similarities to European Americans, would be less academically engaged than African American youth who endorsed a minority ideology, emphasizing their similarities to other African Americans. The Multidimensional Inventory of Black Identity, which is based on the MMRI, was used to assess the participants in the study. The predictions of the MMRI were supported. An assimiliationist identity was associated with more fears of being viewed by peers as high achievers, less persistence with schoolwork, less interest and excitement in academic tasks, and more behavioral problems than was a minority identity.

Research without a theory often leads to post hoc speculation about the meaning of the results and may not advance science as far as providing support or lack of support for a scientific theory. Unfortunately, much racial and ethnic differences research in psychology is atheoretical. For example, researchers found no differences between African American and European American college students on a measure of anxiety (DeLapp, Chapman, & Williams, 2016). They speculated that there might be cultural differences between the groups that could have influenced the results. But they did not measure culture, which seemed to be an afterthought.

Summary

In summary, the purposes of a theory are to explain and predict. A good theory leads to testable hypotheses and can guide the design of a study. Research without a theory leads to post hoc speculation and does little to advance science.

Sampling Issues

Much of what we know in psychology is based on studies of college students. College students are readily available on the campuses where many psychology researchers do their work – college students are a convenience sample. Given that most psychological theories and research are assumed to generalize to all persons, the representativeness of college students either is not addressed in studies or a caveat about college students being not representative is included in the study. The caveat about representativeness is often lip service, as subsequent research on many topics rarely ventures beyond the college campus.

Although college students are a convenience sample, they may be quite relevant for some research topics. Academic achievement studies would logically include college students. The college environment also offers many opportunities for social and sexual interaction, some of which is aggressive. My colleagues and I have found that about one-third of college men admit to perpetrating some form of sexual aggression and that there are not significant ethnic differences in this rate (G. Hall, Teten, DeGarmo, Due, & Stephens, 2005). College students may have more opportunities for sexually aggressive behavior than persons who are not in college. Nevertheless, college students are not representative of all members of any ethnic group. Only about one-third of all adults in the United States have a college degree (Ryan & Bauman, 2016).

Another convenience sample is persons of color who are of lower socioeconomic status. Access to these samples is often achieved via social service agencies, such as hospitals or community mental health clinics. However, persons of color who are of lower socioeconomic status are also not representative of most persons of color, who are not poor (U.S. Bureau of the Census, 2013). Research on persons of color who are of lower socioeconomic status is important because it could guide the development of useful interventions for these populations. Nevertheless, a disproportionate emphasis on these persons has left psychology with a dearth of information on persons of color who are not poor, and generalizations from those who are poor to all members of ethnic groups (G. Hall, 2004).

Patients in mental health centers or psychiatric hospitals are another sample of convenience that is not representative of ethnic communities. It is obvious that persons with psychological disorders do not represent those in a community without disorders. However, psychiatric patients of color also may not be representative of persons of color with psychological disorders. For example, among Asian Americans and Mexican Americans with a probable psychological disorder in national community samples, only about one-third sought mental health services (Abe-Kim et al., 2007; Alegría et al., 2007). Nevertheless, patient populations are of interest because they may represent individuals having psychological disorders that are relatively severe, even if some community members with severe problems are not receiving services.

Within any sample there is much variability. For example, individuals within a sample of Mexican Americans may vary on cultural heritage (e.g., experiences with Mexican cultures), family structure (e.g., nuclear, extended), religion (e.g., Catholicism, no religion), generation (born in Mexico, born in U.S.), acculturation (e.g., relative identification with Mexican and mainstream United States cultures), language use (Spanish, English), legal status, socioeconomic status, and experiences with racism (Bernal, Cumba-Avilés, & Rodriguez-Quintana, 2014). Combining people into a single group (e.g., Mexican Americans) for purposes of generalization or group comparisons overlooks such within-group diversity. This underscores the importance of the multicultural psychology research approach discussed in Chapter 1 in understanding the complexity and nuances of ethnic groups.

Summary

In summary, convenience samples are typically studied in psychology research. These include college students, lower socioeconomic status populations, and clinical populations. Although none of these convenience samples is representative of populations of persons of color, each may be useful depending on the purpose of the research.

Picture 3.1
Source: shutterstock.

Recruitment of Participants

Once a population of interest is identified to study, how is a sample of the population recruited? The process of recruiting persons of color to psychology research may be analogous to how I choose a Japanese restaurant (cf. G. Hall & Eap, 2007). Authenticity of Japanese food is my criterion. If I am in an unfamiliar city, I may peek into the restaurant to see if the cook is Japanese and if the customers are Japanese. Recommendations of a restaurant from Asian friends might also get me to try it. Restaurant reviews by Asian reviewers also could be persuasive. Of course, non-Japanese persons may be quite capable of cooking and evaluating the authenticity of Japanese food. Likewise, some Asian persons may be poor cooks and judges of the authenticity of Japanese food. Nevertheless, Japanese ethnicity suggests that the person is similar to me and is more likely to have similar tastes than someone who is not of the same ethnicity.

A process similar to that in my selection of Japanese restaurants may occur among persons of color who are deciding whether to participate in research. A researcher and participants in the project who are of the same ethnicity as the potential participants may be viewed as a rationale for participation. Also, word of mouth in an ethnic community may facilitate participation. If the researcher and participants are not ethnically similar, a potential participant could view the project as not relevant. These issues of ethnic matching of researchers and participants are analogous to ethnic matching in psychotherapy between therapist and client, which is associated with clients not dropping out of psychotherapy and showing greater improvements (Griner & Smith, 2006).

Even if the intent of the project is to recruit persons of color (e.g., African Americans), potential participants may be suspicious of the motives of a researcher who is not a person of color. For example, some members of ethnic communities may refuse or be reluctant to participate in research out of fear that the researchers will report their immigration status to government authorities. Another example is the distrust of African Americans of research because of the Tuskegee Syphilis Study (see Box 3.1).

BOX 3.1 THE TUSKEGEE SYPHILIS STUDY

Many African Americans may distrust research and the medical community because of the abuses of the Tuskegee Syphilis Study. In 1932, the United States Public Health Service began a study in Alabama of 200 African American men with latent or late syphilis and 200 African American men without syphilis (Paul & Brookes, 2015). Although the men with syphilis were given free medical care, meals, and burial insurance, treatments for syphilis, such as penicillin, were withheld. These men were poor and had almost no access to health services. The study was designed to last 6–8 months but continued for 40 years (Paul & Brookes, 2015). This study did not come to the public's attention until the 1970s, when it was exposed by journalists. Although some compensation was eventually provided to the participants, none of the researchers faced criminal charges.

The Tuskegee study has created a climate of mistrust of medical care among African Americans. African Americans are more likely than European Americans to believe that a similar study could occur again and to distrust the medical care system (Brandon, Isaac, & LaVeist, 2013). This mistrust is reflected in African Americans' attitudes toward AIDS. A third of African Americans in a large study believed that the AIDS epidemic was a government plot to kill African Americans (Russell et al., 2011). Thus, it is not surprising some African American men may distrust medical advice, such as using condoms (Des Jarlais, McCarty, Vega, & Bramson, 2013).

You may know that a study in which necessary treatment is withheld would not be allowed today because of ethics review of research and because participants are asked for informed consent. Neither ethics review nor informed consent was part of the Tuskegee Syphilis Study. The Belmont Report (National Commission for the Protection of Human Subjects of Biomedical and Behavioral Research, 1979) was an investigation of the Tuskegee study by a panel of experts in medicine, law, religion, labor, education, health administration, and public affairs that led to the establishment of the human subjects review boards that we have today.

Discussion

1   The federal government is considering exempting surveys, interviews, and some psychology experiments from Institutional Research Board review (www.chronicle.com/article/Long-Sought-Research/239459). Could such deregulation have an adverse impact on people of color?
2   How can researchers gain the trust of African Americans who are skeptical of research?

To the extent that researchers of color can attract persons of color to research projects, it is important for researchers of color to be represented on research teams (C. Fisher et al., 2002; G. Hall, 2001). This means that it is important to recruit students of color into the field of psychology. Persons of color may have expertise on ethnic communities, and may have valuable contacts within ethnic communities that might facilitate community research participation. Ideally, persons of color should be co-investigators in research, not subordinates, and should be involved in the project from its inception. Of course, not all persons of color are identified with or connected to ethnic communities and may have no more expertise or contacts than someone who is not a person of color.

It has been recommended that culturally competent research teams be established to study communities of color (Chun, Morera, Andal, & Skewes, 2007). *Cultural competence* has been defined as:

- understanding one's own cultural background and how it shapes attitudes and beliefs;
- knowledge of different worldviews of individuals and groups; and
- skills in the use of culturally appropriate communication and intervention (D. Sue, 2001).

In forming research teams, it has been suggested that formal measures of cultural competence, such as the Multicultural Awareness-Knowledge-Skills Survey (D'Andrea, Daniels, & Heck, 1991), be considered to stimulate self-assessment and team discussion and reflection (Chun et al., 2007). Culturally competent research involves the incorporation of culture at every stage of the research design, including its conceptualization (G. Hall, 2001; Yali & Revenson, 2004). Thus, the recruitment of a diverse sample in a project not designed to incorporate culture would not be culturally competent research.

A culturally competent researcher of color can serve as a culture broker between the psychology and ethnic communities. A *culture broker* is one who mediates between two or more cultural groups. A basic form of culture brokering involves language translation. Nevertheless, language skills do not necessarily ensure cultural competence. Culture brokering may involve other mediation, such as explaining cultural norms that differ between groups. For example, participation of persons from a collectivist community in a research project that is framed as a means of helping others in one's own community may be more appealing than a project framed as advancing scientific knowledge or as generally helping unspecified persons.

Even community "insiders" can experience ethnic community resistance to participation in research. Native American psychologist Joseph Gone (2006) thoughtfully describes his experience as an insider/outsider/hybrid in attempting to conduct research in a tribal community. Community members may be suspicious that those who have received training outside the community are no longer part of the community. Social class differences between researchers and participants may transcend ethnic similarity. Graduate education typically is a process of acculturation that may leave the trainee less competent in their ethnic communities to the extent that the trainee has adopted the values of academia and left ethnic community values behind (G. Hall, Lopez, & Bansal, 2001). When a community perceives condescension, entitlement, assumptions of deviance, or self-absorbed career ambition on the part of a researcher, the community is unlikely to be fully cooperative (Harrell & Bond, 2006).

In addition to researchers of color, community leaders who are supportive of research can serve as culture brokers. In some contexts, such as with Native American tribal groups, the approval of community leaders is mandatory for research to take place (P. Fisher & Ball, 2003). It is important to determine that those who appear to be leaders are actually considered leaders in the community. For example, researchers might consider persons in the community who are most educated to be leaders. Yet, the actual community leaders whose guidance is sought and who have decision-making authority may be others, such as elders, who do not necessarily have the most education. Also, leaders must have the cooperation of their community for their leadership to be effective. A leader could agree to have a community participate in research, but this agreement does not necessarily guarantee the community's interest and cooperation.

Community education can also be implemented in the recruitment of ethnic minority participants (C. Fisher et al., 2002). Researchers can educate communities about the research process and content via speakers' bureaus, mass media, social media, schools, health centers, and religious organizations. Such previews of research allow potential participants to make informed decisions about participation.

There also may exist logistical barriers to ethnic minority research participation. These include work schedules, location of research projects, and transportation availability (Chun et al., 2007; C. Fisher et al., 2002). Offering monetary incentives and conducting research in familiar settings, such as the home, are strategies of increasing compliance (Burlew, 2003). However, monetary incentives may attract persons who need the money most, which could reduce the representativeness of a sample. Moreover, high payment levels could be considered coercive if no similar levels of payment are available for other non-research activities. A culture broker may understand these logistical issues and may be able to create bridges from the research to the community that overcome these barriers to research participation.

One possible method of diversifying samples is Internet-based research (Gosling, Vazire, Srivastava, & John, 2004). However, the diversity of Internet samples is dependent upon access to and skills in using the Internet. There are ethnic differences in Internet use. Although a greater percentage of English-speaking Latinx Americans (78%) than European Americans (73%) use the Internet, only 62% of African Americans use the Internet (Pew Internet & American Life Project, 2007). Moreover, representation of ethnic minorities in Internet research samples differs only slightly from traditional research samples. Gosling et al. (2004) reported that 77% of Internet-based research samples and 80% of traditional samples in social psychology research were European American. Nevertheless, Internet-based research samples tend to be quite large and even small percentages of ethnic minority participants may constitute samples of 1000 or more (Gosling et al., 2004).

Summary

In summary, ethnic similarity between researchers and research participants may facilitate recruitment of participants into research studies. Culture brokers from the community, cultural competence on the part of researchers, and offering benefits to a community, such as money or education, also facilitate the recruitment process. Internet-based research is an emerging method of recruiting samples of color.

Ethnic and Racial Identification

Once a diverse research sample is recruited, how is the race or ethnicity of the participants assessed? Perhaps the most common method of assessing race or ethnicity involves a single-item test in which a person chooses a category, such as White, Hispanic, Asian, African American, Native American, or Other. Occasionally, a person is allowed to indicate more than one of these categories. However, these categories are not equivalent to any specific behaviors, traits, or biological or environmental conditions (C. Fisher et al., 2002; Helms, Jernigan, & Mascher, 2005). Moreover, self-designation of race or ethnicity may not correspond well with designations by others. In an analysis of more than 730,000 Veterans Administration files, there was only approximately 60% agreement between patients' self-designated ethnicities versus their ethnicities determined by clinicians or registration clerks (Kressin, Chang, Hendricks, & Kazis, 2003). Agreement was particularly poor for patients who self-designated as Native American or Asian Pacific Islander.

It has been contended that comparisons using racial and ethnic categories should not be used in empirical research (C. Fisher et al., 2002; Helms et al., 2005; Phinney, 1996). Conversely, other researchers have advocated ethnic group comparisons to test the cultural generalizability of theories (Heine & Norenzayan, 2006). Studies purely designed to determine the generalizability of a finding are atheoretical because they do not hypothesize reasons for possible cultural differences (van de Vijver & Leung, 2000). Broad racial/ethnic categories do not correspond with culture. Included within each of these categories is much variability. Therefore, if two ethnic groups differ from one another on some variable (e.g., extroversion), it cannot be concluded that race, ethnicity, or culture is the basis of the difference. The basis of a difference in such a simplistic contrast between ill-defined categories is unknown. Moreover, the absence of differences between two groups could also be a result of within-group variability. Individuals in both groups may vary on a dimension (e.g., extroversion) such that any between-groups differences are obscured.

The assessment of race and ethnicity is much more complex than endorsing one or a few categorical items. Trimble, Helms, and Root (2003) suggested that the assessment of race and ethnicity should address:

- natality;
- subjective identification;
- behavioral expressions of identity; and
- situational or contextual influences.

Natality includes where one and one's ancestors were born, which is objective information. However, one's *subjective identification* of ethnic or racial identity may or may not coincide with natality. A person could be born in the U.S. but identify with an ancestral ethnic or racial group. *Behavioral expressions* of identity may or may not correspond to natality and subjective identification. For example, a person may engage in ancestral cultural customs (e.g., religious ceremonies) because of family or peer pressure, but not be subjectively identified with the group. Finally, opportunities for subjective identification and behavioral expressions of identity may depend on *situational or contextual opportunities*. For example, a person may not develop a subjective identification with a group in the absence of other members of the group. Similarly, one who has a strong subjective identification with a group may live in a situation in which there are not opportunities for behavioral expression (e.g., cultural festivals).

The most commonly used measures of ethnic and racial identity involve individual self-report (Cross & Vandiver, 2001; Helms & Carter, 1990; Phinney, 1992). However, self-report methods usually do not capture the fluid, contextual nature of ethnic and racial identity (Okazaki, 2002). One method of activating identity from the social cognition field is *priming*. Exposure to relevant cues activates an ethnic or racial meaning system in persons, which affects their social judgments and other behaviors. For example, ethnic identity primes (e.g., questionnaire about generational status, non-English language use) have been found to facilitate Asian American women's math performance relative to women who received gender identity primes (e.g., questionnaire about living in single sex vs. coed dorms) or no prime (Shih, Pittinsky, & Ambady, 1999; Shih, Pittinsky, & Trahan, 2006). Priming ethnic identity boosted math performance because of stereotypes about good math performance among Asians, whereas priming gender identity decreased math performance because of stereotypes about poor math performance among women. A *stereotype* is a positive or negative set of beliefs about the characteristics of a group of people. However, seemingly positive stereotypes, such as Asian math skills, can backfire by creating undue performance pressure. Blatant ethnic primes (e.g., "I am a worthy member of the racial group I belong to"; "Overall, my race is considered good by others") created math performance decrements among Asian American women (Cheryan & Bodenhausen, 2000). Issues of stereotype threat will be discussed in more detail in Chapter 6.

To the extent that culture involves the interaction of individuals and the social environment (López & Guarnaccia, 2000), it would appear informative to study how ethnic identity is expressed in group interactions. One method of eliciting interactional data on ethnic identity would be to have a group (e.g., family) discuss issues of race, ethnicity, and culture while being observed by a researcher. Although behavior observational methods have been shown to be valid for assessment of general behavior (e.g., parenting) in ethnic minority groups (e.g., Rodríguez, Davis, Rodríguez, & Bates, 2006), valid methods of observing expressions of ethnic identity have yet to be established. Structuring a discussion of race, ethnicity, and culture could create an artificial situation (e.g., forced discussion) that would not mirror how ethnic identity is actually expressed. Moreover, some cultural practices are not necessarily observable in brief samples of behavior. For example, parents may select "teachable moments" to convey their beliefs about race, ethnicity, and culture, and may not spontaneously do so during a behavioral observation. Moreover, a parent may silently transmit ethnic identity values, such as working hard and not complaining, by behaving as a role model. Unless the parent mentioned such cultural modeling in an interaction with their children and this was observed by researchers, this modeling would not be detected.

Sociometric methods also assess the individual in the context of their peer group (Tsai, Chentsova-Dutton, & Wong, 2002). These methods are most commonly used with children. One method involves nominations of peers with whom they would most or least like to participate in an activity with. Another method involves rating characteristics of peers, such as who are "most Chinese" or "most American." However, sociometric methods have rarely been used in multicultural research.

Summary

In summary, the most common method of assessing race or ethnicity is with a single self-report item in which a person designates a category. However, race and ethnicity involve multiple components. Although the assessment of race and ethnicity typically involves self-report, other methods, such as priming and sociometric ratings, have been developed.

Cultural Equivalence of Constructs and Measures

A psychological *construct* is a variable of interest assessed (constructed) with multiple measures. For example, the construct of intelligence might be assessed via a combination of performance on a cognitive test, grades in school, a measure of verbal skills, and a measure of social skills. A critical issue in research with multiple racial, ethnic, or cultural groups is whether a construct and its measurement are valid for these groups (Trimble, 2007).

Conceptual equivalence refers to whether the construct has the same meaning across groups (Berry, Poortinga, Segall, & Dasen, 2002). For example, the construct of alexithymia involves difficulty in identifying emotions and distinguishing them from bodily sensations in combination with difficulty in communicating emotions to others (G. Taylor, 1984). Asian Americans report greater levels of alexithymia than do European Americans (Le, Berenbaum, & Raghavan, 2002). Yet, if attention to emotions and emotional expression are viewed as maladaptive in East Asian cultural groups that value interpersonal harmony, then attending to and expressing emotions may not be valued (Yen, Robins, & Lin, 2000). Conversely, somatic symptoms may be a prescribed mode of communicating distress (Yen et al., 2000).

Linguistic equivalence involves whether a translated test of a construct has a similar meaning to the original test (Lonner & Ibrahim, 2002). An optimal approach to linguistic equivalence would be to simultaneously develop a measure in multiple cultures, but this approach is rare (van Widenfelt, Treffers, de Beurs, Siebelink, & Koudijs, 2005). To achieve linguistic equivalence, a test is translated from one language to a foreign language. Ideally, translation is conducted by a team that is bilingual, bicultural, and has expertise in psychology (van Widenfelt et al., 2005). Then, the foreign language version is translated into the original language, which is known as back translation. The back translation version of the test is compared with the original version of the test for accuracy. It is useful to have a review team independent of the translators react to the translation and back translation (Geisinger, 1994). This translation–back translation process can continue until an accurate version of the foreign language translation is achieved (Leong, Okazaki, & Tak, 2003). However, because some concepts are not equivalent across cultures, exact translations are sometimes difficult to achieve (Marsella & Leong, 1995). Moreover, the psychometric properties (e.g., reliability, validity) may not be equivalent for translated and nontranslated versions of a test. One method of testing the linguistic equivalence of a test translation is to have bilingual persons take both versions of the test and compare the results. However, even when a person speaks more than one language, it cannot be assumed that they are equally fluent in all languages that they speak (Okazaki & Sue, 1995). Thus, test meaning may vary from language to language even for a bilingual person.

Metric equivalence involves whether the same score on a test has the same meaning for one ethnic group as it does for another (Trimble, 2007). Using the alexithymia example, differences in ability to read one's own emotions may be a function of measurement method. Although Asian Americans in the Le et al. (2002) study reported higher levels of alexithymia than did European Americans, when directly asked, Chinese, Chinese Americans, and European Americans in another study did not exhibit differences in emotional symptoms (Yen et al., 2000). Other research suggests that Asian Americans express higher levels of unpleasant emotions (guilty, irritated, sad, worried) than European Americans, but they may express lower levels of pleasant emotions (happy, joyful; Scollon, Diener, Oishi, & Biswas-Diener, 2004). Thus, the construct of alexithymia may have a different meaning for Asian Americans vs. European Americans, and group differences may be a function of the method of assessment. Conceptualizing alexithymia as a universal deficit may be biased because the validity of the construct and measurement of alexithymia are questionable across ethnic groups.

Another measurement issue pertinent to persons of color involves response style. Measures of social desirability have been developed to identify an impression

Picture 3.2
Source: shutterstock.

management style in which a person tends not to admit to the presence of negative characteristics. There is evidence that African Americans, Latinx Americans, and Asian Americans are more likely to make socially desirable responses than are European Americans (Dudley, McFarland, Goodman, Hunt, & Sydell, 2005). Such socially desirable responding may be a function of heightened skepticism about the testing situation and evaluation concerns among persons of color. Moreover, social desirability is assumed to compromise the validity of personality data. Yet, despite these differences in socially desirable responding, personality scores for ethnic minorities vs. European Americans were not significantly different (Dudley et al., 2005). Thus, socially desirable responding may have a different meaning for groups of color than for European Americans. Moreover, a desire to maintain interpersonal harmony among persons having collectivist orientations may mitigate willingness to express responses that could be perceived as potentially disruptive. For example, persons in China tend not to make extreme responses in responding to tests (Hamid, Lai, & Cheng, 2001).

A common method of demonstrating metric equivalence is the use of factor analysis of the structure of the measure in two or more groups (Trimble, 2007). Factor analysis involves the identification of correlated test items that cluster into factors. If the same test factors are found for multiple groups, the test is assumed to have metric equivalence for these groups. For example, Malcarne, Chavira, Fernandez, and Liu (2006) developed the 32-item Scale of Ethnic Experience. Ethnic identity, perceived discrimination, mainstream comfort, and social affiliation were four factors that were replicated in separate factor analyses for African Americans, European Americans, Filipino Americans, and Mexican Americans. Thus, the Scale of Ethnic Experience has metric equivalence across these ethnic groups.

On the other hand, factor analyses of ethnic group data may mask within-group variability. In a factor-analytic study, Eap et al. (2008) found evidence of a Five Factor personality structure in both European American and Asian American men on the Big Five Inventory (Benet-Martinéz & John, 1998). The Big Five personality factors are neuroticism, extraversion, openness to experience, agreeableness, and conscientiousness. Asian Americans had significantly lower scores than European Americans on extraversion, conscientiousness, and openness, and significantly higher scores on neuroticism (Eap et al., 2008). The Five Factor structure was weaker among Asian American men who were less acculturated to Western culture and more concerned about the East Asian value of loss of face. Although the Five Factor structure on the Big Five Inventory was the same for both ethnic groups, there were important between-groups cultural differences in test means and in the strength of the factor structure, which casts doubt on the metric equivalence of the measure across ethnic groups.

Even when conceptual and metric equivalence exist for a construct, there is not necessarily *functional equivalence* (Dana, 1993; G. Hall, Bansal, & Lopez, 1999). Functional equivalence addresses whether the same behavior elicits the same reaction across groups. For example, verbal participation in classroom discussions and the ability to "think aloud" is valued by many professors and for some is equated with intelligence. Although talking while thinking has been found to facilitate the problem-solving performance of European Americans, it has been found to interfere with performance of Asian Americans (H. Kim, 2002). Asian Americans were found to perform better at problem-solving when they were silent. Asian Americans also have been found to attach less significance to verbal expression as a method of communicating about oneself than do European Americans (H. Kim & Sherman, 2007). Verbal expression may be less critical than actions in cultures that emphasize roles, social status, and relationships (H. Kim & Sherman, 2007). Thus, some Asian Americans may perceive performance on a formal written examination as more diagnostic of their intelligence than verbal participation in class discussion. Silence may not have functional equivalence across cultures, in that it could be interpreted as not being involved in one context and as thinking in another. Similarly, hearing the voices of dead relatives or religious figures might be common in some Latinx American groups, but could be misdiagnosed as symptoms of schizophrenia (Bravo, 2003). Keys to differentially diagnosing culturally normative vs. psychopathological behavior are whether the behavior is common in a cultural group and not maladaptive (e.g., harmful to self or others).

Summary

In summary, equivalence of constructs, language, measures, and behaviors across groups is important in multicultural research. Ethnic group differences may be a result of a lack of equivalence that does not necessarily mean that the differences are cultural differences. Nevertheless, there may be differences in normative behavior across ethnic groups.

Culture-Specific Constructs

Although the previous section addressed the cultural equivalence of constructs, there may be racial and ethnic group differences on some constructs, and other constructs may be culture-specific and not exist across cultures. Western approaches to phenomena are likely to yield Western results (Bodas & Ollendick, 2005). For example, if one has a measure that assesses five personality factors, five personality factors are likely to be identified. When indigenous measures assess personality factors in addition to the commonly assessed five factors, factors in addition to the Big Five may emerge (Katigbak, Church, Guanzon-Lapena, Carlota, & del Pilar, 2002).

A construct can be relatively *distal* (distant) or *proximal* (close) to a behavior. A broad, distal cultural construct along which ethnic groups differ is individualism–collectivism (see Chapter 1). Individualism assumes that individuals are independent of one another, whereas collectivism assumes that individuals are bound together and obligated by groups (Oyserman et al., 2002). It is often assumed that groups of color in North America are less individualistic and more collectivistic than are European Americans. However, as discussed in Chapter 1, African Americans are more individualistic than all other ethnic groups in the United States, including European Americans.

Although individualism–collectivism has been the basis of many cross-cultural psychology studies, it is not a construct that is specific to particular cultural or ethnic groups. Individualists and collectivists exist in all ethnic groups. Moreover, the meaning of individualism–collectivism may differ across groups. For example, Jones (1997) has suggested that individualism may have a different meaning (i.e., individualism in service of the collective) in African American than in European American contexts (see Chapter 1). Although both Asian Americans and Latinx Americans are more collectivistic than European Americans, it is also likely that Asian American and Latinx American collectivism may not be equivalent. For example, to the extent that these two groups differ in expressiveness, collectivism might be commonly expressed among Asian Americans by withholding criticism of others, whereas collectivism among Latinx Americans might be commonly expressed by complimenting others.

Another cultural construct that is particularly relevant to immigrants is acculturation. Proxies for acculturation, such as place of birth or length of residence in the United States, are often used in research. However, such proxies combine vastly different people who may vary on age at immigration, length of time in the country of origin, and generational status (Birman & Simon, 2014). Most measures of acculturation designed for ethnic groups in the

U.S. assess language usage and may not assess identification with particular cultural groups (Zane & Mak, 2003). However, there is not a single widely-accepted measure of acculturation. There are at least 26 measures of acculturation for Latinx alone (Wallace, Pomery, Latimer, Martinez, & Salovey, 2010), which suggests that there is not consensus on Latinx acculturation (G. Hall, Yip, & Zárate, 2016). The majority of acculturation measures assess acculturation as a linear phenomenon – one moves along a continuum from a culture of origin to a host culture. Yet, models of acculturation discussed in Chapter 2 conceptualize the possibility of acculturation to more than one culture (Berry, 1974; LaFromboise et al., 1993). Moreover, acculturation is a relatively broad construct that does not necessarily account for specific behaviors (Zane & Mak, 2003).

More proximal to behavior are specific culture-specific elements of acculturation (Zane & Mak, 2003). One such culture-specific construct for Americans of East Asian ancestry is loss of face. In cultures that are collectivistic, individuals are obligated to preserve group harmony. If an individual's behavior interferes with group harmony, the individual experiences loss of face because they have not fulfilled their obligation to the group. Unlike shame, which involves individual embarrassment and damage to self-image, loss of face occurs because of failed obligations to others. As might be expected, concern about loss of face is a deterrent against aggressive behavior among Asian Americans (G. Hall et al., 2005). This effect is culture-specific insofar as concern about loss of face was a deterrent against Asian American men's sexual aggression but was not associated with European American men's sexual aggression. Loss of face concerns have also been found to deter Asian Americans' disclosure in psychotherapy, as discussing problems could result in face loss not only for oneself but for others in one's social network (Zane & Mak, 2003).

Other culture-specific constructs include African American and Native American spirituality (e.g., Simon, Crowther, & Higgerson, 2007; Stone, Whitbeck, Chen, Johnson, & Olson, 2006), and *machismo* and *marianismo* in Latinx American cultures (e.g., Casas, Turner, & Esparza, 2005; Moreno, 2007). Although a person in any culture might have some of these characteristics, these culture-specific constructs have a particular meaning in specific ethnic contexts. For example, spirituality in African American contexts is much more than attendance at religious services or even personal exploration of faith (see Chapter 8). African American spirituality is often rooted in participation in the African American community and may involve a sociopolitical emphasis. Similarly, gender roles prescribed by values of machismo for men and marianismo for women may appear sexist to outsiders (see Chapter 10). Machismo prescribes that males are strong and provide for their families. Marianismo prescribes that women should serve others and be submissive. Although there may be negative aspects to each of these constructs, positive aspects include a sense of responsibility to one's family and to the community, and adherence to prosocial community norms.

Summary

In summary, culture-specific constructs are likely to be more informative about an ethnic group than constructs that are not sensitive to culture. Moreover, broad cultural constructs are likely to be less sensitive to the behaviors of a particular group than are constructs that are more specific to the particular group. There exist cultural constructs specific to ethnic groups that are likely to be predictive of behavior.

Data Analyses

The purpose of data analyses in multicultural research is to determine the possible cultural bases of behavior. Although I will not go into depth about data analytic strategies, two data analytic issues, moderation and mediation, are important in multicultural research. Moderator and mediator analyses can help in the determination of the psychological bases of ethnic differences.

A categorical variable that is associated with different outcomes based on one's status on the variable is known as a *moderator*. Moderators help identify *when* an effect occurs. For example, Juan is an immigrant from Mexico and does not use drugs. Michael's parents were born in Mexico and he uses marijuana. If drug use is common among United States-born Mexican Americans but is uncommon among Mexican immigrants, country of birth is a moderator of drug use. Drug use mostly occurs *when* a Mexican American is born in the United States. Of course, natality is but one of many factors in determining drug abuse. Another moderator of drug use is access to drugs.

Racial or ethnic group membership (e.g., African American, European American) could be analyzed as a moderator. Moderator analyses can also be conducted within an ethnic group. For example, within Latinx Americans, differences between Puerto Ricans and Mexican Americans could be examined. However, most researchers do not analyze possible ethnic group differences in their samples either because they are not interested, because of the small size of ethnic minority samples, or because they believe it is controversial to do so.

Moderator analyses should be theoretically guided and not simply a "fishing expedition" for possible differences. Otherwise, the meaning of the presence or absence of group differences will be unknown. A good example of theoretically-guided moderator analyses is a large study of the Los Angeles County mental health system by Stanley Sue, Fujino, Hu, Takeuchi, and Zane (1991). Sue and colleagues (1991) observed that ethnic minority clients often dropped out of treatment after only one treatment session and were rated by clinicians as having poorer outcomes even when they remained in treatment. They tested the hypothesis that ethnic match between therapist and client would be beneficial to clients in terms of preventing premature treatment termination and producing better treatment outcomes. Thus, ethnic match (therapist and client of same ethnicity vs. therapist and client of different ethnicities) was the potential moderator in the study. African Americans, Asian Americans, European Americans, and Mexican Americans who were treated by therapists of their own ethnicity were less likely to drop out of treatment after one session and more likely to have better clinician-rated outcomes than clients of these ethnicities who were treated by therapists of ethnicities other than their own. So, the effect (lower dropout, better outcomes) occurred *when* there was an ethnic match. This moderator analysis is diagrammed in Figure 3.1.

A *mediator* is a third variable that serves as the vehicle through which one variable influences a second variable (Baron & Kenny, 1986). A mediator explains *why* an effect occurs. Using the drug use example above, Michael, who was born in the United States and uses marijuana, may be more acculturated than Juan, who was born in Mexico and does not use drugs. If Mexican Americans who are more acculturated (e.g., speak English), regardless of where they are born, are more likely to use drugs, then acculturation is a mediator because it explains why Mexican Americans use drugs. The reason why more United States-born Mexican Americans than immigrants abuse substances is that United States-born Mexican

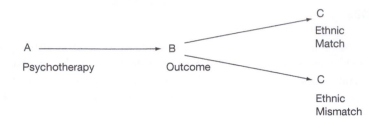

Figure 3.1 Moderation.

Americans are generally more acculturated, although immigrants who are acculturated (e.g., speak English) are also at risk of drug abuse. The ability to communicate in English might allow greater access to drug dealers, regardless of natality.

For mediation to occur:

- variable A must be associated with variable C;
- variable B, the proposed mediator must also be associated with variable C;
- and the association between variables A and C is eliminated or substantially reduced when variable B is accounted for.

For example, Shelly Taylor and colleagues (2004) hypothesized that efforts to maintain group harmony might discourage persons of East Asian ancestry from using social support during times of stress. Indeed, Asian Americans reported using less social support to cope with stress than did European Americans. Thus, ethnicity (variable A) was associated with use of social support (variable C). However, those who perceived using social support as negatively affecting their social network (relationship concerns) were less likely to use social support in both ethnic groups. Thus, perception of the impact of using social support was a mediator (variable B) of the association between ethnicity and use of social support. In other words, perception of the impact of using social support fully accounted for ethnic variation in the use of social support and was the basis of the apparent ethnic difference in use of social support. This mediator analysis is diagrammed in Figure 3.2. Although perceptions of the impact of using social support accounted for ethnic variation in use of social support,

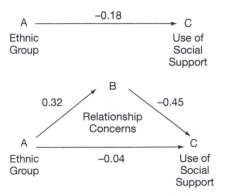

Figure 3.2 Mediation.

ethnicity still mattered in that Asian Americans perceived using social support as negatively affecting their social network more than European Americans did. So, the reason why Asian Americans were less likely to use social support is that they were concerned about how using social support would affect their social network.

Summary

In summary, moderator and mediator variables can help determine the basis of ethnic differences in behavior. Moderators are categorical variables, such as group membership, that are associated with different outcomes based on one's status on the variable. A mediator is a variable that serves as the vehicle through which one variable influences another.

QUALITATIVE RESEARCH METHODS

The approaches discussed up to this point in the chapter have been quantitative and normative, examining how individuals or groups vary on common constructs. However, quantitative approaches are most applicable to relatively large groups of people and do not always capture contextual and individual nuances that are important in the multicultural psychology approach. In contrast to quantitative approaches, qualitative approaches are *exploratory* and *descriptive*. The goal is to explore and describe phenomena, often without a pre-existing theoretical framework or other assumptions. Qualitative approaches are useful when theories and data on a phenomenon do not exist, and can give voice to people who are underrepresented in psychology research, which makes this approach particularly relevant to multicultural psychology (Ponterotto, 2013). Qualitative approaches are not necessarily at odds with quantitative approaches and may be used in conjunction with quantitative approaches. Qualitative work may form the basis of quantitative work (Berry, 2003). For example, focus groups may provide ideas for hypotheses that will be evaluated quantitatively.

Qualitative approaches are idiographic, examining individuals' unique perspectives via qualitative or quantitative data or both (D. Lee & Tracey, 2005). In-depth information about individuals is often lost in quantitative approaches. Moreover, qualitative approaches contextualize behavior, whereas quantitative approaches tend not to emphasize context and often assume that behavior is consistent across contexts (Chun et al., 2007). Unlike quantitative approaches in which hypotheses are developed a priori, hypotheses emerge in qualitative approaches during the research process. Qualitative approaches allow participants to structure the constructs, rather than having researchers impose structure which may be at odds with the participants' perspectives (D. Lee & Tracey, 2005). James, described at the beginning of the chapter, values qualitative methods for this reason. Of course, a limitation of qualitative approaches is that information from individuals is less reliable and generalizable than information from larger groups in quantitative approaches. Nevertheless, reliability and generalizability in qualitative work can be established with the use of multiple interviews of the same person, multiple interviewers, and interviewing several members of the community and identifying consistent themes (L. Suzuki & Quizon, 2012).

Establishing a relationship with research participants is critical for adequate understanding of participants' perspectives in qualitative research (Nagata, Kohn-Wood, & Suzuki, 2012). Collaboration with individuals and communities creates the insider perspective that is valued in multicultural psychology, as discussed in Chapter 1. Les Whitbeck is a European American sociologist and is an excellent example of establishing a collaborative relationship with research participants. Several years ago, he was interested in studying Native American populations and made contact with a tribal leader. The leader took Les to a tribal meeting and instructed him not to speak. Les was introduced to the tribe by the leader as having a "good heart." Les attended these tribal meetings, which were many miles from where he lived, regularly for a year without speaking, and was introduced each time by the leader as having a good heart. After a year of silent participation, Les gained the tribe's trust and has been able to conduct extensive research with this and other Native American communities in the Midwest. Rather than barging into the community pushing his own agenda, Les was effective because he learned and respected the community's norms regarding trust of outsiders.

The *interview* is one of the most commonly used qualitative methods. Qualitative interviews are often open-ended and allow the participant to guide the discussion of topics. It is usually preferable that the interviewer share characteristics with the community (Mertens, 2012), although Les Whitbeck is an exception. A team of interviewers, some of whom share characteristics with the community, may facilitate community access.

Picture 3.3
Source: shutterstock.

In addition to a focus on individuals, qualitative methods often involve small groups. *Focus groups* allow individuals to shape their own views via interactions with others (Chun et al., 2007). This process of individuals influencing the group and the group influencing the individual has been posited as the basis of culture (López & Guarnaccia, 2000). Focus group members may be chosen because they are leaders in the community, have particular expertise or opinions, or represent a particular community group (e.g., adolescents). A group moderator who is of the same ethnicity and speaks the same language as the participants may be desirable for the same reasons that ethnic matching is desirable in psychotherapy (Chun et al., 2007). Participation in a focus group may be appealing to some persons of color because it is consistent with collectivist values of cooperation and group harmony (Iwamasa & Sorocco, 2002). Conversely, groups that are created for research or therapy are dissimilar to community groups in that research or therapy groups are contrived and temporary, which may result in a lack of commitment among people of color who value group involvement (Nagata, 1998).

Another qualitative method involving groups is ethnography. *Ethnography* involves a researcher entering a community or situation as a participant-observer. Data gathering may involve field notes, interviews, and archival material (Chun et al., 2007), as well as storytelling, sharing experiences, and focus groups (Ponterotto, 2013). These data tend to be detailed and comprehensive, as they may constitute the only data gathered. The researcher's involvement and participation in a community may vary, as does the researcher's objectivity. For example, community members may seek help from a researcher and the researcher may or may not become an advocate for the community. Nevertheless, the subjective experiences of the researcher and participants are valued as much as or more than objectivity in qualitative approaches. Data analyses involve the identification of themes across individuals or communities, if more than one community is studied. Themes can emerge from the data or can be determined a priori. As an example of a priori structuring of questions in qualitative research, 18 African American women were specifically asked about the role of spirituality in their breast cancer treatment and health care, which was the focus of the study (Simon et al., 2007). Although the focus was on spirituality, the questions were broad enough to allow the women to describe their own perspectives.

Qualitative Inquiry Approaches

Ponterotto (2013) has identified three qualitative inquiry approaches: (a) grounded theory; (b) consensual qualitative research; and (c) participatory action research. *Grounded theory* is a well-established qualitative research approach (Ponterotto, 2013). It focuses on long interviews lasting from one to three hours. Although it is anchored in past knowledge, it is very open to discovery. The number of participants interviewed and the interview questions emerge over the course of the research process. Interviewing ends when the researcher decides that adding additional participants will not add new knowledge to the data patterns. Themes in the data are identified. The goal of grounded theory is to develop a new theory based on the experiences of the participants. In studying substance abuse in a Mexican American community, a grounded theory researcher might begin by interviewing Michael, who uses marijuana and whose parents were born in Mexico. Depending on the amount and quality of information that Michael provides, the researcher might also interview others, such as Juan, who is a young immigrant from Mexico.

Consensual qualitative research (CQR) is more structured than grounded theory research. It begins with the development of semi-structured interviews, based on existing research, talking with people from the community, or the researchers' own experiences. A sample question might be, "who uses drugs in this community?" Eight to 15 participants are interviewed (Hill et al., 2005). The next step in CQR is coding of the interview responses by three or more coders on the research team, followed by arriving at a consensus among the coders on the meaning of the data. Then, an auditor who is not part of the research team reviews the coding of the researchers to minimize bias. Finally, the interview data are analyzed for recurrent themes. A CQR approach to substance abuse in Mexican American communities might involve interviews with Michael, Juan, their parents, and other Mexican American children and parents. A recurring theme that might be identified is eroding Mexican cultural values being associated with marijuana use.

Participatory action research uses research to empower a community to make social change. This approach is uncommon in psychology (Ponterotto, 2013). In this approach, researchers establish a collaborative relationship with a community and identify a community problem to be addressed. Ethnographic approaches may be used to understand the community. An action plan is then developed and implemented. This approach is less structured than grounded theory or consensual qualitative research. A substance abuse example could be identifying substance use as a community problem, developing a drug education program that is acceptable to the community, and implementing the program in schools.

Summary

In summary, qualitative approaches offer rich descriptions of individuals or small groups of individuals. Although they are usually not guided by theory, theories may emerge from qualitative data. Data analyses involve extracting common themes across individuals. Qualitative and quantitative approaches may complement one another.

CONCLUSION

Cultural competence is important throughout the research process, from the development of theories to designing research to conducting research to interpreting research findings. A well-developed theory will guide each phase of the research process. Identifying, recruiting, and assessing samples of color each are challenging tasks. Data analyses should be oriented toward identifying the bases or mechanisms of racial, ethnic, or cultural influences. Qualitative methods can capture rich contextual data that are often overlooked in quantitative approaches. Unfortunately, much psychology research on race, culture, and ethnicity treats these topics in a superficial way, often as categorical variables, without attempting to address the complexity involved in multicultural research. In the following chapters, I have selected topics for which there exists culturally competent research. Having read this chapter, you may find flaws even in this culturally competent research, which may motivate you to correct these flaws by designing and conducting your own research.

RESOURCES

Blog:
Navel Gazing: Who Has Psychology Research Left Behind? www.psychologytoday.com/blog/life-in-the-intersection/201612/navel-gazing.

Multicultural Issues in the Context of Psychology

CHAPTER 4

Biological Psychology

Stephanie is a 21-year-old Native American junior who is majoring in psychology with an emphasis on neuroscience and minoring in neurobiology. She plans to apply to medical school. The psychology courses she has taken have focused on the biological bases of behavior, which she enjoys because she considers the biological approach to be objective, scientific, and universally applicable. She is taking a multicultural psychology course to fulfill a campus multicultural requirement. Stephanie is somewhat skeptical of this course and considers cultural issues to be peripheral influences on behavior and views the study of race and ethnicity to have political overtones.

Stephen is a 21-year-old African American junior who is working on a bachelor of science degree in psychology. He is interested in culture and racial identity but these issues have not been covered in any of his previous psychology courses, which have presented psychology as a universal and biologically-based science of human behavior. Stephen is minoring in ethnic studies, where there is much more of an emphasis on culture and racial identity. He is interested in how his course on multicultural psychology will integrate cultural and racial issues with the acultural scientific approach to psychology that he has learned so far.

Multicultural psychology has something to offer for both Stephanie and Stephen. If Stephanie goes into medicine, she will need to work with people. If she wants to be an effective physician, she will need to understand her patients' biological makeup and functioning. However, if she wants to fully understand her patients and connect with them, she will need to understand sociocultural influences on their health and behavior. A biological understanding alone will not fully account for her patients' health.

For Stephen, multicultural psychology can elucidate the limits of what are assumed to be psychological universals. Biological phenomena, which are assumed to be universal, are conditioned by sociocultural contexts. However, overlooking biological influences leads to an incomplete understanding of behavior as much as overlooking sociocultural influences does.

Biological approaches to human behavior emphasize universals between and within species. At first glance, the emphasis on universality in biological approaches may appear to be at odds with the emphasis on variability in multicultural psychology. Nevertheless, these approaches inform multicultural psychology because they help elucidate the relative contributions of biology and the sociocultural environment on behavior. In this chapter, we will consider genetic, cultural neuroscience, and health disparities research that is relevant to multicultural psychology.

In comparative psychology, the metaphor for human behavior is animal behavior. Humans share psychological mechanisms with other species, and psychological mechanisms are assumed to be shared within species. In cognitive science, the metaphor for the human mind is the computer. Individual differences, let alone cultural differences, are seldom considered in this metaphor.

An alternative metaphor for the human mind that incorporates variability, including culture, is the toolbox (M. Cole, 1996; Piaget, 1952; Vygotsky, 1978). Tools in the box to solve problems are psychological processes, including cognitive structures, emotions, and motivations (Norenzayan & Heine, 2005). Although all humans may have the same or similar toolboxes, cultural groups may vary in how the tools are used. In the context of the biological approaches in this chapter, humans of all racial and ethnic groups may be biologically similar, but different groups may use their biological resources in different ways to respond to situations.

As an example of cultural differences in the use of biological tools, all humans have cognitive and verbal skills. Western cultures emphasize verbal expression, and "thinking aloud" facilitated problem-solving for European Americans (H. Kim, 2002). Conversely, Asian American cultures value self-restraint and "thinking aloud" interfered with problem-solving for Asian Americans. Both ethnic groups possessed cognitive and verbal skills, yet one group used both and the other used only cognitive skills to solve problems. It could be argued that European Americans effectively used all their available tools or, alternatively, that Asian Americans were more economical by using fewer tools. However, the point is not that one approach is better, but that the two groups used their biological tools in different manners.

GENETIC PSYCHOLOGY

Humans are 99.9% the same genetically (Bonham, Warshauer-Baker, & Collins, 2005). Such biological similarities would seem to support the biological universals that Stephanie enjoys and Stephen eschews. Does this genetic similarity mean that any group differences are trivial?

Genes are pieces of DNA (deoxyribonucleic acid) and are the functional and physical unit of heredity passed from parent to offspring. *DNA* is the chemical inside the nucleus of a cell that carries the genetic instructions for making living organisms. A *genome* is an individual's complete set of DNA, including all of its genes. An *allele* is one of two or more alternative forms of a gene that arise by mutation. *Genotypes* are the actual variations of genes present in an individual. *Phenotypes* are the observable characteristics of an individual that may or may not correspond to genotypes. For example, an individual may have a genotype that creates a risk for antisocial behavior but not engage in antisocial behavior because they live in a tightly controlled environment (e.g., a monastery) in which prosocial norms and few opportunities for antisocial behavior exist. Thus, the environment can influence the expression of genes, which may offer hope to Stephen in his quest to integrate cultural and racial issues with behavioral universals. *Heritability* is the ratio of genetic influence in an attribute, such as temperament (e.g., impulsivity, sadness; Sternberg, Grigorenko, & Kidd, 2005). *Environmentality* is the ratio of environmental influence in a phenotype, such as emotional expression.

There has been enthusiasm about associating particular genes with psychological disorders, such as schizophrenia or antisocial behavior, which would create the possibility of gene therapies to prevent such disorders. However, behavior, including disordered behavior, involves complex interactions of multiple genes and of genes and the environment (Kendler, 2005). Moreover, some genes have undesirable as well as desirable effects. Thus, gene therapies at best might have a limited effect on behavior and at worst might have unwanted effects on behavior (Jaffee, Caspi, Moffitt, & Taylor, 2004).

Just as there is no particular gene exclusively associated with a particular behavior, there is no single gene or genetic variant that is sufficient to classify human populations into racial categories (Bonham et al., 2005; Cavalli-Sforza, Menozzi, & Piazza, 1994). Moreover, there is more variation within than between groups that have been identified as races. Among ancestral population groups whose geographic origins are in Africa, Asia, or Europe, 80–90% of genetic variation occurs within these groups and only 10–15% of genetic variation occurs between them (Jorde & Wooding, 2004). In other words, genetic similarities among people with African, Asian, or European ancestry are far more common than genetic differences.

Additionally, genetic boundaries between purported racial groups are permeable. An increasing proportion of the world's population does not have recent ancestors from a single geographic region, which is the basis of racial grouping (Bonham et al., 2005; Jorde & Wooding, 2004). Thus, concepts of racial groups as distinct genetic entities are of limited utility, given the growing population of mixed race individuals. Moreover, as discussed in Chapter 1, meanings of race are socially constructed and have relatively little to do with biology or genetics. Nevertheless, genes are an important influence on behavior, even if they do not correspond to racial groupings.

A common method of studying genetic influences is twin studies (Whitfield & McClearn, 2005). Identical (monozygotic, MZ) twins, which share 100% of their genes, are compared with fraternal (dizygotic, DZ) twins of the same sex, which share 50% of their genes, as do other sibling pairs. Relative genetic and environmental influence on a characteristic can be determined with the correlations among MZ and among DZ twins on a characteristic, such as impulsivity. Stronger correlations would be expected among MZ twins on characteristics that are genetically influenced.

Are genes an unalterable blueprint for human behavior? Such a deterministic view suggests that humans can do little to change their genetic programming. Thus, maladaptive behaviors (e.g., aggression, sexual infidelity) can be blamed on the genes inherited from our ancestors. However, there is an increasing body of evidence that gene expression interacts with environmental contingencies (Lickliter & Honeycutt, 2003). Humans inherit not only genes, but the ability to use genes as resources in response to the environment (Richardson, 1998). Thus, genes may be considered some of the tools in an individual's cognitive toolbox to be applied or not applied as a function of environmental demands (cf. Lickliter & Honeycutt, 2003; Norenzayan & Heine, 2005; Richardson, 1998).

As an example of environmental and genetic interactions, cultural norms may influence genetic risk for psychopathology (e.g., impulsivity, obsessive-compulsive disorder). For example, the serotonin transporter gene (the short allele of 5-HTTLPR), which is implicated in social sensitivity, is more prevalent in collectivist than in individualist cultures worldwide (Chiao & Blizinsky, 2010). In meta-analytic reviews, this gene has been found to be associated with risk for psychopathology (e.g., impulsivity, anxiety) in primarily White samples (Jonas & Markon, 2014; S. Taylor, 2016). Yet, collectivism is associated with lower levels of psychopathology worldwide relative to individualism. This is because of the lower levels of environmental stress in collectivist cultures associated with "tight" cultural norms in which there is a low tolerance for deviance and a high level of social connectedness (Chiao, 2015; H. Kim & Sasaki, 2014). Thus, genetic risk for psychopathology appears to be offset by cultural norms. The serotonin transporter gene may confer risk for psychopathology in contexts of "loose" cultural norms in which there is greater tolerance of deviance, less social connectedness, and greater environmental stress.

In 2000, the Human Genome Project, which mapped all the genes of the human genome, was completed. The results of this project offered the hopes of genetics-based medicine and of the removal of a biological or genetic basis for differentiating racial groups (Duster, 2015). However, neither of these hopes has been realized. Instead, there has been a quest to establish a genetic basis for putative race differences in risk for and prevalence of disease. For example, high rates of diabetes in Pima Indians in the southwestern United States have been attributed to fat-hoarding genes, also known as "thrifty genes," which ancestors would need to survive cycles of famine (Duster, 2015). These thrifty genes presumably place Pima Indians at risk for diabetes because of modern access to foods with high fat and sugar content. However, global data (New Guinea, Australia, Middle East, Asia) indicate that diabetes is virtually absent in populations that do not consume high fat and sugar diets but occurs at greater rates in populations within the same countries or geographic areas that do consume such diets. These populations around the globe share neither the same race nor the same genes as the Pima Indians. Thus, diabetes does not appear to primarily be a result of racial group membership or genetics.

Genes and Intelligence

One of the most controversial areas in psychology is the study of intelligence, race, and genetics (Nisbett et al., 2012; Sternberg et al., 2005). Studies in psychology of race differences in intelligence began in the early twentieth century with the development of tests of verbal and nonverbal motor performance skills. One's verbal and nonverbal performance on intelligence tests relative to those of others of the same age results in an intelligence quotient (IQ). Psychological studies of intelligence use tests of intellectual functioning, which primarily assess past learning and capture only part of the broader construct of intelligence. In other words, test performance or the IQ derived from these tests is not equivalent to intelligence, but comprise only a part of it. For example, creative, practical, or cultural abilities are typically not assessed by intelligence tests.

It has been argued that racial differences in intelligence developed because those in northern climates were faced with greater survival challenges than those in southern climates (Rushton, 1995b). However, there are equal challenges to surviving in southern climates (Sternberg et al., 2005). Moreover, no gene has been linked to intelligence. The difference between European American and African American IQ scores has decreased over the past five decades and is now about 10 points, or 0.6–0.7 standard deviation (Dickens & Flynn, 2006; Nisbett, 2005). Although there is no evidence that this difference is based on race, in part because race cannot be defined as a genetic or biological entity, there is evidence implicating socioeconomic factors. Children adopted into middle-class homes experience IQ gains relative to those in lower class homes (Nisbett, 2005). The evidence that the test score gap has decreased and that children's IQs can gain suggests that intelligence is not a fixed, unchangeable entity but that it is susceptible to environmental influences.

Current evidence indicates that IQ differences between African Americans and European Americans are accounted for by socioeconomic status (Nisbett et al., 2012). Children of all ethnic backgrounds in higher socioeconomic status contexts have access to resources (e.g., good preschools and schools) that enhance their IQ. Socioeconomic status has often been confounded in comparative studies in which African Americans studied were from lower socioeconomic status backgrounds than European Americans were.

Genetics and Alcohol Use

One difference that is associated with ethnicity is the presence of the aldehyde dehydrogenase gene *ALDH2* and the alcohol dehydrogenase gene *ADH1B*. These genes prevent a person from counteracting toxins that build up as the body metabolizes alcohol and are associated with protection from alcohol dependence (Luczak, Glatt, & Wall, 2006; Luczak et al., 2014). Physiological effects of these genes associated with alcohol use include skin flushing (reddening), headaches, subjective sensations of being drunk with relatively low alcohol dosages, and severe hangovers. Thus, *ALDH2* and *ADH1B* might be considered a form of genetic antabuse. The *ALDH2*2* allele, an alternative form of the *ALDH2* gene, is relatively common in persons of Northeast Asian ancestry but relatively rare in others. Population samples indicate that approximately 31% of Chinese, 45% of Japanese, 29% of Koreans, 10% of Thais, and 0% of Western and Central European Whites possess at least one *ALDH2*2* allele (Goedde et al., 1992). Similarly, population samples indicate that approximately 92% of Chinese, 84% of Japanese, 96% of Koreans, 54% of Thais, and 1–8% of Western and Northern Europe Whites possess at least one *ADH1B*2* allele (Goedde et al., 1992). Although these genes are associated with Northeast Asian ancestry, they are not markers for race or ethnicity, as less than 100% of each ethnic group has these genes and there is some overlap with other ethnic groups.

Alcohol dependence is characterized by: (1) tolerance, which involves either a need for markedly increases amounts of alcohol to achieve intoxication or a markedly diminished effect with continued use of the same amount of alcohol; or (2) withdrawal, involving autonomic hyperactivity (e.g., sweating or fast pulse rate), hand tremors, insomnia, nausea or vomiting, hallucinations, agitation, anxiety, or seizures (American Psychiatric Association, 2000). In a meta-analysis of 15 studies with 1980 cases and 2550 controls, Luczak and colleagues (2006) found that possessing one *ALDH2*2* allele reduces the risk for alcohol dependence to approximately one-fourth and that possessing two *ALDH2*2* alleles reduces the risk to approximately one-ninth. *ADH1B*2* has a protective effect against alcohol dependence above and beyond that of *ALDH2*2*. Possession of one *ADH1B*2* allele reduced the risk for alcohol dependence to approximately one-sixth, and possession of two *ADH1B*2* alleles reduced the risk to approximately one-eleventh (Luczak et al., 2006).

Cultural effects may influence alcohol dependence in addition to these genetic effects. Japanese participants in the studies reviewed were least likely to experience alcohol dependence. Japanese culture places importance on men drinking in social contexts without becoming addicted, which may result in fewer instances of alcohol dependence (Luczak et al., 2006).

Most of the studies reviewed by Luczak et al. (2006) were cross-sectional. In a three-year longitudinal study of Asian American college students, the *ALDH2*2* allele was associated with less heavy drinking and less of an increase in alcohol problems (e.g., hangover, problems at work or school; Luczak et al., 2014). The physiological discomfort associated with drinking may cause persons with the *ALDH2*2* allele to consume less alcohol and thereby develop fewer alcohol-related problems than those without the *ALDH2*2* allele.

This genetic research on alcohol has personal significance. I experience unpleasant physiological sensations, including skin flushing, every time I take a drink of alcohol. I have long suspected that I had the anti-alcohol genes described above, and I joked about this during a paper presentation at the convention of the Association for Behavioral and Cognitive Therapies. In the audience was Tamara Wall, a researcher on genetic and ethnic effects on alcohol, and a co-author of the meta-analytic study discussed above. Dr. Wall said that she could genotype me and sent me a kit that required me to puncture my finger and stain blood on a slide. I mailed the blood sample to Dr. Wall and waited for the results. These results would be a day of reckoning for me, not only in terms of my difficulties in drinking alcohol, but because a large percentage of persons of Northeast Asian ancestry have the *ALDH2*2* allele. My maternal grandparents were from Japan and, although my phenotype is ambiguous, I wanted my genotype to prove that I have something in common with other Japanese people! Sure enough, my genotype indicated that I have the *ALDH2*2* allele. Although there is no gene that distinguishes any ethnic group, I have a gene and experiences with alcohol that are the same as those of many other persons of Northeast Asian ancestry. I consider my *ALDH2*2* allele (and my flushing response to alcohol) as my Asian American membership card.

Recent evidence suggests that genetic effects on alcohol use may be mediated by environmental influences. In a study of American college students with East Asian ancestry with the *ALDH2*2* allele, negative expectancies associated with alcohol

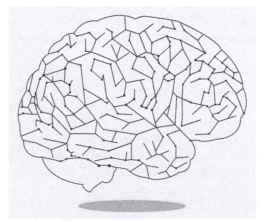

Picture 4.1
Source: shutterstock.

consumption (e.g., cognitive and behavioral impairment, dizziness, nausea) were associated with lower rates of alcohol use (Hendershot et al., 2009). In other words, those who expected drinking to produce negative outcomes were less likely to drink than those who did not expect negative outcomes. In another study of American young adults with East Asian ancestry, it was demonstrated that family influences may be stronger than genetic protective effects against alcohol problems (Bujarski, Lau, Lee, & Ray, 2015). Parental history of alcohol problems (e.g., legal, health, social) was associated with *greater* alcohol use among participants with the *ALDH2*2* or *ADH1B*1*2* allele (Bujarski et al., 2015; Figure 4.1). Thus, genetic protection may not be sufficient to prevent alcohol use and, potentially, abuse in the presence of environmental risk, such as not expecting negative drinking outcomes or parental alcohol problems.

Summary

The promise of genetics research is not that racially- or ethnically-based differences will be identified. Rather, genetics research can help determine relative contributions of the cultural environment to behavior. Genes interact with the environment to produce behavior. Additional research on cultural factors that can promote or prevent the expression of genetic predispositions is needed. In the next section, we will consider how brain functioning that is conditioned by genes is also conditioned by culture.

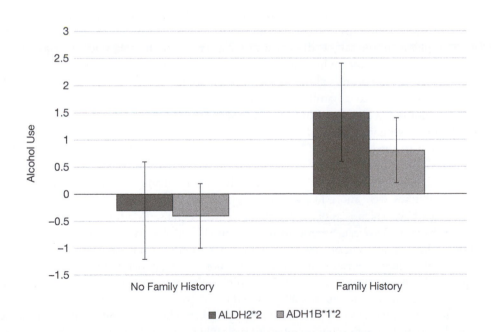

Figure 4.1 Genes, Family History of Alcohol Problems, and Alcohol Use.

Source: Bujarski et al., 2015.

CULTURAL NEUROSCIENCE

The brain is a common set of tools that is accessible to all humans. However, using the toolbox analogy, the ways in which different cultural groups use these tools may differ. Moreover, the ways that tools are used may affect the way the brain functions.

Cultural neuroscience examines how culture and biology mutually influence human behavior (Chiao, 2015). Methods from genetics, cultural psychology, and neuroscience have been integrated in cultural neuroscience. This confluence of biological and cultural approaches addresses the concerns of both Stephanie and Stephen about universality and cultural specificity. *Developmental neuroplasticity* is the concept that the structure, chemistry, and function of the brain can be changed by culture (Li, 2003). This approach typically employs the group differences research approach discussed in Chapter 1, but occasionally within-group variability is examined that is characteristic of multicultural research approaches.

The ability to measure brain activity via fMRI (functional magnetic resonance imaging) has led some researchers to monism, or the tendency to rely on explanations at a single level of analysis, namely the brain (Schwartz, Lilienfeld, Meca, & Sauvigne, 2016). Many in the general public find neuroscience explanations of behavior more convincing than non-neuroscience explanations. fMRI simply measures blood flow to a particular area of the brain during an experimental task. Brain activity is assumed by some to correspond with all important behavior and the measurement of brain activity is all that is needed to understand thoughts, feelings, and behavior. Other types of measurements, such as self-report, are viewed as inherently less reliable and valid. Yet, culture is not reducible to and is much more complex than specific brain functions (Schwartz et al., 2016). Neuroscience may be most useful to complement rather than replace other areas of psychology (Schwartz et al., 2016), including multicultural psychology.

Many of the findings in cultural neuroscience indeed complement and corroborate the findings of multicultural psychology. Collectivist and individualist cultures vary on the relative emphasis on the self, as discussed in Chapter 1. The mesolimbic pathway in the brain transports dopamine, which is associated with pleasure and reward. In an fMRI study, European Americans exhibited more mesolimbic response when receiving cash than when giving it to a family member. Latinx Americans exhibited the opposite pattern, exhibiting greater mesolimbic response when giving cash to a family member than when receiving it (Telzer, Masten, Berkman, Lieberman, & Fuligni, 2010).

In addition to these patterns of ethnic differences in neural responses to reward, ethnic differences in responses to the pain of others have been documented. When viewing members of their ethnic group in an emotionally painful situation (e.g., a natural disaster), African Americans were more likely than European Americans to exhibit cortical midline subsystem activity, which is associated with emotional response (Mathur, Harada, & Chiao, 2012). In contrast, European Americans were more likely than African Americans to exhibit temporal lobe activity associated with memory in response to the same stimuli involving ethnic group members. African Americans were more strongly identified with their ethnic group than European Americans were. It is possible that this stronger ethnic identification causes African Americans to emotionally respond to the pain of other ethnic group members while European Americans may rely on memories of themselves in a similar situation because they are less identified with other members of their ethnic group (Mathur et al., 2012). Thus, having a greater connection to others in one's ethnic group may result in emotional empathy, whereas having less connection may result in thinking about oneself in similar situations.

Although ethnic group differences in brain response have been demonstrated, the brains of people in different ethnic groups are not necessarily wired differently. The brain is responsive to the demands of the cultural context. For example, responses of the amygdala, a brain structure involved in emotion processing, have been found in an fMRI study to be conditioned by cultural influences. In collectivist cultures (e.g., Asian cultures), emotional expression is not encouraged because it has the potential to disrupt interpersonal harmony, which is highly valued. In contrast, emotional expression is encouraged in individualist cultures (e.g., European cultures) as evidence of one's uniqueness. Recent Asian immigrant college students to Europe have been shown to exhibit more amygdala reactivity to emotional faces than Asian immigrant students who have spent more time in Europe (Derntl et al., 2012). Asians who have spent more time in Europe may be less reactive to emotional faces because emotional expression is more common in Europe than it is in Asia. Thus, acculturation, a cultural influence, may condition amygdala response, a biological function. All the participants in this study were of Asian ancestry, yet there was variability in brain responses to emotion within the group. In other words, Asians' brains were not prewired to be less responsive to emotion. Insofar as women are socialized to express and respond to emotions more than men, gender differences might also be expected in amygdala reactivity to emotional faces. However, gender differences were not found (Derntl et al., 2012). Thus, acculturation influenced emotional responding more than gender.

Cultural variables have also been demonstrated to condition impulsivity as measured by brain responses (Telzer, Fuligni, Lieberman, & Galván, 2013). The ventral striatal area of the brain is responsive to reward (e.g., money) and is involved in risk-taking behavior such as drug use. The prefrontal cortex is associated with behavioral inhibition (e.g., not pushing a button in response to the letter X but pushing the button in response to other letters, known as a go/no-go task) and is involved in an individual's deliberate decision-making activities. In an fMRI study of Mexican American adolescents, those who reported higher levels of family obligation showed less ventral striatal activity when receiving money and more prefrontal cortical activity in a behavioral inhibition task than those who reported lower levels of family obligation. Thus, family obligation may decrease reward sensitivity and enhance cognitive control, which reduces risk-taking behavior such as drug abuse and stealing. Once again, all the participants were from the same ethnic background yet there was variability within the group, which suggests that brains respond to cultural demands (e.g., family obligation) rather than brain response being ethnic group-specific.

Summary

Cultural neuroscience complements multicultural psychology. Differences in neural response between and within ethnic groups have been accounted for by sociocultural variables such as connectedness to one's family or ethnic group, acculturation, and family obligation. These findings suggest that sociocultural variables can condition the brain's behavior. The previous sections have examined how genetic and neural bases of behavior are conditioned by sociocultural influences. In the next section, we consider how health is conditioned by sociocultural influences.

BOX 4.1 TOO MUCH NEUROSCIENCE?

Neuroscience holds much promise for understanding human behavior, including health and disease. Direct measurement of neural activity while a task is being performed is much more precise, much less inferential, and more scientific than many other areas of psychology. Most psychology departments have neuroscientists on their faculty and neuroscience dominates some psychology departments.

Neuroscience has also come to dominate federal funding for mental health research. John Markowitz, a professor of clinical psychiatry at Columbia and a research psychiatrist at the New York State Psychiatric Institute, wrote an op ed in the *New York Times*, in which he described the shift from funding studies to develop treatment for mental health problems to neuroscience studies by the National Institute of Mental Health, the primary federal agency that funds mental health research (www.nytimes.com/2016/10/15/opinion/theres-such-a-thing-as-too-much-neuroscience.html?mabReward=CTM&action=click&pgtype=Homepage&region=CColumn&module=Recommendation&src=rechp&WT.nav=RecEngine&_r=1). Although neuroscience has much promise in identifying the causes of mental health problems, the time required to translate a neuroscientific finding to a useful treatment may be decades. Professor Markowitz contended that this emphasis on neuroscience has occurred at the expense of research funding for research on treatments that will address the immediate suffering to individuals and their families caused by mental health problems.

Another criticism of neuroscientists is that they absolve themselves from responsibility to study cultural diversity because they are studying brain structure and functioning, which they contend is universal. Although research is highlighted in this chapter on the influence of sociocultural influences on neural response, cultural neuroscience is a new area and most neuroscientists do not study demographically diverse samples. Neuroimaging is expensive, which means the number of participants in neuroscience studies is relatively small. Thus, neuroscientists may strive to reduce or eliminate variability among their participants, such as ethnic diversity, because such variability may be viewed as an extraneous variable that could compromise their findings.

Discussion

1   Is it important for neuroscience research to have practical applications, such as treatments for mental health problems?
2   What motivation is there for neuroscientists to become interested in cultural diversity?

HEALTH DISPARITIES

Stephanie, who plans to apply to medical school, has a keen interest in health. Multicultural psychology is particularly important in the study of health, as health disparities have been identified between European Americans and people of color. A health disparity is a difference between groups in health status (Bleich, Jarlenski, Bell, & LaVeist,

2012). People of color have been documented to have poorer health than European Americans. Knowing patterns of health disparities among groups of color can help bring attention and services to problems that might otherwise be overlooked.

A national United States study of European Americans, African Americans, and Mexican Americans from ages 51 to 77 ($N = 12{,}976$) revealed the intersectional effects of ethnicity and gender on health (Brown, Richardson, Hargrove, & Thomas, 2016). Participants were asked if their health was poor (1), fair (2), good (3), very good (4), or excellent (5). There were not significant differences between European American men's and women's health, which began at very good at age 51 and declined to good at age 77 (Figure 4.2). European Americans' health was also significantly better at all ages than was the health of African Americans or Mexican Americans, which began in the good range and declined. The two groups with the poorest health were African American and Mexican American women, which implies that the combination of racism and sexism has the worst health effects. However, racism and sexism were not actually examined in this group differences (see Chapter 1) study. With respect to specific diseases, it was found in a review of national data-sets that African Americans and Mexican Americans have higher rates than European Americans of obesity, hypertension, and diabetes (Bleich et al., 2012).

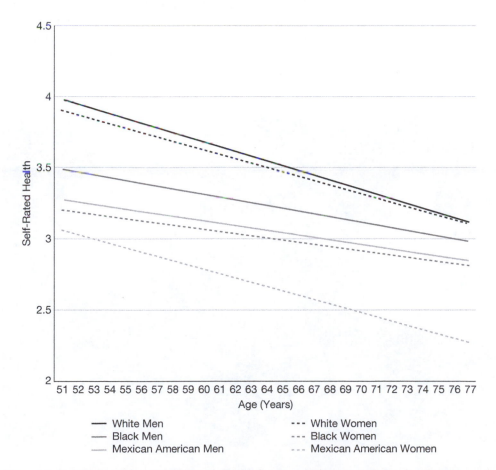

Figure 4.2 Age Trajectories of Self-Rated Health by Race-Ethnicity and Gender (Brown et al., 2016). Used with permission from American Sociological Association.

It might be expected that socioeconomic status (SES) would account for health disparities. For example, a healthier diet and higher activity level might be characteristic of persons with higher SES. Indeed, lower SES is associated with greater obesity among European American and Latinx American youth (Fradkin et al., 2015; Powell, Wada, Krauss, & Wang, 2012). However, there is not an association between SES and obesity among African American youth, possibly because African American women are more accepting of larger body sizes than other groups (Ali, Rizzo, & Heiland, 2013) and this acceptance may vary more by racial identity (Oney et al., 2011 in Chapter 2) than by social class.

In addition to body size acceptance among African Americans, there may be other cultural norms that influence health in addition to the effects of SES. There is some evidence that acculturation, as indicated by being born in the United States, time spent in the United States, and acculturation measures, is associated with greater body mass index among Latinx Americans and Asian Americans (Lommel & Chen, 2016; W. Lu, Diep, & McKyer, 2015; Rosas, Sanchez-Vaznaugh, & Sanchez, 2015). For some immigrants, mainstream United States culture is "obesogenic" relative to their cultures of origin, in areas such as type and amount of food and level of physical activity (W. Lu et al., 2015). Moreover, ethnic discrimination is a stressor in the United States for minority groups that does not occur in their countries of origin. The greater health of immigrants relative to their children who are born in the United States is known as the *immigrant paradox*. Immigrant health is paradoxical to the extent that immigrants experience acculturation stress in adjusting to a new culture that their United States-born children do not experience and would be expected to have poorer health than their children. However, not all Latinx and Asian immigrants experience greater health than their children (Ro & Bostean, 2015).

Picture 4.2
Source: shutterstock.

The inconsistent association of acculturation and health is likely associated with the fact that there are both healthy and unhealthy cultural norms in all cultures. For example, beans and rice are healthy staple foods among immigrant groups but frying them is not healthy, whereas other more healthy cooking methods (e.g., broiling, grilling) are common in the United States. Immigrants may engage in *selective acculturation*, in which they retain some traditional health behaviors while adopting some mainstream protective (e.g., low fat diet) or risky (e.g., sedentary lifestyle) health behaviors (Yeh, Viladrich, Bruning, & Roye, 2009). Thus, acculturation may be a health benefit or liability depending on which behaviors are retained from traditional cultures and adopted from mainstream culture.

Discrimination and Health Disparities

Another factor contributing to health disparities is racial and ethnic discrimination. People of color are more likely to experience racial and ethnic discrimination than European Americans are (Chapter 1; American Psychological Association, 2016). How does racial or ethnic discrimination affect health? Chronic stress may cause the body to adjust in an unhealthy manner. Discrimination provokes a stress response in individuals that has detrimental health effects (Berger & Sarnyi, 2015). An immediate physiological effect of discrimination is an increase in heart rate and blood pressure. Chronic high blood pressure is known as hypertension, which leads to heart disease, the leading cause of death for most Americans. Hypertension in response to discrimination has been studied primarily among African Americans. Hypertension among African Americans does not appear to be a result of biological risk factors (e.g., body mass) and there is less of a Black–White disparity in blood pressure internationally than in the United States (Dolezsar, McGrath, Herzig, & Miller, 2014). In a meta-analysis of 44 studies involving 32,651 participants, 62% of whom were African American, a small, statistically significant association between perceived discrimination and hypertension was found, with the effects strongest among African Americans, men, older persons, and persons with lower education (Dolezsar et al., 2014). The small association means that discrimination is one of many factors that influence hypertension.

Physiological arousal, including increased heart rate and blood pressure, in response to stress activates the *hypothalamic-pituitary-adrenal (HPA) axis* in the brain, which releases cortisol. Cortisol helps the body shut down the acute stress response to maintain homeostasis (Saxbe, 2008). There are mixed results on the effects of chronic discrimination among African Americans and Latinx Americans on cortisol production, with some studies indicating an increased response, others a blunted response, and others a blunted response during the daytime and an increased response at night, which is opposite of the typical daily cortisol production cycle (Berger & Sarnyi, 2015). An increased cortisol response can be an overreaction to stress, whereas a blunted response can be an underreaction.

An altered response to stress can take a toll on the body. *Allostasis* involves constant coping to maintain homeostasis and adapt to acutely stressful events, such as discrimination (Brody et al., 2014; Howard & Sparks, 2016). *Allostatic load* is a biological measure of the effects of exposure to chronic stress on biological systems. Racial discrimination has been found to be associated with subsequent allostatic load, as measured by hormones, blood pressure, inflammation, and body mass index, among African American adolescents but only among those with low emotional support (e.g., sympathy, understanding, help with problems) from parents and peers (Brody et al., 2014). Among African American adolescents with high emotional support, racial discrimination was not associated with subsequent allostatic load. The cumulative effects of allostatic load are poor health and death. Allostatic load was found to be associated with both illness and mortality in a national United States sample of adults and this association was stronger among African Americans than among European Americans (Howard & Sparks, 2016). The more deleterious effects of allostatic load among African Americans versus European Americans may be because of less access to health care resources that could buffer the effects of allostatic load.

Cancer Disparities

Allostatic load is also associated with the development of cancer (Andreotti, Root, Ahles, McEwen, & Compas, 2015). Unlike other ethnic groups in the United States for whom heart disease is the leading cause of death, cancer is the leading cause of death among Latinx Americans and Asian Americans (National Center for Health Statistics, 2011; Yanez, McGinty, Buitrago, Ramirez, & Penedo, 2016). Yet, the rates of cancer among Latinx Americans and Asian Americans are actually *lower* than those for other groups and rates of heart disease are not lower among Latinx Americans and Asian Americans relative to other groups (U.S. Cancer Statistics Working Group, 2013; Yanez et al., 2016). There appear to be cultural and medical reasons for this cancer mortality disparity.

Among Latinx Americans, there is some evidence for the immigrant paradox with respect to cancer. Latinx Americans born in the United States have cancer rates similar to those of European Americans and foreign-born Latinx Americans have lower cancer mortality rates than those born in the United States (Yanez et al., 2016). Greater family support and religion among foreign-born Latinx Americans may contribute to this advantage. Conversely, English language fluency may facilitate communication with medical care providers and improve cancer screening and treatment, which may confer an advantage to United States-born Latinx Americans with respect to cancer outcomes (Yanez et al., 2016).

Colorectal cancer screening and mammography are effective in preventing the development of cancer. Yet, Latinx Americans are less likely than European Americans to receive these screenings. An obvious explanation for limited access to care might be a lack of resources (e.g., no health insurance), but this disparity in cancer screening rates is not fully accounted for by SES. Language barriers, health literacy, and cultural factors, such as fatalism and machismo, may interfere with receiving cancer screening (Yanez et al., 2016). A lack of screening or cancer diagnoses at advanced stages of the disease, which is more common among Latinx Americans than among European Americans, can lead to increased mortality because of the absence of necessary prevention or treatment. Even when Latinx Americans are screened for cancer, they are less likely to adhere to physician cancer screening recommendations than European Americans (Yanez et al., 2016), possibly because of the SES, cultural, and health literacy issues discussed above.

Cancer screening rates have been documented to be lower for Asian Americans than for all other ethnic groups in the United States (U.S. Cancer Statistics Working Group,

2013). Similar to Latinx Americans, there may be cultural issues, such as fatalism, and medical issues, such as health literacy and ability to communicate with health care providers, that influence access to cancer screening. However, another disparity is that physicians recommend necessary cancer screening, including colonoscopies and mammograms, at lower rates for Asian Americans than for other groups (U.S. Cancer Statistics Working Group, 2013). Ibaraki, Hall, and Sabin (2014) proposed that some physicians may not screen Asian Americans for cancer because of model minority health stereotypes. Asian Americans have been stereotyped as a model minority group because they are perceived as more successful than other minority groups in terms of achievements. It is possible that this Asian American model minority stereotype can also be applied to their health. Indeed, there is evidence that Asian Americans have lower rates of smoking, hypertension, and obesity than other ethnic groups (Nguyen, Moser, & Chu, 2014). However, this perception of Asian Americans as healthier than other groups may lead some physicians to conclude they do not require cancer screening, which is actually necessary for all ethnic groups to prevent cancer. Research is currently being conducted to determine if this model minority health stereotype exists and if it influences physician judgment with respect to cancer screening.

HIV Disparities

In addition to the direct effects of discrimination on health, discrimination may indirectly affect health via impaired decision-making. The Stigma and HIV Disparities Model proposes that discrimination against groups that are stigmatized based on racial/ethnic identity, sexual orientation, and other intersecting identities causes some men of color to maladaptively cope with the distress associated with these intersecting stigmas. Maladaptive coping involves having unprotected sex as a temporary escape or as a means of seeking self-validation (Earnshaw et al., 2013).

Structural level discrimination results in residential segregation into communities in which there is a higher concentration of sexually transmitted infections, including HIV. Another structural level risk factor is the mistrust among some men of color of medical advice (e.g., using condoms), which may be viewed as a conspiracy against men of color based on historical evidence of medical abuses against communities of color (e.g., Tuskegee Syphilis Study). Individual and structural level discrimination also increase the likelihood of substance use, including injecting drugs, which increases HIV risk (Des Jarlais et al., 2013).

As a result of these individual and structural factors that create allostatic load, African Americans and Latinx Americans account for a disproportionately high percentage of all new diagnoses of HIV (Centers for Disease Control and Prevention, 2012). Similar to cancer screening, African Americans, Latinx Americans, and Asian/Pacific Islander Americans are tested at a later stage than European Americans after being infected with HIV, which contributes to survival disparities (Earnshaw et al., 2013). Some men of color who have sex with men or who inject drugs may delay testing out of fear of the added stigma of a positive HIV diagnosis. African Americans and Latino Americans have been found to be less compliant with HIV medical care than European Americans and there is evidence that men of color who are HIV patients receive poorer medical care because of provider prejudice and discrimination (Earnshaw et al., 2013).

Reducing Health Disparities

How can health disparities be reduced? Racial and ethnic discrimination is the basis of health problems and disparities. Reducing discrimination could reduce health disparities. Systemic methods of reducing disparities would involve improving education, economic opportunities, and health care for communities of color. Another method would be to educate individual perpetrators of discrimination about the impact of their actions. Increasing contact between European Americans and people of color and creating a common ingroup identity might reduce discrimination (Earnshaw et al., 2013). However, intergroup contact tends to be more beneficial for the majority than the minority and it may be burdensome for the minority to have to educate the majority on reducing discrimination, which is the responsibility of the perpetrator and not the target (Tropp & Pettigrew, 2005). Because of the positive health effects of racial and ethnic identity that were discussed in Chapter 2, health disparities can be reduced and communities of color can be empowered via education and experiences that enhance racial and ethnic identity.

Summary

Health disparities have been documented with European Americans generally having better health than people of color. Discrimination accounts for these health disparities better than SES or acculturation. Cancer and HIV disparities appear to be a function of both patient and provider characteristics. Reducing discrimination and increasing racial/ethnic identity have promise in improving the health of people of color.

CONCLUSION

Biological functioning takes place in a sociocultural context and there are reciprocal influences between biology and culture. Although sociocultural influences are often overlooked or minimized in biological approaches, biological models cannot fully account for human behavior. Biological influences create a context for behavior but genetic and neural effects may be expressed differently in different cultural contexts. Many health disparities between European Americans and people of color are accounted for by discrimination. Biology has been central to the study of human development, the topic of the next chapter, but like all behavior, human development is conditioned by sociocultural influences.

RESOURCES

Blog:
Dying Not to Stand Out: Asian Americans Dying Unnecessarily http://division51.net/homepage-slider/dying-not-to-stand-out-asian-americans-dying-unnecessarily/.

CHAPTER 5

Developmental Psychology

Allison is a 20-year-old Cambodian American who is a junior in college. Her family came to California as refugees following the Vietnam War. Her parents run an Asian market and Allison helped in the market along with her siblings. She and her siblings helped English-speaking customers because of their language abilities. Her parents are pleased to see their children acculturate and become successful in American society. Allison felt that her parents were stricter than her non-Asian friends' parents. They wanted her to become a doctor but she became interested in psychology so she could study Asian Americans. This interest has created some distance not only from her family but also from her Asian American friends, whose interests are in medicine and engineering. Another source of distance from her family and Asian American friends is her attraction to other women. She finds more acceptance of same-sex relationships among her White friends.

Michael is a 21-year-old Cuban American who is a senior in college. His grandparents came to Miami from Cuba to escape the Castro regime. Both parents are successful attorneys and want him and his sister to acculturate. Neither he nor his sister can speak or understand Spanish. The only time he is aware of being Latino is when other Latinx students wonder why he doesn't speak Spanish. His parents taught Michael and his sister to be "color blind" and he considers himself to be an American. He does not want to be associated with negative stereotypes of Latinxs. Michael wants to go to law school, like his parents did. He learns that law schools are interested in recruiting Latinx students. He begins to realize that Latinx individuals might prefer to have a Latinx attorney and that Latinx communities may have legal representation needs that differ from those of other communities.

People of color undergo development in ways similar to others. However, an added developmental task for people of color is racial and ethnic identity. The development of racial and ethnic identity is a normal process for people of color that is not prominent among European Americans. Thus, most courses and textbooks on developmental psychology that focus on European Americans do not focus on racial and ethnic identity development.

In this chapter, we will consider how parents transmit cultural values. For children of color, pressure to acculturate from peers may compete with traditional values. During adolescence, peers may help determine an individual's feelings and strength of association with their ethnic group. The increasing complexity of racial/ethnic identity as one ages will be addressed. We will also consider how race, ethnicity, and racial/ethnic identity impact the development of cross-ethnic friendships, academic identity, and sexual identity.

PARENTS AND FAMILIES

Parenting Styles

Parents of color often view their responsibilities as passing on cultural values to their children. Respect for elders, who carry cultural traditions, is emphasized in communities of color (Ceballo, Kennedy, Bregman, & Epstein-Ngo, 2012). For example, a local African American mother of a middle schooler was horrified that her child's European American teacher wanted students to call her by her first name. The mother insisted that her child address the teacher as "Ms. Smith." Family obligation is also emphasized among families of color. This involves family unity and loyalty, prioritizing family over individual needs, and relying on the family for support (Ceballo et al., 2012).

What does an emphasis on families look like in communities of color? Aren't family values similar for all ethnic groups? Latinx immigrant and European American parents of fifth graders at elementary schools in Los Angeles were asked how to resolve conflict situations (Greenfield & Quiroz, 2013). Latinx parents were interviewed in Spanish. The first conflict situation was:

- Scenario 1: *Credit.* When Tony's and Luis' [pronounced Louis for the English version] mother gets home, she finds that the house has been cleaned, and dinner is almost ready. She thanks them both for being so helpful. Tony says, "Why are you thanking him? I am the one who did most of the work." What do you think the mother should do?

    - An example of a common familistic response was: "Okay, the mother should say that, both of you helped, so it doesn't matter because both of you helped. You helped each other, like you worked as a team."
    - An example of a common individualistic response was: "Well, I guess at that point she should try to figure out who did what and, you know. Give them each a little bit of credit because they care about [the house]."

The second conflict situation was:

- Scenario 2: *Brother.* Ricky tells the teacher that he will probably be absent tomorrow because his mother is sick, and he has to stay home to help take care of his brother. What do you think the teacher should do?

    - An example of a common familistic response was: "Tell him to stay home and help his brother because his mother is sick. Because if he goes to school, the boy, the boy is going ... to do a lot of things, and the mother is not going to be able to watch him. And she's going to, and she's going, and she's going to get more sick, the mother."

- An example of a common individualistic response was: "The teacher should call the mother, and at the same time tell the child that the only time we're supposed to be, kids are supposed to be absent is when they are sick. And that if there is not someone to take care of the mother that she needs to find someone to take care of the mother. That he is a child, and that he needs to be in school."

Figure 5.1 shows that a significantly greater percentage of Latinx parents chose the familistic solution than the European American parents did. In Scenario 1, the familistic solution was equal credit to both boys. In Scenario 2, the familistic solution was excusing Ricky from school to take care of his brother. Family harmony and caring for family members were the goals for most Latinx parents, whereas these goals were much less important for most European American parents.

In contrast to the emphasis on family interdependence in families of color, children's independence (see Chapter 1) is a desirable goal among European American families. Asserting one's own views and self-confidence are components of independence (Rubin & Chung, 2006). *Authoritative parenting,* characterized by firmness and warmth, has consistently been associated with achieving independence more than *authoritarian parenting,* characterized by strictness and lack of warmth, among European Americans. Authoritative parenting has also been found to have positive outcomes among African American families, including lower depression and delinquency among fifth graders, and greater emotional regulation among preschoolers (LeCuyer & Swanson, 2017; Simons, Simons, & Su, 2013). Among Latinx fifth graders, authoritative parenting was associated with better academic performance, better interactions with others, emotional regulation, and lower aggression (Jabagchourian, Sorkhabi, Quach, & Strage, 2014). Authoritative parenting in Asian American families is associated with lower internalizing (e.g., anxiety,

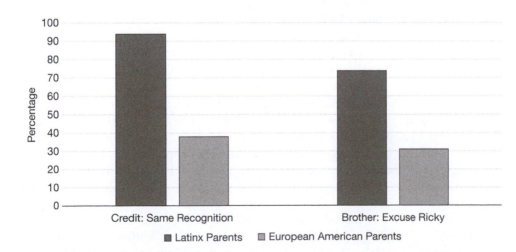

Figure 5.1 Conflict Resolution.

Source: Greenfield & Quiroz, 2013.

depression) and externalizing problems (e.g., rule violations, aggression) among first and second graders (S. Chen et al., 2014).

Unlike European American families in which the effects of authoritarian parenting are generally negative, the effects of authoritarian parenting are somewhat mixed in families of color. Among African American fifth graders, authoritarian parenting was associated with less delinquency but also more depression and less school engagement (Simons et al., 2013). Authoritarian parenting was associated with poorer emotional regulation among African American preschoolers (LeCuyer & Swanson, 2017). There were no associations between authoritarian parenting and emotional, social, or academic outcomes among Latinx fifth graders (Jabagchourian et al., 2014). On the other hand, among Latinx four- and five-year olds, authoritarian parenting was associated with more internalizing and externalizing problems (Calzada, Huang, Anicama, Fernandez, & Brotman, 2012). Among Asian American first- and second-graders, authoritarian parenting was associated with internalizing and externalizing problems (S. Chen et al., 2014). Because the goals of parenting in families of color may be different from those in European American families, authoritative and authoritarian parenting styles may not adequately characterize parenting in families of color.

In contrast to European American independence, the goal in many families of color is children's interdependence. Components of interdependence include conformity, emotional self-control, and humility (Y. Choi, Kim, Kim, & Park, 2013). Respect for elders and family obligation are emphasized in families of color, as discussed above. Among mothers of middle school children, African Americans, Latinas, and Chinese Americans were more likely than European Americans to emphasize respect and obedience to adults (Harding, Hughes, & Way, 2016).

Parents of color are sometimes characterized as harsh and demanding in their efforts to facilitate their children's interdependence. This parenting style might be considered authoritarian. However, parenting in families of color may involve a combination of authoritative and authoritarian practices. African American, Latinx, and European American parents are all found to have high levels of warmth, which is characteristic of authoritative parenting (Deater-Deckard et al., 2011). However, African American and Latinx parents also had higher levels of parental strictness and control, which is characteristic of authoritarian parenting, than European Americans. Similarly, Asian American parents of preschoolers have been found to endorse control strategies (emotional control, shaming) more than European American parents do (Louie, Oh, & Lau, 2013). It might be plausible to believe that authoritarian parenting is more common among less acculturated immigrants. However, Chinese cultural orientation was not associated with authoritarian parenting among Chinese immigrant parents (S. Chen et al., 2014). Thus, both immigrant and non-immigrant Chinese parents were strict. A complaint among many adolescents is that their parents are stricter than their friends' parents are. However, these studies suggest that there may be some truth that parents of color are stricter than other parents. Allison, described at the beginning of the chapter, certainly sees her parents as relatively strict.

A controversial issue in parenting among families of color is the use of corporal punishment, such as spanking, which may be a component of authoritarian parenting. African American and Asian American parents have been found to have more positive attitudes toward corporal punishment and use it more than European American parents (Y. Choi et al., 2013; Lorber, O'Leary, & Smith Slep, 2011). There was some early evidence that corporal punishment did not produce externalizing behaviors in African American children as it did in European American children (Deater-Deckard, Dodge, Bates, & Pettit, 1996). It was assumed that corporal punishment was more acceptable to African American parents and that they did not use it impulsively. In contrast, the impulsive use of corporal punishment among European American parents (e.g., when parents are emotional) was assumed to be the cause of its negative effects. However, recent evidence indicates no ethnic differences in the association of corporal punishment and impulsivity among European American, African American, and Latinx American parents (Lorber et al., 2011). Moreover, in the Early Childhood Longitudinal Study, a large national sample of children beginning in kindergarten, corporal punishment was shown to predict externalizing behavior among European Americans, African Americans, Asian Americans, and Latinx Americans (Gershoff, Lansford, Sexton, Davis-Kean, & Sameroff, 2012). There is also evidence from a longitudinal study of poor African American and Latinx children beginning in preschool that corporal punishment is associated with both externalizing and internalizing behavior (Coley, Kull, & Carrano, 2014).

Parenting in families of color may have culture-specific characteristics that do not fit neatly into mainstream United States notions of parenting. For example, *ga-jung-kyo-yuk* is a family process specific to Korean American culture. It involves parenting via role-modeling, the centrality of the family, family hierarchy, respect for elders, and family obligations and ties (Y. Choi et al., 2013). It is associated with both authoritative and authoritarian parenting among Korean American parents. Similarly, *familismo*, which involves prioritizing family over individual needs, and *respeto*, which involves proper behavior toward elders and authority figures, are emphasized in Latinx families (Ceballo et al., 2012).

Picture 5.1
Source: shutterstock.

BOX 5.1 THE IDEAL MOTHER

What are the characteristics of an ideal mother? Latina mothers of fourth and fifth graders described two characteristics of an ideal mother (Ceballo et al., 2012):

a   close monitoring of her children, including strict curfews and social chaperoning
b   a close relationship with her children.

Think of how your own ideas of an ideal mother might compare to these characteristics:

1   What are your criteria for an ideal mother?
2   Did your own mother fit these criteria?
3   How are these criteria similar to or different from those of Latina mother ideals?
4   What are your criteria for being a parent yourself?
5   How will you parent similarly or differently from your mother? From Latina mothers?

Summary

The parental goal for children in many families of color is interdependence. This includes placing family priorities above those of the individual. The goal of authoritative parenting is independence, yet this parenting style has positive effects among families of color. Authoritarian parenting has somewhat mixed effects in families of color in contrast to their uniformly negative effects in European American families. There may be culture-specific aspects of parenting in families of color that do not map onto European American parenting styles.

Acculturation in Families

Bilingualism. An important responsibility for parents in immigrant families is to help their children adjust to a new culture while maintaining their heritage culture. Within the first six years of life, children are able to differentiate faces based on race (Pauker, Williams, & Steele, 2015). So, it is important for parents to provide meaning about race, ethnicity, and culture early in life. One of the earliest cultural experiences a child has is with language. Children are capable of understanding different languages within the second year of life (DeAnda, Poulin-Dubois, Zesiger, & Friend, 2016). Bilingual children usually learn each language from different sources (Unsworth, 2017). Their parents may be monolingual (e.g., Spanish, Chinese) and their source of English may be outside the family (e.g., peers, teachers). Because their language exposure is split across two languages, bilingual children may have more language breadth but less experience or depth with each particular language (DeAnda et al., 2016).

In immigrant families, learning the heritage language (e.g., Spanish) can help maintain culture and reduce the level of cultural mismatch between parents and children. Cultural mismatch can lead to intergenerational conflict, which is associated with children's poor mental health and educational outcomes (Lui, 2015). Learning two languages enhances executive function, which is the mental process that helps us to plan, focus attention, remember instructions, and juggle multiple tasks successfully (Bialystok, 2015). Executive function is associated with academic success, which in turn is associated with long-term physical and mental health. Thus, becoming bilingual can help a child's adjustment.

Despite the cultural and cognitive advantages that bilingualism confers, some bilingual students may struggle academically because schools are not equipped to address dual language learners (Han, 2012). It has been recommended that teachers become aware of resources and community organizations that can help them understand dual language learners (Zepeda, Castro, & Cronin, 2011). Resources may be available from community ethnic or cultural groups, such as the League of United Latin American Citizens and the Chinese Benevolent Association. Teachers should also learn about the sociopolitical context of dual language learners. For example, some dual language learners may have parents that are undocumented. Teachers should also become aware of their own and others' biases against dual language learners and work to counteract these biases.

One role of children in immigrant families is language translation and interpretation for their parents or *language brokering*. This requires mastery of two languages and responsibilities that children in monolingual families do not have. Language brokering may have positive consequences, such as a sense of contribution to the family and an understanding of parents' struggles and sacrifices for their children (Shen, Kim, Wang, & Chao, 2014). At the beginning of the chapter, Allison and her siblings were described as communicating with English-speaking customers on behalf of their parents at the family's Asian

Picture 5.2
Source: shutterstock.

market. Negative consequences of language brokering include feeling burdened with interpretation, particularly when there are conflicts between parents and children (S. Kim, Hou, & Gonzalez, 2016). Parents may have mixed feelings about having their children translate for them, which is a role reversal (i.e., parent dependent on the child) that can cause parent–child conflict (S. Kim et al., 2014).

Acculturation gap. Differential language abilities can contribute to an acculturation gap between immigrant parents and children. As discussed in Chapter 2, contact between a cultural group and a host culture that changes either or both groups is known as *acculturation* (Berry, 2003). An *acculturation gap* occurs when acculturation occurs at different rates between parents and children. Immigrant parents may expect their children to acculturate to their native culture whereas the expectation in mainstream United States society, such as the school system and peers, is acculturation to mainstream culture (Lui, 2015). For children of immigrants of color, the tension is often between collectivist native cultural values (e.g., family loyalty) and individualistic mainstream cultural values (e.g., personal independence; Chapter 2). These are competing cultural pressures that non-immigrant children do not experience and may be a source of conflict beyond typical intergenerational conflicts in non-immigrant families. Moreover, some degree of intergenerational conflict in mainstream European American families may be viewed as a normative process by which children develop autonomy (Lui, 2015). In contrast, family conflict in collectivist families may be viewed as contrary to cultural goals of interpersonal harmony and interdependence.

Acculturation gaps can occur in different domains, such as language or media use, food choices, choices of friends' ethnicities, cultural values, and ethnic identity. Children in immigrant families might acculturate to mainstream United States culture faster than their parents because of contact with mainstream peers and experiences in school. But there are at least four types of acculturation gaps with respect to mainstream and native cultures (Telzer, 2010), as presented in Table 5.1.

Acculturation gaps in mainstream culture and native culture are separate dimensions. For example, there may be a larger gap between immigrant children and parents in mainstream culture (e.g., child much more acculturated) than in native culture (e.g., children and parents acculturated but parents somewhat more acculturated). Or children and parents may be acculturating to mainstream culture at about the same speed, but children are less acculturated to native culture because of less experience with it than their parents.

The pattern of children acculturating to mainstream culture faster than their parents is common. Immigrant parents were socialized in their native culture, whereas their children are socialized in two cultures. Children may be more open to mainstream culture than their parents are (Telzer, 2010). This type of acculturation gap has been found to be associated with less family conflict than other acculturation gaps, perhaps because it is viewed as normative (Telzer, 2010). Parents may see their children's adaptation to mainstream culture as beneficial for their children who may help the family adapt to the expectations of the new culture. This was true in Allison's family, described at the beginning of the chapter.

Table 5.1 Types of Acculturation Gaps

Acculturation to Mainstream Culture	Acculturation to Native Culture
Child > parent	Child > parent
Parent > child	Parent > child

Some immigrants who come to the United States may desire to acculturate and be more acculturated to mainstream culture than their children. For example, if there are better employment opportunities in the United States than in one's native country, acculturation to mainstream culture may be desirable. If the children in the family did not want to leave the native country, they may resist acculturating to the United States. This may be particularly true for older children who have spent more time in the native country, who are referred to as 1.5 generation immigrants (Lui, 2015; see Chapter 2). These children may have difficulties fitting in with the mainstream culture of their communities and schools.

Some immigrant children remain more acculturated to native culture than their parents are. In some cases, this may result from children's sense of rejection from the mainstream culture. Similar to immigrant families with parents more acculturated to mainstream culture than their children, these children may have been socialized in their native country and may have been less enthusiastic about leaving it than their parents. For example, children may keep in touch with their native culture via media (e.g., K-pop among Korean immigrants). Immigrant children's acculturation to the native culture may be more adaptive in contexts where there is a high concentration of members of the native culture (*ethnic density*) than in contexts where there are few members of the native culture (Stafford, Newbold, & Ross, 2011; Zhou & Kim, 2006).

A fourth pattern of children being less acculturated to the native culture than their parents is common. Many immigrant parents have been socialized in their native culture to adulthood, whereas the children's experience with the native culture may be limited or only through their parents if the children were born in the United States. Children in immigrant families who are born in the United States are known as the *second generation*.

These acculturation gaps are not associated with adjustment problems in children in immigrant families per se. According to a meta-analysis (see Chapter 3 for definition) of 68 studies of over 14,000 Asian and Latinx adolescents and young adults, problems arise when these acculturation gaps result in intergenerational cultural conflict (Lui, 2015). When parent–child acculturation gaps exist, females may experience greater levels of intergenerational cultural conflict than males because mainstream gender roles are more at odds with native gender roles for females than for males. The parent–child acculturation gap also is more likely to result in intergenerational conflict for second generation children born in the United States than 1.5 generation immigrant children. The 1.5 generation children are culturally more similar to their parents than second generation children by virtue of their first-hand experience living in the native culture. Intergenerational conflict was also found to be lower among participants who lived in areas of high ethnic density because of greater opportunities for children to explore native culture than in areas of low ethnic density. Native culture is not experienced as unusual or only something their parents practice for children in areas of high ethnic density.

Intergenerational cultural conflict associated with an acculturation gap in turn results in mental health and academic problems (Lui, 2015). Southeast Asians and East Asians were more likely to experience mental health problems because of intergenerational conflict than Mexican Americans were. This may be because of a greater cultural distance between Asian cultural values and mainstream United States cultural values (Lui, 2015). Although Asian and Mexican cultures both are collectivistic, Mexicans have more exposure to United States mainstream values because of their geographic proximity to the United States. Because family influences are important in collectivist cultures, the negative impact of intergenerational conflict persists into young adulthood among Latinx and Asian immigrant youth (Lui, 2015).

Summary

Children in immigrant families are exposed to more than one culture. Learning two languages has cognitive benefits but schools are not always prepared to support bilingual children. Bilingual children also often have an added responsibility of language interpretation for their parents. Parents and children in immigrant families often acculturate at different rates. Parent–child conflict over acculturation can result in mental health and academic problems.

RACIAL AND ETHNIC IDENTITY

Racial and Ethnic Socialization

In addition to teaching a heritage language, if there is one, parents can shape the identity of their children by communicating or modeling their beliefs, values, norms, and behavior (Peck, Brodish, Malanchuk, Banerjee, & Eccles, 2014). Parents of children of color have the additional responsibility of helping their children develop healthy racial and ethnic identities. The transmission of parental values and perspectives about race and ethnicity to children is known as *racial socialization* or *ethnic socialization* (Hughes et al., 2006). Racial and ethnic socialization of children of color occurs during early adolescence when parents are still more influential in adolescents' lives than peers.

Four themes have emerged in the way parents socialize their children to their own perspectives on race and ethnicity: egalitarianism, cultural socialization, preparation for bias, and promotion of mistrust (Table 5.2; Hughes et al., 2006).

Egalitarianism involves an emphasis on individual qualities (e.g., hard work, self-acceptance) over racial or ethnic group membership and may also involve a silence about race (Hughes et al., 2006). This approach may include a "color blind" perspective on society

Table 5.2 Racial and Ethnic Socialization

Theme	Content	% of Parents Who Communicate
Egalitarianism	"Color blind" perspective	20–50
Cultural socialization	Exposure to culture and language	20–47
Preparation for bias	Awareness of and coping with discrimination	4–47
Promotion of mistrust	Suspicion in interethnic interactions	13–21

Source: Hughes et al., 2006.

(Neville et al., 2013). Of parents of color, 20 to 50% do not discuss race and ethnicity with their children. A parent of color who emphasizes egalitarianism might be attempting to have their child assimilate into the mainstream, as discussed in Chapter 2 (Sellers et al., 1998). This was the case with Michael's parents, discussed at the beginning of the chapter. Conversely, an emphasis on egalitarianism might reflect a humanist ideology, which emphasizes similarities among all humans and de-emphasizes the importance of race.

Cultural socialization includes: (1) talking about important historical or cultural figures; (2) exposing children to culturally relevant books, artifacts, music, and stories; (3) celebrating cultural holidays; (4) eating ethnic foods; and (5) encouraging children to use their family's native language (Hughes et al., 2006). Of African American parents, 20 to 47% culturally socialize their children (Dunbar, Perry, Cavanaugh, & Leerkes, 2015; Peck et al., 2014). Cultural socialization is associated with the development of healthy racial and ethnic identity (Hernandez, Conger, Robins, Bacher, & Widaman, 2014; Peck et al., 2014).

Education and economic status are factors that have been found to influence the amount of cultural socialization parents engage in. Parents of color with higher education and income are more likely to culturally socialize their children and prepare them for bias than parents with a lower income and educational attainment (Peck et al., 2014). These parents of higher socioeconomic status are more likely to have the resources (e.g., time, knowledge) to be able to culturally socialize their children (Caughy, O'Campo, Randolph, & Nickerson, 2002) and also may be more aware of prejudice and discrimination (D. Williams, 1999). Moreover, higher education and income are associated with more interactions with persons of different racial and ethnic backgrounds, which create more opportunities for interracial and interethnic prejudice (Brody et al., 2006).

Experiences with discrimination can influence parents' cultural socialization behavior. African American and Latinx Americans mothers of adolescents who experienced workplace discrimination were more likely to culturally socialize their children than parents of adolescents in these groups who did not experience it (Hagelskamp & Hughes, 2014). For the mothers who experienced workplace discrimination, cultural socialization may be perceived as offsetting the effects of discrimination that their children might experience. The opposite finding was true for Chinese immigrant mothers of adolescents; those who experienced greater discrimination were less likely to culturally socialize their children. It is possible that Chinese immigrant mothers may attribute discrimination to stereotypes of being a perpetual foreigner. Less emphasis on Chinese culture may be seen as a way to help their children fit in better in the United States (Hagelskamp & Hughes, 2014).

Because of their direct connections to their cultures of origin, it might be expected that immigrant parents culturally socialize their children more than do parents of color born in the United States. However, Asian American and Latinx college students born in the United States reported being culturally socialized as much as immigrants from these groups did (Juang & Syed, 2010). Thus, cultural socialization is as important to immigrant families as it is to families of color born in the United States. Unlike traditional immigration patterns of coming to a country and remaining, international migration has become transnational where a family may reside in more than one country for periods of time. For these families, cultural socialization in their culture of origin may occur remotely via media such as foreign media, Skype, and brief visits (Ferguson, Costigan, Clarke, & Ge, 2016).

Preparation for bias involves making children aware of discrimination and teaching them how to cope with it (e.g., problem-solving, social support). Parents prepare their children for bias in 4 to 47% of African American families (Dunbar et al., 2015; Peck et al., 2014).

Preparation for bias may be more frequent among African Americans than among other groups because of long-standing racism against African Americans (Caughy et al., 2002; Hughes et al., 2006). African American, Latinx, and Chinese mothers who have experienced workplace discrimination were more likely than mothers who had not experienced discrimination to prepare their children to cope with workplace discrimination (Hagelskamp & Hughes, 2014). Unlike the findings in this same study in which workplace discrimination resulted in more cultural socialization behavior among African American and Latinx mothers and less among Chinese mothers, workplace discrimination resulted in preparing their adolescent children for bias for *all* groups of mothers. Personally experiencing bias makes one want to prepare one's children to handle it.

Promotion of mistrust involves the need for wariness and distrust in interethnic interactions. Of parents of color, 13 to 21% communicate these messages to their children (Barr & Neville, 2008; Dunbar et al., 2015). Parental messages that promote caution and wariness about other groups are different from preparation for bias messages because they contain no advice for coping with or managing discrimination (Hughes et al., 2006). Promotion of mistrust typically is targeted at European Americans, but also may target other groups of color.

Racial socialization messages associated with promotion of mistrust were less common among African American parents living in primarily European American neighborhoods than among African American parents who had less contact with European Americans (Caughy, Nettles, O'Campo, & Lohrfink, 2006). In addition to neighborhood demographics, interracial conflicts in neighborhoods may also influence parents' racial and ethnic socialization behavior (Hughes et al., 2006). In a study of urban African American first graders, parental messages emphasizing racism and mistrust were associated with negative neighborhood social climate (perceived physical/social disorder, fear of retaliation and fear of victimization; Caughy et al., 2006).

So far we have reviewed the effects of racial and ethnic socialization on people of color. What are the effects of racial and ethnic socialization on European Americans? In a recent study of college students, European Americans were less likely than people of color to have received racial and ethnic socialization from their parents (Tran, Mintert, & Jew, 2016). When European Americans were racially or ethnically socialized by their parents, this was associated with anti-egalitarian attitudes or with a preference for dominance of European Americans over other groups. Thus, the positive effects of racial and ethnic socialization on racial identity for people of color (see Chapter 2) do not necessarily hold for European Americans.

Summary

Most parents of color engage in some form of racial/ethnic socialization with their children. Such socialization ranges from a "color blind" message to exposure to cultural traditions to preparation for societal bias. European American parents less commonly racially/ethnically socialize their children and the effects are different than they are in families of color.

Development of Racial and Ethnic Identity

Racial and ethnic socialization are the processes by which racial and ethnic identity develop. As discussed in Chapter 1, a person is not born with a racial or ethnic identity. Attitudes about one's group and how other groups interact with it develop and change over time. Adriana Umaña-Taylor and her colleagues in the Ethnic and Racial Identity in the 21st Century Study Group (2014), which consists of 13 psychologists from across the United States, have detailed the *process* by which individuals explore, form, and maintain the ethnic or racial identity, and the *content* of racial and ethnic identity, which involves attitudes and beliefs about one's own group and its relations to other groups, in early childhood, middle childhood, and adolescence.

The racial and ethnic identity process during early childhood involves differentiating the self from others in terms of ethnicity and race (Umaña-Taylor et al., 2014). During early childhood, racial and ethnic identity content includes labeling self and others by ethnicity, knowledge about the characteristics of ethnic groups, and a recognition that one's ethnicity is constant and does not change. The primary social and environmental influences during early childhood are family and the media. Family and the media can provide accurate information about one's group's characteristics and traditions, as well as inaccurate information, such as stereotypes.

When a child enters school during middle childhood, peers begin to influence behavior in addition to family and the media. The racial and ethnic identity process at this time involves becoming aware of bias against groups and an understanding of the social hierarchy among racial and ethnic groups. Content issues involve one's identity becoming salient (often by some triggering event such as discrimination), the centrality or importance of identity, affect toward one's own identity, the ingroup's identity, outgroup identities, and how the public views one's ingroup. These issues become salient as a child interacts with same- and different-ethnic peers. Family and media messages about one's ethnic group and other ethnic groups may or may not be consistent with peer messages. Similarly, *private regard* (positive or negative feelings about one's race/ethnicity and racial/ethnic group; Sellers et al., 1997; see Chapter 2) may or may not be consistent with *public regard* (perceptions of societal views of one's racial/ethnic group; see Chapter 2).

Positive feelings about one's racial or ethnic group tend to increase from early to middle adolescence (French, Seidman, Allen, & Aber, 2006). These positive feelings about one's racial or ethnic group that develop during adolescence are associated with positive social, psychological, and health outcomes among adolescents of color, as indicated in Chapter 1. In a meta-analysis (see definition in Chapter 1) by Rivas-Drake and colleagues (2014) of 46 studies of African American, Latinx American, Asian American, and Native American adolescents, positive feelings about one's racial or ethnic group (e.g., I feel good about the people in my ethnic group) were significantly associated across studies with positive social functioning (e.g., social competencies, peer acceptance), fewer depressive symptoms, and lower health risks (e.g., risky sex, substance use). These findings did not vary by age, gender, or ethnic group of the participants. In another meta-analysis of 47 studies of children, adolescents, and adults from multiple ethnic groups, ethnic/racial identity had a small but significant positive correlation with academic achievement (Miller-Cotto & Byrnes, 2016).

Although ethnic and racial group identification is generally associated with positive outcomes, in some cases it may be associated with negative outcomes. For example, positive feelings about ethnic identity were associated with declining academic perform-ance among Latinx adolescents from seventh to eighth grades (Umaña-Taylor et al., 2012). An explanation of this finding is that Latinxs may have begun to underperform, consistent with negative academic stereotypes about their group.

An important feature of identity development during adolescence is merging one's personal identity with one's ethnic or racial group and developing an understanding of a *shared destiny* with others in this group. As discussed in Chapter 2, this shared destiny with a group differentiates ethnic and racial identity from the development of general personal identity. This shared destiny based on group membership becomes prominent during adolescence because of the increasing influence of peers and exposure to multiple groups and perspectives. Discrimination because of one's racial or ethnic group member-ship may also solidify a sense of shared destiny.

Lack of exposure to one's own racial group, such as being a child of color adopted by European American parents with only European American social contacts, could prevent a sense of shared destiny and interfere with identity development. In such cases, *identity self-denial*, which involves minimization of one's ethnic-racial background, may occur (Umaña-Taylor et al., 2014). Such identity denial may be intentionally or unintentionally encouraged by European American adoptive parents who may have a color-blind ideo-logy, as discussed in Chapter 1 (Neville et al., 2013). Nevertheless, there is evidence that European American parents can effectively culturally socialize their adopted children of color (Arnold, Braje, Kawahara, & Shuman, 2016).

Children who are socialized outside racial and ethnic communities, such as by Euro-pean American adoptive parents or by parents of color in settings where there are extremely few people of color, may experience challenges in connecting with com-munities of color. They may be seen as "not ethnic enough" by other group members who may view them as "whitewashed." Such exclusion may also occur for someone who does not speak a language associated with an ethnic group or who is mixed race (Umaña-Taylor et al., 2014). Michael, described at the beginning of the chapter, experi-enced exclusion from other Latinxs because of his inability to speak Spanish. Children's reactions to such challenges might involve "proving" themselves by immersing them-selves in cultural activities (e.g., Black church, taking Spanish in school) or, alternatively, finding sources of identity other than race/ethnicity (e.g., academic, sports).

In late adolescence, perspective-taking skills become more advanced and individuals begin to explore their identity by seeking information about their ethnic or racial group (Umaña-Taylor et al., 2014). Exploration may include thinking about identity, discussing it with others, or participating in activities with one's group. Joining an ethnic club at school would be an example of such exploration. Resistance to peer pressure may cause some adolescents to engage in ethnic and racial exploration independently of their peers. Such resistance might happen if an adolescent felt that their same-ethnic peers were too acculturated and might involve reading about one's group or joining an ethnic organiza-tion (e.g., NAACP) whose primary membership is adults.

During early adulthood, ethnic and racial identity becomes more complex (Umaña-Taylor et al., 2014). Many early adults are in college. This means increased or decreased exposure to intellectual and cultural diversity, depending on one's background. For example, a person of color from a setting in which European Americans constitute 90% of the population will probably experience greater intellectual and cultural diversity in college, unless the college is similarly homogeneous. In contrast, someone from a multicultural setting, such as New York or Los Angeles, may experience less intellectual and cultural diversity in most colleges, which are not as diverse as either of these cities.

Because of increasing cognitive abilities, early adults develop an intersectional identity. Ethnic and racial identity intersect with other identities, such as gender identity, sexual identity, social class, religious identity, and political identity (Umaña-Taylor et al., 2014). For example, a person is not simply Latinx but may be a Latinx working class lesbian woman who is a feminist. The interaction of racial/ethnic and sexual identities is discussed later in this chapter. The salience of any particular identity may depend on the context. For example, a common feminist identity might be more salient when the person in the example is among European American women, whereas a Latinx working class identity might be more salient when this person is among other Latinx working class people.

Part of the intersectional identity for Latinx and Asian college students, particularly if they or their parents are immigrants, is bridging their ethnic heritage and American culture. During their four years in college, these students were more likely to add American to their labeling of themselves (i.e., Latinx American, Asian American; Tsai & Fuligini, 2012). Because these students continued to search for their ethnic identity, referring to oneself as an American was an integration of cultures rather than a detachment from their heritage cultures.

Summary

The development of racial/ethnic identity begins in early childhood and becomes increasingly complex. As a child ages, peer influences supplement family and media influences on racial/ethnic identity development. The development of racial/ethnic identity is generally associated with positive outcomes, although there may be negative outcomes associated with stereotypes of a racial or ethnic group. Intersectional identities develop for early adults who have increased cognitive abilities.

INTERSECTIONAL IDENTITIES

Racial and ethnic identities develop in the context of different-ethnic peers, school, and sexual relationships. Racial/ethnic identity has a varying degree of impact on the development of other identities. In this section, we consider how being a person of color and being racially/ethnically identified affect cross-ethnic friendships, academic identity, and sexual identity.

Cross-Ethnic Friendships

As discussed previously, a major part of racial/ethnic identity development involves peers. Many peers are from the same ethnic group, which may strengthen racial and

Picture 5.3
Source: shutterstock.

ethnic identity. *Homophily* is the tendency to make friends with similar characteristics, such as gender, race, or ethnicity (Graham, Munniksma, & Juvonen, 2014). This tendency toward homophily is strong among adolescents. However, if adolescents are in an ethnically diverse environment, there are opportunities for cross-ethnic friendships, which is known as *propinquity*. Cross-ethnic friendships are associated with better attitudes about and better treatment by others (Graham et al., 2014).

Graham and colleagues (2014) asked African American and Latinx sixth graders in 10 Los Angeles middle schools to list the names of classmates that they considered to be friends. Five schools were predominantly Latinx, three were predominantly African American, and the other two were ethnically diverse with no ethnic group (African Americans, Latinx, Asians, Whites) constituting more than 50% of the population. All schools were in predominantly low socioeconomic status neighborhoods.

The African American and Latinx students had more same-ethnic than cross-ethnic friends, consistent with other research on homophily (Graham et al., 2014). The more friends these two groups had from their own ethnic group, the stronger their positive feelings about being a member of their ethnic group, which is an aspect of ethnic identity. Same-ethnic peers share cultural experiences (e.g., language) and discrimination, and are a source of social support.

Cross-ethnic friendships were more likely to occur if there was propinquity (Graham et al., 2014). Unlike same-ethnic friendships, cross-ethnic friendships were associated with feelings of safety and fewer experiences of victimization. This is because adolescents with cross-ethnic friendships have widespread social acceptance and support from their peers. Cross-ethnic friendships were not associated with ethnic identity because friends outside one's ethnic group do not share the same cultural experiences and may have different experiences of discrimination, as well.

Homophily can influence cross-ethnic friendships. Asian American sixth graders were more likely to have White friends than Latinx or African American friends (X. Chen & Graham, 2015). This was because Whites were more similar to Asian Americans on grade point average (GPA) than Latinx or African Americans were. The Latinx and African American friends that Asian American students had were relatively similar to them in GPA. These sixth-grade students had not yet been segregated by academic performance and self-selected their friends. However, "tracking," which does segregate students based on academic performance and which often begins in high school, can reduce cross-ethnic contact between students.

Academic Success and Social Acceptance

Homophily may also influence social acceptance among students of color who are academically successful. In the Add Health study, Asian American middle- and high-schoolers had the highest GPAs, followed by European Americans, Latinx Americans, African Americans, and Native Americans (Fuller-Rowell & Doan, 2010). Social acceptance was measured by whether students felt socially accepted, whether others were unfriendly, whether people disliked them, and how often they felt lonely. For Asian Americans and European Americans, greater academic success was associated with greater social acceptance. The opposite was true for African Americans, Latinx Americans, and Native Americans. Greater academic success was associated with *lower* social acceptance in these groups. Figure 5.2 shows the results for European Americans,

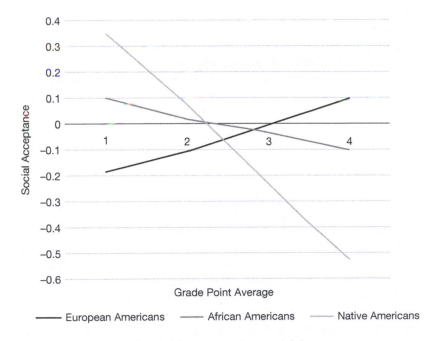

Figure 5.2 Academic Success and Social Acceptance Among Adolescents.

Source: Fuller-Rowell & Doan, 2010.

African Americans, and Native Americans. The results for Asian Americans and European Americans were not significantly different from each other nor were the results for African Americans and Latinx Americans. Thus, within all ethnic groups, those whose academic performance was unlike that of other group members were the least socially accepted.

This pattern of Asian Americans and European Americans academically outperforming African Americans, Latinx Americans, and Native Americans is consistent across multiple academic achievement measures (Kurtz-Costes, Swinton, & Skinner, 2014). Unfortunately, these achievement disparities lead to stereotypes that may interfere with academic performance for members of some groups. These achievement disparities may also result in academic tracking, which results in ethnic segregation, as discussed above.

Why do ethnic academic achievement disparities exist? Student attitudes, parents, and schools all influence academic achievement (Kurtz-Costes et al., 2014). Student awareness of stereotypes of ethnic differences in intellectual ability (see Chapters 1 and 6) may interfere with their performance. For example, some Latinx students may underperform in school, consistent with negative academic stereotypes about their group, as discussed previously in this chapter (Umaña-Taylor et al., 2012). Perceived barriers may lead many students of color to believe that education will not lead to success. Parents of color with low income may have difficulty providing health care and nutrition, books and other educational enrichment, and assistance with studying. Language barriers may also limit parents' involvement in students' schooling. An Asian American child of immigrants once told me that there came a point when she was in elementary school where her parents could no longer help her study because they could not understand the study materials. Parents with limited work flexibility may not have time to be involved in their child's school, which keeps them out of the information loop and may inadvertently communicate to teachers that they are uninvolved in their child's education.

Ethnic academic achievement disparities also exist because students of color are disproportionately located in public schools in low income areas (Kurtz-Costes et al., 2014). Many of these schools have limited resources, such as libraries, laboratories, computers, college preparation, extracurricular activities, and well-trained teachers. The student to teacher ratio is also often high. These limitations contribute to achievement disparities. In addition, a meta-analysis (see Chapter 2) indicates that teachers have been demonstrated to hold lower achievement expectations for Latinx and African American students than for European American students or for Asian American students, for whom expectations were the highest (Tenenbaum & Ruck, 2007).

Academic success and seemingly positive stereotypes are not uniformly beneficial for Asian Americans. Although Asian Americans' academic success may be associated with social acceptance among other Asian Americans, non-Asians may resent this success and teacher favoritism that results from it. Among high school students in New York City, Latinx and African Americans harassed Asian Americans because of perceived teacher favoritism (Rosenbloom & Way, 2004). Even being interested in an academic field that is somewhat atypical for Asian Americans, such as psychology, can lead to social isolation among other Asian Americans, as it did for Allison, described at the beginning of the chapter.

BOX 5.2 ASIAN AMERICAN ACADEMIC ACHIEVEMENT

East Asian, Filipino, Southeast Asian, and South Asian students in the United States have been documented to have better academic performance compared to other ethnic groups, as indicated by teacher ratings and grades (Hsin & Xie, 2014). They are also more likely to complete high school and attend college, including elite colleges. Three explanations have been proposed for Asian American academic achievement:

- cognitive abilities
- cultural values
- career opportunities.

In a large national sample of school-aged children, ethnic differences in academic achievement between Asian Americans and European Americans were minimal (Hsin & Xie, 2014). So, superior cognitive abilities are an unlikely explanation for Asian American academic achievement. Confucian teachings about the value of education have also been invoked as a cultural value that motivates academic achievement. Although Confucian values might explain the academic achievement of East Asian Americans (Confucius was a Chinese philosopher), they do not explain the academic achievement of other Asian American groups.

A third explanation is that the career opportunities available for Asian Americans require education. For example, Asian Americans have succeeded in medicine, science, and business. Education is required to enter these fields. On the other hand, Asian Americans have been less prominent in fields that are less directly tied to education, such as entertainment, sports, and politics. Thus, Asian Americans have focused on academic achievement because it is seen as the only path to career success. This idea is known as *relative functionalism* (S. Sue & Okazaki, 1990).

Rather than a result of an inherent cognitive or cultural advantage relative to other groups, Asian American academic success is a result of hard work. For example, according to the National Center for Education Statistics, Asian Americans spend an average of 10 hours per week studying vs. six to seven hours for students in other ethnic groups (Aud, Fox, & KewalRamani, 2010). Teachers also rate Asian American students as working harder than European American students (Hsin & Xie, 2014).

Asian American academic achievement comes at a high cost. Asian American students experience greater parental academic pressure than European American students do (Fu & Markus, 2014). Seemingly positive academic stereotypes of Asian Americans may create high expectations that actually interfere with academic performance (Cheryan & Bodenhausen, 2000). Compared to European American students, Asian American students have lower self-esteem and are more alienated from their peers and parents (Hsin & Xie, 2014). As discussed earlier in this chapter, Asian American students may be harassed by peers because of perceived teacher favoritism (Rosenbloom & Way, 2004). Moreover, the education-related fields that Asian Americans aspire toward are highly competitive and do not have room for everyone who is qualified.

Discussion

1   How can academic stereotypes of Asian Americans be changed?
2   Is there a way to reduce the pressure for academic achievement among Asian Americans?

Sexual Behavior and Identity

Cultural values and racial/ethnic identity also influence sexual behavior and identity among adolescents and young adults of color. In a study of Latinx adolescents in the southeastern United States, higher levels of Latinx cultural orientation (e.g., speaking Spanish at home, enjoying Latinx-oriented places) were associated with greater *self-efficacy* (belief in ability) to resist and avoid peer pressures to engage in sexual behaviors, fewer sexual partners for females, and greater condom use self-efficacy for both males and females (Ma et al., 2014). Greater endorsement of *respeto* was associated with a lower intention to have sex during secondary school and greater condom use self-efficacy. Greater endorsement of *simpatia* (belief in interpersonal relationship harmony) was associated with sexual abstinence and greater self-efficacy in resisting and avoiding peer sexual pressure for all adolescents, and with being older at sexual debut for females. In contrast, American cultural orientation (e.g., speaking English at home, enjoying American-oriented places) was associated with less condom use. Consistent with these results, in the Add Health study, Latina adolescents who spoke English and were born in the United States were more likely to engage in risky sexual behavior, including sexual debut before 17, greater number of sexual partners, non-use or inconsistent use of condoms, and having sex under the influence of alcohol or drugs (Smith, 2015). The data from these studies are consistent with the *immigrant paradox* (see Chapter 4), in which less acculturation is associated with better health.

Acculturation, in terms of generation in the United States and English speakers at home and in one's neighborhood, among Asian Americans in the Add Health study was also associated with earlier sexual debut and multiple partners (Tong, 2013). Although a gender-based double standard exists among Asian cultures in which female sexuality is restricted, acculturated Asian American females had an earlier age of sexual debut and more partners than Asian American males. This gender discrepancy in sexual behavior may be associated with stereotypes of Asian American females as more sexually attractive than Asian American males (Galinsky, Hall, & Cuddy, 2013).

Similar to the protective effects of ethnic cultural orientation among Latinx and Asian American youth, racial identity is associated with fewer sexual partners among young African American heterosexual men (Oparanozie, Sales, DiClemente, & Braxton, 2012). Racial identity in the study involved *centrality* (importance of race relative to other identities) and *private regard*. In another study of young African American heterosexual men, ethnic identity (as measured by Phinney's belonging, attachment, and pride components; see Chapter 2), was associated with greater relationship mutuality, which involved empathy, engagement, and authenticity in relationships (Corneille, Fife, Belgrave, & Sims, 2012). Despite sexualized stereotypes of African American men (Galinsky et al., 2013), African American racial/ethnic identity may redefine Black masculinity as associated with healthy sexual behavior and respectful relationships (Corneille et al., 2012).

Ethnic/racial and sexual identity may develop concurrently for people who are members of ethnic and sexual minority groups (Jamil, Harper, & Fernandez, 2009). Parallel to stage models of minority ethnic identity (see Chapter 2), minority sexual identity stage models have been proposed (Cass, 1979; Coleman, 1982; Troiden, 1989). A first stage involves same-sex attraction followed by feelings of confusion about differences from heterosexual peers. First wondering about same-sex attraction occurs about age 12 across ethnic groups (Balsam et al., 2015). Awareness of heterosexism and withdrawal from the heterosexual community occurs in the next stage. The following stage involves relationships with "out" gay and lesbian individuals as well as exploration of the gay and lesbian community. Integration of sexual orientation into one's identity is the final stage.

People who are both ethnic and sexual minorities may be marginalized by heterosexuals in ethnic minority communities and by European Americans in sexual minority communities (Jamil et al., 2009). For example, lesbians of color are less "out" to family members than are European American sexual minority persons (Balsam et al., 2015). Allison, described at the beginning of the chapter, felt her same-sex attraction was more accepted by European Americans than by Asian Americans. However, lesbians of color are less connected to the lesbian community than are European American lesbians (Zimmerman, Darnell, Rhew, Lee, & Kaysen, 2015).

In a study of Latino and African American male youth identified as gay, bisexual or questioning, differences in ethnic minority and sexual minority development were identified (Jamil et al., 2009). Awareness of ethnic identity was triggered externally by experiences of racism, being the only member of their ethnic group, or positive experiences with dissimilar others. In contrast, sexual identity awareness was triggered internally by feelings of same-sex attraction. Development of ethnic identity occurred via family and peer networks, whereas sexual identity development was private and solitary. This lack of public exploration was associated with rejection from the predominately European American gay community. However, the young men also experienced rejection from the heterosexual community. Nevertheless, these men were able to maintain connections with both their ethnic and their sexual minority communities.

There may be positive effects of racial identity on sexual behavior in same-sex relationships similar to those in heterosexual relationships discussed above. In a sample of young African American gay and bisexual men, *centrality* and *public regard* were associated with fewer anal sex acts and fewer unprotected anal sex acts (Walker, Longmire-Avital, & Golub, 2015). On the other hand, in a sample of gay Latinos, traditional *machismo*, a measure of hypermasculinity, was associated with internalized homophobia (i.e., negative attitudes about being gay) and risky sex, as measured by number of non-monogamous partners, knowledge of STD/HIV transmission issues, and risky sexual situations (e.g., drunk while having sex; Estrada, Rigali-Olier, Arciniega, & Tracey, 2011).

Summary

Children and adolescents of color have identities in addition to their ethnic/racial identity that may or may not be impacted by their ethnic/racial identity. Cross-ethnic friendships do not have a bearing on ethnic/racial identity but help create social acceptance and support. Students of color tend to associate with, accept, and emulate peers with academic performance similar to their own. Ethnic racial/ identity is generally associated with healthy sexual behavior but minority ethnic/ racial identity and minority sexual identity develop largely independently.

CONCLUSION

Parenting and the development of children and adolescents look different for families of color than for European American families. A culture-specific goal in families of color is interdependence. Parenting behaviors to promote interdependence include transmission of cultural values and strictness. As children become adolescents, peers begin to have a major influence on private and public regard with respect to racial/ethnic identity. Adolescents and young adults tend to affiliate with others who have similar identities to themselves. The development of racial/ethnic identity generally has a positive impact on health and behavior. This chapter has focused on childhood through early adulthood. The next chapter will focus primarily on adults of color.

RESOURCES

Blog:
Secret Asian Man?: There is No "Secret" to Academic Success www.psychologytoday.com/blog/life-in-the-intersection/201612/secret-asian-man.

Videos:
A Conversation with My Black Son www.nytimes.com/2015/03/17/opinion/a-conversation-with-my-black-son.html.
A Conversation About Growing Up Black www.nytimes.com/2015/05/07/opinion/a-conversation-about-growing-up-black.html.

CHAPTER 6

Social Psychology

Jamaal is a 20-year-old African American sophomore in a predominantly White elite college. He notices that many White students don't make eye contact with him on campus and seem uncomfortable when they pass him. Despite being his high school valedictorian, he is aware that some students may not believe he is as smart as they are and that he is on campus because of affirmative action. These thoughts about not belonging have been particularly salient when taking exams in his chemistry class, where he felt extra pressure to disprove negative academic stereotypes of African Americans. Although some White students want to be "color blind," others seem to be genuinely interested in him and how his perspectives might be similar to and different from their own.

Katie is a 19-year old European American freshman at a large state university. She has an African American roommate. Following the election of Donald Trump, she is concerned that people of color will think she is like people who voted for Trump because she is White. Katie starts wearing a safety pin to communicate to others that it is safe to talk about political climate issues with her. Her roommate tells her that the safety pin may make Katie feel good but it doesn't necessarily make people of color feel any better. Katie's roommate invites her to a Black Lives Matter meeting, which Katie attends.

In Chapter 5, we focused on development in individuals and families. Social psychology focuses on intergroup relations. Most social psychology research on prejudice, racism, and discrimination is on the perspectives of perpetrators and most of this research has been on European Americans. In the late 1990s, studies began to focus on the perspectives of persons being targeted by prejudice, racism, and discrimination (Mays, Cochran, & Barnes, 2007). Although much research in social psychology focuses on the attitudes and behavior of European Americans in relation to persons of color, the focus of this chapter will primarily be on the attitudes and behavior of persons of color in relation to other groups.

People of color have lived in North America and have been involved in North American society for centuries, and constitute over one-third of the U.S. population, but they are perceived as less American than European Americans. Devos and Banaji (2005) found that European American, African American, Latinx American, and Asian American college students rated African Americans and Asian Americans as less American than European Americans, and Asian Americans as less American than African Americans. "American" for many Americans means White or European American. To the extent that persons of color are viewed as less American than are European Americans and because of other social inequities that result in discrimination (see Chapter 1), persons of color are devalued in American society.

European Americans and people of color may agree that White = American but they diverge on perceptions of racism. African Americans view discrimination as more of a problem than European Americans do and perceive less of a decrease in anti-Black bias than European Americans do (Carter & Murphy, 2015). This may be because a smaller percentage of European Americans than African Americans experiences discrimination (American Psychological Association, 2016; see Chapter 1). Many African Americans also may have a low threshold for perceiving racism (Carter & Murphy, 2015). Being alert to potential racism serves a protective function. Maltreatment of African Americans in society may cause African Americans to be vigilant about remarks (e.g., racial jokes) or behavior (e.g., having comments in class being discounted by a professor) that could lead to problems. In contrast, European Americans may have a higher threshold for racism that also serves a protective function to avoid confirming stereotypes of European Americans as racist (Richeson & Shelton, 2007).

So, whose perceptions of racism are accurate? Is racism subjectively in the eye of the beholder or is there an objective method of determining the accuracy of people's perceptions? Nelson, Adams, and Salter (2012) examined the accuracy of African American and European American college students in detecting cases of racism on an established measure of racism (e.g., stereotypic portrayal of African Americans in entertainment media, preferential treatment of Whites in a restaurant). African Americans were more accurate. In addition, for both groups, better ability to distinguish 11 historical events (e.g., FBI wiretapping of civil rights leaders) from five false events (e.g., shooting of a fictitious African American for trying to integrate professional football) about racism was associated with more accurate perception of racism. However, African Americans were better than European Americans at distinguishing these historical facts from fiction, which was why they were also better able to accurately detect racism. Thus, education about racism may improve the ability to accurately detect it. Katie, described at the beginning of the chapter, attended a Black Lives Matter meeting and probably had an opportunity to learn about racism from African Americans' perspectives.

European Americans also have relatively low thresholds when it comes to racial progress. Whereas European Americans measure racial progress in terms of how bad things were in the past, African Americans consider how much better things could be in the future (Carter & Murphy, 2015). European Americans also may base estimates of progress on a few salient examples of successful people of color (Critcher & Risen, 2014). Calling to mind Barack Obama and Oprah Winfrey may cause European Americans to overlook racism. Similarly, the expression of valuing diversity in a company's mission statement may cause European Americans to overlook imbalances in the company's promotion of minority employees (Kaiser et al., 2013).

Picture 6.1
Source: shutterstock.

People of color and European Americans also have different thresholds for perceiving diversity in an organization. Do you consider your campus diverse? It may depend on whether you are a person of color or a European American. Both *numerical representation* (i.e., 28% of the employees are minorities) and *hierarchical representation* (i.e., 42% of high-level administrators are minorities) are required for people of color to perceive an institution as diverse (Unzueta & Binning, 2012). In contrast, *either* numerical representation *or* hierarchical representation was sufficient for European Americans to perceive an institution as diverse. So, in a university context, many European Americans may perceive that an increase in the number of students of color equals diversity even if it is not accompanied by a change in the power structure. Or, a few high-level administrators of color may be perceived as evidence of diversity without additional student diversity. Many people of color, on the other hand, may not perceive a campus as making progress on diversity until both numerical and hierarchical diversity are achieved.

CURRENT FORMS OF DISCRIMINATION

Another perception of racial progress was that following the 2008 election of Barack Obama as President of the United States, some contended that the United States was a post-racial society. However, the rise in hate speech and crimes following the 2016 election of Donald Trump tells another story (Yan, Sgueglia, & Walker, 2016). These are reminders that discrimination is not a thing of the past. Trump eschewed "political correctness," which dictates sensitivity in intergroup relations. Blatant "old fashioned" forms of racism, such as treating minority persons as if they are inferior, may become more common than they have been in the last few decades. European Americans recognize blatant forms of racism but are less likely than people of color to detect more subtle forms of racism (Carter & Murphy, 2015).

Racism and discrimination may not be obvious when they occur in a more subtle fashion (J. Jones, 1997). Subtle forms of racism have been referred to as *modern racism*

(McConahay, 1986), *symbolic racism* (Sears, 1988), and *aversive racism* (Dovidio, Gaertner, Kawakami, & Hodson, 2002). Subtle racism may involve explicitly positive statements about people of color accompanied by discomfort around people of color (Carter & Murphy, 2015; Richeson & Shelton, 2003). Ostensibly non-racial reasons are used as a rationale for attitudes that are anti-African American or against other racial or ethnic groups (Gaertner & Dovidio, 2000). Modern racists disclaim personal bigotry by strong and rigid adherence to traditional American values (e.g., individualism, self-reliance, hard work) and view responsibility for success or failure as residing within the individual (D. Sue et al., 2007). An example of symbolic racism would be opposition to affirmative action not ostensibly because of overt prejudice toward ethnic minority groups but based on a belief that ethnic minority groups already have the benefits that affirmative action is intended to provide. Thus, racism is not overt or direct, but symbolic in that it opposes a policy that provides benefits to multiple racial and ethnic groups. Aversive racists are strongly motivated by egalitarian values, which operate at a conscious level, as well as anti-minority feelings, which are less conscious and usually covert (D. Sue et al., 2007). Thus, an aversive racist might philosophically oppose affirmative action because it discriminates among groups and is not egalitarian, conveniently ignoring the fact that in many cases diversity and opportunities for minority groups will not exist without affirmative action. Moreover, the status quo of European Americans providing opportunities for people like themselves is a form of affirmative action.

Although some might assume that persons who are politically liberal might be considered less racist than those who are politically conservative, modern and symbolic racism are associated with political conservatism whereas aversive racism is associated with political liberalism (Dovidio & Gaertner, 1996, 2000). The assumption of each of these forms of subtle racism is that treating all persons equally without regard to race or ethnicity will result in equal outcomes for all persons. However, this "color blind" approach results in bias in favor of the majority group (Neville, Awad, Brooks, Flores, & Bluemel, 2013; see Chapter 1).

How is subtle racism expressed? Everyday occurrences of subtle racism involve *microaggressions*, which involve "brief, everyday exchanges that send denigrating messages to people of color because they belong to a racial minority group" (D. Sue et al., 2007, p. 273). The forms of microaggressions are: (a) microassaults; (b) microinsults; and (c) microinvalidation. *Microassaults* involve "verbal or nonverbal attacks intended to hurt another person via name-calling, avoidant behavior, or purposeful discriminatory actions" (D. Sue et al., 2007). Examples include racial epithets, or calling someone "colored" or "Oriental" (terms considered derogatory by persons of color), or deliberately serving a European American patron before a patron of color. Microassaults tend to be overt and intentional.

Less intentional and conscious are microinsults and microinvalidation. A *microinsult* involves "communications that convey rudeness and insensitivity and demean a person's racial heritage or identity" (D. Sue et al., 2007). Microinsults communicate that a person is less valued because of their membership in a racial category, which may be associated with different levels of intelligence, abnormality, and criminality. For example, asking an employee of color, "How did you get your job?" could convey the assumption that the person is not qualified for the job and got it for some reason other than ability (e.g., racial quota). A nonverbal microinsult might involve ignoring the input of a person of color. *Microinvalidation* involves communications that exclude, negate, or nullify the

Table 6.1 Microaggressions

Type	Definition	Examples
Microassault	Verbal or nonverbal attacks intended to hurt another person	• Racial epithets • Using derogatory terms for a group • Differential treatment of a group
Microinsult	Communications that convey rudeness and insensitivity and demean a person's racial heritage or identity	• Questioning a person's competence • Ignoring a person's input
Microinvalidation	Communications that exclude, negate, or nullify the psychological thoughts, feelings, or experiential reality of a person of color	• Assumptions of foreignness • Color blindness • Belief in the myth of meritocracy • Denial of personal responsibility for racism

Source: D. Sue et al., 2007.

psychological thoughts, feelings, or experiential reality of a person of color (D. Sue et al., 2007). For example, a person whose ancestors immigrated to the U.S. from Asia might be complimented on how well they speak English, despite the fact that the person and their ancestors were born in the U.S. Included in microinvalidation is the belief that racial or ethnic minority citizens are foreigners, color blindness (e.g., "I don't see color"; see Chapter 1), the belief in the myth of meritocracy that race or ethnicity plays a minor role in life success, and the denial that one has personal responsibility for racism. Most research on microaggressions has focused on microinsults and microinvalidation, and not on microassaults (G. Wong, Derthick, David, Saw, & Okazaki, 2014).

Being the target of microaggressions is a common experience among people of color. Nearly all (98%) Native American young adults in a recent study had experienced at least one microaggression (Jones & Galliher, 2015). Microinvalidations (98% experienced) were slightly more common than microinsults (92% experienced), but both were experienced by nearly everyone (Jones & Galliher, 2015). In a sample of Asian American first-year college students in New York, 78% had experienced at least one microaggression over a two-week period (Ong, Burrow, Fuller-Rowell, Ja, & Sue, 2013). Experiencing microinvalidations was more common than experiencing microinsults among Asian Americans, accounting for 75% of the microaggressions in the study.

Although perpetrators or bystanders may minimize the intention or impact of micro-aggressions (e.g., "you are being too sensitive"; "he really didn't mean to insult you"), they are a form of discrimination. As discussed in Chapter 1, people of color experience more discrimination than European Americans do (American Psychological Association, 2016). So, someone who has had relatively few experiences with discrimination or microaggressions may not be as sensitive to their impact as someone who has, as discussed previously in this chapter. Moreover, microaggressions can be perpetrated by anyone, including people of color.

A single microaggression incident may not appear particularly impactful but constant exposure to microaggressions creates a cumulative, harmful impact (D. Sue et al., 2007). In a two-week daily diary study with Asian American college students, the impact of a microaggression (i.e., negative affect, somatic symptoms) was worse if a microaggression had been experienced the previous day (Ong et al., 2013). In addition, microinvalidations had more detrimental psychological effects (i.e., negative affect, somatic symptoms) than microinsults among Asian Americans (Ong et al., 2013). Microinvalidations were also more upsetting than microinsults for Native American women but not for men (Jones & Galliher, 2015). The greater impact of microinvalidations may be because microinsults are similar to common, everyday rudeness that one might experience regardless of race, whereas microinvalidations reflect a more comprehensive rejection of a racial group.

Expressions of microaggressions may be group-specific. For African American men, this may involve White people: (a) seeming uncomfortable when they pass on the street; (b) avoiding eye contact; and (c) locking their car doors when an African American passes by (Bowleg et al., 2016). These were some of the experiences of Jamaal, described at the beginning of the chapter, as an African American man at a predominantly White elite college. Microaggressions that target African American women include: (a) assumptions of beauty and sexual objectification, (b) being silenced and marginalized, (c) the strong Black woman stereotype, and (d) the angry Black woman stereotype (J. Lewis & Neville, 2015). Latinx Americans and Asian Americans often experience microaggressions involving foreignness (Huynh, 2012). Microaggressions can also be region-specific, with Asian Americans on the West Coast, where they are more numerous, less likely to report microaggressions than those in the Northeast and Midwest (Nadal, Wong, Sriken, Griffin, & Fujii-Doe, 2015). For multiracial individuals, microaggressions may take the form of racial identification inquiries (e.g., "what are you?"), sometimes from strangers (Tran, Miyake, Martinez-Morales, & Csizmadia, 2016). Sexual minority groups also experience microaggressions but there are few studies of intersectional microaggressions, such as those targeted against people who are both sexual and racial/ethnic minorities (Nadal, Whitman, Davis, Erazo, & Davidoff, 2016).

What can offset the effects of microaggressions for people of color? Among African American college students, microaggressions were associated with anxiety (Liao, Weng, & West, 2016). However, being socially connected to the African American community buffered the effects of microaggressions. In other words, African Americans who experienced microaggressions were less anxious if they had African American friends. On the other hand, social connections to European Americans did not reduce anxiety. Thus, social support from one's ethnic community appears important in reducing the effects of microaggressions.

Ethnic identity has been found both to offset the effects of microaggressions and to sensitize people of color to them. In a study of Latinx adults, microaggressions were associated with traumatic stress (Torres & Taknint, 2015). *Traumatic stress* is defined as the negative responses, including avoidance, physiological arousal, and hypervigilance, that correspond to an adverse, sudden, and uncontrollable event (Carlson, 1997). However, ethnic identity buffered the effects of microaggressions on traumatic stress. Conversely, African Americans, Latinx Americans, and Native Americans who are more strongly ethnically identified are also more likely to report microaggressions than those who are less strongly ethnically identified (Burrow & Ong, 2010; Jones & Galliher, 2015; Torres & Ong, 2010).

It could be concluded that being less ethnically identified would be desirable for people of color because they would be less likely to be aware of microaggressions. However, there are many other physical and mental health benefits of racial/ethnic identification previously reviewed in Chapters 2 and 5. Moreover, not being aware of microaggressions may leave a person poorly prepared for other more overt forms of discrimination. The most effective method of reducing the impact of microaggressions would be to reduce the perpetration of microaggressions. If there were less perpetration of microaggressions, targets of microaggressions would not be affected nor would they be burdened with getting perpetrators to stop.

Summary

Discrimination comes in blatant and subtle forms. Subtle forms of racism are more common and have been the focus of recent research. Being the target of micro-aggressions is a common experience among people of color. Specific forms of microaggressions may be group-specific. Racial/ethnic identity may both sensitize people of color to microaggressions and buffer their effects.

STEREOTYPE THREAT

Repeated discrimination makes people of color aware of stereotypes about their group. The discomfort persons feel when they are at risk of fulfilling a negative stereotype about their group has been termed *stereotype threat* (Aronson, Quinn, & Spencer, 1998; Steele, 1997). Anxiety about poor performance may interfere with performance. For example, an African American student in an elite university in which there are few students of color may be aware of a stereotype that African Americans are less capable than other students and less qualified because they are in the university only because of affirmative action. This was Jamaal's situation, described at the beginning of the chapter, despite the fact that he was the valedictorian of his high school. Extra pressure about this belief may interfere with this student's academic test performance, beyond the general pressure that all students may feel about test performance. In this chapter we focus on stereotype threat involving persons of color but it affects other identities, such as gender and age.

In a classic test of stereotype threat, African American and European American students at Stanford University were given instructions that a test (the Graduate Record Exam Verbal test): (a) was not diagnostic of intellectual ability; or (b) was diagnostic of intellectual ability (Steele & Aronson, 1995). They then took the test. European Americans performed the same whether the test was non-diagnostic or diagnostic. However, a different pattern of results emerged for African Americans. There were no ethnic differences when the test was non–diagnostic. But in the diagnostic condition, African Americans' scores were significantly lower than those of European Americans (Figure 6.1). Thus, taking a difficult exam at Stanford that was diagnostic of intellectual ability may have activated stereotypes about African Americans' intellectual abilities. African Americans in the study may have experienced extra pressure to disprove these stereotypes that interfered with their performance. European Americans, who are not targeted by negative academic stereotypes, were not affected by stereotype threat. These effects have been replicated across studies (Spencer, Logel, & Davies, 2016).

The effects of stereotype threat are not specific to African Americans. Schmader and Johns (2003) told one group of Latinx American college students that a memory test was

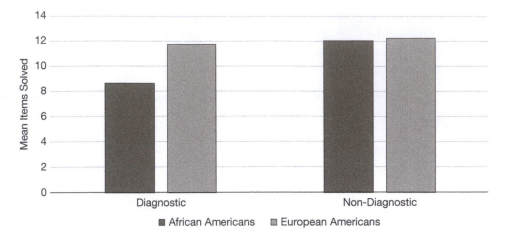

Figure 6.1 Stereotype Threat: Test Performance by Condition.
Source: Steele & Aronson, 1995.

highly predictive of performance on intelligence tests and that their performance would be used to help establish norms for different groups. This group also was asked to indicate their ethnicity before taking the test. A second group of Latinx American college students was told that the memory test was a test of working memory capacity and was asked their ethnicity before the test. Groups of European Americans were given the same instructions as either the first or the second Latinx American group and were asked their ethnicity before the test. The first Latinx American group in the intelligence condition performed more poorly on the memory test than any of the other groups (Schmader & Johns, 2003). Thus, Latinx Americans may be susceptible to academic performance stereotypes similar to those of African Americans.

There are three requirements for stereotype threat to occur (N. Lewis & Sekaquaptewa, 2016). The first requirement is *stereotype awareness*, which involves the existence of a stereotype that the target is aware of. The second requirement is *domain identification*. The more one is invested in a domain (e.g., school) and cares about performing well, the more vulnerable they may be to stereotypes. The third requirement is *task difficulty*. A person is not threatened if a task is easy. Jamaal, described at the beginning of the chapter, particularly experienced stereotype threat during chemistry exams, which are challenging. Persons do not need to believe a stereotype to be threatened by it. For example, an African American may be aware of negative stereotypes about African American academic performance but not believe them. If this person cares about doing well in school, however, they may experience excess pressure to disprove such stereotypes that may interfere with their performance on difficult academic tasks. For Jamaal, a chemistry test was not only a test of his individual chemistry knowledge but a test of whether he and other African Americans were smart.

For members of stigmatized groups, any cue that reminds them of a stereotype may induce a threat to performance (Steele, 1997). These cues include: (a) *numerical minority status*; (b) *physical objects* that suggest that one's group members do not belong in a domain (e.g., a photo of the past department chairs who are all White); and (c) *maltreatment*, such as discrimination or microaggressions (N. Lewis & Sekaquaptewa, 2016). These cues can interfere with performance in a particular situation but can also decrease a sense of belonging in an institution or field, such as science (Woodcock, Hernandez, Estrada, & Schultz, 2012).

Repeated experiences of rejection for stigmatized groups lead to expectations of rejection, which is known as *rejection sensitivity* (Mendoza-Denton, Downey, Purdie, Davis, & Pietrzak, 2002). Rejection sensitivity may be particularly acute in contexts in which stereotyping has occurred, such as in academic contexts for ethnic minority groups. For someone who is rejection sensitive, even innocuous events, such as an instructor paying less attention to them than to other students in class, may signal rejection (Spencer et al., 2016). In a study of African American students at a predominantly European American university, those who were sensitive about race-based rejection experienced a steady decline in their GPAs over their first five semesters, whereas the GPAs of those who were less sensitive about race-based rejection remained consistent (Mendoza-Denton et al., 2002; Figure 6.2). Thus, decreasing expectations of rejection and increasing a sense of belonging might be beneficial in reducing stereotype threat.

Relatively simple interventions to increase a sense of belonging have been demonstrated to reduce the effects of stereotype threat (Walton & Cohen, 2007). Most college students experience self-doubt about their abilities when they observe the abilities of others. If a person belongs to a stigmatized group, such self-doubt may lead them to question whether they belong in college. In a study by Walton and Cohen (2007), experimenters told African American and European American college students in an experimental condition that most students during their first year of college, regardless of race, worry about whether they belong in college, but that these worries decrease with time. Students in a control condition were told that their political views would become increasingly sophisticated over time. All students' GPAs were assessed in the fall semester of their freshman year in college before the experiment and again in the fall semester of their sophomore year. The GPA increase of African American students in the experimental condition was significantly greater than that of students in the other conditions. Thus, reducing stigmatization by creating a sense of belonging (i.e., self-doubt is characteristic of all college students) improved the performance of a stigmatized group but did not affect the performance of a non-stigmatized group.

Are there ethnic group stereotypes that might enhance academic performance? A stereotype about Asians is that they have superior quantitative skills compared to other groups. Asian American college women who were asked about being an Asian American (e.g., non-English language knowledge, generation in the United States) performed significantly better on a quantitative task than when they were not asked about being an Asian American or when they were asked about being a woman (e.g., questions about coed/single-sex dorms; Shih et al., 1999; see Chapter 3). Thus, the stereotype about Asians having superior quantitative skills appears beneficial.

Could there be situations in which a seemingly positive stereotype could create undue pressure? The Asian identity cues in the Shih et al. (1999) study were relatively subtle, involving language spoken and generation in the United States. Cues that are more blatant, such as "Overall, my race is considered good by others," "I am a worthy member of the racial group I belong to," and "Asian Americans are good at mathematics," have been demonstrated to create pressure that interferes with math performance (Cheryan & Bodenhausen, 2000; Shih, Ambady, Richeson, Fujita, & Gray, 2002). Even a seemingly positive stereotype is still a stereotype. People of Asian ancestry do not excel at math in all circumstances nor are all Asians inherently good at math and such stereotypes can interfere with identifying students who are in need of help.

Stereotypes, whether they are positive or negative, characterize people in terms of group membership (e.g., Asians are good in math, Asians are bad drivers). A person whose group is positively stereotyped may also believe that others who view their group in terms of the positive stereotype also view their group in terms of the negative stereotypes associated with the group. Siy and Cheryan (2016) had Asian Americans in an experimental condition read this statement:

> Imagine you are at the local cafe studying for an upcoming math final. While you are studying, you are approached by a classmate who says: "Can you help me with these two problems? I know Asians are typically good at this stuff."
>
> (p. 945)

Asian Americans in the control condition read the same statement without the last sentence. Participants in the experimental condition were more likely to believe that the person asking for help held negative stereotypes of Asians (cheap, cold, bad drivers, narrow-minded, antisocial, bad at English) and was racist. Thus, even positive stereotypes can cue stereotype threat because they may signal unstated negative stereotypes.

Stereotype threat also has effects in non-academic contexts, such as intergroup relations and stress response (N. Lewis & Sekaquaptewa, 2016). In Black–White interactions, Whites may be aware and concerned that they may appear racist (Richeson & Shelton, 2007), whereas Blacks may be aware and concerned that they may be the targets of racism (Najdowski, Bottoms, & Goff, 2015). As discussed at the beginning of the chapter, Katie was concerned about being categorized with Trump supporters, some of whom could be considered racist, because she was White. Stereotype threat may make intergroup interactions uncomfortable or unsuccessful and result in future avoidance. Brief interactions with strangers from other racial or ethnic groups tend to result in more negative outcomes (e.g., anxiety, discomfort) than longer term contact between members of different racial or ethnic groups (MacInnis & Page-Gould, 2015; Zárate, Quezada, Shenberger, & Lupo, 2014).

Interactions with health care providers can also be impaired by stereotype threat (Aronson, Burgess, Phelan, & Juarez, 2013). People of color may feel a sense of threat in medical settings about fulfilling negative stereotypes (e.g., unintelligent, unhealthy). Stereotype threat may make interactions with health professionals uncomfortable. Some people of color may avoid health care for this reason. When people of color are in medical settings, the cognitive load of stereotype threat may impair their ability to communicate necessary information or recall what the health care provider recommends. Some patients of color may even attempt to present themselves as healthier than they actually are to avoid fulfilling stereotypes. If the interaction with the health care provider is uncomfortable, patients of color may mistrust the treatment advice that the health care provider offers.

Similar to discrimination, stereotype threat can activate physiological stress responses, as discussed in Chapter 4. Situations in which group stereotypes are salient (e.g., academic settings) may be viewed as threatening, which may activate stress response (Levy, Heissel, Richeson, & Adam, 2016). Repeated physiological arousal associated with these threatening situations may alter cortisol production in the HPA axis.

How does one deal with membership in a devalued group? Tajfel and Turner (1986) have described three strategies: (a) individual mobility; (b) social creativity; and (c) social competition. *Individual mobility* involves disidentifying with a devalued group. For example, a person of color may emphasize their other group memberships (e.g., student, professional) that are valued by others and de-emphasize their racial or ethnic group membership. This is similar to the Cross (1971) pre-encounter stage of racial identity or low racial centrality in the Sellers et al. (1998) model of racial identity discussed in Chapter 2. Moreover, a person focusing on individual mobility may be attempting to assimilate into mainstream American society (Sellers et al., 1998). African Americans and Latinx Americans who believe that individuals from all ethnic backgrounds are able to advance in American society have been found to perceive less discrimination than those from the same groups who do not believe in individual mobility (Major et al., 2002). Those who believe that they can move away from a devalued group may also believe that they can escape discrimination. Moreover, they may view members of their group as personally responsible for their devalued status (Major, Kaiser, O'Brien, & McCoy, 2007). However, when persons from devalued groups who believe in individual mobility do perceive discrimination, it may be more harmful to their self-esteem than it is for persons from devalued groups who do not believe in individual mobility and realize that others devalue their group (Major et al., 2007; Sellers & Shelton, 2003).

Social creativity involves redefining the meaning of racial or ethnic group membership by comparing one's ingroup with the outgroup on a dimension on which the ingroup is superior or by changing the values assigned to the ingroup from negative to positive (Tajfel & Turner, 1986). For example, persons of color who are interdependent on their family and community might be viewed by others as overly dependent on these groups. Alternatively, interdependent behavior could be defined by persons of color as a type of social skill and that they have a greater degree of social skills than those who are independent of others. Social creativity is consistent with aspects of Cross's (1971) immersion-emersion stage. In the Sellers et al. (1998) model, race or ethnicity may be central to the identity of a socially creative person of color, they may have high private regard for their racial or ethnic group, and they may have a nationalist ideology in that they may desire limited input from others concerning their group. Social creativity may be a risky strategy unless the ingroup is large and powerful enough to define valued behavior and reward it.

Social competition involves fighting the current system to change the societal hierarchy of group membership. For example, as depicted in the film *Glory Road*, the Texas Western College (now the University of Texas at El Paso) men's basketball team, with an all African American starting lineup, defeated the powerhouse and all-White University of Kentucky men's basketball team for the 1966 National Collegiate Athletic Association championship. Although it may seem incredible, given the dominance of African Americans in basketball today, many Americans in the South in the 1960s considered African Americans to be inferior basketball players to European Americans. The Texas Western victory was a first step in desegregating college basketball teams in the South, eventually including the University of Kentucky. Social competition is also consistent with the Cross (1971) internalization stage and with the oppressed minority ideology in the Sellers et al. (1998) model in which one identifies with the oppression of others. As with social creativity, the size and power of the ingroup may determine the effectiveness of a social competition strategy.

Summary

Persons of color are susceptible to stereotype threat because of influential stereotypes. Stereotype awareness, domain identification, and task difficulty must be present for stereotype threat to occur. Interventions to create a sense of belonging may reduce stereotype threat. Positive stereotypes of a group may create stereotype threat because they may signal that the stereotyper holds unstated negative stereotypes of a group. Persons of color may adopt various strategies to cope with being members of stereotyped groups, including individual mobility, social creativity, and social competition.

BOX 6.1 STEREOTYPING OF PEOPLE OF COLOR IN THE MEDIA

How do stereotypes of people of color become prominent? Think about popular television shows, news media, and movies. Are people of color represented? When they are represented, how are people of color portrayed? A survey of over 20 years of characters in prime-time television shows showed that people of color are largely excluded, particularly Latinx Americans, Asian Americans, and Native Americans (Tukachinsky, Mastro, & Yarchi, 2015). However, African Americans are disproportionately portrayed in the news media as criminals, which causes viewers of all ethnic backgrounds to view African Americans as more culpable than European Americans for the same crimes (Hurley, Jensen, Weaver, & Dixon, 2015). Stereotypic portrayals of Latinx American movie actors (e.g., focus on crime, money, sex) result in shame, guilt, anger, and less positive affect among Mexican Americans (Schmader, Block, & Lickel, 2015).

Discussion
1   What media images of people of color can you identify?
2   How might media images influence people's attitudes toward people of color?

Picture 6.2
Source: shutterstock.

INTERGROUP RELATIONS

Stereotype threat can be reduced if a stereotyped person feels a sense of belonging with groups other than their own. A major focus in social psychology has been intergroup relations. There is evidence that intergroup relations have improved over the past half century. For example, racism, as measured by prejudiced attitudes and interracial marriages, has generally decreased (Zárate et al., 2014). It remains to be determined if the 2016 election in the United States will undo this progress in intergroup relations. Richeson and Sommers (2016) identified social identity theory, social categorization/group cognition, and social dominance theory as the prevailing social psychological theories of intergroup relations (Table 6.2). A more recent social psychological theory of intergroup relations is dehumanization.

Social identity theory posits that intergroup relations are shaped by cognitive and motivational processes by which there is a bias in favor of the ingroup and against the outgroup (Tajfel & Turner, 1986). Ingroup bias may have an evolutionary basis. Our hunter-gatherer ancestors lived in bands and came into conflict with neighboring bands. Survival involved distinguishing friends from enemies. A primitive method of detecting coalitions and alliances was shared appearance (Cosmides, Tooby, & Kurzban, 2003). Thus, humans developed neurocognitive machinery that processes phenotypic characteristics as a means of *alliance detection*. Even when people are arbitrarily assigned to groups (e.g., by month of birthday), they become biased toward the ingroup. Such arbitrary group assignment is known as the *minimal group paradigm*. The minimal group paradigm demonstrates that ingroup and outgroup categorizations may change (Brewer, 1996). For example, a Native American woman's ingroup may be Native Americans during a pow wow, but it may become women from multiple groups in other contexts, such as the Women's March on Washington following Donald Trump's inauguration.

In the *social categorization/group cognition approach*, placing people into groups activates stereotypes and prejudice that result in discrimination (Fiske, 1998). Race perception begins almost immediately after initial face perception, with the activation of neural regions that detect racial group distinctions (Ito & Bartholow, 2009). Once race is perceived, accompanying stereotypes are activated (e.g., African American men are dangerous). These stereotypes affect behavior toward the group via prejudice and discrimination (see Chapter 1).

According to *social dominance theory* (Sidanius & Pratto, 1999), societies are group-based hierarchies with dominant groups controlling resources. Hierarchies are based on age, gender, and socially constructed categories, including race, ethnicity, and religion. High-status groups perceive their group as superior to other groups and do not allocate resources (e.g., educational opportunities, jobs) equally. Unlike the previous two theories, social dominance theory focuses on the systemic power disparity between groups that perpetuates group disparities (e.g., health disparities, see Chapter 4). People of color in the United States are rarely the socially dominant group. The perception of American = White by European Americans and people of color preserves the group-based hierarchy (Devos & Mohamed, 2014). Moreover, people of color who view group-based hierarchies as legitimate are less likely to perceive prejudice (Jost & Hunyady, 2002). Conversely, socially dominant people tend to be prejudiced against groups that threaten their superiority (Sidanius & Pratto, 1999).

Table 6.2 Theories of Intergroup Contact

Theory	Definition
Social identity	Bias towards the ingroup and against outgroups
Social categorization/group cognition	Categorizing people into groups activates stereotypes and prejudice that result in discrimination
Social dominance	A dominant group controls others in a group-based hierarchy
Dehumanization	The perception of a person or group as less than fully human with animalistic and mechanistic characteristics

Dehumanization is the perception of a person or group as lacking humanness (Haslam & Loughnan, 2014). For example, during the 2016 presidential election, Syrian refugees were referred to as "rabid dogs" and Muslims were referred to as "Trojan horses." Indeed, there is research evidence that non-Muslims and non-Latinxs of multiple ethnic backgrounds in the United States dehumanize Muslims and Latinx, associating them with characteristics such as being savage, aggressive, and lacking morals (Kteily & Bruneau, 2017). Such characteristics are often infra-human or *animalistic* (Haslam, 2006). In addition to attributing animalistic characteristics to outgroups, those who dehumanize also attribute *mechanistic* characteristics characteristic of inanimate objects, such as lack of warmth, emotion, and individuality. Dehumanization of one group by another has been found to be separate from prejudice and to contribute to intergroup aggression. Those who dehumanize other groups tend to support the social hierarchies of a social dominance orientation, discussed previously (Kteily, Bruneau, Waytz, & Cotterill, 2015). A silver lining of sorts is that perceptions of outgroups are reciprocal. For example, when non-Muslims in the United States learned that Muslims humanized Americans (i.e., saw them as having human rather than non-human characteristics), they tended to humanize Muslims in return (Kteily, Hodson, & Bruneau, 2016).

Given these prejudices against outgroups, how are intergroup relations improved? A classic finding in the social psychology literature is that contact between ingroups and outgroups reduces prejudice (Allport, 1954; Pettigrew, 1998). A meta-analysis (see Chapter 3) of over 500 studies confirms that intergroup contact does reduce prejudice (Pettigrew & Tropp, 2006). Extended intergroup contact may reduce prejudice toward outgroups via a three-step process (Pettigrew, 1998): (a) *decategorization*; (b) *mutual intergroup differentiation*; and (c) *group recategorization*.

In the first step, actual experiences with individuals from outgroups may demonstrate that stereotypes are not true, which may cause outgroup members not to be viewed in terms of categories. Prejudice is reduced by an increase in knowledge about the outgroup. Jamaal, described at the beginning of the chapter, met some White students who were not color blind and who were interested in his perspectives. Once contact is established with an outgroup member, prejudice is further reduced in a second step if group members maintain their distinctiveness. The second step involves a recognition that group differences are positive. Intergroup prejudice is reduced in the third step by developing a common intergroup identity (e.g., member of the student body) that is a combination of multiple distinct group identities (Hornsey & Hogg, 2000). Becoming friends with an outgroup member also creates a common intergroup identity that reduces prejudice. The mechanisms by which intergroup contact reduces prejudice, according to another meta-analysis of the 500 studies in the Pettigrew and Tropp (2006) study, are: (a) reduced anxiety about intergroup contact; and (b) increased empathy and understanding the perspectives of others (Pettigrew & Tropp, 2008).

Prejudice reduction may be more effective among European Americans when intergroup contact occurs within a multicultural perspective vs. a color-blind perspective. European American college students expressed less racial bias (attitudes, reaction time in associating Black and White characteristics with good and bad) after being presented with a multicultural perspective than after being presented with a color-blind perspective (Richeson & Nussbaum, 2004; see Chapter 1 on multicultural and color-blind perspectives). The multicultural perspective was that intergroup harmony can be achieved by appreciating diversity and recognizing and accepting each group's positive and negative qualities. The color-blind perspective was that intergroup harmony can be achieved by recognizing people's similarities and that we are a nation of individuals. The ineffectiveness of the color-blind perspective in reducing prejudice may be because people are being asked to ignore obvious group differences (Devos, 2014). In fact, efforts to suppress stereotypes actually backfire (Wyer, Sherman, & Stroessner, 1998), analogous to asking someone not to think about a flying pink elephant. However, when there is intergroup disagreement (e.g., on abortion rights), multiculturalism may actually increase hostility, resentment, and anger among European Americans (Vorauer & Sasaki, 2011). The focus on differences in the multicultural approach (vs. on similarities in the color-blind approach) may create extreme reactions when ingroup and outgroup members disagree on an issue.

It is important for European Americans for intergroup contact to be positive if racism is to be reduced. In an online study of European Americans, reporting positive/good contact (1 = never, 7 = extremely frequently) with Black people was associated with decreased levels of racism (e.g., "Most Black people are dirty and unkempt," "Discrimination against Black people is no longer a problem in America"; 1 = strongly disagree, 7 = strongly agree) and less avoidance of African Americans (e.g., "I would rather study for an exam than talk to a Black stranger on the street," "I would go out of my way to avoid talking about race with a Black person"; 1 = strongly disagree, 7 = strongly agree; Barlow et al., 2012; Figure 6.2). However, reporting negative/bad contact with Black people was associated with increased levels of racism and avoidance of African Americans. Moreover, negative contact was more strongly associated with increased levels of racism and avoidance than positive contact was with decreased levels of these characteristics. Put another way, negative intergroup contact can be particularly damaging when it comes to European Americans' racism and avoidance of African Americans.

Another risk of intergroup contact is stereotype confirmation. People tend to seek evidence that confirms rather than disconfirms their stereotypes (Devos, 2014). Stereotypes are strengthened when people observe stereotype-consistent information. For example, if a person believes that Asian Americans are inscrutable, they may perceive an Asian American to be uncommunicative in an interaction and believe that this piece of data confirms the inscrutable stereotype. Counter-stereotypic information, such as meeting a self-disclosing Asian American, might be viewed as an exception that does not apply to the rest of the group (Devos, 2014). Moreover, because people seek stereotype-confirming evidence, a single stereotype-confirming experience may be more powerful than multiple stereotype-disconfirming experiences (Czopp, Mark, & Walzer, 2014).

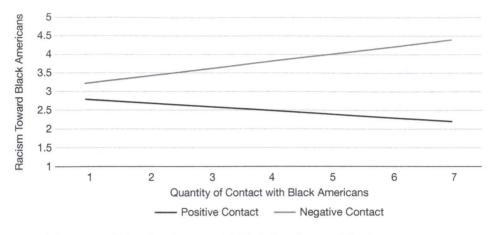

Figure 6.2 Positive and Negative Contact with Black Americans and Racism.
Source: Barlow et al., 2012.

The effects of intergroup contact in reducing prejudice are weaker for people of color than they are for European Americans, according to the results of another meta-analytic study (Tropp & Pettigrew, 2005). Whereas intergroup contact may cause members of the majority to become aware of their prejudiced attitudes, intergroup contact for ethnic minority persons may become a reminder of their devalued status in society. Moreover, in their everyday lives, ethnic minority persons may have more intergroup experiences with majority persons because the majority tends to be well-represented in most settings, such as school, business, and government. Conversely, majority persons may not have as many opportunities for interactions with ethnic minority persons. Katie, described at the beginning of the chapter, likely learned more from students at the Black Lives Matter meeting than they learned from her. Intergroup contact interventions to reduce prejudice usually attempt to create optimal conditions, such as equal status, common goals, cooperation, and institutional support (Tropp & Pettigrew, 2005). However, members of ethnic minority groups may be skeptical about how successfully such conditions can be implemented.

Summary

Racism has decreased over the past half century in part because of improved intergroup relations. Theories of intergroup relations include social identity, social categorization/group cognition, social dominance, and dehumanization. Extended intergroup contact reduces prejudice via a three-step process of decategorization, mutual intergroup differentiation, and group recategorization. Intergroup contact is more effective in reducing prejudice when it occurs within a multicultural perspective and when it is positive. However, a risk of intergroup contact is stereotype confirmation. Moreover, the effects of intergroup contact in reducing prejudice are stronger for European Americans than they are for people of color.

CONCLUSION

Despite progress over the past half century, prejudice and discrimination are not things of the past. Microaggressions are a current form of discrimination that has negative mental and physical health effects. Racial/ethnic identity may moderate the effects of micro-aggressions by sensitizing people of color to them or by buffering their effects. Stereotype threat is the product of repeated discrimination and has been found to interfere with performance for multiple ethnic groups. People of color have developed various strategies to reduce the effects of stereotype threat. Intergroup contact has generally been found to reduce prejudice.

RESOURCES

Blog:
The Platinum Rule: Treat Others the Way They Wish to Be Treated www.psychology today.com/blog/life-in-the-intersection/201702/the-platinum-rule.

Video:
How Microaggressions Are Like Mosquito Bites http://fusion.net/video/354460/how-microaggressions-are-like-mosquito-bites/.
If White People Had to Deal with Microaggressions http://everydayfeminism.com/2015/08/white-people-microaggressions/.

CHAPTER 7

Clinical Psychology

Richard is a 19-year-old Korean American freshman. His parents are immigrants and very tradi-
tional. Getting As in high school was easy for him, but college is much more challenging. He
feels pressure to achieve and is constantly worried about doing well in courses. Richard has been
feeling sick and has had a lack of energy. He wonders if feeling sick has something to do with
being worried about his grades – or vice versa. Richard has considered going to the university
counseling center for help in school but he is reluctant to talk about feeling pressured and worried
about his grades.

Ana is a 19-year-old Puerto Rican American freshman. Her parents were from Puerto Rico and she
grew up in a Puerto Rican community in New York. College is her first experience away from
home. She was sexually assaulted at a party earlier in the year by a man who she thought was a
friend. Ana reported this to the authorities and the perpetrator is banned from having contact with
her. However, she experiences panic any time she goes to a place on campus where she used to see
the perpetrator. She has been in counseling at the university counseling center. The counseling has
made her feel better, but she feels that her European American counselor does not understand her
culture and how it might affect her reaction to the sexual assault.

Clinical psychology applies psychological science to the diagnosis and treatment of
mental disorders, also known as psychopathology. In this chapter, we will review research
on ethnic differences in psychopathology and culture-specific psychopathology. Then we
will examine why people of color underutilize mental health services and conclude with
a review of the research on culturally-adapted interventions.

According to the current nomenclature: "a mental disorder is a syndrome characterized by clinically significant disturbance in an individual's cognition, emotion regulation,
or behavior that reflects a dysfunction in the psychological, biological, or developmental
processes underlying mental functioning" (American Psychiatric Association, 2013,
p. 20). Clinically significant means a problem outside the normal range of behavior that

Picture 7.1
Source: shutterstock.

causes distress and interferes with daily functioning, such as hygiene, work, or school. The definition indicates that the cause could be psychological, biological, *or* developmental. However, the cause could also be an interaction of the three. For example, a biological risk for depression might be exacerbated if a child is in an abusive or neglectful environment. A mental disorder is not under the control of the patient and is not a choice or a lifestyle (Kraemer, 2014). In the absence of intervention, a mental disorder can be prolonged and may get worse.

By the American Psychiatric Association (2013) definition of mental disorders, 46% of United States adults have experienced at least one mental disorder during their lifetime (Kessler et al., 2005). Commonly studied mental disorders include schizophrenia, bipolar disorder, depressive disorders, anxiety disorders, obsessive-compulsive disorders, trauma-related disorders, eating disorders, impulse control disorders, substance use disorders, and personality disorders (American Psychiatric Association, 2013). The most common disorders experienced during one's lifetime are anxiety disorders (29% of U.S. adults), mood disorders (e.g., depression, bipolar disorder; 21%), and substance use disorders (15%; Kessler et al., 2005).

Although a particular disorder (e.g., obsessive-compulsive disorder) is characterized by a particular set of symptoms, persons with the same disorder may vary from one another (Kraemer, 2014). They may express different symptoms, have different severity levels, and be at a different stage of the disorder. Moreover, the expression of symptoms may differ across cultures, and some cultural groups may have unique forms of mental disorders.

PSYCHOPATHOLOGY

Diagnostic and Statistical Manual of Mental Disorders (DSM)

A clinical diagnosis is an informed opinion by a clinical psychologist or other clinician that a mental disorder exists in a person (Kraemer, 2014). The *Diagnostic and Statistical*

Manual of Mental Disorders (DSM) has been the official diagnostic system in the United States since 1952 (Blashfield, Keeley, Flanagan, & Shannon, 2014). A reliable diagnostic system is a useful communication tool for researchers studying the same disorder (e.g., depression). DSM is also useful for guiding treatments for mental disorders.

DSM was first developed after World War II. Many veterans were returning from military service and there was an acute need for mental health services. This need led to the development of the field of clinical psychology and to the first accreditation of clinical psychology PhD programs in 1948. DSM, published in 1952, was an attempt to create a standard diagnostic classification system that did not previously exist. It was developed by a committee of leading psychiatrists and researchers, resulting in 128 categories of mental disorders. Disorders were divided into those that were biologically-based and those that were not. They were further divided into psychotic (severe), neurotic (less severe), and character disorder (enduring) categories. There was not attention to potential cultural variations in the disorders.

DSM was revised by clinicians and researchers in 1968 as part of a World Health Organization effort to standardize the classification of mental disorders. The result was DSM-II, which was expanded to 193 diagnostic categories. Despite an international committee that worked to create a consensus, DSM-II essentially was a Western classification system that did not account for cultural variation in disorders.

Based on research that established more specific and reliable criteria for mental disorders (Feighner et al., 1972), the DSM was revised a second time in 1980. DSM-III also represented a departure from the psychoanalytic basis of DSM and DSM-II to a non-etiologic focus on symptoms. The number of diagnostic categories increased to 228 but there was still no attention to cultural variation.

Soon after DSM-III was released, studies began to be published using the Research Diagnostic Criteria and focused on psychotic and depressive disorders (Spitzer, Endicott, & Robins, 1975). Incorporating these studies, the DSM-III-R was published in 1987 and included 253 diagnostic categories. Diagnoses were now made with the Structured Clinical Interview for DSM-III-R (Spitzer, Williams, Gibbon, & First, 1990). Feminists criticized DSM-III-R for including premenstrual syndrome and masochistic personality disorder as new diagnostic categories (Blashfield et al., 2014). As with the previous editions of DSM, there was inattention to culture.

Culture made its debut in DSM-IV in 1994, albeit in an appendix. Cultural considerations were presented as a supplement to the other 383 diagnostic categories in DSM-IV. The impetus for DSM-IV was evidence-based medicine. Data from previous studies were considered to modify the existing DSM-IV diagnostic categories as needed and to add new categories. DSM-IV was developed by 13 workgroups of professionals.

DSM-V was published in 2013 and included input from a group of professionals who considered cross-cultural issues. The Cultural Formulation Interview was based on research on 12 clinical samples in the United States, Canada, Peru, the Netherlands, Kenya, and India. The Cultural Formulation Interview addressed:

- cultural identity of the individual
- cultural explanations of the individual's illness
- cultural factors related to psychosocial environment and levels of functioning
- cultural elements of the relationship between the individual and the clinician.

DSM-V also attempted to incorporate dimensional models of personality into the diagnostic criteria (Blashfield et al., 2014). Dimensional models acknowledge that normal and abnormal personalities are not separate but lie on a continuum. Over 500 professionals were involved in the development of DSM-V. Input also was solicited from the public on a website, which drew 10,000 comments. DSM-V burgeoned to 541 diagnostic categories.

The National Institute of Mental Health (NIMH) rejected DSM-V as exclusively symptom-based without attention to etiological mechanisms. NIMH developed the Research Domain Criteria (RDoC; Insel et al. 2010), which includes levels of analyses from the molecular to the social. RDoC emphasized biological etiologies with an emphasis on genetics and neuroscience. Although RDoC has stimulated research, it is less valuable for clinicians. And in not considering culture, the RDoC took diagnosis back three decades to the time when culture was absent from DSM. Moreover, less than 7% of research funded by NIMH from 1997–2015, the primary federal funding agency for mental health research, focused on people of color (McKay et al., 2016).

Summary

DSM was slow to incorporate culture. When culture was first incorporated into DSM, it was done so peripherally. The latest DSM-V has a more central focus on culture. However, DSM-V was rejected by NIMH, whose alternative RDoC again ignored culture.

Ethnic Differences in Psychopathology

A logical question in the discussion of diagnostic categories is whether people of color differ in their rates of mental disorders compared to European Americans. Epidemiological studies focus on the patterns of health and disease in populations and make it possible to compare groups. The Collaborative Psychiatric Epidemiological Surveys included the National Survey of American Life (NSAL) and the National Latino Asian American Study (NLAAS). In both surveys, professional interviewers interviewed nationally representative samples in English, Spanish, Mandarin, Cantonese, Tagalog, or Vietnamese as needed. NSAL examined mental disorders and mental health service use among African-American and Afro-Caribbean populations in the United States as compared with White respondents living in the same communities. NLAAS examined mental disorders and mental health service use among Latinx and Asian Americans. The results of these Collaborative Psychiatric Epidemiological Surveys generally suggest that the rates of mental disorders are *lower* for people of color than for European Americans (Miranda, McGuire, Williams, & Wang, 2008). Latinx Americans (except Puerto Ricans), Asian Americans, and African Americans had *fewer* mental disorders than European Americans did (Figure 7.1).

These consistent findings of lower rates of mental disorders among people of color relative to European Americans seem paradoxical given what we have covered so far in

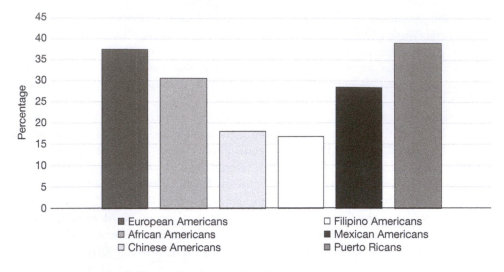

Figure 7.1 Prevalence of Lifetime Psychiatric Disorders.
Source: Miranda et al., 2008.

this textbook. After all, people of color experience greater levels of racial/ethnic discrimination than European Americans do, which is stressful (Chapter 1; American Psychological Association, 2016). The Collaborative Psychiatric Epidemiological Surveys indicate that perceptions of racial/ethnic discrimination among African Americans, Latinx Americans, and Asian Americans are associated with major depressive disorder, panic disorder, agoraphobia (avoidance of places where a panic attack has occurred or could occur), post-traumatic stress disorder, and substance use disorders (Chou, Asnaani, & Hofmann, 2012). Discrimination was associated with these mental disorders regardless of socioeconomic status, level of education, age, and gender. Moreover, meta-analyses of 27 studies of African Americans (D. Lee & Ahn, 2013), 51 studies of Latinx Americans (D. Lee & Ahn, 2012), and 23 studies of Asian Americans (D. Lee & Ahn, 2011) support this discrimination–psychopathology link. In addition, a meta-analysis of 81 studies of over 44,000 people indicates that discrimination has negative effects on the well-being of people of color, regardless of socioeconomic status, age, and gender (T. Smith & Trimble, 2016).

So, why are there lower rates of psychopathology among people of color relative to European Americans? There are three major possible explanations:

1   People of color are mentally healthier than European Americans
2   Measurement error
3   Culture-specific expressions of psychopathology

The first explanation is that people of color are *mentally healthier* than European Americans are. Lower rates of mental disorder among people of color suggest resilience despite discrimination and other stressors associated with being a minority. One source of resilience may be racial/ethnic identity. In the meta-analyses of studies involving African Americans (D. Lee & Ahn, 2013) and Asian Americans (D. Lee & Ahn, 2011), racial/ethnic identity was negatively correlated with psychopathology. However, the strength of these correlations was relatively weak. Moreover, ethnic identity for Latinx Americans was *positively* associated, albeit weakly, with psychopathology in the meta-analytic study (D. Lee & Ahn, 2012).

Unlike the weak racial/ethnic identity correlations, there were strong negative correlations for Asian Americans and Latinx Americans in these meta-analyses between self-esteem and psychopathology (D. Lee & Ahn, 2011, 2012). Although self-esteem was not examined in the meta-analysis of studies of African Americans (D. Lee & Ahn, 2013), a consistent research finding is that African Americans have higher self-esteem than European Americans (Erol & Orth, 2011; Gray-Little & Hafdahl, 2000). Although Latinx American adolescents have been found to have lower self-esteem than European American adolescents, Latinx American self-esteem surpasses European American self-esteem at age 20, and this gap persists (Erol & Orth, 2011). Thus, greater self-esteem is a possible source of better mental health among people of color relative to European Americans.

Another explanation of lower psychopathology among people of color is "tight" cultural norms, as discussed in Chapter 4. Interdependent cultural groups are characterized by a low tolerance for deviance and a high level of social connectedness (Chiao, 2015; H. Kim & Sasaki, 2014). Accountability and social support in communities of color may be protective factors against psychopathology.

A second explanation of lower rates of psychopathology among people of color is measurement error. Interviews, which are commonly used to diagnose psychopathology, can be susceptible to error (Alcantara & Gone, 2014). In the Collaborative Psychiatric Epidemiological Surveys, diagnostic interviews were conducted in participants' first language, which likely enhanced accuracy. Still, some participants may associate stigma with psychological problems and may have been reluctant to disclose such problems to a stranger. There is evidence of higher reports of psychopathology among people of color during self-report than during interviews (S. Sue, Cheng, Saad, & Chu, 2012). Mistrust of researchers or health care providers out of concerns about being exploited may also inhibit disclosure (Whaley, 2001). For example, awareness of the Tuskegee Syphilis Study (see Chapter 3) may make African Americans suspicious of researchers (Brandon et al., 2013). In addition, measures of psychopathology are not necessarily equivalent across cultural groups (see Chapter 3). If there is not conceptual, linguistic, metric, and functional equivalence of measures across cultural groups, apparently different rates of psychopathology may result (Liang, Matheson, & Douglas, 2016; Trimble, 2007).

There is other evidence to suggest that measurement underestimation may be minimal and that it might be expected that people of color would be diagnosed with *greater* levels of psychopathology than European Americans. Measures of psychopathology have been found to be reliable (i.e., consistent results) and valid (i.e., correlate with other measures of psychopathology) for multiple ethnic groups (e.g., G. Hall, Bansal, & Lopez, 1999; Ritschel, Tone, Schoemann, & Lim, 2015). Moreover, patients interviewed in their first language report a greater number of psychopathology symptoms than when they are interviewed in their second language (Brown & Weisman de Mamani, 2017). Clinicians also may be biased toward making more severe diagnoses of people of color (Alcantara & Gone, 2014; Liang et al., 2016). If they are aware of stereotypes of people of color, they may intentionally or unintentionally attend to evidence during an interview that is consistent with these stereotypes.

The third explanation of relatively low rates of psychopathology among people of color is culture-specific expressions of psychopathology. Most measures of psychopathology are not culture-specific. An example of culture-specific expression of psychopathology is *somatization*, the tendency to express distress via physical symptoms, such as insomnia, fatigue, poor appetite, dizziness, heart palpitations, or pain (Ryder et al., 2008). Somatic expression of distress is common among persons of East Asian ancestry. Cultural reasons for somatic expression include mind–body integration, stigma surrounding mental vs. physical illness, and cultural proscriptions against emotion expression which might upset group harmony. The somatic symptoms experienced by Richard, described at the beginning of the chapter, may be a culturally acceptable way of expressing distress. In contrast, a culture-specific expression of psychopathology for European Americans is *psychologization*, the tendency to express distress via emotions, such as feeling sad or worthless and crying. Similarly, African Americans may express anxiety somatically because of the salience of physical illnesses in their lives (e.g., hypertension, cardiovascular disease, diabetes) combined with the stigma of mental illness (Hunter & Schmidt, 2010). Once again, it is more culturally acceptable to be physically than mentally ill. These somatic aspects of psychopathology may not be adequately assessed by European American conceptualizations and measures of distress that emphasize psychologization.

In addition to these general tendencies to somatize across groups of color, there may be other *culture-bound* forms of psychopathology that do not map onto European American syndromes. For example, *ataque de nervios* involves symptoms of panic, depression, and dissociation (feelings of detachment from one's emotions or body) and is found in Latin American and Caribbean cultures (Alcantara, Abelson, & Gone, 2012). *Ataque de nervios* involves screaming, falling, lack of communication, and agitated motor activity. Similarly, *neurasthenia* is mental and physical exhaustion with chronic fatigue, weakness, and pain, which was found in 7% of a community sample of Chinese Americans in Los Angeles (Zheng et al., 1997). Culture-specific panic syndromes among Cambodian Americans include neck-focused panic attack and orthostasis-triggered panic attack (Hinton et al., 2005). In *neck-focused panic attack*, there is worry about neck vessel rupture accompanied by dizziness, blurry vision, and heart palpitations. *Orthostatis-triggered panic attack* involves standing and experiencing dizziness and other symptoms, such as heart palpitations, after which the person sits, fearing fainting. A person experiencing one of these group-specific syndromes would not necessarily be detected as experiencing psychopathology on measures that do not assess these symptoms.

Although culture-bound syndromes may be regarded as "folk" medicine because they do not map onto mainstream diagnostic categories, they are discrete entities. There is even some evidence of a neural basis of culture-bound syndromes. *Hwa-byung* is a Korean culture-bound syndrome that may affect Korean American immigrants. It involves suppression of anger despite social bullying (Chiao, 2015). Symptoms include sighing, tearing, and talkativeness, as well as somatic symptoms including heat sensations, chest compression, heart palpitations, and respiratory problems. Relative to normals, *hwa-byung* patients show heightened fusiform and lingual gyri brain activity while viewing angry and sad faces (B. Lee et al., 2009). These brain areas are involved in face perception. *Hwa-byung* patients also exhibited blunted anterior cingulate cortex activity, which is involved in emotions, relative to normal, while viewing these emotional faces. This combination of neural responses is consistent with the social sensitivity and anger suppression in *hwa-byung*.

Culture-bound syndromes may also interact with syndromes common to European Americans. Post-traumatic stress disorder (PTSD) develops in some people who have experienced a traumatic (shocking, scary, dangerous) event. For at least one month after the event, the person re-experiences the event, avoids reminders of the event, experiences arousal and reactivity (e.g., feels tense, easily startled), and has thought and mood disturbance (e.g., memory loss, feelings of guilt or blame; American Psychiatric Association, 2013). Latinx Americans have been found to be at greater risk than European Americans for the onset of PTSD following a traumatic event (Alcantara, Casement, & Lewis-Fernandez, 2013). An example is the reactions following the September 11, 2001 terrorist attacks of over 1000 New York City residents who lived near the World Trade Center (Galea et al., 2002). The rates of onset of PTSD among European Americans, African Americans, and Latinx Americans in this sample are shown in Figure 7.2. It is possible that the higher rates of PTSD among Latinx Americans were because PTSD was exacerbated by *ataques de nervios*, a response to overwhelming stress specific to Latinx communities (Hinton & Lewis-Fernandez, 2011). Unfortunately, *ataques de nervios* were not assessed in the study. Ana, described at the beginning of the chapter, could have been experiencing PTSD.

Of interest in addition to rates of psychopathology between European Americans and people of color is variation with groups of color. In Chapter 4, we reviewed the immigrant paradox in which some immigrants experienced better physical health than persons from the same ethnic group who were born in the United States. Is there an analogous immigrant paradox for mental health? Within ethnic groups, Mexican, African, Caribbean, and Asian women immigrants have lower rates of mental disorders than members of these groups who have spent more time in the United States (Miranda et al., 2008). However, the correlation between assimilation to mainstream American culture and psychopathology generally is weak (Gupta, Leong, Valentine, & Canada, 2013; Yoon et al., 2013). It is possible that this weak correlation is a result of difficulties in measuring acculturation and the complexity of psychopathology (Gupta et al., 2013).

Another explanation of the weak association between assimilation and psychopathology is that the effects of acculturation are mixed. As discussed in Chapter 4, many immigrants engage in *selective acculturation*, which involves both healthy and unhealthy

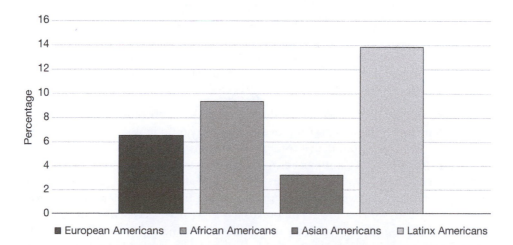

Figure 7.2 Onset of PTSD 5–8 Weeks Following 9/11/01 Among New York City Residents.
Source: Galea et al., 2002.

behaviors (Yeh et al., 2009). For example, acculturation may make Asian Americans more likely to seek help for mental health problems (Sun, Hoyt, Brockberg, Lam, & Tiwari, 2016), but also more likely to abuse substances (Salas-Wright, Vaughn, Todic, Cordova, & Perron, 2015). Thus, the correlation between acculturation and psychopathology is neither uniformly positive nor negative.

Yet another reason for the weak association between acculturation and psychopathology is that the acculturation process often is not linear. As discussed in Chapter 2, only about one-fourth of immigrants assimilate by moving to a new country and leaving their home culture behind while adopting the new country's culture (Berry et al., 2006). More common was the *integration* strategy, which involves maintaining one's culture while interacting with the host culture. Integration is associated with lower levels of psychopathology and higher levels of positive mental health than other acculturation strategies (Yoon et al., 2013; see Chapter 2). On the other hand, *marginalization* from one's culture of origin and from the host culture is more strongly associated with psychopathology than the other acculturation strategies.

Although acculturation is not unequivocally associated with psychopathology, it can be stressful. As discussed in Chapter 5, intergenerational cultural conflict associated with an acculturation gap between parents and children results in children's mental health problems (Lui, 2015). Cultural distance between a family's culture of origin and mainstream American culture may be associated with greater psychopathology. Conflicts often arise when one's parents seem "old school" (e.g., traditional, overly strict) and when one's children are learning things that seem completely foreign (e.g., curse words that parents don't understand, new styles of music).

BOX 7.1 SAME-SEX RELATIONSHIPS AND HOMOPHOBIA

Before 1973, homosexuality was considered a mental disorder by the American Psychiatric Association. Based on research and changing social norms, the American Psychiatric Association dropped homosexuality from its nomenclature of Diagnostic and Statistical Manual of Mental Disorders (DSM) in 1973. The American Psychological Association followed suit in 1975, at which time they no longer considered homosexuality a mental disorder. The distress associated with homosexuality came to be viewed as imposed by others rather than arising within the individual (Kraemer, 2014).

Despite the fact that psychiatry and psychology have not considered same-sex relationships to be pathological for over 40 years, homophobic attitudes persist. There may be a perception that African Americans may be less accepting than European Americans of same-sex relationships because of the importance of religion and church. However, in a large study of Midwest college students, there were no differences between African Americans and European Americans in views toward gays and lesbians (e.g., homosexuality is wrong), acceptance of gay and lesbian rights (e.g., gays and lesbians should have the same rights as everyone else), or willingness to socialize with gays and lesbians (e.g., comfortable having a gay or lesbian as a close friend; Jenkins, Lambert, & Baker, 2009). Compared to European

Americans, African Americans rated religion as more important in their lives and attended religious services more frequently. However, these two indicators of religiosity were associated with homophobia, but only for European Americans. Men, regardless of ethnic group, were more homophobic than women.

Discussion

1 Did you expect ethnic differences in homophobia?
2 Why was religiosity not associated with homophobia for African Americans despite religion and church attendance being important in their lives?
3 Why were men more homophobic than women, regardless of ethnic group?

Summary

People of color have been found to have lower rates of psychopathology than European Americans. Greater self-esteem, "tight" cultural norms, and undetected culture-specific psychopathology may explain this finding. For immigrants, there is a weak association between assimilation to mainstream United States culture and psychopathology. Integration of two cultures is associated with low psychopathology and high positive mental health. Acculturative conflict between parents and children can result in children's psychopathology.

UNDERUTILIZATION OF MENTAL HEALTH SERVICES

A consistent finding over the past 40 years is that some groups of people of color underutilize mental health services relative to European Americans (J. Chang, Chen, & Alegría, 2014; T. Smith & Trimble, 2016; S. Sue, 1977). In a meta-analysis of 130 studies involving 4,771,472 participants, rates of lifetime mental health service utilization were lower for African Americans, Latinx Americans, and Asian Americans relative to European Americans (T. Smith & Trimble, 2016; Figure 7.3). Mental health services are most commonly offered in English, which might partially explain why Asian American and Latinx American groups, which both include a large percentage of immigrants whose first language is not English, use mental health services at lower rates than African Americans and European Americans, who are primarily English-speaking groups (Bauer, Chen, & Alegría, 2010). In Chapter 4, we reviewed physical health disparities. Mental health service underutilization is a mental health disparity.

The lower rates of mental health service utilization among people of color are consistent with their relatively low rates of psychopathology in the Collaborative Epidemiological Surveys (Miranda et al., 2008). However, the epidemiological surveys also reveal that people of color underutilize mental health services even when they have a mental disorder. Among those in the community with mental disorders, only 33% of African

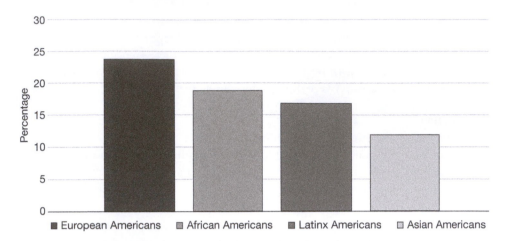

Figure 7.3 Lifetime Mental Health Service Utilization Rates by Ethnicity.

Source: T. Smith & Trimble, 2016.

Americans (Jackson et al., 2007) and 28% of Asian Americans (Meyer, Zane, Cho, & Takeuchi, 2009) used mental health services within the past 12 months vs. 54% of European Americans (estimate from Meyer et al., 2009; Figure 7.3). Although comparable 12-month data for Latinx Americans with mental disorders are not available in the Collaborative Epidemiological Surveys, less than 11% of all Latinx Americans (those with and without mental disorders) used specialty mental health services in the past 12 months (Alegría et al., 2007). The T. Smith and Trimble (2016) meta-analysis of 130 studies of over 4 million people, described earlier, indicated that across studies African Americans were the ethnic group least likely to use mental health services when mental disorders were present. So, most European Americans seek mental health services when they experience psychological distress whereas most people of color do not.

There are several possible reasons for this underutilization, including:

- socioeconomic status
- high distress threshold
- stigma associated with the use of mental health services
- use of alternative services
- lack of cultural responsiveness of mental health services.

Socioeconomic status may affect access to mental health care. People who do not have mental health insurance may not receive services. Geographic distance from services may also affect access. However, the results of research on the direct effects of socioeconomic status on underutilization of mental health services are mixed (T. Smith & Trimble, 2016). Socioeconomic status likely interacts with other variables, such as immigration status.

The high distress threshold hypothesis is that people of color can tolerate high levels of distress and may not immediately seek mental health services (Liang et al., 2016). This may be because they are used to coping with stressors. Thus, treatment may be postponed until a problem is chronic or severe. There is evidence that parents of color do not seek mental health services until their children's problems are severe (Liang et al.,

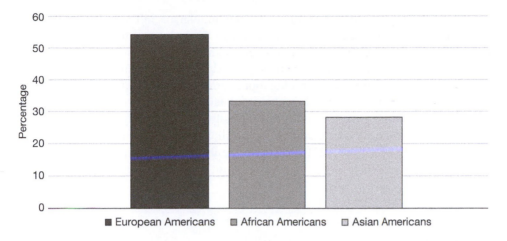

Figure 7.4 Mental Health Specialty Service Usage in the Past 12 Months Among Persons With a Mental Disorder.

Source: Jackson et al., 2007; Meyer et al., 2009.

2016). However, a recent study of African American, Asian American, European American, Latinx American, and Native American college students indicated no significant differences in psychological distress at intake (Ibaraki & Hall, 2014).

Stigma associated with the use of mental health services may explain why Asian Americans are the ethnic group least likely to utilize mental health services. Asian Americans associate greater levels of stigma with seeking mental health services than do European Americans (J. Kim & Zane, 2016). Stigma associated with someone who is mentally ill was found to decrease the likelihood that South Asian American students would seek mental health services (Loya, Reddy, & Hinshaw, 2010). In a meta-analysis of 207 studies involving over 37,000 Asian American, Latinx American, and African American participants, racial/ethnic identification was significantly associated with greater levels of public stigma, the perception that the public holds negative stereotypes and prejudices about mental illness, only among Asian Americans (Sun et al., 2016). Many Asian Americans may believe that seeking mental health services is not normative behavior for their group (N. Choi & Miller, 2014).

For some clients, there may be less stigma in seeking help outside of mental health service settings. Some clients may also seek help outside mental health services settings because they are unfamiliar with these settings or mistrust them (T. Smith & Trimble, 2016). Between 5 and 17% of the participants in the Collaborative Psychiatric Epidemiological Surveys sought mental health services in primary care settings (e.g., physicians). Another 10 to 20% sought mental health services from alternative providers, such as religious and spiritual advisers, and complementary medicine providers (e.g., herbalists, chiropractors). Nevertheless, most African Americans, Latinx Americans, and Asian Americans who did seek help for distress sought it in mental health service settings.

A fourth reason for mental health service underutilization is the lack of culturally-responsive mental health services. As mentioned above, most mental health services are provided in English. Non-English speaking Latinx Americans and Asian Americans use mental health services at lower rates than those who speak English (Bauer et al., 2010). In a study of college-age European, African, Asian, and Latinx immigrants in the United States, acculturative stress was associated with *negative* attitudes toward using mental health services (Rogers-Sirin, 2013). Perhaps this is because mental health services are seen as irrelevant in addressing stressors that immigrants experience associated with acculturation.

Beyond language barriers and acculturation, some people of color may view mental health services as foreign because they have not been developed or adapted for people of color. For example, if a person believes that their distress is primarily spiritual, cultural, or physical, mental health services that focus on psychological issues may be viewed as irrelevant (T. Smith & Trimble, 2016). The culturally-adapted interventions movement, reviewed in the next section, has been a response to the lack of culturally-responsive mental health services.

Summary

People of color tend to underutilize mental health services relative to European Americans. Underutilization is particularly pronounced among people of color who have a mental disorder. Stigma associated with mental health service use and lack of culturally-responsive mental health services are likely reasons for underutilization.

CULTURALLY-ADAPTED INTERVENTIONS

During the 1980s, United States mental health policy began to focus on improving the quality of treatment (Kiesler, 1992). Mental health services began to be provided in the context of managed health care that was covered by insurance. Short-term, cost-effective mental health treatments were emphasized. The NIMH began to fund randomized clinical trials to evaluate mental health treatments. *Randomized clinical trials* are modeled after evaluations of drug treatments, in which participants are randomly assigned to a treatment or comparison condition, which may involve no treatment or a comparison treatment. This policy emphasis on quality of treatment and funding for randomized clinical trials spawned the empirically-validated treatments movement in clinical psychology (Rosner, 2005).

In 1996, the American Psychological Association Division 12 (Clinical Psychology) Task Force on Promotion and Dissemination of Psychological Procedures reported a list of treatments that were considered to be empirically-validated (Chambless et al., 1996). The criteria for *well-established treatments* were: (a) at least two experiments demonstrating that a treatment is more efficacious than a drug or another treatment; or (b) more than 10 single case experiments demonstrating the efficacy of a treatment; (c) experiments conducted with treatment manuals; (d) characteristics of client samples clearly specified; and (e) experiments conducted by at least two different investigators or investigatory teams. For *probably efficacious treatments*, the criteria were: (a) two experiments demonstrating that the treatment is more effective than a waiting list control group; or (b) one experiment or more by a single investigator or team meeting the well-established treatment criteria (a), (c), (d), and (e); or four or more single case experiments meeting well-established treatment criteria (c) and (d).

It was determined by the Task Force that well-established treatments existed for anxiety and stress, depression, some health problems (e.g., headache, bulimia), childhood enuresis, childhood oppositional disorder, marital discord, and sexual dysfunction (Chambless et al., 1996). Probably efficacious treatments were identified for these disorders, as well as for substance abuse and dependence. These treatments were initially known as empirically-validated treatments and later became known as evidence-based treatments.

Most of the well-established and probably efficacious treatments were behavioral or cognitive-behavioral. Behavioral therapies involve changing behavior via conditioning methods. For example, if a person fears public speaking, the person is gradually exposed to public speaking (e.g., visualizing it, going to an auditorium, practicing speaking without an audience, practicing speaking with a small audience, public speaking with a larger audience) while simultaneously engaging in a response incompatible with fear, such as relaxation. The premise of cognitive-behavioral therapies is that a person's thoughts affect the way they feel and act. Biased information processing leads to disorders (Beck & Haigh, 2014). For example, a person's belief that they are a failure may cause them to be depressed. A cognitive-behavioral therapist would help the person assess the accuracy of the belief, identify contrary evidence, modify biased beliefs, and develop goals and behavioral skills that will enhance success with these goals.

The Task Force reported that none of these well-established or probably efficacious treatments was based on studies that included ethnic minorities (Chambless et al., 1996). This spawned the culturally-adapted evidence-based treatment movement. Cultural adaptation has been defined as "the systematic modification of an evidence-based treatment or intervention protocol to consider language, culture, and context in such a way that it is compatible with the client's cultural patterns, meanings, and values" (Bernal, Jiménez-Chafey, & Domenech Rodríguez, 2009, p. 362). Cultural adaptations have ranged from surface adaptations, such as matching clients and therapists on language or ethnicity, to deep adaptations that change the content of treatment. Whereas unadapted treatments primarily focus on the individual, culturally-adapted treatments for people of color focus on the individual in the context of relationships and community norms (G. Hall, 2001).

Culturally-adapted treatments were not welcomed with open arms by those in the evidence-based treatment movement. Proponents of evidence-based treatments emphasized fidelity, or strict adherence to the procedures in the treatment manuals. Any modifications of the established approaches were assumed to compromise treatment effectiveness (Elliott & Mihalic, 2004). Competing with demands for fidelity is the cultural fit of a treatment (Castro, Barrera, & Martinez, 2004). The evidence for evidence-based treatments was not based on populations of color, as indicated above. However, evidence-based treatment proponents proceeded to disseminate and implement the unadapted treatments in communities of color (G. Hall & Yee, 2012). This insistence on fidelity emphasized internal validity at the expense of external validity (S. Sue, 1999). Those who began to develop culturally-adapted treatments sought a better balance between internal and external validity, and between fidelity and flexible fit.

Proponents of unadapted evidence-based treatments have created a false dichotomy between fidelity and fit. A treatment manual is a guide to the structure of each treatment session, but it does not provide statements to be read verbatim. Thus, even those who use treatment manuals adapt their treatment to the particular client's concerns. It

Picture 7.2
Source: shutterstock.

has been contended that *all* treatment is culturally adapted (Benish, Quintana, & Wampold, 2011).

Despite the resistance of evidence-based researchers to culturally-adapted treatments and funding directed more toward dissemination and implementation of unadapted treatments than to cultural adaptations, multiple studies on culturally-adapted treatments have been conducted. A recent meta-analysis (see Chapter 3) was conducted on 78 studies of cultural adaptations conducted over the past 25 years involving over 13,000 participants, 95% of whom were people of color (G. Hall, Ibaraki, Huang, Marti, & Stice, 2016). Overall, culturally-adapted treatments produced effects that were two-thirds of a standard deviation better than no treatment or comparison treatments in reducing psychopathology. This is considered a medium effect size, which is substantive. Ana, described at the beginning of the chapter, may have experienced additional benefits from a therapy approach that was responsive to Latinx American culture.

What is impressive about the findings of the G. Hall, Ibaraki et al. (2016) meta-analysis is that the outcomes were unadapted measures (other than language translation in some cases) of psychopathology, such as depression, anxiety, or psychosis. In other words, culturally-adapted treatments beat unadapted treatments at their own game. Had the outcome measures been adapted to address culture-specific forms of psychopathology (e.g., *ataque de nervios*), it is possible that the difference in effectiveness between unadapted and culturally-adapted treatments would have been even larger (cf. Helms, 2015).

A common type of cultural adaptation is matching therapists and clients on ethnicity. This may be helpful because of shared language and culture. A therapist of the same ethnicity may signal that the therapist has similar experiences to the client (Meyer, Zane, & Cho, 2011). Having similar experiences in turn may be associated with the therapist's perceived credibility. Therapist–client ethnic match may be particularly important in preventing premature termination from treatment. A meta-analysis of 53 studies involving over 62,000 clients indicated that therapist–client ethnic match was associated with attending more therapy sessions among clients of color (T. Smith & Trimble, 2016). Therapist–client ethnic match did not affect attendance among European Americans. The results of a recent study on therapist–client ethnic match in a sample of 4924 clients at a college counseling center are consistent with these results (Ibaraki & Hall, 2014; Figure 7.5). Ethnic match may have been most influential for Native Americans who may have been relatively unacculturated to mainstream culture and less influential for Latinx Americans who were relatively acculturated.

One might wonder why staying longer in treatment is better. Doesn't being in treatment a shorter time mean that the treatment is more effective? Clients need to be in treatment long enough to receive a therapeutic dosage. This is similar to taking an antibiotic. Antibiotic pills need to be taken for several days to receive a therapeutic effect.

Therapist–client ethnic match may also influence the issues addressed in treatment (Ibaraki & Hall, 2014). African Americans were over 10 times more likely to discuss substance abuse when ethnically matched vs. mismatched. This may be because they assumed that an African American therapist would have a more culturally-informed perspective on substance abuse whereas there might be fears of confirming stereotypes about African Americans (see Chapter 6) in discussing substance abuse with a non–African American therapist. In contrast, Asian Americans were less likely to discuss alcohol abuse when ethnically matched, possibly because they were concerned about losing face in the presence of another Asian American. On the other hand, Asian Americans were more likely to stay in treatment longer if the therapist, regardless of ethnicity, discussed academic issues. Academic achievement is emphasized in many Asian American families (see Chapter 5) and discussion of academic issues may carry less stigma for Asian Americans than psychological problems. Richard, described at the beginning of the chapter, wanted to discuss academic issues with a therapist despite experiencing other

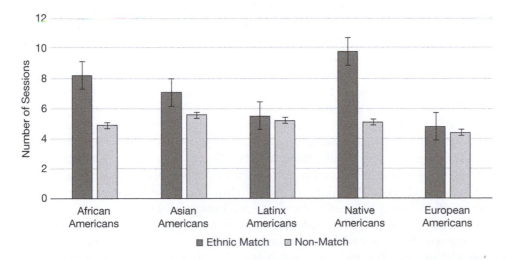

Figure 7.5 Therapist–Client Ethnic Matching and Number of Counseling Sessions Attended.
Source: Ibaraki & Hall, 2014.

problems. Latinx American clients were also nearly five times more likely to discuss sexual orientation issues when ethnically matched. This may indicate a greater sense of safety in discussing these issues with a person of one's own ethnic background. As can be seen from these study results, the effects of therapist–client ethnic match may vary by ethnic group.

Although therapist–client ethnic match may have some initial positive effects in preventing termination from therapy and promoting discussion of certain topics, the effects on therapy outcome are limited. Therapist–client ethnic match did not reduce psychopathology in the G. Hall, Ibaraki et al. (2016) meta-analytic study relative to therapist–client ethnic mismatch. The importance of ethnic match in preventing premature termination from treatment in combination with its lack of influence on psychopathology outcomes suggests that initial impressions of a therapist are based on surface characteristics and outcome is based on deeper components, such as therapist multicultural competence.

Multicultural competence (D. Sue, Arredondo, & McDavis, 1992) involves:

- *awareness* of one's own assumptions, values, and beliefs and how they can affect interactions with a client
- *knowledge* of clients' cultures and worldview
- *skills* in providing culturally-relevant treatment.

Multicultural competence differs from general competence. Some therapists who are effective in working with European American clients are less effective in working with clients of color and vice versa (Hayes, Owen, & Bieschke, 2015). Thus, competence with one group does not necessarily mean competence with another.

Therapist multicultural competence is associated with better working alliance, which involves the collaboration between the therapist and the client, and client satisfaction (Tao, Owen, Pace, & Imel, 2015). In a meta-analysis of 18 studies, client ratings of therapist multicultural competence were moderately associated ($r = 0.29$) with clinical outcomes (lower psychological distress and better psychological functioning, such as life satisfaction and social interactions; Tao et al., 2015). However, these studies involved client self-report of both therapist multicultural competence and clinical outcome measures. An improved methodology would be observer ratings of therapist multicultural competence based on actual session content (e.g., rating videos). There have been few studies of therapist multicultural competence in the 25 years since multicultural guidelines have been developed (D. Sue et al., 1992). This relative lack of attention may reflect the field's priorities, such as treatment content adaptations discussed previously.

A limitation of the culturally-adapted interventions field is that most research is from a "top down" perspective in which an approach developed for European Americans is modified for application to other groups (G. Hall, Ibaraki et al., 2016). An alternative is a "bottom up" approach, developed within a particular cultural context to address culture-specific issues (G. Hall, Ibaraki et al., 2016). The "bottom up" approach is consistent with the insider's perspective of multicultural psychology (G. Hall, Yip, & Zárate, 2016), discussed in Chapter 1. These approaches are particularly relevant in cultural contexts in which the worldview of health and healing differs from that of mainstream United States culture (Pomerville, Burrage, & Gone, 2016). Unfortunately, there are few studies of "bottom up" approaches currently available.

BOX 7.2 MINDFULNESS

Mindfulness-based interventions have become quite popular in the United States during the past two decades. Mindfulness involves focusing on the present moment without judgment. Because of the roots of mindfulness in Asian cultural traditions, such as Buddhism, mindfulness may be considered to be particularly relevant for Asian Americans. However, Asian mindfulness approaches have been culturally adapted by therapists for the United States. In this chapter, we have discussed cultural adaptations to make treatments developed for European Americans more relevant for people of color. Mindfulness adaptations are the opposite — cultural adaptations of approaches developed for people of color to make them more relevant for European Americans.

Therapists in the United States who implement mindfulness typically have selected the aspects that are focused on the self. For example, mindfulness meditation in the United States is designed to help the individual focus on their own sensations. In contrast, Asian mindfulness traditions emphasize social connection (Hall, Hong, Zane, & Meyer, 2011). For example, loving-kindness meditation that is often practiced in Asian cultures focuses on directing compassion and wishes for well-being toward others.

Buddhist traditions that form the basis of some mindfulness approaches may not be particularly relevant for many Asian Americans. Most Buddhists in the United States are not Asian Americans and most Asian Americans are not Buddhists (Pew Research Center, 2015). Thus, both Asian-based mindfulness traditions and Buddhism have been culturally adapted for practice by non-Asians in the United States.

Discussion
1 What cultural traditions of non-United States cultures (e.g., food, fashion, music) have been culturally adapted for use in the United States?
2 Does cultural adaptation improve quality?

Summary

The evidence base for evidence-based treatments did not include persons of color. Cultural adaptations of evidence-based treatments are more effective in reducing psychopathology than non-adapted treatments. Therapist–client ethnic matching may prevent premature dropout from therapy and may also facilitate discussion of certain topics but is not associated with reductions in psychopathology. Therapist multicultural competence shows promise in improving psychotherapy process and outcomes. Most culturally-adapted interventions are "top down" and there is a need to develop and evaluate "bottom up" approaches.

CONCLUSION

People of color have been overlooked in psychopathology research until recently. Relative to European Americans, people of color have been found to have better mental health, which may be an actual difference or may be because of undetected culture-specific psychopathology. People of color underutilize mental health services relative to European Americans, possibly because of stigma and the lack of culturally-responsive services. Culturally-adapted interventions are more effective in reducing psychopathology than unadapted interventions but there is a need for the development and evaluation of "bottom up" interventions.

RESOURCES

Blogs:
Getting Better or Getting Well?: How Culture Can Improve Your Health https://psycho logybenefits.org/2016/10/27/getting-better-or-getting-well-how-culture-can-improve-your-health/.
Occidental Tourist: Lost in (Mindful) Translation www.psychologytoday.com/blog/life-in-the-intersection/201701/occidental-tourist.

Video:
Challenges and Rewards of a Culturally-Informed Approach to Mental Health – Jessica Dere www.youtube.com/watch?v=VrYmQDiunSc.

Psychology in the Context of Multicultural Issues

CHAPTER 8
African Americans

Will is a 21-year-old African American junior majoring in political science at a historically Black university. He is part of a Black men's group that has multiple purposes. One purpose is providing social and political support to Black men who have been the targets of multiple racist acts nationwide. A second purpose is to explore the meaning of healthy Black masculinity and to counteract stereotypes outside and within the Black community. He and the group leaders have included gay men, although this has been met with resistance from a few group members. A third purpose is to mentor younger African American men, including high school students.

Angela is a 20-year-old African American sophomore majoring in business administration at a predominantly White university. Her classmates of all ethnic backgrounds consider her to be a leader. She can be assertive or nurturing, depending on the demands of the context. However, a few of her male classmates view her as a bit too assertive, to the point of being angry at times. Angela is in the choir and is very involved in social justice projects at her Black church. Her White friends can't understand how she can be involved in a church and still be politically progressive.

The previous chapters in this book provide a context for a more focused consideration of racial/ethnic groups. This chapter and the following chapters have three sections: (a) group history; (b) gender roles; and (c) a prominent issue for each group based on its coverage in the literature. For each group, the intersections of racial/ethnic, gender, and sexual identities are considered. We begin this section of the book with African Americans.

At 46.3 million people, African Americans are 13.3% of the United States population (U.S. Bureau of the Census, 2017, January). Most African Americans' families have been in the United States for centuries, although about 8% of the population consists of immigrants, primarily from the Caribbean and Africa (Waters, Kasinitz, & Asad, 2014). These immigrant groups may have more in common with other recent immigrant groups than African Americans, who are native to the United States. Most of the research in psychology on people of color has focused on African Americans.

Picture 8.1
Source: shutterstock.

HISTORY

Since 1976, February has been African American History Month. Although it is important for all Americans to give special recognition to African American history, it is also important to understand that African American history is part and parcel of American history. African Americans have been influenced by and have influenced American history. Many of the historical issues of African Americans, such as racism and civil rights, are issues of all people of color in the United States. A synopsis of African American history follows to provide a context for current theory and research in psychology.

1600s–1800s: Slavery and the Civil War

The earliest African immigrants to the United States probably were not slaves. Twenty Africans came to America in 1619 as servants (Takaki, 1993). Similar to many other European immigrants, these Africans were probably indentured servants who were bound by contract for four to seven years to pay for their transportation expenses. Unlike slaves, these servants could eventually earn their freedom.

Black and White servants began to be treated differently during the 1640s (Takaki, 1993). Unlike Black servants, when White servants escaped they could blend into European American communities (Spickard, 2007). Native Americans were enslaved by European Americans for a brief period, but they also could easily escape into non-slave Native communities. European Americans also felt less guilty enslaving Blacks because they regarded Native Americans as human savages but regarded Blacks as subhuman beasts (Spickard, 2007).

Although the slave trade was controlled by Europeans, slaves were kidnapped in Africa by Africans from outside their communities who worked for the Europeans. The slaves were chained together and transported across the ocean to the United States in tightly packed ships. Many Africans died in transit, and dead bodies were simply thrown overboard. When they arrived in North America, the slaves were kept in forts or cages to be auctioned as merchandise for the purpose of performing unpaid labor on European American tobacco and cotton plantations. Tobacco and cotton were extremely labor-intensive to produce. A slave auction staging area that I saw in Charleston, South Carolina several years ago was a depressing reminder of the area's past.

Despite originating from culturally diverse ethnic groups in West Africa, Blacks who came to North America became generically regarded as Negroes (Spickard, 2007). However, many African Americans retained their African cultures in terms of language when communicating with other African Americans. The struggle to survive slavery became a common bond for these Americans from diverse African backgrounds. These cultural and sociocultural aspects of unity were the beginnings of Black identity in the United States.

Black servants began to be treated as slaves for life in 1642 in Virginia. In 1648, the children of slaves began to be regarded as slaves. To keep the part-White children of European American slave owners and African American slave women as slaves, the one-drop rule established that any person with any known African ancestry was regarded as Black (Spickard, 2007). Laws also explicitly indicated that conversion to the European Americans' Christianity did not change slave status.

Between 1720 and 1760, 159,000 Africans came to the United States as slaves, whereas only 105,000 Europeans immigrated to the United States during this period (Spickard, 2007). This increase in African slaves in the South decreased the need for White servants, and African labor was less expensive than White labor. The Virginia legislature formally began to define a slave as property in 1669. Later, in 1691, the Virginia legislature denied slaves the right to vote, to hold office, and to testify in court. Although they could not vote, each slave was counted as three-fifths of a person for states to be represented in Congress and in the Electoral College. Despite not having rights as citizens, approximately 25% of George Washington's Continental Army in the Revolutionary War was African American (Spickard, 2007).

Slavery did not develop on a large scale in New England because of the absence of a staple crop that required slaves (Takaki, 1993). In 1777, when Vermont became a state, its constitution outlawed slavery, and Massachusetts outlawed it in 1781 (Spickard, 2007). However, ship captains in New England continued to profit from transporting slaves. New York and Philadelphia also depended on slave labor for their docks and industries (Spickard, 2007). Nevertheless, children born to slaves after 1780 were declared free (although their parents and other existing slaves were not) by the Pennsylvania legislature, and New York gradually began freeing slaves in 1799. Unlike the South, the abolition of slavery in Northern states had limited economic impact.

The slave trade was abolished by Congress in 1807. However, ending the slave trade did not free those who were already slaves. Slavery continued to flourish from 1820 to 1850 in Alabama, Mississippi, and Louisiana because of cotton production. Slave owners depended on slave women to bear children. African American men were used as breeders, and frequent changes of partner were common for African American men and women (Hines & Boyd-Franklin, 1996). Slaves had been prohibited from marrying to prevent family bonds from being established that would interfere with the trade of individual slaves. Such destruction of family unity is at odds with African communal traditions. Some European American slave owners would rape slave women to produce children (Takaki, 1993).

By the Civil War, 4 million African Americans were enslaved (Takaki, 1993). The Civil War freed African Americans by law from slavery with the 13th Amendment of the Constitution in 1865. African Americans played a critical role in the Civil War. Approximately 86,000 African Americans served, one-third of whom were subsequently missing or dead. In 1865, near the end of the Civil War, Union Army general William Tecumseh Sherman issued Special Field Order 15, which awarded 40 acres of farmland and a mule to each of the former slaves. President Andrew Johnson quickly rescinded this order, returning the land to the former slave owners. This would have been a token form of reparations for slavery and other forms of oppression but would have represented a recognition of the debt owed to African Americans. No other form of reparations or even an apology has been issued by the U.S. government since then.

Following the Civil War, the vestiges of slavery were prominent despite laws to create civil rights for African Americans. The 14th Amendment in 1868 stated that all persons born or naturalized in the U.S. are citizens and are entitled to the privileges and protections of citizens. The Civil Rights Act of 1875 gave African Americans the right to equal treatment in public settings, inns, theaters, and public amusement places, but the act was ruled unconstitutional in 1883. The 1896 Supreme Court's "separate but equal" decision in Plessy v. Ferguson legalized racial segregation of schools. Nevertheless, the separate schools were anything but equal, with European American schools and other facilities having far superior resources (Spickard, 2007).

1900s–1930s: Racism and Separatism

Racism consists of beliefs, attitudes, institutional arrangements, and acts that tend to denigrate individuals or groups because of phenotypic characteristics or ethnic group affiliation (Clark, Anderson, Clark, & Williams, 1999). Racism can be attitudinal or behavioral. Some individuals may suffer the negative effects of racism without attributing their problems to racism. For example, institutional racism may reduce access to resources (Clark et al., 1999), but individuals may attribute their lack of resources to their own inabilities. Although slavery was abolished in the nineteenth century, racism continued in the United States as a legacy of slavery in the twentieth century.

Conflicts between European Americans and African Americans continued during the early 1900s. From 1900 to 1910, anti-Black race riots occurred in the North, and lynching and burning in the South (J. Jones, 1997). Lynch mobs were as likely to consist of European American employers and their henchmen trying to terrorize African Americans into accepting lower wages as they were to consist of Ku Klux Klan members (Spickard, 2007). In response, the National Association for the Advancement of Colored People was established in New York City in 1909. Between 1910 and 1920, there was a large migration of African Americans north for jobs. However, many European Americans did not want African Americans in their neighborhoods.

The Social Darwinism and eugenics movements contended that there was an evolutionary basis for the inferiority of African Americans. Natural selection, or "survival of the fittest," favored European Americans. African Americans were viewed as a burden to the progress of European Americans. The field of social psychology, which emphasized the interdependence of individual personality and societal influences, developed in response to the biological emphasis of Social Darwinism (J. Jones, 1997). Race relations problems were redefined as a problem of European American prejudice rather than African American inferiority. Unfortunately, Social Darwinian thought did not cease in the early 1900s but continues to have proponents among those who posit biologically-based race differences (e.g., Rushton, 1995a, 1995b).

Separatist movements also developed during the early 1900s. Marcus Garvey made plans for African Americans to return to Africa but was later deported by the U.S. government. W. E. B. Dubois, the leader of the NAACP, had initially supported integration but began to support the establishment of a separate African nation. Dubois immigrated to Ghana shortly before his death.

1940s–1970s: Civil Rights

Several landmark civil rights events occurred during the late 1940s and 1950s. President Truman desegregated the military in 1948. One year later, Jackie Robinson became the first African American Major League Baseball player. In 1954 in the Brown v. the Board of Education of Topeka decision, the Supreme Court declared the "separate but equal" doctrine invalid. On December 1, 1955, Rosa Parks sat at the front of the colored section of a bus in Montgomery, Alabama, and refused to move farther back for a White patron when the White section became full. This incident sparked the Montgomery bus boycott, led by the Rev. Dr. Martin Luther King, Jr.

Picture 8.2

Source: courtesy of Pixabay.

Civil rights activism and legislation continued to blossom during the 1960s. The decade began with four students from North Carolina A & T State University staging a sit-in at a Greensboro lunch counter in February of 1960. These students had been refused service because they were African Americans. The Student Nonviolent Coordinating Committee (SNCC) was organized in 1960 and coordinated sit-ins. In 1961, an integrated busload of freedom riders traveled south from Washington, DC. In Montgomery, Alabama, the riders were beaten and the bus burned. Attorney General Robert Kennedy sent 600 federal marshals to restore order. The March on Washington for jobs and freedom occurred in 1963, culminating in the "I Have a Dream" speech by Rev. Dr. Martin Luther King, Jr.

The Civil Rights Act of 1964 mandated constitutional rights without discrimination or segregation on the grounds of race, color, religion, or national origin. Affirmative action legislation was signed by President Lyndon Johnson in 1965. Whereas the Civil Rights Act of 1964 created equal opportunity, the purpose of affirmative action was to take proactive steps to include underrepresented groups such that equal outcomes could be achieved. In the equal opportunity approach, employers are able to adopt a passive stance by claiming that they do not actively discriminate against persons or groups. However, affirmative action goes beyond creating opportunities by assessing whether outcomes reflect the goals of diversity (Crosby & Cordova, 1996).

Parallel to these efforts toward integration, the separatist movement that began in the early part of the century continued. Elijah Muhammad and Malcolm X led the Black Muslim movement. Goals of Black Muslims were to replace the negative effects of slavery with positive values and behavior and to develop independence from the dominant culture. Malcolm X broke away from Elijah Muhammad to practice orthodox Islam. In 1965, SNCC moved from the goal of integration to Black power under the leadership of Stokely Carmichael. European American members were informed that their role would be secondary. The Black Panther Party was formed as a protective vigilante group in Oakland, California, in 1966. The progress of the 1960s spilled over into the early 1970s. The Kwanzaa celebration was established as an integration of African, European American, and Jewish influences (J. Jones, 1997). Afro-American studies were established at universities, followed by the initiation of women's studies, Asian American studies, Latino studies, and American Indian studies.

The progress of the 1960s and 1970s began to be halted near the end of the 1970s. A sense of community responsibility began to be replaced by individualism, where individuals were expected to fend for themselves (Etzioni, 2007). The Supreme Court ruled in the Bakke case in 1978 that a separate admissions process for minority groups was illegal. Allan Bakke, who was White, was initially denied admission to medical school at the University of California, Davis, because 16 of 100 slots were allotted to African American, Latinx American, and Native American students who had lower test scores than his. As a result of the Supreme Court decision, Bakke was later admitted to the medical school. Nevertheless, the Bakke decision allowed that race could be taken into account in the admissions process. Justice Blackmun wrote, "In order to get beyond racism we must first take account of race. ... In order to treat persons equally, we must treat them differently" (Regents of the University of California v. Bakke, 1978).

Psychology in the 1960s and 1970s shifted from individual to cultural and societal explanations of prejudice (J. Jones, 1997). Childhood socialization and conformity were viewed as causal mechanisms of prejudice. Desegregation, which allowed social contact between African Americans and European Americans, was viewed as the solution to prejudice. However, psychology's optimism about solutions to prejudice decreased when the civil rights movement began to focus on institutional racism, including voting rights, jobs, and income disparities, which affected both the North and the South (J. Jones, 1997).

By the 1960s, there was a critical mass of African American psychologists that allowed the development of African American psychology (Holliday, 2009). In 1968, the Association of Black Psychologists (ABPsi) was established in San Francisco at the American Psychological Association (APA) convention in protest of APA's lack of responsiveness to African American psychologists and communities. ABPsi presented APA with a Petition of Concerns that included: (a) the low numbers of Black psychologists and psychology graduate students; (b) APA's failure to direct its efforts to social concerns, including poverty and racism, and to address social problems in communities of color; and (3) the inadequate representation of Blacks in the APA governance structure (Holliday, 2009). The Black Students Psychological Association (BSPA) was established at the Western Psychological Association meeting in Vancouver, BC, in 1969. Later that year, at the APA convention, the group interrupted the APA presidential address and voiced their concerns, which they were allowed to present the next day to the APA Council of Representatives, the governing body of APA. BSPA demanded greater recruitment and retention of Black faculty and students. APA's council supported the students' concerns. In 1969, ABPsi called for a moratorium on educational testing that was biased against African American children and in 1970 developed a 10-point plan for recruitment and retention of African American students. In 1974, ABPsi launched the *Journal of Black Psychology*, which focuses on psychological theory and research involving African Americans. Some of the studies reviewed in this textbook are drawn from this journal.

1980s–2000s: Dismantling of Affirmative Action, but Some Hope

Many Americans in the 1980s, led by President Reagan proclaiming that it was "morning in America," contended that racism was no longer existent. Reagan's policies that favored the rich hurt African Americans more than any other group (Zinn, 2015). By the end of the 1980s, a third of African Americans were below the official poverty level. Although blatant forms of racism may have decreased somewhat, subtle racism continued (Dovidio & Gaertner, 1996; J. Jones, 1997). Subtle forms of racism include the belief that discrimination no longer exists and valuing a single way of life. African Americans may be sensitive to subtle racism because of negative personal experiences with racism (Franklin, 1999).

What may have been morning for some Americans was dusk for many others. Whereas many Americans would not express overt antagonism toward African Americans, they did believe that many gains of African Americans were undeserved. Many of the civil rights gains of the previous four decades began to be dismantled. Because many Americans believed that discrimination was a thing of the past, they believed that fairness involved not providing special treatment to African Americans or any other historically disadvantaged group. These critics were not without data to support their arguments. African Americans with college and graduate degrees earned more than their White counterparts from the mid-1970s until 1980. Nevertheless, the reverse occurred from 1981 to 1993, which may reflect changing attitudes concerning affirmative action (J. Jones, 1997). Adversarial relationships between European Americans and people of color continued, resulting in the Hate Crimes Act of 1989. However, those who opposed acts of intolerance were viewed by some as hypersensitive and driven by political correctness.

A positive development in psychology in 1986 was the founding of the Society for the Psychological Study of Ethnic Minority Issues, which is a division (Division 45) of APA. Division 45 adopted a multicultural model with leadership that has included African Americans, Asian American/Pacific Islanders, Latinx Americans, and Native Americans. This group has attracted many psychologists and students of color to become active in APA.

Racism and its negative consequences were overlooked as the dismantling of affirmative action continued in the 1990s. The Civil Rights Act of 1991 forbade adjustment of test scores or the use of cutoffs based on race, color religion, sex, or national origin, which modified the Civil Rights Act of 1964 (Wittig, 1996). However, the 1991 Act pronounced it unlawful for employers to engage in practices that have a disparate impact on racial/ethnic, sex, religious, national origin, or disability groups when not required by business necessity. Thus, qualified applicants from any of these groups should not be discriminated against. Although such legislation may seem fair, the broader issue of how to get qualified ethnic minority applicants into the employment pipeline was not addressed, nor were actions or resources for training potential ethnic minority applicants provided.

Subsequent legislative decisions in education even more directly outlawed affirmative action. The 1996 Hopwood decision in Texas pronounced the preferential admission of Black and Latinx students to the University of Texas Law School unconstitutional. This decision overturned the clause from the Bakke decision that race could be taken into account during the admissions process. During the same year, affirmative action was effectively dismantled by the Board of Regents of the University of California, when Proposition 209 was approved. Similar anti-affirmative action legislation followed in Washington state.

While these legal decisions reversed previous protections of African Americans and other people of color, racism continued in the United States during the 1990s. This included police brutality against people of color, higher rates of infant mortality among African Americans, a lack of jobs for young African Americans, and disproportionate incarceration of African Americans (Zinn, 2005). Efforts to organize African Americans were sporadic. One of these efforts was African American men traveling from all over the country to Washington, DC for the Million Man March in 1995.

Despite these political and legal setbacks, psychological theory and research in the 1980s and 1990s offered hope for understanding African American identity and multicultural relations. Against the backdrop of conservativism and the much broader context of centuries of African American oppression, the construct of Afrocentrism was being developed. Afrocentrism espouses African ideals at the center of one's approach to problem-solving (Asante, 1987). Another important development in psychology over the past two decades is the multicultural movement (D. W. Sue, Bingham, Porché-Burke, & Vasquez, 1999). This movement emphasizes that different cultural groups have differing worldviews. Recognizing and understanding these worldviews allows intercultural communication. Psychology has developed within a Western worldview. However, many persons of color have non-Western worldviews. Multicultural psychology attempts to understand persons within their own cultural context and in their own terms.

A counterpoint to the multicultural movement has been the Decades of the Brain. In 1989, President George H. W. Bush proclaimed the 1990s to be the "Decade of the Brain." Brain-based biological approaches to research became more valued than psychological science (G. Miller, 2010). This emphasis on brain research at the expense of psychosocial research has continued to the current decade (Markowitz, 2016; see Chapter 4). Unfortunately, this emphasis on brain research has also diverted attention away from research on people of color (McKay et al., 2016).

By 2000, the 1954 Brown v. Board of Education ruling invalidating segregation seemed to have been reversed (Pettigrew, 2004). During 2000, 70% of African American children went to predominantly African American schools, and 30% went to schools that had 90% or greater African American students. Such segregation was the result of the rulings of five conservative justices (Rehnquist, Kennedy, O'Connor, Scalia, and Thomas) appointed to the Supreme Court by Republican Presidents (Nixon, Reagan, and Bush). These justices emphasized local over federal authority and providing resources for segregated schools, rather than affirming Brown and integrating schools (Pettigrew, 2004).

Despite a conservative Supreme Court, subsequent decisions upheld affirmative action. Barbara Grutter, a White woman who was denied admission to the University of Michigan Law School, sued the school because of discrimination against Whites. Nevertheless, the Grutter v. Bollinger Supreme Court decision in 2003 allowed the consideration of race in a college's admissions process to achieve a diverse student body. In a similar case, Abigail Fisher, a White woman, sued the University of Texas at Austin because she was denied admission based on race. The 2016 Fisher v. the University of Texas at Austin Supreme Court decision also allowed the consideration of race in college admissions if there is no other realistic alternative that would create a diverse student body.

Barack Obama made history in 2008 when he was elected the first African American and first non-White President of the United States. One of his signature accomplishments as President was the 2010 Patient Protection and Affordable Care Act, which provided health insurance to many who were previously uninsured, including many people of color. Part of this health care reform law was the establishment of the National Institute on Minority Health and Health Disparities (NIMHD). The purpose of NIMHD is to promote minority health and ultimately eliminate health disparities (see Chapter 4) for ethnic minority groups.

Some viewed Obama's election as evidence of a post-racial society. However, racism persists in subtle forms, as discussed in Chapter 6, and in blatant hate speech and crimes following the 2016 election of Donald Trump (Yan et al., 2016). Moreover, the Trump administration has made efforts to repeal or at least modify the Patient Protection and Affordable Care Act.

GENDER ROLE IDENTITY

African American Males

In the United States, normative masculinity is defined by European American, heterosexual, middle class men (Griffith, Gunter, & Watkins, 2012). However, masculine gender roles for men are defined by stereotypes, which are inconsistent and frequently violated (Pleck, 1995). Masculine gender role norms have been defined as winning,

Picture 8.3
Source: shutterstock.

emotional control, risk-taking, violence, dominance, sexual promiscuity, self-reliance, primacy of work, power over women, disdain for homosexuals, and pursuit of status (Mahalik et al., 2003). "Real men" are not feminine or gay (Fasula, Carry, & Miller, 2014). Violating masculine gender roles can lead to social condemnation and distress (J. Wong & Schwing, 2014). Men often will prefer to risk their physical health and well-being rather than be associated with traits they or others may perceive as feminine (Evans, Frank, Oliffe, & Gregory, 2011).

Conformity to masculine gender role norms can also lead to distress. In a meta-analysis (see Chapter 3) of 74 studies of more than 19,000 men, conformity to masculine gender role norms was associated with poorer mental health (e.g., depression, stress, substance abuse, body image problems, loneliness) and a lower likelihood of seeking psychological help (Y. Wong, Ho, Wang, & Miller, 2017). Self-reliance, sexual promiscuity, and power over women were the components of masculine gender role norms that were most consistently associated with poorer mental health. African Americans, Asian Americans, Latino Americans, and European Americans were included in the studies reviewed. Ethnicity did not moderate (see Chapter 3) the effects. It is likely that heterosexual men who strongly adhere to these norms have poorer mental health because of impaired relationships with women. However, all the studies in the meta-analysis were correlational. Thus, it is unknown if masculine gender role norms cause mental health problems or vice versa.

Masculine gender role norms can also have deleterious effects on the health of gay and bisexual men of color. Same-sex relationships are a violation of traditional masculine gender role norms. African American men have been found to be more prejudiced against gay men than European American men are (Daboin, Peterson, & Parrott, 2015). Will, described at the beginning of the chapter, encountered some of this prejudice in his Black men's group. In a study of Canadian gay and bisexual men of color, 22% of whom were of African ancestry, a focus on body image as a definition of masculinity (e.g., weight, muscle tone, physical appearance, penis size) was associated with internalized homophobia (e.g., "I wish I weren't gay or bisexual"; Brennan et al., 2015). A focus on body image as a definition of masculinity was also associated with having anal intercourse without a condom with a partner whose HIV status was serodiscordant (one partner infected by HIV and the other is not) or unknown.

Compared to other ethnic groups, African Americans are perceived as more masculine. African Americans were rated by European Americans, Asian Americans, and African Americans as more associated with masculine traits than European Americans or Asian Americans (Galinsky et al., 2013; Figure 8.1). Nevertheless, being perceived as more masculine than other groups has not afforded African American men the privileges that European American men have (Fasula et al., 2014). Conceptions of African American masculinity have devolved into hypermasculine stereotypes, in an effort by European Americans to make it non-normative. These hypermasculine stereotypes have been conditioned by the centuries of racism reviewed at the beginning of this chapter.

J. Wong and Schwing (2014) have identified three racist gender role stereotypes of African American males that compromise their conceptualizations of masculinity. The first are stereotypes about *intellectual competence*. As discussed in Chapter 6, such stereotypes can interfere with African Americans' academic performance (Spencer et al., 2016; Steele & Aronson, 1995). One method of coping with intellectual and other stereotypes of African American men is "cool pose" (Majors & Billson, 1992). Cool pose is a ritualized expression of Black masculinity in dress, speech, and behavior in combination with emotional restraint in high-pressure situations. A costly consequence of cool pose is underachievement and disidentification with academics.

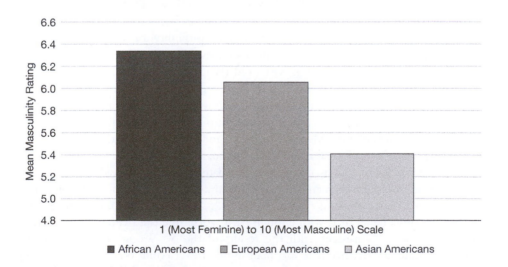

Figure 8.1 Masculinity Ratings By Ethnic Group.

Source: Galinsky et al., 2013.

African American males who underidentify with academics may overidentify with athletics because of stereotypes about *athletic abilities* (J. Wong & Schwing, 2014). These stereotypes are based on the belief that athletic abilities are genetically determined. They are limiting in that sports are viewed as the only visible and high-status occupation for African American males. An additional limitation is that there are extremely few opportunities for professional careers as athletes.

Stereotypes about *violence* are the third type of stereotypes of African American males (J. Wong & Schwing, 2014). These stereotypes started during slavery as an excuse to subjugate African American males. Violent African American men are glorified in the hip hop industry (Worsley, 2010). The message perceived by African American males is that violence is necessary for survival and to beat the system (J. Wong & Schwing, 2014). African Americans are disproportionately portrayed as criminals in the media (Hurley et al., 2015; see Chapter 6). The overrepresentation of African American males who are incarcerated reinforces violence stereotypes. However, incarceration is based on the actions of decision-makers in the criminal justice system who also are exposed to violence stereotypes of African Americans. Therefore, disproportionate incarceration is not necessarily evidence that African Americans are more violent than others. Nevertheless, stereotypes about intelligence, athletic abilities, and violence dehumanize African Americans (Kteily et al., 2015; see Chapter 6).

Men of color may redefine and modify mainstream masculine ideals to be adaptive in their own cultural context (cf. Griffith et al., 2012). This was one of the purposes of Will's Black men's group, described at the beginning of the chapter. Based on focus groups with 71 African American men, definitions of health for African American men include being able to fulfill social roles, such as holding a job, providing for family, protecting and teaching their children, and belonging to a social network (Ravenell, Johnson, & Whitaker, 2006). In keeping with these components of health, healthy masculinity includes respect and responsibility, according to focus groups with 30 African American fathers of preadolescent sons (Doyle, Magan, Cryer-Coupet, Goldston, & Estroff, 2016). Respect involves both self-respect (e.g., self-worth, pride) and respect for others (e.g., courteous, tolerant). Responsibility involves becoming independent, developing a strong school and work ethic, and taking responsibility for one's mistakes.

Similar themes of healthy African American masculinity were reported among 17 African American men aged 18 to 53 years old (Rogers, Sperry, & Levant, 2015). The most common theme was leadership, which involved being a positive role model, provider, and protector. African American values, consisting of religion and spirituality (see discussion later in this chapter), a quality education, and historical knowledge, were another theme of masculinity. Mental toughness and physical strength/control of one's body were aspects of a traditional masculinity theme.

Culture-specific forms of masculinity may mediate the effects of traditional masculinity on health. John Henryism is an active coping strategy used by African American men to cope with racist environments (James, Hartnett, & Kalsbeek, 1983). It is characterized by persistence and a belief that, with enough hard work, one can overcome the demands of the environment. Consistent with the results of the Y. Wong et al. (2017) meta-analysis, masculine self-reliance (e.g., "A man should never count on someone else to get the job done") was associated with depression among a sample of 458 African American adult men (Matthews, Hammond, Nuru-Jeter, Yasmin, & Melvin, 2013). Most of the men in the study were moderately self-reliant. The autonomy that is characteristic of masculine self-reliance may isolate African American men and make them depressed. However, John Henryism (e.g., "When things don't go the way I want them to that makes me work even harder") buffered the effects of masculine self-reliance on depression. The persistence and optimism associated with John Henryism may reduce the depressive effects of traditional masculine self-reliance for African American men.

Summary

Masculine gender role norms have been associated with poor health. African Americans are perceived to be more masculine than other ethnic groups. This perception has led to stereotypes of African American men. African American men have modified mainstream masculine ideals to conceptualize healthy forms of masculinity.

BOX 8.1 SHOOTER BIAS EXPERIMENTS

From January 1999 to May 2015, 78 police killings of unarmed African American male civilians occurred (A. Hall, Hall, & Perry, 2016). African Americans are 2.5 times more likely to be killed by police than European Americans are (Lowery, 2016). Sadly, it is likely that this trend will continue. Why does this discrepancy exist?

Shooter bias experiments may offer an explanation. These experiments involve a shoot/don't shoot video game simulation. The participant has to determine as quickly as possible whether to shoot at the person in the picture. The requirements are to:

- shoot if the person is armed with a gun
- don't shoot if the person is unarmed (e.g., has a wallet or cell phone).

Errors involve: (a) shooting an unarmed person; or (b) not shooting an armed person. Any pattern of errors based on a person's group membership is known as shooter bias.

Figure 8.2 shows the results of a shooter bias experiment that was conducted with a group of college students that was primarily European American but also included African Americans, Asian Americans, and Latinx Americans (Plant, Goplen, & Kunstman, 2011). Unarmed African American men were shot nearly one out of four times. This error of shooting of unarmed African American men exceeded errors in shooting unarmed persons in the other groups. Shooters made relatively few errors in deciding to shoot an armed African American man. With European American men and women, and African American women, the tendency was to not shoot someone who was armed. This tendency was particularly pronounced with European American women – armed European American women were less likely to be shot than any other group. This study involved college students but has been replicated with police officers.

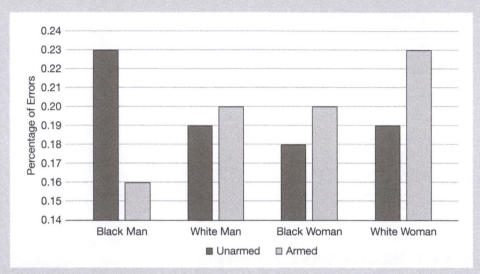

Picture 8.2

Source: Plant et al., 2011.

Discussion

1   Why might people be more inclined to shoot unarmed African American men than unarmed members of other groups?
2   Why might people be disinclined to shoot armed European American women?
3   What can be done to decrease shooter bias?

African American Females

Gendered racism (Essed, 1991) addresses the intersectionality of racism and sexism that women of color experience. Similar to the stereotypes of African American men, there are specific stereotypes of African American women. Also, similar to stereotypes of African American men, the stereotypes of African American women have been conditioned by centuries of racism. These include: (a) assumptions of beauty and sexual objectification; (b) silenced and marginalized; (c) strong Black woman stereotype; and (d) angry Black woman stereotype (J. Lewis & Neville, 2015).

Assumptions of beauty and sexual objectification involve others' perceptions of unattractiveness based on physical features and assumptions that a woman is exotic and sexualized (e.g., sexually promiscuous). This stereotype might be expressed in catcalls, stares, or disparaging comments about physical features (e.g., butt, hips, thighs) or communication styles (e.g., assumption that the person speaks African American vernacular English). Consistent with sexualized stereotypes, a group of college students in the Northeast consisting primarily of European American and Asian American women perceived an African American woman as having more sexual partners and less likely to use birth control than a European American woman (Rosenthal & Lobel, 2016). Sexual stereotypes of African American women are dehumanizing (Kteily et al., 2015; see Chapter 6) and have been contrasted with European American women's sexuality, which is considered pure and ideal (Collins, 2000). Stereotyping women as tainted, promiscuous "bad girls" is a justification for men to sexually objectify them (Fasula et al., 2014).

Silenced and marginalized involves being unheard, ignored, disrespected, and excluded. Being silenced and marginalized renders African American women invisible in school and in the workplace. African American women are invisible not only compared to women from other ethnic groups but also compared to African American men. When asked to write a story about an African American individual, European American, Asian American, and African American participants were more likely to write about a man than a woman (Schug, Alt, & Klauer, 2015).

The *strong Black woman* stereotype is of a woman who is independent and assertive but at the same time dominating and emasculating (Collins, 2000). Another component of the strong Black woman is to prioritize others' needs at the expense of one's own needs. This can include not seeking necessary health care (Belgrave & Adams, 2016) and not negotiating safe sex practices, which may put African American women at risk for contracting HIV (L. Brody et al., 2014). Because the comparison group is European American women, the strong Black woman is too assertive and less feminine than European American women.

The *angry Black woman* stereotype is the perception that a woman is angry and this perception persists even when the woman is calm. Characterizing someone as angry may also serve to silence them, as they may become reluctant to risk being stereotyped if they speak up. Some of Angela's male classmates, described at the beginning of the chapter, perceive her as too assertive and sometimes angry.

Over 90% of African American women in on online survey had been the target of all four of these stereotypes, as measured by the Gendered Racial Microaggressions Scale (J. Lewis & Neville, 2015). Moderate correlations between these stereotypes and another measure of sexist events ($rs = 0.3$ to 0.6) suggest that these stereotypes are similar but distinct. In other words, these four stereotypes do not target all women but target African American women in particular. Each of these stereotypes was a source of psychological distress.

The strong Black woman stereotype was less stressful than the other stereotypes (J. Lewis & Neville, 2015). This may be because there are positive aspects of being a strong Black woman (Abrams, Maxwell, Pope, & Belgrave, 2014). Forty-four African American women aged 18 to 91 from the Mid-Atlantic area identified these themes as important aspects of being a strong Black woman:

- Embodies and displays multiple forms of strength
- Possesses self/ethnic pride in spite of intersectional oppression
- Embraces being every woman
- Anchored by religion/spirituality

Embodies and displays multiple forms of strength involves independent leadership in both families and communities (Abrams et al., 2014). Resilience in the face of adversity is part of this theme, analogous to John Henryism among African American men, discussed previously. *Possesses self/ethnic pride in spite of intersectional oppression* involves positive feelings about being a woman and African American and not being defined by others. Psychological connections to other African Americans are an important aspect of this theme. *Embraces being every woman* involves having multiple roles and expectations. Multiple roles allow for competence in multiple domains, such as mother, father, caretaker, and leader. *Anchored by religion/spirituality* is a theme in which religion and spirituality serve as sources of strength and coping with adversity. Religion involves outward practices (e.g., church attendance), whereas spirituality is an inward personal experience. Religion and spirituality are discussed in more depth later in the chapter.

Because African American women assume multiple roles, they tend to be less gender role stereotyped than European American women (Belgrave & Abrams, 2016). Traditional masculine gender roles are to be instrumental and agentic. In contrast, traditional feminine gender roles are to be expressive and nurturing. African American women tend to be more androgynous (i.e., share masculine and feminine characteristics) than women in other ethnic groups. Indeed, studies of African American women have revealed both agency (e.g., independence, strength, resilience) and caretaking (e.g., supportive, caregiver, keeps family connected) as gender role beliefs (Belgrave & Abrams, 2016). Among the benefits of androgyny are higher self-esteem, lower anxiety and depression, fewer eating disorders, better body image, and better health practices (e.g., exercise, safety precautions; Belgrave & Abrams, 2016). The gender role flexibility of androgyny may provide a greater repertoire in coping with stress than a single gender role identity.

Both the agentic and nurturing aspects of African American women's behavior may be valued as leadership skills. Angela, described at the beginning of the chapter, is both agentic and nurturing, which are assets in a business career. Non-African American participants in an online study were randomly assigned to eight conditions in which a leader's race (Black vs. White), gender (male vs. female), and behavior (dominant vs. communal) were manipulated (Livingston, Rosette, & Washington, 2012). They were shown photos of a fictitious senior vice president of a Fortune 500 company. Dominant leaders were described as demanding action (i.e., "I demand that you take steps to improve your performance") and assertive (i.e., "I am a tough, determined boss and intend to do everything in my power to ensure that your performance improves"). Communal leaders were described as encouraging (i.e., "I encourage you to take steps to improve your performance") and compassionate (i.e., "I am a caring, committed boss and intend to do everything in my power to ensure that your performance improves"). Participants rated the leaders' status on these questions:

- "How well do you think the leader handled the situation with the employee?"
- "How effective is the leader at maximizing the employee's performance?"
- "How much do you think the leader is admired by his or her employees?"
- "How respected is this leader by the other executives at the company?"

Figure 8.3 shows that African American women were rated favorably as leaders whether they were dominant or communal (Livingston et al., 2012). This pattern was similar for the ratings of European American men. In contrast, African American men and European American women were rated favorably as leaders only when they were

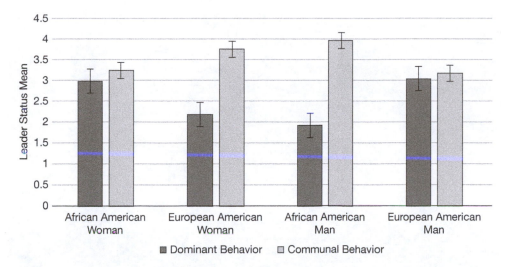

Figure 8.3 Leader Status, Race, Gender, and Behavior.

Source: Livingston et al., 2012.

communal. Although African American women were valued as leaders on a par with European American men in this study, this does not reflect their status in real life. There are few African American women executives relative to European American men executives (Sanchez-Hucles & Davis, 2010). Perhaps this is because of the glass ceiling, which prevents women of color from advancing in organizations.

Summary

African American women have been stereotyped similar to African American men. Although it can be stereotypic, being a strong Black woman has positive attributes. African American women are perceived as having leadership attributes similar to those of European American men. However, these attributes have not resulted in greater leadership opportunities for African American women.

RELIGIOUS AND SPIRITUAL IDENTITY

Have you ever gone to church? If so, has church been important in your life? Religion and spirituality are prominent among African Americans. Of African Americans, 82% are religiously affiliated, the highest of any United States major ethnic group (Pew Research Center, 2015). Christianity is the dominant religion among African Americans but some African Americans practice other religions, such as Islam (Mattis & Grayman-Simpson, 2013).

Religiosity and spirituality have different meanings among African Americans (Mattis & Grayman-Simpson, 2013). *Religiosity* involves prescribed beliefs and devotional

Picture 8.4 Refreshing Spring Church of God Choir Sings the 50th Anniversary of the March on Washington and Martin Luther King's I Have A Dream Speech, August 24, 2013, Lincoln Memorial, Washington, D.C.

Source: shutterstock.

practices associated with worshipping God. *Spirituality* is more comprehensive, involving an awareness of the sacredness of all things, a relationship between humans and others, including the transcendent, and a commitment to live a life of virtue. The Black church has been a hub for both religion and spirituality, as well as a source of social networking and political action (Reed & Neville, 2014).

The influence of religion and spirituality differs in the lives of African Americans compared to European Americans. Spirituality and the practice of religion are more interconnected for African Americans than for European Americans. As can be seen in Figure 8.4, data from the National Survey of American Life (see Chapter 7) indicate that African Americans are more likely than European Americans to indicate that they are both religious and spiritual and less likely to indicate that they are spiritual only or neither religious nor spiritual (Chatters et al., 2008). It is likely that the greater interconnection of religion and spirituality for African Americans is because of the central role of the Black church in their lives (Reed & Neville, 2014). In contrast, European Americans may be more likely to seek spiritual experiences outside the church because European American churches may focus more on religiosity and are a less comprehensive social institution than they are in African American communities (G. Hall, 2001).

Both religious service attendance, a component of religiosity, and guidance provided by religion, a component of spirituality, buffer the effects of racism (Ellison, Musick, & Henderson, 2008). In the National Survey of American Life, experiences with racism during the previous month were associated with psychological distress

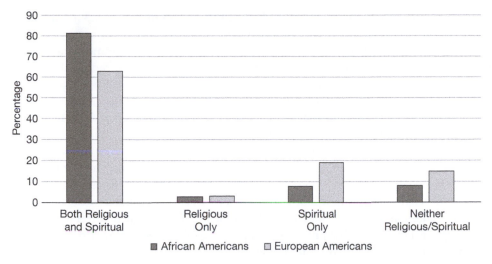

Figure 8.4 Ethnic Differences in Religiosity and Spirituality.

Source: Chatters et al., 2008.

(e.g., stress, low spirits, moody, depression, anxious, upset). However, African Americans who had been targeted by racism and who attended religious services or were guided by religion experienced less psychological distress. The social support and spiritual identity provided by religion may offer protection against the deleterious effects of racism (Ellison et al., 2008).

The effects of religiosity and spirituality on well-being, as measured by mental health and life satisfaction, have been elucidated in a study of African American women (Reed & Neville, 2014). Religiosity was measured by religious participation and core religious values. Spirituality was measured by relationships (e.g., with a higher power), eco-awareness (e.g., nature should be respected), and self-discovery (e.g., sense of purpose). Consistent with previous research, religiosity and spirituality were positively correlated. Both religiosity and spirituality were also positively associated with well-being. However, a mediation analysis (see Chapter 3) revealed that the positive effects of religiosity on mental health were accounted for by spirituality. Thus, religiosity is beneficial to well-being to the extent that it provides an opportunity for relationships and meaning in life.

Religious participation does not have uniformly positive effects for African Americans. In another study on African American adolescents from the National Survey of American Life, religious involvement, as defined by church attendance, participation during church service, and church-related activities, was *negatively* associated with positive well-being (Rose, Joe, Shields, & Caldwell, 2014). Positive well-being was a construct (see Chapter 3) involving self-esteem (e.g., satisfaction with self), active coping (e.g., hard work), and mastery (e.g., able to accomplish tasks). In addition, religious involvement was *positively* associated with negative well-being, which was a construct involving perceived stress and mental disorders (see Chapter 7). In other words, religious involvement was associated with poorer mental health.

It is possible that these negative effects of religious involvement on mental health were because African American adolescents were involved in religious services because their parents required them to do so. Indeed, religious commitment, involving a personal choice to attend religious services and activities, was associated with better well-being among these adolescents (Rose et al., 2014). In fact, religious commitment mediated the association between religious involvement and well-being. This means that African American adolescents who had high religious involvement and were involved by their own choice had better well-being. As discussed previously, the African American church is a source of social connections, which may be one of the reasons that African American adolescents would choose to be involved.

Religious commitment is often associated with political conservativism. Angela's White friends, described at the beginning of the chapter, assumed that because she went to church that she would be politically conservative. However, this is another area in which the meaning of religiosity/spirituality for European Americans and African Americans diverges. Religious commitment, as measured by the Religious Commitment Inventory-10 (e.g., "My religious beliefs lie behind my whole approach to life"), was more strongly associated with political conservatism (i.e., regarding foreign policy, economic, and social issues) among European American than among African American college students (D. Davis et al., 2016). This is because African Americans tend to be both more religious *and* politically liberal than European Americans (Mattis & Grayman-Simpson, 2013). For example, 89% of African Americans voted for Hillary Clinton in the 2016 presidential election whereas only 37% of European Americans voted for her, by far the lowest percentage of any major racial/ethnic group (CNN, 2016).

A negative aspect of religious commitment is homophobia, which is prejudice against sexual minority people. In a sample from the Deep South of African American men who have sex with men, religious commitment as measured by the Religious Commitment Inventory-10 was positively associated with internalized homonegativity (e.g., "I believe it is morally wrong for men to be attracted to each other"; Smallwood, Spencer, Ingram, Thrasher, & Thompson-Robinson, 2017). Religious commitment was also negatively associated with gay affirmation (e.g., "I see my homosexuality as a gift"). Similarly, religiosity (e.g., religious service attendance, how religious a person is) was positively associated with homonegativity (e.g., "I wish I were not attracted to other men") in samples from Milwaukee, Cleveland, and Miami of African American men who have sex with men (Quinn & Dickson-Gomez, 2015).

Sexual minority men and women experience homophobia in the Black church (Lassiter, 2016; Miller & Stack, 2014). However, the Black church is central to life in many African American communities and provides social support, so sexual minority African Americans may conceal their sexual orientation in church to avoid homonegativity. The homophobia of the Black church may also deter many African American sexual minorities from attending. Two-thirds of a national sample of African American men who have sex with men attended church once a month or less (Lassiter, 2016). Yet, these men considered themselves to be moderately to highly religious.

Despite the homophobia in many churches, religious faith may be a source of resiliency for African American sexual minority persons. In a study of African American lesbian, gay, and bisexual emerging adults, aged 18 to 25 years old, internalized homonegativity (e.g., "I feel ashamed of my homosexuality") was negatively associated with resiliency, the ability to handle changes or misfortunes in their lives (Walker & Longmire-Avital, 2013). However, religious faith (e.g., "My religious faith is extremely important to me") interacted with homonegativity. Among those who reported high internalized homonegativity, better resilience was associated with higher religious faith. Because of this influential role of religion in the lives of many African Americans, churches that affirm their congregants' sexual orientation may reduce homonegativity and improve mental health (Walker & Longmire-Avital, 2013).

One method of making church congregations more affirming of sexual minorities is personal contact. In a study of two African American and three Latinx church congregations, knowing someone with HIV was associated with less stigmatizing attitudes toward HIV (e.g., homosexuality is immoral, avoidance of homosexuals; Derose et al., 2016). Thus, churches could reduce HIV stigma and increase acceptance of sexual minority persons with activities that promote care and support for people with HIV.

Summary

Religion and spirituality have different meanings for African Americans. Both generally have positive effects on African Americans' well-being. Religious commitment is not as strongly associated with political conservatism among African Americans as it is among European Americans. Although religious commitment is associated with homonegativity, religious faith is a source of resilience among African American sexual minorities with internalized homonegativity.

CONCLUSION

African Americans have made important contributions to the history and culture of the United States for centuries. These contributions have occurred despite a long history of racism. Racism has resulted in gender role stereotypes of African Americans. Nevertheless, African Americans have developed healthy masculine and healthy feminine identities. Religious and spiritual identities have also facilitated African American health.

RESOURCES

Blog:
What is Healthy Masculinity?: It May Involve Femininity www.psychologytoday.com/blog/life-in-the-intersection/201703/what-is-healthy-masculinity.

Videos:
A Conversation with Black Women on Race www.nytimes.com/2015/12/01/opinion/a-conversation-with-black-women-on-race.html.
If Black People Said the Stuff White People Say www.youtube.com/watch?v=A1zLzWtULig.

CHAPTER 9

Asian Pacific Americans

Chris is a 21-year-old Samoan American senior. He is from Hawaii but is in college on the main-land. Some of the best-known Samoan Americans on his campus are athletes. Chris is not an athlete. He is majoring in psychology because he finds that the courses help him better understand himself and others. Chris has been sexually attracted to other males since he was a teenager. He has come out as gay to his parents and to some of his close Samoan American friends, who have been supportive. The LGBTQ groups on campus are primarily White and he doesn't see a place for himself there. Chris wants to become a clinical psychologist and focus on the mental health of LGBTQ people of color.

Kim is a 21-year-old Vietnamese American senior in college. Her grandparents came to the United States in 1975 after the Vietnam War. Both of her parents were born in California and completed college. Although they were well-educated, her parents adhered to traditional gender roles, with her father focusing on his work and her mother focusing on their family despite also working. Her parents saved enough money over Kim's lifetime so that she would not have any college debt. Kim is completing an engineering degree. Most of her classmates are men, and some are dismissive of women in the field. Her parents want her to get married and start a family but she is focused on her career as a way of repaying her parents for their sacrifices for her.

Asian Pacific Americans are immigrants and descendants of immigrants from East and South Asia and the Pacific Islands. They constitute at least 29 different groups whose cultural customs are distinct from most other groups in the United States. "Asian Pacific American" will be used as a term in this chapter to include Americans of East Asian (e.g., China, Japan, Korea), Southeast Asian (e.g., Vietnam, Thailand, Cambodia), South Asian (e.g., India), and Pacific Island (e.g., Philippines, Hawaii, Samoa) ancestry, whereas the term "Asian American" will be used to refer to persons of East Asian ancestry and not to the other groups. Most research in psychology has been on Americans of East Asian ancestry, with a developing literature on Southeast Asian and South Asian Americans. The literature on Pacific Island Americans is quite limited.

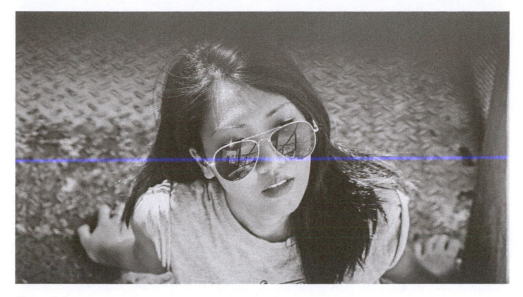

Picture 9.1
Source: courtesy of Pixabay.

Chinese, Japanese, and Korean Americans are influenced by Confucian traditions, although each culture has developed these traditions in somewhat unique ways. Hong Kong has been influenced by Chinese culture as well as its former status as a British colony. Vietnamese Americans have been influenced by Chinese culture as well as by French colonization. Vietnamese, Cambodian, and Thai Americans all are likely to have been influenced by the Buddhist religion. Indian Americans may have multiple religious influences, including Buddhism, Hinduism, Islam, Sikhism, and Jainism (Min, 1995). British colonization resulted in the adoption of English as the official language in India. Spanish colonization exposed Filipino Americans to Roman Catholic influences. Colonization by the United States introduced American influences in the Philippines, including the English language. Over 70% of Korean Americans are Protestant as a result of American missionary influences in Korea beginning in the late 1800s (Kitano & Daniels, 1995; E. Lee, 1997).

Of the total U.S. population, 6% (21 million people) have Asian ancestry (U.S. Bureau of the Census, 2017, March). The Chinese American population numbered 4.5 million, followed by Asian Indian Americans (3.8 million), Filipino Americans (3.8 million), Vietnamese Americans (2.0 million), Korean Americans (1.8 million), Alaska Natives/Pacific Islanders (1.5 million), and Japanese Americans (1.4 million).

HISTORY

Early Immigration

The late 1700s was the first period of Asian Pacific immigration to America, although the total number of immigrants was small. Chinese and Filipino sailors who arrived on Spanish ships founded settlements in Louisiana during this time, and South Asians and Malaysians arrived on English ships on the East Coast as slaves (Agbayani-Siewert & Revilla, 1995). During the nineteenth century, approximately 250,000 Chinese persons immigrated to the United States (Spickard, 2007). A cohort of Chinese men came to the United States in the 1820s seeking work in railroads or mines, as did a larger group to California following the Gold Rush in 1849. The Burlingame Treaty between China and the United States encouraged Chinese immigration for a period. By the 1860s, there were 24,000 Chinese men working in the mines (Takaki, 1993). Asian miners were subjected to a Foreign Miners' Tax, which provided European Americans a competitive advantage.

Following the gold rush, Chinese farm laborers' agricultural knowledge helped transform California agriculture from wheat to fruit (Takaki, 1993). Over 12,000 Chinese men were hired to build the transcontinental railroad. They received lower pay than the European American workers, and 1000 died during the railroad construction. Chinese and African American workers were conspicuously absent from drawings depicting the Golden Spike ceremony in the Utah Territory in 1869, signifying the completion of the transcontinental railroad (Spickard, 2007).

The American economy was depressed at the end of the 1800s, and Chinese immigrants were often scapegoats. Additional Chinese immigration to the United States ended in 1882 with the Chinese Exclusion Act, motivated in part by perceived competition between Chinese and European American laborers. This was the first law that excluded immigrants on the basis of nationality, and it was not repealed until 1942. In 1885 and 1886, Chinese residents of Tacoma and Seattle, Washington and Rock Springs, Wyoming, were attacked, killed, and driven out of these communities by European Americans (Spickard, 2007).

Most Chinese immigrants had families in China and intended to eventually return there. However, these men could not have become United States citizens even if they had wanted to. A 1790 federal law reserved naturalized citizenship for Whites, and Asians were not allowed to become naturalized citizens until 1952 (Takaki, 1993).

Because there were very few Chinese women in California, only 4% of Chinese in the United States in 1900 were American-born (Takaki, 1993). Roles for Chinese women were extremely limited in the United States. In 1870, 61% of the 3536 Chinese women in California listed their occupation as prostitute (L. Lee, 1998). This statistic must have come to federal attention, as the 1875 Page Law prohibited immigration of women who were being brought into the United States for "lewd and immoral purposes" (Spickard, 2007). Selective enforcement of this law further reduced the immigration of Chinese women to the United States. Chinese men were unable to marry European American women in California as a result of an 1880 California law that prohibited marriage between a White person and a "negro, mulatto, or Mongolian" (Takaki, 1993).

Chinatowns were developed at the end of the 1800s for economic and social support. Many Chinese Americans were forced into self-employment, including stores, restaurants, and laundries, as a result of discrimination and language barriers. These occupations required limited English language skills. Thus, the existence of Chinese restaurants and laundries in the United States is not necessarily a result of a Chinese affinity for these businesses. However, many European Americans began to view Asian American men as feminized, as cooking and washing were traditionally female tasks for European Americans (Spickard, 2007). Asian American men continue in the present to be perceived as less masculine than men in other ethnic groups (Galinsky et al., 2013; see Chapter 8).

Over 6000 Asian Indian men immigrated to California between 1904 and 1911 (Jensen, 1988). Most of these men worked as farmers. About half were married, but most were unable to bring their wives to the United States until legislation allowed this in 1946. Similar to the Chinese immigration experience, the relative absence of women prevented a lasting Asian Indian presence. Indeed, many of the 1000 Indian students who came to the United States in the 1920s intended to learn science and technology and to return to India and apply this knowledge (Sheth, 1995). Financial hardships caused by British colonial rule motivated many Indians to immigrate to the United States (Sheth, 1995). However, improved social, political, and economic conditions following India's independence from Great Britain in 1947 curtailed Indian immigration to the United States until 1965.

A wave of immigrants to the United States from Japan followed the Chinese Exclusion Act in 1882. The 1908 Gentleman's Agreement between the United States and Japan allowed Japanese family members to immigrate to the United States. This law allowed many Japanese immigrants to remain with their families in the United States, unlike the Chinese immigrants whose families remained in China. Japanese immigrants came to California to seek employment and economic opportunities, finding independent employment in shop keeping and in farming. However, the immigrants' opportunities were restricted by the Alien Land Law of 1913, which prohibited noncitizens from owning land. Nevertheless, their American-born children were able to own land as citizens. By 1940, Japanese Americans grew 95% of beans, 67% of tomatoes, 95% of celery, 44% of onions, and 40% of green peas in California (Takaki, 1993).

Asian Pacific Americans in Hawaii

The Asian Pacific American diversity in Hawaii is a result of labor force issues. During the early 1900s, many Asian Pacific groups were brought by European Americans to Hawaii to prevent any particular Asian group from becoming the majority (Takaki, 1993). However, the Asian workers in Hawaii united across ethnic groups, eventually became the majority, and unionized (Takaki, 1993). Over 60% of the current population of Hawaii has Asian Pacific American ancestry.

The recruitment in Hawaii of Asian laborers resulted in over 7200 Koreans emigrating from 1903 to 1905 (Min, 1995). Between 1906 and 1923, the primary groups of Korean immigrants to the United States were the wives of the workers, students, and political refugees (Min, 1995). Asian immigration to the United States, other than that of Filipinos, was completely halted in 1924 with the Asian Exclusion Act.

The United States gained possession of the Philippines in 1898 after the Spanish–American War. Between 1906 and 1940, Filipinos were brought to Hawaii and the West Coast of the United States as a cheap source of farm labor (Agbayani–Siewert & Revilla, 1995; Edman & Johnson, 1999). Similar to Chinese immigration, Filipino immigration primarily involved men (Agbayani–Siewert & Revilla, 1995). During the Depression in the 1930s, 2000 Filipino Americans left the United States under pressure from the federal government to "repatriate" to the Philippines (Spickard, 2007). Such repatriation occurred on a much larger scale during the 1930s with Mexican Americans, who were also perceived as a threat to the employment opportunities of European Americans (see Chapter 8). Many Filipinos served in the United States armed forces during World War

II, and those who served were allowed to become U.S. citizens in 1943. The Philippines gained independence from the United States in 1946.

Before and after World War II, European Americans controlled the social and political systems of Hawaii (Spickard, 2007). Their goal with Japanese Americans was to Americanize them in the public schools by teaching standard English and other U.S. customs, such as table manners. However, Japanese Americans used these tools to take political control of Hawaii.

Japanese American Incarceration During World War II

The largest act of discrimination by the United States government against any Asian Pacific American group occurred against Japanese Americans during World War II. Japanese American agricultural productivity, discussed previously, was perceived as an economic threat to European American farmers in California and provided much of the impetus for the incarceration of 120,000 Japanese Americans in United States internment camps during World War II.

Two-thirds of the Japanese Americans who were incarcerated were United States citizens. The official reason for Japanese American wartime internment was that they were a threat to national security. However, no acts of sabotage against the United States by Japanese Americans were committed before or during World War II (Nakanishi, 1988). Even military leaders debated over the actual threat that Japanese Americans posed to national security (Commission on Wartime Relocation and Internment of Civilians, 1982). All Japanese Americans on the West Coast of the United States were incarcerated, whereas very few Japanese Americans in Hawaii were similarly incarcerated, nor were

Picture 9.2 Manzanar Relocation Center. Photo by Ansel Adams.
Source: shutterstock.

Japanese Americans who lived in other parts of the United States. Moreover, the United States was also at war with Germany and Italy, but there were not mass incarcerations of German and Italian Americans. Another irony is that Japanese American men were recruited from the internment camps to serve in the United States military in Europe and the Pacific. Somehow these men's parents and younger siblings constituted a threat to the national security, but they did not.

It took 35 years for the United States government to apologize to the incarcerated Japanese Americans (Spickard, 2007). In 1988, the U.S. government enacted redress legislation to provide $20,000 to each camp survivor or the children of those who died. Considering the traumas that Japanese Americans endured in the areas of education, employment, and health, $20,000 is a token sum. In 2008, colleges and universities in Oregon and Washington states made symbolic efforts to recognize how the internment interrupted the education of internees by awarding honorary degrees to their former students who were removed from college because of the internment. Colleges and universities in California later did the same. However, many of the former internees had died before these degrees were awarded.

Repeal of Immigration Restrictions

In 1943, Congress repealed the Chinese Exclusion Act because China had become a U.S. ally (Takaki, 1993). This allowed 105 Chinese persons to immigrate annually to the United States. Many of these Chinese immigrants were women, which resulted in a population of American-born Chinese. Chinese wives of Chinese American soldiers were allowed to come to the United States via war brides acts, which were intended to allow American soldiers to bring home women they had married abroad during World War II (Spickard, 2007). Chinese students and professionals who were in the United States after the 1949 Communist Revolution in China and did not wish to return were also permitted to remain in the United States because of refugee status.

Immigration opportunities were opened for Filipinos and Asian Indians in 1946 in separate congressional acts that allowed the annual immigration of 100 persons from each group (Fong, 1998). The legislation also allowed Filipinos and Asian Indians to apply for United States citizenship. However, it was not until the Immigration and Naturalization Act of 1965 that Asians were again allowed to immigrate in large numbers to the United States. During and following the Korean War in the early 1950s and through 1964, Korean and Japanese women immigrated to the United States as wives of American soldiers. Orphaned Korean children were also part of this wave of immigration. Asian immigrants for the first time became eligible for U.S. citizenship in 1952 with the passage of the McCarran-Walter Act (Nishi, 1995). Exposure to Americans during the Korean War caused over 27,000 Koreans to come to the United States between 1950 and 1964 as nonimmigrant students (Min, 1995). During the 1970s and 1980s, over 3000 Korean orphans were adopted by U.S. citizens per year (Min, 1995). This wave of adoptions ended, in part, because of negative world publicity during the 1988 Seoul Olympics about Koreans not caring for their own orphans.

The Immigration Act of 1965 repealed the restrictions of the 1924 Asian Exclusion Act. Immigrants from all countries were allowed into the United States if they had valuable occupational skills, were being reunified with family members, or were vulnerable to political or religious persecution. A quota of 20,000 immigrants per country was established. Before 1965, approximately two-thirds of the Asian American population was born in the United States. Since then the opposite has occurred – approximately two-thirds of current Asian Americans were born in Asia.

Southeast Asian Immigration

Following the Vietnam War in 1975, refugees began emigrating from Southeast Asia. These Southeast Asians had become refugees because of the political conflicts that had resulted from United States political and military involvement in Southeast Asia. Many of the first-wave immigrants were Vietnamese, educated, and spoke English (Nishio & Bilmes, 1987). This group included Vietnam government and military personnel (Fong, 1998). The 1975 Indochinese Resettlement Assistance Act was passed by Congress to assist these refugees. The immigration of this initial wave of Southeast Asians was relatively smooth and complete by the time the Resettlement Assistance Act expired in 1977.

After the Immigration Act of 1965, many Asian professionals immigrated to the United States. However, the flow of Asian professional immigrants was severely restricted by the Eilberg Act and the Health Professions Assistance Act in 1976 (Min, 1995). These acts eliminated valuable occupational status as an eligibility criterion for immigration. Thus, a large portion of the Asian immigrants since 1976 has been family members of persons already in the United States and refugees.

From 1979 to 1984, Vietnamese, Cambodian, Laotian, and Hmong refugees settled across the United States. Many were involuntary immigrants because they had become refugees in their own countries for assisting the United States' war effort. These groups had been evacuated from their homes, placed in "reeducation camps," forced to labor in rural regions, attacked with bombs and chemical weapons, had family members executed, and forced to flee to refugee camps in Thailand. At least half of these refugees experienced post-traumatic stress (Sack & Clarke, 1996). Thousands of refugees attempted to escape in boats on the South China Sea, with at least 100,000 drowning in these escape attempts (Rumbaut, 1995). Immigrants in this second wave were primarily rural, of lower socioeconomic status, and unable to speak English (Nishio & Bilmes, 1987). The 1980 Refugee Act allowed 50,000 refugees to enter the United States annually and initially provided 36 months of assistance, after which time the refugees could become eligible for welfare benefits. The length of assistance was reduced to only 18 months in 1981.

Recent Immigration

Over half a million Koreans came to the United States between 1970 and 1990 (Min, 1995). The Korean American community has been highly cohesive because of language barriers and because many immigrants are immersed in the Korean American community, including Korean Christian churches and businesses. Most Korean Americans are either self-employed or work for Korean companies (Min, 1995). Korean businessmen have been described as a middleman minority, which distributes products produced by the group in power to the masses (Min, 1995). Following the not guilty verdict in 1992 involving the

White police officers who assaulted Rodney King in Los Angeles, the media focused on African Americans vandalizing and destroying Korean businesses. However, the media coverage of these riots has been perceived by Korean Americans as an attempt by the media to shift public attention from African American–European American conflicts, which were likely the primary source of dissatisfaction in the African American community. Less than half of the property damage during these incidents involved Korean American businesses (Spickard, 2007). Moreover, there were more Latinx Americans among the 12,000 arrested than African Americans (J. Gonzalez, 2000).

Korean Americans have described those who were born in Korea but came to the United States with their families as young children as the 1.5 generation (Spickard, 2007; see Chapter 2). They are more likely to speak the Korean language better and are usually more identified with Korean culture than Korean Americans born in the United States. However, 1.5 generation Korean Americans are able to speak English and are acculturated to Western traditions as well, which makes them similar to Korean Americans born in the United States. All immigrant groups have similar individuals who immigrated as children, but Korean Americans have coined the 1.5 generation term for themselves (Spickard, 2007).

The Asian Pacific American population has continued to change during the past two decades. Since 1971, Filipinos have been the largest group of Asian Pacific immigrants to the United States and will be the largest group of Asian Pacific Americans within 30 years. The United States has been particularly attractive to Filipinos because of cultural influences during American colonization and because of intermarriage of Filipinos and U.S. military personnel (Agbayani-Siewert & Revilla, 1995). Many nurses were trained in the Philippines during the Vietnam War to serve the U.S. troops who were hosted there. The United States experienced a shortage of nurses, and in 1989 Congress passed the Immigration Nursing Relief Act, which attracted many nurses to the United States from the Philippines, where there was a surplus of nurses after the Vietnam War (Spickard, 2007).

Since 1965, approximately 1 million South Asians, from India, Pakistan, Bangladesh, Sri Lanka, Nepal, Bhutan, and Sikkim, have immigrated to the United States. Many of these immigrants were well-educated and had the occupational skills that were desirable in the 1965 Immigration Act (Spickard, 2007). Their economic resources allowed them to travel to South Asia and maintain contact with their families, unlike other Asian immigrants who seldom were able to return to their ancestral homelands. Immigration may not be a linear process of moving from one country to another. Some immigrants live in multiple places during their lifetimes. This is known as transnational immigration (E. Lee, 2015).

Asian American Identity and Civil Rights

Asian American identity began to galvanize in the late 1960s, particularly on the West Coast, in the context of the civil rights movement. The Asian American movement demanded civil and political rights for Asian Americans, created pressure for universities to begin Asian American studies programs, and helped established community services for disadvantaged and poor Asian Pacific Americans (Fong, 1998). The movement was pan-Asian, including Asian Pacific Americans of all ethnic groups. Asian American activists recognized the similarities of their own concerns to those of other ethnic minority groups and the power in uniting with these groups in common struggles. One of the major events of the movement was the Third World Strike in 1968–1969, which shut down San Francisco State College for five months. This strike resulted in the establishment of the first school of ethnic studies, which included Asian American studies. Permanent Asian American studies programs were also established at major universities in California, including UCLA and the University of California at Berkeley, and at the University of Washington. Asian American student groups were also formed at universities in other parts of the country, and Asian American studies programs were established in response to student initiatives.

Coinciding with the civil rights movement in the late 1960s was the perpetration of the myth of Asian Americans as a "model minority" (Petersen, 1966). The myth was initially based on Japanese Americans, who were the largest Asian American group at the time, but has since been blanketly applied to other Asian American groups. Critics of affirmative action argued that Asian Americans had become successful in society without the benefit of affirmative action, so why couldn't other minority groups succeed as well without affirmative action? The model minority stereotype advanced a color-blind ideology (see Chapter 1) to deny special attention or privileges for people of color (Poon, Squire, Kodama, Byrd, & Chan, 2016). This argument ignored the centuries of oppression in the United States faced by non-Asian groups of color that has placed them at a competitive disadvantage in society, as well as discrimination against Asian Americans. Although Asian Americans may be regarded as competent, they are also regarded as unsociable and threatening to the opportunities of other groups, which may exclude them from full acceptance and participation in mainstream U.S. culture (Lin, Kwan, Cheung, & Fiske, 2005; Maddux, Galinsky, Cuddy, & Polifroni, 2008). The model minority myth is reviewed in greater detail later in the chapter.

The Asian American Psychological Association (AAPA) was founded in 1972 by a group of Asian American psychologists in the San Francisco Bay area (Leong & Okazaki, 2009). AAPA was formed to exchange ideas and to provide social support, and the emphasis has been on education and training of psychologists and improving mental health services for Asian Americans. Derald Wing Sue served as the AAPA's first President, and the association has grown from 185 members in 1979 to over 500 currently. AAPA has an annual professional convention and a professional journal.

Asian Americans from many ethnic backgrounds became united following the murder of a Chinese American man, Vincent Chin, in 1982. Chin was murdered by two White autoworkers because they were angry at the competition of the Japanese auto industry and mistook him for being Japanese. The two men were convicted of relatively minor offenses, and neither served jail time (Spickard, 2007). This is yet another example of a failure to distinguish Asian Americans from Asians, let alone a failure to distinguish within Asian American ethnic groups.

Such a failure to distinguish Asian Americans from Asians appears to be the basis of the U.S. government's handling of Wen Ho Lee. Lee was a scientist who came to the United States in the 1960s, earned a PhD at Texas A&M University, and became a naturalized citizen (Spickard, 2007). In the 1990s, the Los Alamos National Laboratory, where Lee worked as a physicist, came under criticism for lax security because other countries, including China, were making advances in weapons technology that were presumed to be based on stolen information. Lee became a suspect in 1996 because he had met some Chinese scientists and also probably was a suspect because of his Chinese ancestry. Based on a 1999

New York Times story that indicated that Lee was probably a spy, although the story did not name him, the Los Alamos Laboratory fired Lee (Spickard, 2007). The Justice Department subsequently indicted Lee on 59 counts of sharing bomb secrets with a foreign country. Lee was placed in solitary confinement for 278 days, during which time it was unknown how long he would spend in prison. Asian Americans and scientists criticized the government's mistreatment of Lee. The government ultimately dismissed all but one count of mishandling classified information, to which Lee pled guilty, and he was released from prison. Lee had downloaded to his home computer information that was not classified at the time. The purpose was to work on the information at home, something his colleagues commonly did (Spickard, 2007). Thus, it appears that Lee became the scapegoat for the Los Alamos Laboratory, in part because of his Chinese ancestry.

Another case of mistaken identity was the backlash against South Asian Americans following the attacks on the World Trade Center and the Pentagon on September 11, 2001. Harassment, racial profiling, and hate crimes spiked against South Asian Americans following 9/11/01. Nearly 40% of those detained on suspicion of terrorism following the attacks were believed to be Pakistani nationals (E. Lee, 2015). Although some of these Pakistanis may have been Muslims, those who attacked on 9/11 were not from Pakistan and they were extremists who did not follow the peaceful tenets of Islam. In 2002, Attorney General John Ashcroft proposed that men from 25 primarily Muslim countries be fingerprinted, photographed, and registered with the Immigration and Naturalization Service (E. Lee, 2015). This is not unlike President Trump's 2017 travel ban of several predominantly Muslim countries that was quickly overturned in court. These forms of racial profiling that are not based on actual danger are reminiscent of the incarceration of Japanese Americans during World War II.

Stereotypes of successful Asian Americans were revisited in 2011 with the publication of the memoir "Battle Hymn of the Tiger Mother," by Yale law professor Amy Chua. She attributed her children's academic success to her emphasis on working hard in academics and music at the expense of leisure activities, such as play dates and sleepovers (E. Lee, 2015). Chua portrayed this "Tiger Mother" parenting style as Chinese. As discussed in Chapter 5, Asian American academic achievement is more likely a result of hard work than cultural values. Moreover, the greater parental pressure to succeed that Asian American students experience has the costs of low self-esteem and alienation from peers (Hsin & Xie, 2014).

GENDER ROLES

Asian American Males

Asian American men perceive the same masculine gender role norms as other men do. These include winning, emotional control, risk-taking, violence, dominance, playboy, self-reliance, primacy of work, power over women, disdain for homosexuals, and pursuit of status (Hsu & Iwamoto, 2014). Marginalized men may attempt to cope with their devalued status by adhering to stereotypic masculine roles. However, rather than alleviating stress, adherence to masculine roles increases it (Y. Wong et al., 2017). Attempts by men of color to cope with being devalued by becoming hypermasculine are known as *minority masculinity stress theory* (A. Lu & Wong, 2013).

Picture 9.3
Source: shutterstock.

Although Asian American men may perceive their own gender role norms as similar to those of other groups of men, they are not perceived by others to be similar to other groups of men. As presented in Chapter 8, Asian Americans are perceived as less masculine than African Americans or European Americans (Galinsky et al., 2013). In addition, college students primed (see Chapter 3 on priming) with the word "Asian" more accurately identify briefly-presented feminine words (feminine, graceful, gentle, beautiful, delicate) than masculine words (masculine, vigorous, strong, muscular, burly; Galinsky et al., 2013). When asked to write a story about an Asian American vs. a European American individual, participants were more likely to write about a woman when writing about an Asian American individual (Schug et al., 2015). These perceptions of Asian American male femininity are not restricted to non-Asians, as Asian American men and women were also in these studies (Galinsky et al., 2013; Schug et al., 2015).

Stereotypes of Asian American men in LGBTQ communities are similar to those in heterosexual communities. They are often assumed to be effeminate, passive, dependent, unmasculine, and unattractive (A. Choi & Israel, 2016). In contrast, masculine attributes which are regarded more positively are associated more with European American men than with Asian American men in LGBTQ communities. Asian American men's issues are also secondary to LGBTQ activist efforts that privilege European Americans (A. Choi & Israel, 2016). Chris, who is discussed at the beginning of the chapter, found the LGBTQ groups of his campus to be primarily White and he did not want to join them.

Either fulfilling or violating these feminized stereotypes may be punished (Iwamoto & Liu, 2009). According to the *Asianized attribution* framework, Asian American men who are polite, modest, and agreeable are viewed positively because they fit the stereotype of Asians as being passive. However, such men are also considered unassertive and poor leaders. In the *transgressive attribution* framework, violating the passive stereotype is viewed negatively. An assertive Asian American man who talks about his accomplishments may be perceived as aggressive and arrogant.

Stereotypes of Asian American men may affect them in the workplace. Asian American men born in the United States have lower incomes than European American men with comparable education and jobs (C. Kim & Sakamoto, 2010). Consistent with the Asianized attribution framework, individuals who do not stand out or do not advocate for themselves may not be paid as much as those who do. In a national sample of scientists and engineers, Asian American men were less likely than European American, African American, Latino American, or Native American men to be in managerial or supervisory positions (Zeng, 2011). Once they are in managerial positions, Asian Americans tend to leave them (Zeng, 2011). Consistent with the transgressive attribution framework, Asian American men may perceive or have experienced negative consequences of leadership positions.

Asian American men are aware of others' stereotypes of them. A group of 159 Asian American male college students identified these stereotypes: (a) interpersonal deficits; (b) intelligence; (c) intense diligence; (d) unflattering physical attributes; (e) physical ability distortions; (f) perpetual foreigner; and (g) sexual/romantic inadequacies (Y. Wong, Owen, Tran, Collins, & Higgins, 2012). Interpersonal deficits included descriptions such as boring, bad tippers, and wacky. Intelligence was the implication of being smart, such as good at math. Intense diligence involved a strong work ethic and intense concern about work or studies. Unflattering physical attributes included being short, unattractive, and having slanted eyes. Physical ability distortions included being unathletic, physically weak, or, in contrast, knowing kung fu. Perpetual foreigner included having a strong accent and sticking to Asian culture and friends. Finally, sexual/romantic inadequacies included sexual inabilities and being bad at relationships. As can be seen in Figure 9.1, intelligence and interpersonal deficits were the most common self-perceived stereotypes whereas intense diligence and sexual/romantic inadequacies were the least common. Although they were relatively uncommon, sexual/romantic inadequacies, perpetual foreigner, and intense diligence were associated with higher self-reported depression among the participants than the other stereotypes.

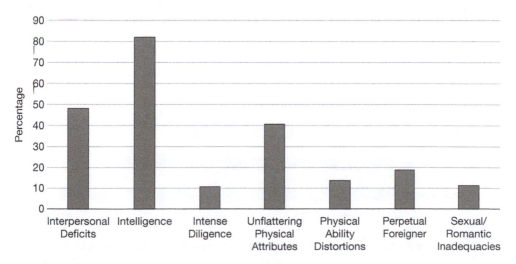

Figure 9.1 Self-Perceived Stereotypes of Asian American Men.

Source: Y. Wong, Owen et al., 2012.

Being intelligent and hard-working may appear to be positive stereotypes. However, as reviewed in Chapter 6, positive stereotypes may create undue pressure that creates negative mental health outcomes (Hsin & Xie, 2014). Moreover, a person who holds positive stereotypes of a group may simultaneously hold negative stereotypes of them (Siy & Cheryan, 2016).

Despite these general stereotypes of Asian American men, Asian Americans as a group have been found to be more accepting of gay men and lesbians that other ethnic groups in the United States. In a national study in which respondents rated their feelings toward gay men and lesbians on a scale of 0 (coolest) to 100 (warmest), Asian Americans reported the warmest feelings (Adamczyk, Boyd, & Hayes, 2016; see Figure 9.2). This acceptance of gays and lesbians among Asian Americans is consistent with the experiences of Chris with his parents and with his Samoan American friends, described at the beginning of this chapter. This acceptance may be because many Asian Americans do not have religious proscriptions regarding same-sex relationships. Asian Americans are more likely than other ethnic groups in the United States to be unaffiliated with a religion and less likely to be Christian (Pew Research Center, 2012). In contrast, the religiosity of African Americans may contribute to their relatively cool feelings toward gays and lesbians, as discussed in Chapter 8 (Smallwood et al., 2017). Nevertheless, some Asian American groups, such as Filipino Americans, have strong religious influences that prevent acceptance of minority sexual identities (Nadal & Corpus, 2013). Also, many Latinx Americans are Catholic but Latinx Americans report relatively warm feelings about gays and lesbians. Perhaps Latinx cultural values associated with interpersonal warmth outweigh religious proscriptions about people in same-sex relationships.

The research on Asian American men has focused on stereotyped masculinity but not on healthy masculinity. Healthy Asian American masculinity must be decoupled from stereotypes. One component of healthy masculinity may be characteristics typically associated with femininity, including empathy and a focus on interpersonal relationships (Hall & Barongan, 1997). In a 17-year study of men, femininity (e.g., affectionate, sympathetic, sensitive to the needs of others, understanding, compassionate, eager to soothe hurt feelings, warm, tender, loves children, gentle) was associated with lower rates of death from coronary heart disease (Hunt, Lewars, Emslie, & Batty,

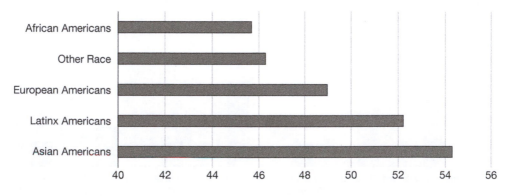

Figure 9.2 Means of Feelings About Gays and Lesbians by Ethnic Group.

Source: Adamczyck et al., 2016.

2007). However, feminine behavior is not valued, particularly when men engage in it (Hall & Barongan, 1997). Moreover, being perceived as feminine has negative consequences for Asian American men, as discussed above. Nevertheless, given the negative mental health consequences of traditional masculinity (Y. Wong et al., 2017), as discussed in Chapter 8, new definitions of healthy masculinity need to be explored for all ethnic groups.

Summary

Asian American men are perceived as less masculine than men in other ethnic groups. Complying with or violating this stereotype both have costs. Other stereotypes of Asian American men are also negative, despite being seen as intelligent and hard-working. Asian American communities generally may be more accepting of gays and lesbians than other communities.

Asian American Females

Stereotypes of Asian American women are similar to those of men. Because Asian American men are perceived as feminine, gender-specific stereotypes may be less prominent among Asian Americans than among other groups, including European Americans, African Americans, Latinx Americans, and Middle Eastern Americans (Ghavami & Peplau, 2013). Students from multiple ethnic backgrounds, including Asian Americans, at a public university in Southern California were asked to list cultural stereotypes of various groups. Common stereotypes for both Asian American men and women were: (a) intelligent; (b) short; (c) quiet; (d) bad drivers; (e) shy; and (f) skinny.

Although these gender similarities exist, Asian American women are perceived as more feminine and less masculine than other groups, including Asian American men. A national sample of participants that included Asian Americans chose the 10 traits that characterized European American, African American, and Asian American men and women (E. Hall, Galinsky, & Phillips, 2015). As can be seen in Figure 9.3, Asian American women were rated the most feminine and the least masculine.

Being perceived as feminine may make Asian American women more acceptable than Asian American men among European Americans. In a national sample of college students, 13% of European American men had dated an Asian American woman vs. only 5% of European American women who had dated an Asian American man (Herman & Campbell, 2012). Similarly, 66% of European American men were willing to marry an Asian American woman, whereas only 43% of European American women were willing to marry an Asian American man.

Being perceived as feminine may disadvantage Asian American women in the workplace. As discussed above, Asian American male scientists and engineers are less likely than men of other ethnicities to be in managerial or supervisory roles (Zeng, 2011). However, Asian American female scientists and engineers are the *least* likely of any ethnicity or gender to be managers or supervisors.

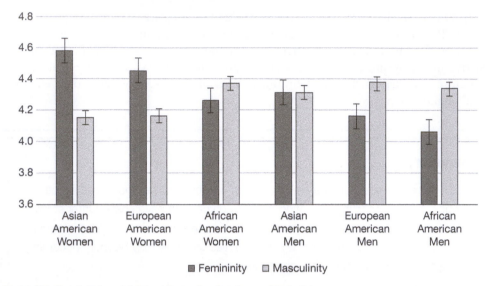

Figure 9.3 Femininity and Masculinity by Gender and Ethnicity.
Source: E. Hall et al., 2015.

Asian Americans have been found to endorse traditional gender role ideology more than other groups. Traditional gender role ideology is that men should earn money and that women should take care of the home and children. This traditional ideology restricts the roles of both men and women. A component of traditional gender role ideology is that maternal employment outside the home comes at a cost to her children's well-being. In a study at a large public university in the Western United States, Asian Americans endorsed traditional gender role ideology more than European Americans or Latinx Americans (Goldberg et al., 2012). Asian Americans more than the other groups also perceived costs to children of maternal employment. Asian American men perceived these costs more than Asian American women did. Moreover, Asian Americans who had a parent who was not born in the United States held these gender role and maternal employment beliefs more strongly than European Americans with two parents born in the United States. Traditional gender role beliefs may be a source of stress for Asian Americans, as they are at odds with the beliefs of other groups in the United States. In other words, these traditional gender role values are a poor cultural fit in much of the United States.

There may be both similarities and differences in gender role beliefs between Asian American women and other women of color. In a focus group (see Chapter 3) study of Vietnamese American immigrant women from faith-based institutions and African American women from community settings and a university, both ethnic groups emphasized women's roles as chief caretakers and their responsibility to fulfill multiple roles (Abrams, Javier, Maxwell, Belgrave, & Nguyen, 2016). However, caretaking for Vietnamese American women was more connected to traditional gender role ideology, as discussed previously. Vietnamese women more strongly endorsed a patriarchal hierarchy in which men are providers and women are caretakers. These are the gender roles of Kim's parents, described at the beginning of the chapter. Both Vietnamese American and African American women discussed multiple roles, such as mothers, wives, caregivers, support systems, and employees, as part of womanhood. Kim's mother had at least three roles as wife, mother, and employee. However, Vietnamese women emphasized cooking as more of a role responsibility whereas African American women focused more on being providers. The provider role is more typically a man's role in Asian American families than in African American families (Kulkarni, 2015). Another difference was that Vietnamese American women were more deferent to and dependent on others than African American women were (Abrams et al., 2016).

Asian American women who defy traditional gender roles may pay a price. In a study of Asian American college students at a Southwest university, Asian American women who sought family recognition through achievement (e.g., "One should achieve academically since it reflects on one's family") were more depressed than men who did so or than women who did not (Y. Wong, Nguyen et al., 2012). Although family recognition through achievement is considered to be an Asian value, it may be more acceptable for Asian American men. Asian American women pursuing family recognition through achievement may experience a poor fit with gendered cultural norms. Kim, described at the beginning of the chapter, felt that she would honor her family with a successful engineering career, but her parents wanted her to start a family of her own.

Despite the generally greater acceptance of gays and lesbians among Asian Americans relative to other groups discussed previously (Adamczyk et al., 2016), same-sex relationships violate Asian American women's prescribed gender role as procreator (A. Choi & Israel, 2016). Moreover, nonheterosexuality is viewed by many Asian Americans as a European American or Western phenomenon. Because of stereotypes of passivity and dependence, Asian American sexual minority women may be vulnerable targets of abuse.

Similar to healthy masculinity among Asian American men, there is limited research on healthy Asian American femininity. The intense cultural pressure to fulfill traditional gender roles creates a challenge to creating alternative identities for Asian American women that are less exclusively tied to procreation and family responsibilities. Violating prescribed gender roles may have negative consequences for Asian American women, as discussed previously. Nevertheless, a bicultural balance of being nurturant and agentic may be most adaptive across Asian American and non–Asian contexts.

Summary

Similar to Asian American men, stereotypes of Asian American women involve femininity and passivity. Such stereotypes may severely restrict opportunities for Asian American women. Moreover, traditional gender role ideology has been found to be more prominent among Asian American women than among women in other ethnic groups. Defiance of traditional gender roles may be costly to Asian American women.

BOX 9.1 LOSS OF FACE

Loss of face occurs when someone in an interdependent culture fails to live up to their prescribed social role (Zane & Mak, 2003). A person's moral reputation is preserved by performance of social roles. Prescribed social roles might include husband, wife, father, mother, child, family member, student, or employee. Face is not gained by personal achievements. But it can be lost by violating a social role norm that brings shame to one's reference group, such as the family or community. For example, if an individual is depressed and this interferes with her ability to fulfill a social role (e.g., student), this can reflect poorly on her family or her teachers who are supposed to be caring for her. If the individual discloses her depression to someone else (e.g., friend, therapist), face loss could occur not only for her but also for her family and teachers. Face concerns are common among people of East Asian ancestry.

Loss of face can have positive and negative consequences. On the plus side, it is associated with impulse control. For example, Asian American men who are concerned about loss of face are less likely to be sexually aggressive (G. Hall et al., 2006). Loss of face is not predictive of European American men's sexual aggression. Conversely, loss of face is associated with anxiety and a lower likelihood of seeking help among Asian American men and women (Liu, Lieberman, Stevens, Auerbach, & Shankman, 2017). Loss of face is also associated with depression among Asian American men and women (Y. Wong, Kim, Nguyen, Cheng, & Saw, 2014).

Discussion

1   What advantages does concern about face loss have in Asian American contexts?
2   Does loss of face exist for people whose ancestry is not in East Asia?

Picture 9.4

Source: shutterstock.

MODEL MINORITY MYTH

In addition to gender role stereotypes, Asian American men and women are both subjected to model minority stereotypes. As discussed earlier, the model minority myth portrays Asian Americans as hard working, successful, financially secure, and assimilated into United States society (Iwamoto & Kaya, 2016). Think of someone who:

> is diligent and hardworking. They do well in school, particularly in the area of math and sciences. Both of them are on the honor roll. Despite the superior academic performance, they are quiet in class most of the time. With their achievements, they are expected to excel in their career in the future – with a well-paid and prestigious occupation.
>
> (Chao, Chiu, Chan, Mendoza-Denton, & Kwok, 2013, p. 86)

Which ethnic group does this image fit best? This is a chapter on Asian Americans, so you are already thinking about characteristics and stereotypes of Asian Americans. A large group of Asian American college students, 39% of whom were European Americans and 34% of whom were Asian Americans, associated this image much more strongly with Asian Americans than with either European Americans or African Americans (Figure 9.4; Chao et al., 2013). Moreover, in a second study of primarily European American and Asian American college students, participants estimated that nearly two-thirds of the adult population in the United States would associate the same image with Asian Americans (Chao et al., 2013). The participants also estimated that only 39% of the adult population in the United States would associate the image with European Americans and only 17% would associate the image with African Americans.

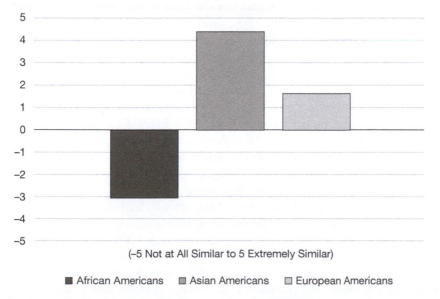

(–5 Not at All Similar to 5 Extremely Similar)

■ African Americans   ■ Asian Americans   □ European Americans

Figure 9.4 Perceived Similarity of the Model Minority Description to Images of Ethnic Groups
Source: Chao et al., 2013.

The model minority myth consists of two assumptions (Yoo, Burrola, & Steger, 2010):

• Asian Americans are more successful than *any* other racial/ethnic minority group.
• Asian Americans have stronger values emphasizing work and achievement.

The assumption behind this myth is that anyone can succeed if they work hard. If they fail, they are personally responsible.

The idea that Asian Americans are more successful than other minority groups is a "divide and conquer" aspect of the model minority myth. If Asian Americans can be successful, one should not have sympathy for other minority groups who are less successful. European American college students who were exposed to a news story of an Asian American whose accomplishments had received statewide recognition were more likely to perceive social acceptance (e.g., friendship, marriage) toward Asian Americans than toward African Americans (Chao et al., 2013). European Americans' social acceptance of the two groups did not significantly differ when the news story was about a European American's accomplishments or was not about success. A limitation was that the study did not include exposure to a news story about an African American's accomplishments.

Hidden in the model minority myth is the variability among Asian American groups (Yoo et al., 2010). Some South and East Asian groups, such as Asian Indian Americans and Japanese Americans, have high rates of bachelors and advanced degrees. However, many Southeast Asians, including Hmong Americans, Cambodian Americans, and Laotian Americans, never completed high school. Lumping all Asian Americans into one group as a model minority can cause schools and colleges to overlook the educational problems that Asian Americans from any group, including those that are relatively successful (e.g., South Asians, East Asians), may experience (B. Suzuki, 2002).

Another hidden aspect of the model minority myth is selective immigration. As discussed previously in this chapter, an effect of the 1965 Immigration Act was selection of immigrants with occupational skills. Thus, many Asian immigrants to the United States since then were already educationally and economically successful *before* they immigrated. These immigrants did not have to overcome centuries of discrimination, which other groups of color have experienced, to become successful. Moreover, many Southeast Asian Americans immigrated to the United States as refugees, as discussed previously in this chapter, which has been a major barrier to educational and economic adjustment in the United States. The model minority myth also hides discrimination against Asian Americans, which is as common for Asian Americans as it is for other groups of color in the United States (see Chapter 1; American Psychological Association, 2016).

Although the model minority myth originated outside the Asian American community, some Asian Americans have internalized it. Yoo and colleagues (2010) have developed the Internalization of the Model Minority Myth Measure based on a study of Asian Americans at a large public university in the Southwest. The largest groups of Asian Americans in the study were Chinese, Vietnamese, Filipino/a, and Korean. First- (immigrants), second- (born in the U.S.), and third-generation (parents born in the U.S.) students were included. Using factor analysis (see Chapter 3), two factors were identified: (a) *achievement orientation*; and (b) *unrestricted mobility*. Achievement orientation involves belief in the myth that Asian Americans are more successful, are more motivated to succeed, and work harder than other groups. Unrestricted mobility is the belief in the myth that Asian Americans are treated fairly and do not experience prejudice, racism, discrimination, or barriers at work.

The model minority myth could be construed as a positive stereotype that might enhance Asian Americans' success. Nevertheless, the achievement orientation and unrestricted mobility factors were associated with psychological distress among Asian Americans (Yoo et al., 2010). Similar to other seemingly positive stereotypes of Asian Americans discussed earlier in this chapter and in Chapter 6, model minority stereotypes may create undue pressure to succeed. Distress may occur when an Asian American perceives that they have failed to live up to the high expectations of their group.

European Americans who endorse the model minority myth do not have favorable attitudes toward Asian Americans. Those who believe that Asian Americans have unrestricted mobility are likely to hold negative attitudes toward Asian Americans (e.g., Asian Americans are perpetual foreigners; Parks & Yoo, 2016). European Americans who believe in unrestricted mobility may resent Asian Americans because they are competing for resources. Moreover, color-blind racial attitudes (e.g., racism is a problem of the past) mediated (see Chapter 3) the association between unrestricted mobility and negative attitudes. In other words, European Americans who believed that Asian Americans have unrestricted mobility had color-blind racial attitudes which in turn were associated with negative attitudes toward Asian Americans. Because no ethnic group should come out ahead in a color-blind society, those who have color-blind racial attitudes may resent Asian Americans because they are an ethnic group that is successful. Thus, these seemingly positive beliefs about unrestricted mobility and color-blind racial attitudes do not result in favorable attitudes toward Asian Americans.

If Asian Americans actually have unrestricted mobility, they should have parity with European Americans on economic indicators and social acceptance by European Americans. A review by J. Lee and Kye (2016) suggests otherwise. Asian Americans are paid less than European Americans with similar educational levels. Access to living in European American neighborhoods is still limited, particularly for Vietnamese Americans, but also for Chinese Americans and Asian Indian Americans. Although Asian Americans have high rates of intermarriage with European Americans, rates are lower for those who are unacculturated and for men. Relative to their percentage of the population in the United States, Asian Americans are underrepresented among registered voters and among those who actually vote. This may be because political campaigns usually do not target Asian Americans. All these differences suggest that Asian Americans have not achieved economic parity with, or full social acceptance of, European Americans.

The intent of the model minority myth is not to create parity between Asian Americans and European Americans (Poon et al., 2016). European Americans still view Asian Americans as a minority group in the myth, not as equals, and control the narrative about the myth. Chinese American psychologist Alice Chang has contended that Asian Americans are treated as a "minority of convenience." It is convenient to include Asian Americans as a minority group in statistics concerning recruitment, retention, and graduation for educational institutions. It is also convenient for businesses and communities to tout their diversity by including Asian Americans. However, it is inconvenient to include Asian Americans as minorities when it comes to funding for ethnic minority programs or affirmative action efforts to increase ethnic minority representation. It is also inconvenient for Asian Americans to be regarded as ethnic minorities when they are perceived by other groups as competing for educational, employment, or other opportunities.

Rather than being pawns in someone else's political game, Asian Pacific Americans need to determine their own destiny. This will require Asian Americans to move into positions of leadership and power where they can influence policy (G. Hall & Yee, 2012). The creation of opportunities for leadership will require the cooperation of those already in power and the initiative of Asian Pacific Americans.

Summary

The model minority myth of Asian American success has driven a wedge between Asian Americans and other groups of color. Because of immigration circumstances, not all Asian Americans are equally successful. Some Asian Americans have internalized the achievement orientation and unrestricted mobility aspects of the model minority myth. European Americans' beliefs in unrestricted mobility for Asian Americans are associated with color-blind attitudes, which in turn are associated with unfavorable attitudes toward Asian Americans. Asian Americans have not achieved parity with, and social acceptance of, European Americans that would be expected if they actually did have unrestricted mobility. Instead of being a model minority, Asian Americans have been characterized as a minority of convenience.

CONCLUSION

Large scale Asian Pacific American immigration to the United States occurred more recently than it did for the other groups discussed in this book. Various laws have controlled the number and type of Asian Pacific Americans allowed into the United States. Despite notable accomplishments, Asian Pacific Americans have not been fully accepted into mainstream United States society. Both Asian Pacific American men and women have been stereotyped as feminine. This stereotyping has not been advantageous for either group. Both groups have also been stereotyped as a model minority, which also has not been beneficial, despite the stereotype's seemingly positive connotations. It is necessary for Asian Pacific Americans to be in positions of leadership and power for these stereotypes to dissolve.

RESOURCES

Blogs:
Only Penguins Look Alike: Internment Camps are Still a Bad Idea www.psychology today.com/blog/life-in-the-intersection/201611/only-penguins-look-alike.
Life as a Banana: Asian American Identity www.psychologytoday.com/blog/life-in-the-intersection/201704/life-banana.

Videos:

A Conversation with Asian Americans on Race www.nytimes.com/2016/04/05/opinion/a-conversation-with-asians-on-race.html?_r=1.

If Asians Said the Stuff White People Say www.youtube.com/watch?v=PMJI1Dw83Hc.

What Kind of Asian Are You? www.google.com/search?q=what+kind+of+asian+are+you%3F&ie=utf-8&oe=utf-8.

CHAPTER 10
Latinx Americans

Eduardo is a freshman at a Hispanic-serving college in Texas. His parents were born in Puerto Rico. Although some of his male Latino American classmates are stereotypically masculine, Eduardo's parents have taught him to care about others and to be respectful, consistent with Puerto Rican culture. He is more popular among his Latina American women classmates than his stereo-typically masculine friends are. Eduardo feels that his many family obligations of providing income for the family and caring for his two younger siblings are interfering with his education. His desire to become independent from his family has been a source of conflict between him and his parents.

Carla is a sophomore at a public university in California. Her parents were born in Mexico and came to California before she was born for better employment opportunities. She is the oldest of four children, has always had childcare responsibilities, and is seen as a source of strength for her family.

Picture 10.1
Source: shutterstock.

Although neither of her parents attended college, they want her to complete her degree. Unlike many of her non-Latinx friends in college, she maintains close relationships with her family and relies on them for support and advice. Although she is close to her family, she has not revealed to them that she is in a same-sex relationship.

What is the appropriate term to refer to the largest group of color in the U.S.? The search for a term for ethnic self-designation empowers ethnic groups and involves a rejection of colonization (Comas-Díaz, 2001). The terms "Hispanic" and "Latino" are political terms used within a U.S. context (Bernal & Enchautegui-de-Jesús, 1994). Hispanic is an English term and refers to persons having Spanish ancestry, including Puerto Rico, Cuba, Central and South America, and Spain. The federal government began to use the term Hispanic in the 1970s for census and federal program purposes (Bernal & Enchautegui-de-Jesús, 1994).

"Latinx" refers to Latin American origins. The term Latino is masculine while Latina is feminine. Latinx is used to include males and females. Those who prefer the term Latino or Latina may disidentify with Spain and the term Hispanic because of the associations of the latter with colonization (Comas-Díaz, 2001). Some Mexican Americans prefer the term Chicano/a. Chicano/as view themselves as outsiders to both mainstream United States and Mexican cultures (Falicov, 1998). Those Latinx Americans who have a panethnic Latinx American identity tend to be female, more educated, born in the U.S., involved in politics, and to perceive discrimination (Masuoka, 2006). Because of Spanish influences, many Latinx Americans speak Spanish. About 55% of Latinx Americans are Roman Catholics, although the number of practicing Latinx American Catholics may be decreasing, with 24% considering themselves to be former Catholics (Pew Research Center, 2015).

Latinx Americans can be from any racial group. There are large groups of Latinxs having African ancestry, as well as large groups having European ancestry. Many Latinxs are racially mixed. Those having Spanish and Indian ancestry are known as *mestizos*. Those with Spanish and African ancestry are known as *mulattos*. Skin color has created a social hierarchy among Latinx Americans (see Box 10.1).

Race may be a problematic concept for many Latinx Americans, as two-thirds of a national sample of Latinx American adolescents chose No Race or Other rather than White, Black, Asian, or Native American to describe themselves (Kao & Vaquera, 2006). Ethnicity may be a more useful basis of identity, as Cuban Americans, Mexican Americans, and Puerto Rican Americans identify more with their particular Latinx American ethnic group than with Latinx Americans as a whole (Huddy & Virtanen, 1995). Moreover, Latinx American adolescents tend to form close friendships on the basis of ethnicity (i.e., Mexican, Chicano, Puerto Rican, Cuban, Central or South American, other Hispanic; Kao & Vaquera, 2006).

Latinx Americans are 17.6% of the United States population at 56 million persons and constitute the largest non-White group in the country (U.S. Bureau of the Census, 2016, October). Immigrants are the minority of Latinx Americans, as nearly two-thirds of Latinx Americans were born in the United States. Since 2000, Latinx Americans have been the fastest growing ethnic minority in the United States. People of Mexican origin are the largest group of Latinx Americans, representing 63% of the nation's total Latinx American population. Percentages of other Latinx groups are presented in Figure 10.1. California's Latinx American population is 15.2 million, which is the largest of any state.

BOX 10.1 COLORISM

Colorism is discrimination within Latinx groups based on skin color (Chavez-Dueñas, Adames, & Organista, 2014). During Spanish colonization, Latin America was stratified based on skin color. A person's placement in the hierarchy determined their power and privilege, including access to education and social class. Spaniards placed themselves at the top and people of African descent at the bottom. The hierarchy from top to bottom was:

- Spaniards – phenotypically White individuals born in Spain
- Criollos – offspring of the Spaniards born in the Americas
- Mestizos – people of mixed European and indigenous ancestries
- Mulatos – people of mixed European and African ancestries
- Zambos – people of mixed indigenous and African ancestries
- Indigenous – phenotypically of indigenous descent
- Africans – phenotypically of African descent

The impact of this colonial social stratification persists. In the United States, people with European ancestry remain at the top of the social hierarchy and non-Whites are at the bottom. Currently, darker-skinned Latinx Americans have been found to complete less education, have lower income, experience greater discrimination, and have more mental health problems than lighter-skinned Latinx Americans. Colorism also exists within African American communities (Breland-Noble, 2013).

Discussion

1   What are some current examples of people of color benefitting from lighter skin color?
2   Can privilege associated with Whiteness be dismantled?

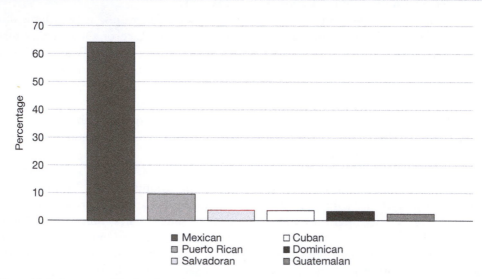

Figure 10.1 Ancestry of Latinx Americans.

Source: U.S. Bureau of the Census, 2016, October.

HISTORY

Highly developed cultures, with achievements in agriculture, textiles, and medical practices, existed in the regions that are now Central and South America long before the
Spanish arrived there (Comas-Díaz, Lykes, & Alarcón, 1998). The Mayan, Incan, and
Aztec empires were part of these cultures. Much of Central and South America was conquered by the Spanish in the late fifteenth and early sixteenth centuries. The Spanish also
conquered the indigenous peoples of what are now New Mexico, Texas, and California
in the 1500s. In the view of Spaniards, indigenous people in the Americas were viewed
as "heathens" who needed to be civilized (Chavez-Dueñas et al., 2014). By the early
1800s, Spaniards were about one-fourth of the population of the Americas.

Mexican Americans

Spanish missions were established throughout what is now California beginning in 1769.
Mexican settlers, most of whom were poor, came to live and work at these missions. By
1821 there were 3000 Mexicans in California (Takaki, 1993). European American settlers were initially welcomed by the Mexicans, although tensions developed between the
groups. The Mexicans were viewed by the European Americans as idle and thriftless,
while the Mexicans viewed the European Americans as having a sense of entitlement to
the land (Takaki, 1993).

Mexico became independent from Spain in 1821 and began to encourage immigration (Spickard, 2007). By 1836, the majority of the people in the region of Mexico that
is now Texas were European Americans. European Americans in Texas battled the
Mexican army and proclaimed independence after capturing Mexican President Santa
Ana. The Texas Republic applied for admission to the United States as a state, but was
initially denied because of the practice of slavery (Spickard, 2007).

The Mexican–American War, led by European American Texans, began in 1846 to
gain the Southwest for the United States. Robbery, murder, and rape of Mexicans were
common during the war (Takaki, 1993). In 1848, the Treaty of Guadalupe Hidalgo
ceded Texas, California, New Mexico, Nevada, parts of Colorado, Arizona, and Utah to
the United States. Mexico lost 45% of its national territory and over 100,000 of its people
(Bernal & Enchautegui-de-Jesús, 1994). The treaty promised citizenship, freedom of
religion and language, and maintenance of lands (Garcia-Preto, 1996a). However, similar
to the many treaties between the United States government and American Indians,
Mexicans in the United States were oppressed by these supposed agreements. The
English language, United States laws and courts, and United States food and dress were
imposed on these Mexicans, and lynching of Mexicans occurred (Spickard, 2007).
Mexican landowners lost their land when it was decided by the United States government in 1851 that land grants under former Spanish and Mexican rule were no longer
valid (Takaki, 1993). Those who did not lose their land by legal rulings often lost it
because of an inability to pay high taxes.

The gold rush in 1849 resulted in a huge influx of European Americans to California.
Before 1849, Mexicans outnumbered European Americans by 10 to 1 in California
(Takaki, 1993). This situation was reversed in 1849, by which time there were 100,000
European Americans and 13,000 Mexicans in California. Although European Americans

learned gold mining methods from Mexicans, foreign miners' taxes were imposed on Mexican miners, including United States citizens of Mexican ancestry. The tax was intended for anyone who was not White, as it was not levied against Europeans who were not United States citizens (Spickard, 2007).

Many Mexicans migrated to the United States during the early 1900s for better opportunities. The available work planting cotton, on railroads, and in mining was menial and often dangerous. Mexicans were a cheap source of labor, as they were paid less than European Americans for the same work (Takaki, 1993). Many Mexicans were migrant laborers, performing strenuous work alongside their families, including small children, and living in shacks or tents with no plumbing or running water (Spickard, 2007).

Mexican laborers organized strikes in California in the early 1900s. In 1903, Japanese and Mexicans formed the Japanese-Mexican Labor Association, which successfully orchestrated a strike in Oxnard, California that forced a pay raise. This labor association attempted to join American Federation of Labor (AFL), but decided not to when the AFL would not accept Japanese members (Takaki, 1993). Anti-Asian immigration laws later caused European American farmers to rely on Mexican labor.

Mexicans in California faced segregated public buildings and their children were educated in segregated schools (Takaki, 1993). European American teachers taught Mexican children to be obedient so that they could eventually replace their parents as workers. Mexican children were taught domestic skills and manual labor skills in school.

Mexicans began to be perceived as a source of competition for jobs during the Depression in the 1930s. Approximately 300,000 Mexicans were "repatriated" – deported on trains and dropped off at the Mexican border during the early 1930s (Bernal & Enchautegui-de-Jesús, 1994). Many were children who were born in the United States, which made them American citizens. However, the rights of American citizenship have been suspended for ethnic minority groups during other times of perceived national emergency, such as when over 120,000 Japanese Americans were later incarcerated during World War II (see Chapter 9).

During World War II, a farm labor shortage in the United States occurred because of involvement in the war effort (Bernal & Enchautegui-de-Jesús, 1994). The United States and Mexico issued Mexicans temporary permits to work in the United States. These temporary workers were known as *braceros*, who worked 10-hour days with few breaks, lived in tents or shacks, and had no medical care (Spickard, 2007). Over 5 million *braceros* came to the United States between 1942 and 1964. Mexican immigrants during and following World War II were primarily from rural areas (Bernal & Enchautegui-de-Jesús, 1994).

In 1962, Cesar Chavez, Dolores Huerta, and other Mexican American farmworkers organized the National Farm Workers Association in the San Joaquin Valley of California (Spickard, 2007). They began a strike against grape growers in 1965, which became a national boycott of table grapes. The strike ended in 1970 when better pay and working conditions were negotiated for the farmworkers. In 1966, the National Farm Workers merged with a Filipino union and the combined groups eventually became the United Farm Workers of America in 1973. Strikes and boycotts were organized against lettuce and other crops. Chavez adhered to a strict ethic of nonviolence in these strikes (Spickard, 2007).

"Chicano Power" was proclaimed in 1968 by 10,000 students who walked out of classrooms in East Los Angeles in protest over poor educational conditions (Spickard,

2007). This movement was modeled after the antiwar, civil rights, and Black Power movements. These students were also angry about the Vietnam War, in which a disproportionately high number of Mexican Americans served and died.

Latinx American psychologists began to unite in the late 1960s as well. Edward Casavantes founded the Association of Psychologists por la Raza in 1969 (Padilla & Olmedo, 2009). Later in 1980, the National Hispanic Psychological Association was established, which is now known as the National Latino Psychological Association.

Mexican Americans and other Latinx Americans suffered in the 1980s during the Reagan administration. In 1984, 42% of all Latinx American children lived below the poverty line as did 25% of all Latinx American families (Zinn, 2003). The Immigration Reform and Control Act of 1986 punished employers for hiring undocumented immigrants (Spickard, 2007). However, employers of seasonal agricultural workers were not punished under this act. Moreover, this act provided amnesty for 3 million undocumented immigrants in the United States and allowed a path to citizenship. In California, Mexican American farmworkers were experiencing abnormal rates of cancer, likely caused by exposure to pesticides on the farms (Zinn, 2003). Cesar Chavez fasted for 35 days in 1988 to protest these conditions.

In 1994, the United States began to invest in the United States/Mexico border region following the North American Free Trade Agreement (NAFTA). This agreement caused many Mexicans to leave farming and seek jobs in the northern border region of Mexico and the United States because the reduced agricultural tariffs on United States crops, such as corn and wheat, drove the Mexican farmers out of business (J. Gonzalez, 2000). Mayan peasants in the Chiapas region of Mexico protested NAFTA in the Zapatista revolt. Mexican workers often took construction, crop picking, restaurant, and domestic work in the United States that paid too little for other workers or was too unhealthy, monotonous, or dangerous. Also in 1994, the Clinton administration began Operation Gatekeeper, which involved building steel walls topped by barbed wire at the San Diego-Tijuana, El Paso-Ciudad Juarez, and Brownsville-Matamoros borders, to keep Mexicans out of the United States (Spickard, 2007). Ironically, President Clinton's wife, Hillary Clinton, was a presidential candidate in 2016 running against Donald Trump, who promised to build a wall along the United States–Mexico border.

Mexicans who wished to find temporary work in the United States began to rely on *coyotes*, who smuggled them into the United States via desert routes (Hernandez, 1996; Spickard, 2007). The trips lasted weeks or months, and the refugees were often taken advantage of by these guides. Many refugees were ultimately captured by immigration officers and deported.

Puerto Rican Americans

Puerto Rico was colonized by Spain in 1493. Its native Taino Indian inhabitants were enslaved and killed (Comas-Díaz et al., 1998). Taino emphases on tranquility, kinship, and group dependence continue to persist in current Puerto Rican culture (Garcia-Preto, 1996b). These are characteristics that Eduardo's parents tried to instill in him, described at the beginning of the chapter. Spanish influences included language, the Roman Catholic religion, and patriarchy (Garcia-Preto, 1996b). The Spanish brought African slaves, who also contributed language, religion, and medicine (Garcia-Preto, 1996b). During the Spanish American War in 1898, Puerto Rico, Cuba, Guam, and the Philippines were invaded by the United States (Bernal & Enchautegui-de-Jesús, 1994). Puerto Rico has remained a colony of the United States since then. English was mandated as the official language of instruction in Puerto Rican public schools, although few Puerto Ricans, including teachers, spoke English (Garcia-Preto, 1996b). Congress allowed Puerto Ricans to become United States citizens in 1917. Nevertheless, many Americans do not regard Puerto Ricans as citizens.

Large numbers of Puerto Ricans immigrated to the northeastern United States in the 1940s and 1950s for economic reasons. Puerto Ricans often took menial, low-paying jobs that no one else wanted (Inclán & Herron, 1998). Available employment often involved domestic labor (e.g., housecleaning), which women were more willing to accept. Thus, female immigrants became more employable than male immigrants, which resulted in a power shift and gender conflicts in many families (Hernandez, 1996). Puerto Rico became a commonwealth in 1952 and Spanish was reinstituted as the language of instruction in public schools (Garcia-Preto, 1996b). Nevertheless, Puerto Rico still often functions as a colony of the United States (Comas-Díaz et al., 1998).

Cuban Americans

Cuba gained its independence from the United States in 1902, but continued to trade with the United States until the revolution in 1959. The revolutionary government created social, economic, and political changes in Cuba, as well as an economic embargo by the United States (Bernal & Enchautegui-de-Jesús, 1994). Political reasons were the motivation for initial waves of Cuban immigrants to the United States between 1959 and 1965. These initial immigrants were predominantly White and upper and middle class (Bernal & Enchautegui-de-Jesús, 1994). They also received over $1 billion in financial assistance from the United States government (Spickard, 2007).

The second wave from 1965 to 1973 included middle class, lower middle class, and working class persons, who were allowed to leave to be united with relatives in the United States. The third wave began in 1980 when Fidel Castro allowed anyone who wanted to leave Cuba to do so via boatlifts at the port of Mariel. This third migration wave included a broader spectrum of persons in terms of race, education, gender, and socioeconomic status (Bernal & Enchautegui-de-Jesús, 1994). This third wave also included a greater percentage (30%) of Afro-Cubans than the earlier waves (Bernal & Shapiro, 1996).

The higher socioeconomic status of the first two waves of Cuban immigrants in combination with federal resources that have not been available for other Latinx groups has placed Cuban Americans in relatively better standing than other Latinx groups. Indeed, most Cuban Americans, Mexican Americans, and Puerto Rican Americans perceive Cuban Americans as having the highest status among these Latinx American groups (Huddy & Virtanen, 1995). Cuban Americans also have the strongest ethnic identity of Latinx American groups, although most Latinx Americans are strongly ethnically identified (Guarnaccia et al., 2007). Cuban Americans have been considered by some to be a "model minority," but the same stereotypes and disadvantages of being a model minority for Asian Americans that were discussed in Chapter 9 apply to Cuban Americans.

A fourth wave of Cuban immigration to the United States occurred in the 1990s (Bernal & Shapiro, 1996). Economic hardships became severe at the end of the Soviet Union, which had been sending aid to Cuba, combined with the United States economic blockade. In 1994, thousands of *balseros* (rafters) attempted to elude coastal police and come to Florida on makeshift rafts. The Cuban government again allowed persons to leave Cuba. The United States and Cuba entered an agreement to allow 20,000 Cubans to legally emigrate each year.

Diplomatic relations between the United States and Cuba were restored in 2015. This involved lifting the economic blockade and allowing civilian travel between the countries.

Other Latin Americans

Several waves of immigration to the United States from Latin America have occurred for economic and political reasons. Argentineans and Chileans left their countries for the United States in the 1960s and 1970s because of repressive regimes. Poor economic conditions caused Mexicans from urban areas to come to the United States during the 1970s and 1980s. Political conflicts in Nicaragua, El Salvador, Peru, and Guatemala in the 1980s caused many persons in these countries to leave for the United States. Conflicts have resulted from historic tensions between indigenous peoples and those with Spanish ancestry who have controlled the government. Maoist and Marxist groups have also engaged in guerilla warfare. Many women joined these guerilla efforts and participated in changing national politics, which constituted a shift in gender roles (Hernandez, 1996).

In an effort to oppose communist influence, the United States backed the governments of some Central American countries (Hernandez, 1996). Thousands of civilians, including children and youth, have been murdered and indigenous cultures have been destroyed in conflicts involving the United States (Comas-Díaz et al., 1998). Nicaraguans were welcomed in the United States as political refugees of the Sandinistas, who the United States opposed, whereas Salvadorans and Guatemalans were viewed as emigrating for economic reasons and were often deported (Bernal & Enchautegui-de-Jesús, 1994). Beginning in 1982, the Sanctuary movement, led by more than 200 United States churches, provided refuge for Central American refugees (J. Gonzalez, 2000).

In addition to these political and economic motivations for emigration, Latin American countries have been susceptible to the effects of natural disasters, including floods and earthquakes, which has been an additional motivation for immigration to the United States (Hough, Canino, Abueg, & Gusman, 1996). However, the United States has often not been hospitable to these refugees. In 1994, Proposition 187 in California denied public services to undocumented immigrants and compelled employers to report undocumented immigrants to immigration officials (Falicov, 1996; Spickard, 2007). Latinx Americans living in ethnic enclaves are particularly susceptible to investigations and deportation by immigration officials. The 1996 Personal Responsibility and Work Opportunity Act went further than Proposition 187 in that even legal immigrants were not eligible for Supplemental Security Income or food stamps until they became citizens (Spickard, 2007). Federal government efforts to deport undocumented immigrants increased under the Trump administration, although many local communities and police forces have refused to comply with these efforts.

GENDER ROLES

Latino American Males

Latino American masculinity is complex and includes both positive and negative aspects (Ojeda & Organista, 2016). One research focus has been on *machismo*, which involves hypermasculine traits, including aggression, dominance, and chauvinism. It also includes beliefs that women should be in traditional roles and encourages male dominance over women (Nuñez et al., 2016). Younger, less educated, and less acculturated men tend to endorse *machismo*. Although there is variability across Latinx American men and women, there were not significant differences on a measure of *machismo* among Central Americans, Cuban Americans, Dominican Americans, Mexican Americans, Puerto Rican Americans, or South Americans living in New York, Chicago, Miami, and San Diego (Nuñez et al., 2016). Thus, *machismo* is a common characteristic across Latinx American groups. However, the concept of *machismo* is present in many cultures and is not restricted to Latinxs (Casas, Wagenheim, Banchero, & Mendoza-Romero, 1994).

As discussed in Chapters 8 and 9, traditionally masculine characteristics are associated with mental health problems (Y. Wong et al., 2017). Similar to the research on traditionally masculine characteristics, there is evidence that negative aspects of *machismo*, including dominance, sexism, and emotional restrictiveness, are associated with mental health problems. In a multiethnic sample of over 2000 Latino American men, these negative aspects of *machismo* were associated with anxiety and cynical hostility, which involves hostility toward and mistrust of others (Nuñez et al., 2016). Also, similar to the research on traditionally masculine characteristics, *machismo* in a community sample of Latino Americans was associated with a lower likelihood of seeking help for mental health problems (J. Davis & Liang, 2015).

Picture 10.2

Source: shutterstock.

It might be possible that gay Latino American men, who create alternative identities to stereotyped heterosexual masculinity, may be less susceptible to the effects of *machismo*. However, *machismo* also has deleterious effects among gay Latino American men. In a study of 152 gay Mexican American men, *machismo* was associated with internalized homophobia (e.g., "I am ashamed of my homosexuality," "I believe it is morally wrong for men to be attracted to each other"; Estrada, Rigali-Oiler, Arciniega, & Tracey, 2011). Moreover, in a study of Latinx American undergraduates in Texas, *machismo* was associated with negative attitudes toward gay men (Hirai, Winkel, & Popan, 2014).

Machismo may exacerbate other psychological disorders. As discussed in Chapter 7, Latinx Americans are at greater risk than European Americans for the onset of post-traumatic stress disorder (PTSD) following a traumatic event (Alcantara, Casement, & Lewis-Fernandez, 2013). In a study of Latino American male veterans, the restricted emotionality aspects of *machismo* were associated with PTSD (Herrera, Owens, & Mallinckrodt, 2013). Thus, adherence to *machismo* may partially explain why Latinx Americans are at particular risk for PTSD.

An alternative form of Latinx masculinity is known as *caballerismo*, which includes nurturance, being chivalrous, honor, bravery, social responsibility, and emotional connectedness (Ojeda & Organista, 2016). The term originates in the Spanish word *caballero*, for horseman. A caballero is a Spanish gentleman with proper and respectful manners, living by a code of chivalry (Arciniega, Anderson, Tovar-Blank, & Tracey, 2008). *Machismo* and *caballerismo* are not mutually exclusive, and Latino American men may have both characteristics to varying degrees. Figure 10.2 shows that both heterosexual and gay Mexican American men endorse *caballerismo* to a greater degree than *machismo* on seven-point Likert scales (Arciniega et al., 2008; Estrada et al., 2011). Thus, contrary to stereotypes, Mexican American men are better characterized as nurturing and respectful than as dominant and sexist (Estrada et al., 2011). Eduardo, described at the beginning of the chapter, was socialized by his parents to have *caballerismo* characteristics.

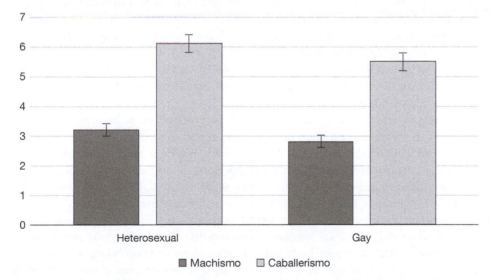

Figure 10.2 Heterosexual and Gay Mexican American Men's Endorsement of *Machismo* and *Caballerismo*.

Source: Arciniega et al., 2008; Estrada et al., 2011.

In a study of Mexican American men, *caballerismo* was associated with affiliation with others, emotional connectedness to others, and satisfaction with life (Arciniega et al., 2008). In contrast, *machismo* was associated with fighting and arrests. *Caballerismo* and *machismo* also had opposite effects with respect to alexithymia (i.e., unawareness of feelings) and practical problem-solving. *Caballerismo* was associated with awareness of feelings (i.e., negatively associated with alexithymia) and practical problem-solving. On the other hand, *machismo* was associated with being unaware of feelings and impulsivity. *Caballerismo* also was found to be associated with positive academic attitudes (i.e., satisfaction, motivation, low skepticism), which were in turn associated with higher academic aspirations among adolescent Mexican American males in Texas (Piña-Watson, Lorenzo-Blanco, Dornhecker, Martinez, & Nagoshi, 2016).

Recent research suggests that *caballerismo* and *machismo* are not mutually exclusive. In a study of Mexican day laborers in Texas, men who adhered to *machismo* but not to *caballerismo* had low self-esteem (Ojeda & Piña-Watson, 2014). However, self-esteem was high for men who adhered to *both machismo* and *caballerismo* rather than one or the other (Ojeda & Piña-Watson, 2014). *Machismo* may be necessary for Latino Americans' self-preservation against barriers such as discrimination (Ojeda & Organista, 2016). The benefits of adherence to both *machismo* and *caballerismo* may be analogous to the benefits of being bicultural, as discussed in Chapter 2 (LaFromboise et al., 1993). However, self-esteem was also high for Mexican day laborers who did not adhere to either *machismo* or *caballerismo* (Ojeda & Piña-Watson, 2014). These men may not feel obligated to conform to male gender role norms, which may enhance their self-esteem.

Because emotional connectedness with others is a component of *caballerismo*, it might be expected that *caballerismo* would be a protective factor against psychological problems. For these reasons, Herrera and colleagues (2013) hypothesized that *caballerismo* would be associated with lower levels of PTSD in the study of Latino American veterans described above. However, *caballerismo* was not significantly correlated with PTSD. Similarly, *caballerismo* was not significantly correlated with internalized homophobia in a study of gay Mexican American men (Estrada et al., 2011).

The chivalry, honor, and bravery aspects of *caballerismo* are not always adaptive. In the multi-city study of 2000 Latino American men described above, *caballerismo* was associated with a greater tendency to experience anger when provoked (Nuñez et al., 2016). Provocation may threaten honor and some Latino American men may become angry in an effort to defend honor.

The effects of *machismo* and *caballerismo* might be pronounced in heterosexual relationships. Men's and women's consistent or conflicting expectations of gender roles might affect relationship satisfaction. In a study of 112 Mexican American married couples, negative *machismo* (e.g., control of emotions, risk-taking, personal honor) and positive *machismo* (e.g., honor, assertiveness, responsibility, reputation) were assessed (Pardo, Weisfeld, Hill, & Slatcher, 2013). Positive *machismo* included elements of *caballerismo*. Husbands' and wives' endorsement of positive *machismo* was similar but husbands endorsed negative *machismo* more than wives did. The total *machismo* score (positive + negative) was associated with greater marital satisfaction among husbands in low acculturated couples but not among high acculturated couples. This may be because low acculturated couples adhere to traditional gender roles. However, adherence to *machismo* was not associated with marital satisfaction among wives in low acculturated couples. Thus, traditional gender roles may be more satisfying for Latinx American men than women in low acculturated couples.

Machismo and marital satisfaction for wives and husbands also differed among high acculturated couples (Pardo et al., 2013). Wives' endorsement of positive *machismo* was associated with greater marital satisfaction. In contrast, positive *machismo* was not associated with husbands' greater marital satisfaction. Taking the acculturation findings together, it appears that aspects of *machismo* are important to low acculturated men and high acculturated women. As Latino American men become more acculturated, *machismo* becomes less important. As Latina American women become more acculturated, positive *machismo*, or men being "gentlemen," becomes more important. Eduardo, described at the beginning of the chapter, was more popular with his Latina peers than his stereotypically masculine Latino peers because of his positive *machismo* characteristics.

Supporting one's family is also part of the Latino masculine role. Latino American men may express *familismo*, which involves prioritizing one's family, by providing for and protecting their family of origin in addition to their own family (Ojeda & Organista, 2016). Many Latino men immigrated to the United States to find work opportunities to support their families who remained in their country of origin (Ramirez, 2011). *Familismo* will be discussed in more detail later in the chapter.

Summary

Positive and negative aspects of Latino American masculinity have been identified. *Machismo* consists of dominance and sexism whereas *caballerismo* consists of nurturance and respect. *Machismo* is generally associated with adjustment difficulties, whereas the evidence on *caballerismo* is mixed, although there are associations with prosocial behavior in several studies. *Machismo* is associated with marital satisfaction among low acculturated husbands whereas elements of *caballerismo* are associated with marital satisfaction among high acculturated wives. *Familismo* is also part of Latino American masculinity.

Latina American Females

Similar to Latino masculinity, Latina femininity is complex and often misunderstood. *Marianismo* involves being virtuous and chaste, subordinate to others, self-silencing to maintain harmony, and a family and spiritual source of strength (Piña-Watson et al., 2016). The ideal woman for Roman Catholic Latinx Americans is the Virgin Mary. *Marianismo* is grounded in other Latinx cultural values, including *simpatía*, *respeto*, and *familismo*. *Simpatía* involves preserving social cohesion via agreeableness, modesty, and consideration of others' needs (Ojeda & Organista, 2016). *Respeto* involves respect and deference to those with superior status, such as elders, males, and professionals. *Familismo* involves prioritizing one's family, sometimes at the expense of one's own needs. A more extended discussion of *familismo* occurs later in this chapter.

Marianismo may involve both positive and negative components. Being virtuous and chaste, a family pillar (i.e., source of strength), and a spiritual pillar were associated with positive academic attitudes (i.e., satisfaction, motivation, low skepticism), which in turn were associated with higher educational goals among 524 Mexican American adolescent females in Texas (Piña-Watson et al., 2016). These positive aspects of *marianismo* may reflect sexual decision-making and leadership roles within the family. Carla, described at the beginning of the chapter, was a source of strength for her family. However, being self-silencing and subordinate to others was negatively associated with positive academic attitudes. In other words, being self-silencing and subordinate were negative components of *marianismo* that interfered with school attitudes. These characteristics may be associated with a lack of control and disempowerment.

Marianismo may become more burdensome for Latina Americans as they become adults with greater family responsibilities. In a multiethnic study of over 2000 Latina American women, the effects of *marianismo* were mostly negative (Nuñez et al., 2016). *Marianismo* was associated with depression, anxiety, and anger. The components of *marianismo* that were most consistently associated with these negative emotions were family and spiritual pillar. The responsibility of being a source of strength for the family may create a psychological burden for Latina American women. Also, being subordinate to others and self-silencing to maintain harmony were associated with anxiety and cynical hostility (Nuñez et al., 2016). Interestingly, similar effects of *marianismo* were found for Latino American men (Nuñez et al., 2016). Thus, endorsement of traditional gender roles is generally associated with poorer mental health for both Latina and Latino American adults.

A belief that women should be virtuous and chaste had positive effects for both Latinx American men and women (Nuñez et al., 2016). This belief was associated with lower levels of depression, anxiety, and anger. This may be because having high moral standards is consistent with cultural norms involving sexual behavior. In another study of 11–14-year-old Latina Americans in Texas, primarily of Mexican descent, the belief that women should be virtuous and chaste was significantly associated with low rates of initiation of sexual activities (Sanchez, Whittaker, Hamilton, & Zayas, 2016).

Latinx immigrants might be expected to adhere to gender-stereotyped roles. However, in a study of 120 primarily Mexican immigrant heterosexual couples with young children in North Carolina, three common gender role patterns were identified (Wood, Helms, Supple, & Perlman, 2015). These patterns were based on each member of the couple's masculinity (e.g., ambitious, assertive) and femininity (e.g., compassionate, sensitive). The first pattern involved both members of the couple reporting high levels of both masculinity and femininity. This pattern was known as *Androgynous*. The second pattern was characterized by the opposite – both members of the couple had low levels of both masculinity and femininity. This pattern was termed *Undifferentiated*. The third pattern, which was most common, was characterized by men who reported low levels of both masculinity and femininity and by women who reported high levels of both of these characteristics. This pattern was known as *Mismatched*.

Marital satisfaction (e.g., communication, decision-making, satisfaction with spouse's support of Mexican traditions) for both members of the couples was greater among Androgynous and Mismatched couples than among Undifferentiated couples (Wood et al., 2015). Androgynous and Mismatched couples did not significantly differ from one another in marital satisfaction. Thus, women having feminine characteristics of being attuned to the needs of others is particularly important for marital satisfaction among

Mexican immigrant couples. Femininity is consistent with traditional feminine gender roles in Latinx and other cultures. However, femininity may also have benefits for men. Both men's and women's femininity were associated with greater marital satisfaction. This finding is consistent with the benefits of femininity for men with regard to death from heart disease discussed in Chapter 9 (Hunt et al., 2007). Neither men's nor women's masculinity was significantly associated with marital satisfaction.

Given the emphasis on traditional gender roles among many Latinx Americans, it might be expected that Latina sexual minority women would be less accepted in Latinx American communities and experience more distress. However, the attitudes of Latinx Americans toward lesbians and gay men (e.g., female homosexuality is a threat to many of our basic social institutions, male homosexuality is a perversion) did not differ from those of European Americans or African Americans in a large online sample of adults (Elias, Jaisle, & Morton-Padovano, 2017). Nevertheless, some Latinx Americans may be biased against lesbians. In a study of Latino and Latina American undergraduates in Texas, traditional *machismo* attitudes were associated with negative attitudes toward lesbians (Hirai et al., 2014).

There are similarities and differences between Latina sexual minorities and other sexual minority women. In an online study of lesbian and bisexual women aged 18–25, Latina American women did not differ from European American, Asian American, or African American women on negative lesbian/gay/bisexual identity (e.g., "I keep careful control over who knows about my same-sex romantic relationships," "I would rather be straight if I could," "Admitting to myself that I'm an LGBTQ person has been a very painful process"), involvement in LGB activities (e.g., pride march, clubs, bars), or connectedness to the LGBTQ community (Balsam et al., 2015). Moreover, depression, anxiety, and PTSD did not differ among the ethnic groups. However, women of color were less likely to have disclosed their sexual orientation to family members than European American women. Latina American lesbians and other lesbians of color may not disclose their sexual orientation to their families, in an effort to maintain harmony (Balsam et al., 2015). Carla, described at the beginning of the chapter, did not disclose her same-sex relationship to her family.

Summary

The traditional gender role aspects of *marianismo* have mixed effects on Latina Americans. Being virtuous and chaste has some positive effects in terms of academic attitudes, mental health, and low rates of sexual initiation among adolescents. However, being a family and spiritual pillar, subordinate to others, and self-silencing generally have negative effects for Latina American adults. Latinx immigrants do not necessarily adhere to traditional gender roles. For both men and women, femininity is associated with marital satisfaction. Lesbian and bisexual Latina Americans' sexual identities are no more negative than those of other ethnic groups. However, lesbian and bisexual Latina Americans are less likely to come out to their families, possibly in an effort to maintain family harmony.

Picture 10.3
Source: shutterstock.

FAMILISMO

Family values are common in many cultural groups. *Familismo*, which involves dedi-cation, commitment, and loyalty to family, is a central Latinx cultural value (Marin & Marin, 1991). The Latinx family provides its members with emotional and material support. At the same time, the family's needs may come at the expense of the individ-ual's needs.

Parenting styles in Latinx American families may differ from those in European American families (Domenech Rodríguez, Donovick, & Crowley, 2009). In addition to authoritative and authoritarian parenting, discussed in Chapter 5, permissive and neglect-ful parenting styles have been identified among European Americans. A permissive parent is highly responsive to their children and allows high levels of autonomy and is not demanding. A neglectful parent is disengaged, and is not responsive or demanding, nor do they allow autonomy. However, these four parenting styles did not characterize most Latinx immigrant parents (46 fathers, 49 mothers), most of whom were from Mexico (Domenech Rodríguez et al., 2009). A *protective* parenting style, in which parents were high on warmth, high on demandingness, and low on autonomy granting, characterized 61% of these parents.

Latinx parenting goals for young children are *respeto* and compliance plus family obligations as children become older (Stein et al., 2014). *Respeto* may involve being quiet, obedient, and respectful of elders. Parent–child conflict during adolescence is considered contrary to *familismo*, similar to the way in which parent–child conflict is seen as contrary to the cultural goals of interpersonal harmony and interdependence in other collectivist cultural groups (Lui, 2015; see Chapter 5). The emphasis on independence and assertiveness in mainstream culture in the United States may create parent–child conflicts in Latinx American families (Stein et al., 2014). Eduardo, described at the beginning of the chapter, wanted to become more independent, which caused conflicts with his parents. As discussed in Chapter 5, acculturation gaps between children and parents may contribute to parent–child conflict (Telzer, 2010).

As might be expected, *familismo* is associated with traditional gender role attitudes among Latinx Americans. In a sample of primarily immigrant Latinx American adolescents from Mexico, Central America, South America, and Puerto Rico, *familismo* (e.g., "parents should teach their children that the family always comes first") was associated with traditional gender roles (e.g., "families need to watch over and protect teenage girls more than teenage boys"; Velazquez et al., 2017). Similarly, among primarily United States-born Mexican American college men, *familismo* (e.g., "My family is always there for me in times of need") was associated with traditional masculinity ideology (e.g., "A guy will lose respect if he talks about his problems"; Ojeda, Piña-Watson, & Gonzalez, 2016).

Although *familismo* is associated with traditional gender role attitudes, which are generally associated with adjustment difficulties, as discussed earlier in this chapter, *familismo* has been found to have positive effects. In a study of 80 Latinx American youth aged 11–17 years, most of whose parents were born in Mexico, youths' reports of *familismo* were negatively associated with parents' reports of externalizing behavior (e.g., rule violations, aggression). The *familismo* measure assessed feelings of duty and responsibility to family (e.g., "parents should teach their children that the family always comes first") and a desire to maintain close family relationships (e.g., "children should be taught that it is their duty to care for their parents when their parents get old"; Kapke, Grace, Gerdes, & Lawton, 2017). Children who adhere to *familismo* share their parents' cultural values, which may result in less intergenerational conflict. As discussed in Chapter 5, children in immigrant families may experience adjustment difficulties when an acculturation gap exists between them and their parents (Lui, 2015).

College is a time of increasing independence from their family for many students, but *familismo* is beneficial for Latinx American college students. Unlike her non-Latinx peers, Carla, described at the beginning of the chapter, maintained relationships with her family and relied on them for advice. Among primarily United States-born Latinx American college students with parents from Mexico, Central America, South America, and the Caribbean, *familismo* was negatively associated with stress, depression, and anxiety (Corona et al., 2017). Thus, connections to one's family may be a buffer against the stressors of college for many Latinx American students.

Familismo was also associated with resilience, as indicated by personality characteristics that enhance adaptation and quality of life among 124 Mexican American college students (Morgan Consoli & Llamas, 2013). When these students experienced problems, they looked to their families for support and family input was valued above friends' input. Moreover, *familismo* was more strongly associated with resilience than other Latinx cultural values, including *respeto*, religiosity, and traditional gender roles.

Family obligations, such as working to support the family and caring for family members, might be seen as competing with and even interfering with one's educational goals. Eduardo, described at the beginning of the chapter, certainly thought so. However, for Mexican American men, *familismo* has a role in their intentions to stay in college. College is challenging for students of many ethnic backgrounds, which creates a risk of dropout. In a study of 186 mostly United States-born Mexican American men who were students at a Hispanic-serving college in the Southwest, *familismo* was associated with intentions to stay in college. This association between *familismo* and intentions to stay in college was mediated (see Chapter 3 for definition) by parental encouragement to stay in college. In other words, Mexican American men who were connected to their families with supportive parents were the most likely to intend to stay in college. Carla, described at the beginning of the chapter, had parents who had not attended college but were supportive of her completing college.

On the most widely-used measures of *familismo* (Sabogal, Marin, Otero-Sabogal, Marin, & Perez-Stable, 1987; Steidel & Contreras, 2003), central components of *familismo* include:

- familial obligations (e.g., "One should help economically with the support of younger brothers and sisters")
- family as a source of support (e.g., "When one has problems, one can count on the help of relatives")
- family as a referent (e.g., "Much of what a son or daughter does should be done to please the parents")
- family support (e.g., "A person should live near his or her parents and spend time with them on a regular basis")
- family interconnectedness (e.g., "A person should often do activities with his or her immediate and extended families, e.g., eat meals, play games, go somewhere together, or work on things together")
- family honor (e.g., "A person should feel ashamed if something he or she does dishonors the family name")
- subjugation of self (e.g., "A person should respect his or her older brothers and sisters regardless of their differences in views").

Some of these family characteristics may sound similar to the emphasis on family in Asian American cultural groups discussed in Chapter 9. Indeed, similarities as well as differences in *familismo* were found among 173 Latinx American, 642 Asian American, and 257 European American college students (Campos, Ullman, Aguilera, & Dunkel Schetter, 2014). Of the Latinx Americans, 80% in the study were born in the United States, as were 72% of the Asian Americans. Figure 10.3 shows group comparisons on the different components of *familismo*. Latinx Americans and Asian Americans had higher scores than European Americans on most of the components of *familismo*. However, the pattern of endorsement was similar, with all groups adhering less to family as a referent (e.g., pleasing parents) and family honor (e.g., dishonoring the family with one's actions) than to the other components of *familismo*. Moreover, *familismo* contributed to better mental health for all groups. These findings suggest that family connections are beneficial for college students from multiple ethnic backgrounds. Although independence is typically encouraged during college, seeking family support is adaptive for college students and should be encouraged.

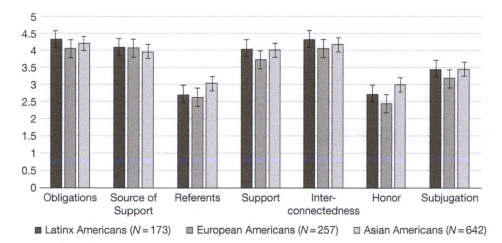

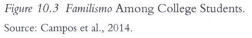

Figure 10.3 Familismo Among College Students.
Source: Campos et al., 2014.

Summary

Familismo is a Latinx cultural value that involves family connections and commitments that differ from those of European American families. Although *familismo* is associated with traditional gender role values, it is also associated with psychological health. Patterns of *familismo* are similar among Latinx American and Asian American college students. However, *familismo* is also beneficial not only for these groups but also for European American college students.

CONCLUSION

Latinx Americans are the largest group of color in the United States. Mexican Americans are the largest group of Latinx Americans but Latinx Americans are diverse. Interactions with, and sometimes colonization by, Spain and the United States characterize the history of most Latinx Americans. *Machismo* and *marianismo* are culturally-prescribed gender roles which include both adaptive and maladaptive aspects. *Familismo* is another Latinx value that has primarily positive effects on psychological adjustment.

RESOURCES

Blog:
Familismo: The Importance of Family for College Students' Mental Health www.psychologytoday.com/blog/life-in-the-intersection/201704/familismo.

Video:
A Conversation with Latinos on Race www.nytimes.com/2016/02/29/opinion/a-conversation-with-latinos-on-race.html.

CHAPTER 11

Native Americans

Elizabeth is a 20-year-old sophomore who grew up in South Dakota and whose family is Cheyenne. She lived near a reservation and spent much time there participating in Native cultural activities. Her grandparents had been in an Indian boarding school and told her awful stories of the abuse they experienced. Both her grandparents and parents want her to go to college to become a doctor. Her family has known of her attraction to other females since she was in high school and is accepting of her. However, she finds many of her classmates at the university to be conservative and not accepting of sexual minorities.

John is a 20-year-old sophomore whose family is Navajo. He grew up in Los Angeles with limited contact to Native culture. John is going to college in New Mexico because he wanted to learn more about the Navajo tribe and its traditions. He is familiar with negative media images of Native Americans, including the focus on alcoholism and suicide. John is seeking a more accurate image in his Native Studies courses and by becoming involved with a reservation. The reservation requires him to document his Native ancestry before they accept him.

The current existence of Native Americans, Alaska Natives, and their cultures is a tribute to their resilience. These groups have survived attempts of outsiders toward extermination, relocation, and destruction of their language, culture, and religion. Native Americans and Alaska Natives could not escape this oppression because it was occurring in their own homeland (Duran, Duran, Brave Heart, & Yellow Horse-Davis, 1998). The oppression that Native groups have experienced in this country has been conceptualized as hate crimes, although Native Americans and Alaska Natives receive limited attention as hate crime victims (Herring, 1999). Yet, Native Americans and Alaska Natives remain vibrant and growing groups in the United States.

Native Americans and Alaska Natives number 6.6 million or 2% of the United States population (U.S. Bureau of the Census, 2016, November). The state with the largest population of Native Americans and Alaska Natives is Alaska, where they constitute

Picture 11.1
Source: shutterstock.

19.5% of the population. Native Americans and Alaska Natives are the most diverse group in this textbook, with 567 federally recognized tribes. A *tribe* is a social organization based on ancestry with its own history, traditions, and culture (Spickard, 2007). The Bureau of Indian Affairs (BIA) defines an Indian as an enrolled or registered member of a federally-recognized Indian tribe or as at least one-fourth Indian or more in blood quantum who can legally demonstrate that to BIA officials (Trimble & Thurman, 2002). As presented as the beginning of the chapter, John had to prove his Native ancestry before a reservation would allow his involvement.

Being a Native American not only involves ancestry but also cultural identity (Herring, 1999). Because many Indian tribes are sovereign nations, many Indians have dual citizenship in their tribal nation and in the United States (Castro, Proescholdbell, Abeita, & Rodriguez, 1999). Moreover, at least 100 tribes are not federally recognized but have members with a strong Indian identity (Trimble & Thurman, 2002). Most tribes have their own languages. Of Native Americans and Alaska Natives, 27% speak a language other than English in their home, which is greater than the 21.5% for the United States as a whole (U.S. Bureau of the Census, 2016, November).

The term "Indian" is a misnomer, coined by Europeans who, when they reached this continent, believed that they had reached India. All the indigenous people living on this continent were referred to by Spanish explorers as "*indios*," despite the diversity among these indigenous groups (Sutton & Broken Nose, 2005). Although the many diverse groups that were on this continent before Europeans arrived did not consider themselves to be part of a single group, the European perception of Indians as a single group persists (Spickard, 2007). The term "Native American" is confusing, insofar as many who are not native who were born in the U.S. consider themselves native Americans. Canada's indigenous peoples refer to themselves as First Nations Peoples.

There are nine major geographic areas in which Indian nations have shared an ecological environment (Hodge & Fredericks, 1999). These areas are the Northeast, Southeast, Southwest, Northern Plains, Northwest Coast, Plateau/Great Basin/Rocky Mountains, Oklahoma, California, and Alaska. Although different tribes have shared the same geographic environment, their cultures and languages are not necessarily shared. The cities having the largest populations of Native Americans are Los Angeles and New York (Sutton & Broken Nose, 2005).

HISTORY

Native American and Alaska Native history did not begin with European contact (Hays, 2006; Page, 2003). Native cultures were highly developed by the time European explorers first reached this continent (Hodge & Fredericks, 1999; Spickard, 2007). Many tribes had sophisticated systems of agriculture, government, and commerce with other tribes. Knowledge in medicine, astronomy, and the arts was also developing. There was more cultural and linguistic diversity on this continent when Columbus arrived than there was in Europe (Duran & Duran, 1999).

Indian tribes treated the environment with respect. Agriculture, hunting, and fishing were primarily for subsistence purposes. The land was not misused or polluted, nor were animals killed other than for food. Native attempts to maintain a balance between the land's resources and their own survival needs were consistent with the spiritual value of harmony within nature (Hodge & Fredericks, 1999). Non-Natives have desecrated the land by polluting the air, water, and soil, creating health hazards for many Natives (Hodge & Fredericks, 1999). Pollution and industrialization have also limited farming and fishing opportunities. For example, Natives cannot hunt buffalo, which were exterminated by settlers.

Displacement by Europeans

Despite the existence of advanced Native cultures, European explorers viewed Natives as savages, dominated by passions, especially sexuality (Takaki, 1993). Native Americans have been treated as part of the natural landscape, similar to antelopes and cougars (Spickard, 2007). When the natural landscape becomes threatening, it can be removed and exterminated. Natives may have viewed the unfamiliar White explorers as gods or at least may have feared them because of their metal weapons (Spickard, 2007). They soon learned that Europeans were out to exploit them, their land, and their possessions.

Within 50 years of Columbus' arrival to the continent, European settlers began to displace Natives in the Southeastern area of the country (Hodge & Fredericks, 1999). These early European settlers can be considered our country's first illegal immigrants (Spickard, 2007). English settlers in Virginia during the early 1600s believed that the Natives, who grew corn, were not using the land properly. Thus, confiscating Native land was not considered robbery (Takaki, 1993). Although the Natives had initially assisted the English settlers, the English attacked Natives in 1608 and destroyed their villages to get food supplies. The European settlers' need for land increased in 1613 when they began exporting tobacco to England. In 1622, the Natives attempted to forcibly drive the settlers out.

Migration from the East to the Plains began in 1650 when European settlements drove Natives west (Hodge & Fredericks, 1999).

The Native population decreased dramatically between 1610 and 1675 because of the introduction of European diseases (e.g., smallpox), to which they were not immune (Spickard, 2007; Takaki, 1993). The Native population in what is now the U.S. is estimated to have dropped from 5 million in 1600 to only 1.3 million in 1800 (Spickard, 2007). Many colonists interpreted Native deaths as divine intervention and confirmation that they should take the land (Takaki, 1993).

Wars were another cause of Native deaths. In 1637, 700 Pequots were killed by colonists, and 6000 Natives died from combat and disease during 1675–1676 in King Philip's War (Takaki, 1993). Violence against Natives was justified by Europeans as driving out the Devil. Sadly, the ethnic group that was once the largest on this continent is now the smallest (McDonald & Gonzalez, 2006).

Another source of health problems that was introduced to Natives by Europeans was alcohol use. Most Natives did not have experience with alcohol prior to European contact (Beauvais, 1998). European colonists produced large amounts of potent, distilled alcoholic beverages and modeled heavy drinking. The stereotype of the drunken Indian was a projection of European colonists' own behavior. Drinking alcohol for European colonists was a means of avoiding contaminated drinking water and fighting illness (Spillane & Smith, 2007). Fur traders and political officials also used alcohol as a currency of trade for Native resources.

BOX 11.1 THE FIREWATER MYTH

The firewater myth is the stereotype that Native Americans are sensitive to the effects of alcohol and vulnerable to alcohol problems because of biological or genetic differences between themselves and other groups (V. Gonzalez & Skewes, 2016). As discussed previously in this chapter, the stereotype of a drunken Indian was a projection of the behavior of European colonists, who had introduced alcohol to Native Americans. The genetic contribution to alcohol problems is no different for Natives than it is for other ethnic groups (Ehlers & Gizer, 2013). In fact, there is some evidence of the protective effects of alcohol metabolizing genes, similar to the patterns among Asian Americans discussed in Chapter 4 (Wall, Carr, & Ehlers, 2003). However, as discussed in Chapter 4, genetic effects on alcohol use may be mediated by environmental factors, such as family history of alcohol problems (Bujarski et al., 2015).

Although there is not a specific biological risk for alcohol abuse among Native Americans, the firewater myth persists and may influence drinking behavior. The Firewater Myth Scale was developed to measure this belief (V. Gonzalez & Skewes, 2016). Sample items include:

- Alaska Natives and American Indians are more likely to have a genetic vulnerability to problems with alcohol.
- Alaska Natives and American Indians metabolize alcohol differently than non-Native people.

- Alaska Natives and American Indians feel the effects of alcohol, or feel intoxicated, more easily than people of European descent.
- Because of biological or genetic differences, it would be best for Alaska Natives and American Indians to never drink or stop drinking completely.
- Drinking even small amounts of alcohol is harmful for many Alaska Natives and American Indians.
- Alaska Natives and American Indians are more likely to be born with a tendency to develop problems with alcohol.

Among 159 Natives at two colleges in Alaska, belief in the firewater myth was associated with drinks consumed per week, frequency of heavy drinking, and drinking problems (V. Gonzalez & Skewes, 2016). Although there is not an actual biological propensity for alcohol problems among Natives, this association between a belief in the firewater myth and drinking behavior and problems may be a self-fulfilling prophecy both for Natives and for non-Natives. The danger in this myth is that, for those who believe it, alcohol abuse may be viewed as biologically-determined and not amenable to change.

Discussion
1   Does the firewater myth still exist?
2   How can stereotypes of Native drinking be reduced among Natives and non-Natives?

Early American History

American statesman and founding father Thomas Jefferson's view of Native culture mirrored that of the early European settlers. In 1776, Jefferson believed that Natives should either be civilized, which meant adopting European methods of farming, or exterminated (Takaki, 1993). "Civilizing" the Natives would limit their needs for hunting lands. Jefferson contended that lands had been fairly and legally purchased from Natives. He blamed Native cultural practices for the decline in numbers of Natives. Ironically, he publicly stated that both Natives and colonists were Americans, born in the same land, and hoped the two could be friends. Such duplicity was not unknown to Jefferson, who publicly opposed slavery but personally owned hundreds of slaves who were never freed.

The United States government, not long after it was established, began a repeated pattern of removing Natives from their lands and marginalizing them from American society. Even the leftover lands that Natives were given were often taken from them. The Northwest Ordinance of 1783 and the 1790 Trade and Intercourse Acts gave Native tribes sovereignty and protection in exchange for their lands (Carson & Hand, 1999). Although sovereignty and protection might appear to be at least somewhat beneficial, the Naturalization Act of 1790 excluded non-White immigrants and American Indians from U.S. citizenship (Takaki, 1993). Native land in the South became valuable for cotton production, and the government forced Natives to sell their land in Alabama, Mississippi, and Louisiana between 1814 and 1824. The Bureau of Indian Affairs was created within the United States War Department in 1824 to oversee relationships with tribes.

Andrew Jackson was elected President of the United States in 1828 in part because he had been a hero in wars against the Natives (Takaki, 1993). Jackson believed that efforts to civilize Natives had failed and that Natives should be removed. In 1830, the Indian Removal Act moved 70,000 Natives west of the Mississippi (Carson & Hand, 1999). Most of the Natives in Oklahoma settled there because they were removed from other areas, primarily the South (Hodge & Fredericks, 1999). In 1829 and following, over 10,000 Cherokee, Choctaw, Chickasaw, Creek, and Seminole Indians were forced to leave their sacred homelands and burial grounds in the South without their belongings, often during winter. Between 4000 and 8000 Natives died in transit (Takaki, 1993). This forced exodus is known as the "Trail of Tears."

Throughout American history, over 600 treaties were made with Native tribes, often by force or with subgroups of Natives who did not represent tribal wishes (Duran et al., 1998; Takaki, 1993). Ancestral tribal lands are considered sacred by Natives (Trujillo, 2000). Thus, the government's removal of Natives from their ancestral tribal lands is analogous to a church being seized by the government and the prohibition of its members from worshipping there. By the mid-nineteenth century, European Americans had developed an ideology, *manifest destiny*, in which seizing the lands of non-Whites on the North American continent was viewed as their God-given right (Spickard, 2007).

Natives in California were also exploited during Spanish colonization during the nineteenth century. Spanish settlers sought to turn these Natives into laborers and to convert them to Christianity. Diseases introduced by Europeans and violence from non-Native settlers and the U.S. military completely exterminated some tribes.

Government Interventions

Banishing Natives to previously uninhabited regions of the nation was not the end of government interference. In order to connect the country for commerce, railroads through Native territories were needed (Takaki, 1993). The Indian Appropriation Act of 1871 stated that "no Native nation or tribe within the territory of the United States shall be acknowledged or recognized as an independent nation, tribe or power with whom the United States may contract by treaty." This Act allowed railroads to be built through the Plains and also allowed buffalo, which were the Plains Natives' sustenance, to be killed by non-Natives.

A major provision of the Indian Appropriation Act was the establishment of Indian reservations. The purpose of these reservations was a temporary support to help Natives make the adjustment to assimilate into U.S. society (Takaki, 1993). Forced marches to reservations from one's homeland were common (Rouse, 2016). United States' policies regarding reservations were arbitrary, sometimes forcing enemy tribes onto the same reservation, such as the Modoc, Klamath, and Paiutes in Southern Oregon (Spickard, 2007). Conditions on the reservations varied, but often involved inadequate food, non-pure water, fuel shortages, disease, abuse by military personnel, and even raids by other tribes. Communal living was forbidden and Native communities were required to take up farming (Rouse, 2016). Christianity was also imposed.

Because Natives were federally mandated to live on reservations, those who refused to be displaced to reservations could be attacked with impunity. For example, the Nez Perce, led by Chief Joseph, attempted to flee to Canada after European Americans discovered gold on their reservation in northeast Oregon and ordered the Nez Perce to a far smaller reservation in Idaho in 1877 (Spickard, 2007). Following many battles that killed tribal leaders, Chief Joseph capitulated to the United States government, which imprisoned the Nez Perce in Kansas. By 1911, 98% of Nez Perce territory was leased by the United States government to non-Natives (Wilkinson, 2005).

Native children were taken from their families and forced to live in boarding schools, often hundreds of miles from their families, beginning in 1879 in Pennsylvania at the Carlisle Indian Industrial School (Brucker & Perry, 1998). The schools were often run by Christian churches or missionaries and in other cases by military personnel who had fought in the Indian Wars (Rouse, 2016). The government withheld food and other economic resources from parents who refused to have their children taken to boarding schools (Warne & Lajimodiere, 2015). Parents whose children were taken to the boarding schools experienced extreme guilt about not being able to prevent their children from being taken. Boarding schools were also established in Canada.

Church attendance was mandatory at boarding schools, and Native traditions and religions were regarded as pagan and uncivilized (LaFromboise, Berman, & Sohi, 1994). The curriculum consisted of general education and vocational training: industrial arts for boys and domestic skills for girls. Teachers at these boarding schools often physically punished children for any displays of traditional culture (Thompson, Hare, Sempier, & Grace, 2008). The motto of the founder of the Carlisle School, Captain Richard Henry Pratt, was "Kill the Indian and save the man" (Spickard, 2007; Wilkinson, 2005). Corporal punishment was foreign to many Natives who entered these schools, as was sexual abuse that occurred (Rouse, 2016). As described at the beginning of the chapter, Elizabeth's grandparents told her of the physical abuse they endured in the boarding schools.

Boarding schools were later established in Alaska for Alaska Native children (Hays, 2006). The schools were underfunded and the teachers were often unqualified (Kaspar, 2014). Students in the boarding schools were not being prepared for higher education. They received mostly religious instructions and vocational training for employment in industrial or manual labor jobs (Kaspar, 2014). This training for subordinate jobs is similar to the training Mexican children received in California from European American teachers during the early twentieth century (see Chapter 10). Most Native boarding school students did not progress beyond the ninth grade. Disease was also rampant at the overcrowded schools (Warne & Lajimodiere, 2015).

Figure 11.1 shows the effects of Canadian boarding schools on Natives' self-perceived health (Kaspar, 2014). The participants in the study were First Nations Canadians aged 15 years or older. Those who attended boarding schools had significantly poorer health than those who did not. A greater percentage of boarding school attendees had poor or fair health and a lower percentage had very good or excellent health. Boarding school attendees had lower socioeconomic status, which restricted their access to health care. Boarding schools have been demonstrated to have intergenerational effects among First Nations People, with the children of those who were in Canadian boarding schools experiencing greater depression than the children of those who did not (Bombay, Matheson, & Anisman, 2013).

Federal policy in the late 1800s outlawed traditional Native religion and spirituality (Trujillo, 2000). It is possible that the removal of these coping mechanisms may have contributed to Natives seeking maladaptive coping mechanisms, such as alcohol abuse (Spillane & Smith, 2007). Christian churches collaborated with the U.S. government to

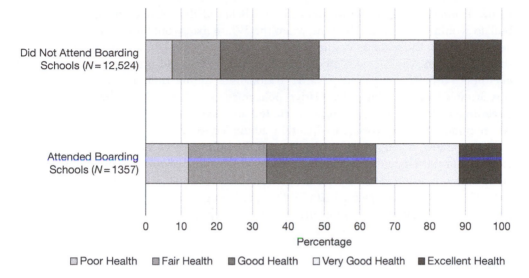

Figure 11.1 Boarding School Attendance and Health in Canada.
Source: Kaspar, 2014.

"civilize" Natives by attempting to convert them to Christianity (Garrett & Pichette, 2000). In 1882, Presbyterian missionary Sheldon Jackson and other Protestant Christian leaders divided Alaska into religious territories in which specific Protestant denominations could work without interference from other groups (Hays, 2006). Catholics already had influence in Alaska. However, neither the Protestants nor the Catholics consulted with Alaska Natives about their plans to spread Christianity in Alaska.

Sixteen years after reservations were established, Congress passed the 1887 Dawes Act, which sought to discontinue reservations and help Natives become property owners and United States citizens (Takaki, 1993). Part of the rationale for making Natives property owners was to convert them to farmers, rather than hunters and gatherers (McDonald & Gonzalez, 2006). Farming was considered to be more "civilized" than hunting and gathering, and involved limited access to the lands that were formerly inhabited by Natives. Those considered by the United States government to be the "Five Civilized Tribes" (Cherokee, Chickasaw, Choctaw, Creek, and Seminole) adopted European American agricultural systems, government, churches, and schools (McDonald & Gonzalez, 2006). However, these tribes learned that European Americans were more interested in their land than in their assimilation into United States society.

The Dawes Act encouraged individual landownership and each Native family was given 160 acres for 25 years. Ironically, 19 years after the Dawes Act, the Burke Act nullified the 25-year trust provision of the Dawes Act. Large areas of land from the reservations were taken from the Natives and sold to non-Natives. "Last arrow" pageants that marked the transition to American citizenship were established (Takaki, 1993). In these pageants, Natives wore a traditional costume and shot an arrow. They then entered a teepee and changed into "civilized" clothing, emerged from the tepee, and were given a plow and an American flag.

Despite the oppression that Natives suffered as non-Natives began to occupy their lands, many were undaunted and maintained their ancestral traditions. In 1890, Wovoka of the Paiutes claimed to be the messiah and believed that Native customs, lands, and buffalo would be restored. The time when the White man would leave Native lands was celebrated with the tradition of ghost dancing (Takaki, 1993). Ghost dancers wore muslin shirts decorated with sacred symbols that they believed would protect them from their enemies. To quell this growing Native nationalism, Sitting Bull, a ghost dance leader, was arrested and then killed by Native policemen who worked for the United States government. Sioux Natives were also arrested and taken to the Wounded Knee camp, where hundreds were massacred when they attempted to escape.

The presence of Europeans in the Natives' homelands forced them into a peripheral existence in the United States. Whereas there were estimated to be 6 million Natives in what is now North America before the arrival of Europeans, this number was reduced to only 250,000 by 1900 (Spickard, 2007). Disease, killing, and poor conditions on reservations were the primary reasons for this population decline.

Civil Rights

Native Americans and Alaska Natives gained some civil rights during the early twentieth century. They became official United States citizens in 1924, although this act alternatively could be viewed as an effort by the United States government to abolish a Native identity separate from other Americans (Spickard, 2007). The 1934 Indian Reorganization Act allowed tribal land acquisition and self-government. Nevertheless, these rights were in many ways empty to people whose presence on this continent predated those who were offering these rights. Also, as with many other government treaties and laws involving Natives, the apparent freedom that these acts provided proved to be temporary. From 1933 through 1945, the federal government reorganized Native groups into councils that adopted Western structures (Hodge & Fredericks, 1999).

Many Natives have felt an obligation to their communities to serve in the United States military as a way of honoring government treaties with tribes (Rouse, 2016). Native code talkers served in the armed forces during World War II using Native languages to transmit messages that could not be decoded by the enemy. Following World War II, Natives returning from military service or from work in factories in the war effort were offered a bus ticket, low-cost housing, and new clothing as incentives to move to urban areas, as part of the Voluntary Relocation Program (Garrett & Pichette, 2000). Beginning in 1946, the government sought to terminate tribes by taking their land, Native status, and services, and by relocating them from reservations to urban areas (Hodge & Fredericks, 1999; Norton & Manson, 1996). Despite their status as natives to North America, being granted citizenship in 1924, and their loyalty demonstrated by their military service, Native Americans did not receive the right to vote in all 50 states until 1948.

The Indian Relocation Act of 1956 was an effort by the United States government to end support for Native Americans by moving them from reservations to urban areas (Rouse, 2016). There were some funds for moving and vocational training. However, many found cities to be unfriendly and returned to reservations.

During the 1960s, a supra-tribal identification began to develop (Nagel, 1995). In 1968, the American Indian Movement (AIM) was founded in Minneapolis by a group of urban Natives (Spickard, 2007). During the same year, the Indian Civil Rights Act that allowed Native self-governance was passed and self-determination became the government's policy toward Natives (Hodge & Fredericks, 1999). In 1969, students from San Francisco State University, with involvement of the AIM, took over Alcatraz Island, a former penitentiary in the San Francisco Bay (Nagel, 1995). According to the 1868 Fort Laramie Treaty between the United States and the Sioux, abandoned federal facilities could be claimed by Natives (Spickard, 2007). The island was reclaimed in the name of all Natives. The purpose of the occupation was to establish cultural and training centers on the island. The protesters were removed from Alcatraz in 1971 by local and federal authorities. Although the cultural and training centers were not established, Alcatraz spawned other Native protests and became a rallying point for Red Power activism during the 1970s.

The 1970s saw the passage of the Alaska Native Claims Settlement Act (1971), the Indian Self-Determination Act (1975), the Indian Child Welfare Act (1978), and the Religious Freedom Act (1978). These acts all provided increased authority and autonomy to Native tribes. The Indian Child Welfare Act limited the removal of Native children from their tribe for purposes of adoption or foster care, whereas such removal was common before this act. The first Native gay and lesbian organization, Gay American Indians, was founded in San Francisco in 1975 (Lang, 2016). In 1976, a lawsuit by an Alaska Native student forced Alaska to support the rights of students to be educated in their home villages rather than in boarding schools (Hays, 2006). Oil revenues in the 1970s allowed the state to build schools in villages that had 15 or more high school-age children (Haycox, 2002). Federal funding for Native tribes declined in the 1980s, but Natives continued to work for control over reservation government and industry.

Native fishing rights created conflict with non-Native fisherman in the Pacific Northwest. During the 1940s and 1950s, dams built on the Columbia and Snake rivers in the Pacific Northwest flooded Native fishing areas, such as Celilo Falls in Oregon, and made Native net fishing impossible (Wilkinson, 2005). Although Natives took just 6% of the overall fishing harvest in the Puget Sound area of Washington state, state officials in the 1960s began to restrict Native fishing because of complaints from non-Native commercial and sport fishermen. This resulted in the court case *United States v. Washington*, in which conservative Judge George H. Boldt ruled in favor of Native fishing rights in 1974.

Conflicts between the AIM and the FBI developed in 1973 at the Pine Ridge reservation in South Dakota. Tribal chairman Richard Wilson asked the FBI for help in removing the AIM from the reservation (Spickard, 2007). The FBI, armed with machine guns, helicopters, and armored vehicles, surrounded the AIM group and engaged in gun battles in which two Natives were killed. The AIM was removed from the reservation after two and a half months. There was continued violent conflict between the FBI and AIM in which several Natives were killed. In 1975, two armed FBI agents entered an AIM encampment and engaged in a battle that killed the agents and one Native. The AIM leader, Leonard Peltier, was incarcerated, and still remains so, for the officers' deaths, although there is inconclusive evidence that he was responsible for the deaths. Human rights organizations consider Peltier to be a political prisoner (Spickard, 2007).

GENDER ROLES

Before European colonization, Native gender roles were largely undifferentiated. Work was shared and there was a balance of power between men and women. A person's role was not based on biological sex but on one's spiritual or interpersonal purpose (e.g., leader, healer; Rouse, 2016). However, Europeans introduced a male/female binary. Native women were forced into passive roles of servitude (Peters, Straits, & Gauthier, 2015). Communal family systems were supplanted by European hierarchical family systems. Gender roles were imposed on Natives.

Native American Males

A prominent stereotype of Native men is the warrior chief (Rouse, 2016). This stereotype developed during European Americans' wars with Natives, described in the first part of this chapter. Portrayals of Natives as heathen, violent savages justified wars against them. The warrior chief stereotype is dehumanizing, as discussed in Chapter 6. This stereotype is expressed in the use of Natives as mascots for sports teams. Natives (e.g., Indians, Chiefs, Braves, Redskins) are placed on a par with other sports team mascots that are animals, such as lions, tigers, and bears. Because Native Americans are a relatively small group and so rarely portrayed in the media (Leavitt, Covarrubias, Perez, & Fryberg, 2015), such mascot portrayals may be the only images of Native American men available to many people. Native Americans may even view themselves through the lens of these stereotyped images.

Proponents of Native mascots contend that the mascots focus on positive characteristics of Native masculinity, including aggressiveness, bravery, and strength (I. Davis, 1993). These are characteristics admired by sports fans. Critics contend that mascots stereotype Natives as "frozen in time," dismissing genocide and colonization, as well as the richness of contemporary Native cultures (Jacobs, 2014; Leavitt et al., 2015). Moreover, stereotypes of Native Americans as aggressive have been used to justify their subjugation.

How do these mascots affect the mental health of Native Americans? Chief Wahoo, a red-faced caricature with a grin and red feather, is the mascot of the Cleveland Indians baseball team. Forty-eight Native American male and female high school students were shown:

- Chief Wahoo
- Pocahontas, which is a popular and stereotypic representation of Native women in a Disney film
- data on high school dropout rates, suicide, alcoholism, and teen pregnancy among Native Americans, or
- control instructions that participation in the study involves completing a series of questionnaires about yourself and your community (Fryberg, Markus, Oyserman, & Stone, 2008).

Then they completed a self-esteem questionnaire. Exposure to Chief Wahoo, Pocahontas, or the negative outcomes for Native Americans was associated with lower self-esteem (the average of 20 items with a five-point scale) than the control instructions (see Figure 11.2). In fact, exposure to the stereotypic visual images depressed self-esteem even more than exposure to the negative outcomes for Native Americans. Thus, stereotypic images of Native Americans have negative effects on Native Americans' mental health.

How do Native mascots affect non-Natives' perceptions of Natives? A direct test of whether Chief Wahoo honors or dishonors Natives was examined among non-Natives (Freng & Willis-Esqueda, 2011). One hundred and nineteen non-Native students at a

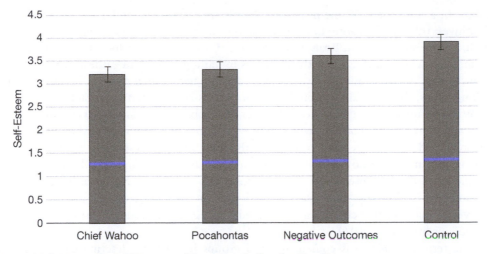

Figure 11.2 Means for Self-Esteem of American Indians by Condition.
Source: Fryberg et al., 2008.

Great Plains university were briefly exposed (17 ms) to the Chief Wahoo mascot, the Pittsburgh Pirates' mascot, or the New York Yankees' logo, and then required to identify words or non-words (i.e., a string of letters) as quickly as possible. The words included positive stereotypes of Natives (generous, noble, faithful, nature, proud, artistic), negative stereotypes of Natives (savages, primitive, dirty, drunk, lazy, suspicious), baseball words (e.g., shortstop, outfield), or control words (e.g., intention, slope). Participants more quickly identified the negative stereotype words after seeing the Chief Wahoo mascot vs. the other mascots. Exposure to any of the three mascots did not influence how quickly participants identified any of the other words, including positive stereotypes. Thus, exposure to a Native mascot activated negative stereotypes of Native masculinity.

A second stereotype of Native men is the mystic shaman (Rouse, 2016). This stereotype has been romanticized as a noble character and is a darling of the New Age movement. The New Age movement incorporates Western, Eastern, and indigenous spiritual traditions with popular psychology. Native communities have criticized this movement as culturally appropriating their spiritual practices (Deloria, 1998). *Cultural appropriation* is the adoption and misuse of another culture's practices. This is similar to European American therapists selecting aspects of Asian mindfulness that focus on the self rather than others for their interventions (G. Hall, Hong et al., 2011; see Chapter 7). Who becomes an actual Native spiritual leader or healer is decided by other Native leaders, the Native community, and the spirits (Rouse, 2016). Outsiders may fail to understand the diversity of Native spirituality and may attribute some element of Native spirituality (e.g., sweat lodge) to all Natives.

As discussed at the beginning of the chapter, Native Americans are the most diverse group discussed in this textbook because there are many Native tribes and each tribe has its own history, traditions, and culture. Gender roles also differ according to tribe. Hunting and fishing would seem to be ways that Native men could contribute to the household. Among Northern Plains tribes, hunting and fishing are traditional ways of living. In contrast, raising sheep and cattle is a traditional way of living in Southwest tribes. In a study of 1638 members of a Northern Plains tribe and 1446 members of a Southwest tribe, participating in activities inconsistent with their traditions was associated with depression (Kaufman, Beals, Croy, Jiang, & Novins, 2013). Men from the Northern Plains tribe who contributed to their families by raising sheep and cattle were depressed, as were men from the Southwest tribe who contributed to their families by hunting and fishing. Thus, the cultural fit of one's activities affects Native men's mental health.

When Spaniards first encountered Natives, they observed men who were doing what they considered to be women's work, who were dressing as the Spanish thought women to dress, and having sex with other men (Rouse, 2016). These men were viewed as having lost masculine power. The Spanish termed these men *berdache*, derived from an Arabic word for male prostitute. This depiction was based on a European heterosexual/homosexual dichotomy that was not relevant in Native cultures (Nanda, 2011). However, many Native communities adopted the negative attitudes of Europeans toward homosexuality (Lang, 2016).

The term *two spirit* was coined by tribal groups in 1990 to describe gender variant people who possess both male and female characteristics (Rouse, 2016). However, this term has also been criticized for its focus on the male/female binary. Moreover, not all LGBTQ Natives identify as two spirit (Lang, 2016). A term more consistent with a Native worldview is genderqueer, which is neither masculine nor feminine (Rouse, 2016). This identity falls outside the binary of male and female constructs and does not ascribe sexual orientation based on gender or sex. Unlike many European American LGBTQ people, ethnic identity is more primary than sexual identity for many Native American LGBTA people (Lang, 2016).

Summary

Stereotypes of Native American males are harmful. These stereotypes, as embodied in sport mascots, have been found to negatively affect Native Americans' mental health. The cultural fit of one's activities (e.g., hunting, raising sheep) with one's gender role also affects mental health. Male gender roles and sexual orientation are more flexible in Native communities than they are in European American communities.

Native American Females

Many of the negative stereotypes of Native American men, discussed previously, are applied to Native American women. This may be because non-Natives have limited experience with Natives and may not differentiate Native men and women. Natives are viewed by many non-Natives as a group that has multiple problems, such as high school dropout, suicide, alcoholism, and teen pregnancy (Fryberg et al., 2008). These may be based on the few images of Native Americans available in the media. Native Americans, such as John who is described at the beginning of the chapter, are also exposed to and influenced by these negative images.

Picture 11.2
Source: courtesy of Pixabay.

As discussed above, exposure to an image of Disney's Pocahontas reduced self-esteem among both Native women and men (Fryberg et al., 2008). You might wonder why, as Pocahontas was the heroine in the movie. However, Disney's depiction of Pocahontas was inaccurate. In the movie, she was portrayed as a young adult with an idealized European American body figure who had a romantic affair with John Smith. The actual Pocahontas, whose real name was Matoaka, was about 10 years old. The artificial nature of this image of a Native woman may be what is harmful to Natives.

Discrimination against Native men and women does not appear to be gender-specific. As discussed in Chapter 1, over 80% of Native Americans have ever experienced discrimination, which is higher than all other ethnic groups in the United States (American Psychological Association, 2016). A study of over 3000 Native Americans from 138 different tribes identified the specific types of discrimination experienced (Gonzales et al., 2016). There were no gender differences in the type and frequency of gender discrimination that was experienced. The most common type of discrimination was people acting as if they are better than you and the least common was being threatened or harassed (Figure 11.3). Discrimination experiences were relatively uncommon. However, when they did occur, there were negative consequences. Discrimination was associated with both distress and anger.

Similarly, there do not appear to be gender differences in the occurrence of microaggressions (see Chapter 6) among Native Americans. In a sample of 114 Native young adults from 70 indigenous groups in the United States, Canada, and Mexico, the most common forms of microaggressions experienced were assumed universality of the Native experience and denial of individual racism, experienced by over 85% of the participants

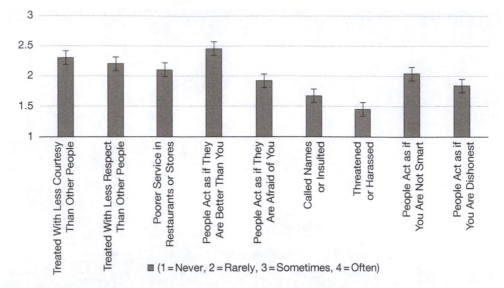

Figure 11.3 Means of Everyday Discrimination Among Native American Men and Women.
Source: Gonzales et al., 2016.

(Jones & Galliher, 2015). Men and women did not significantly differ in the number of times that they experienced microaggressions. However, Native women were particularly upset by specific microaggressions, including ascription of a lack of intelligence, myth of meritocracy (i.e., race or ethnicity plays a minor role in success), denial of individual racism, and assumed universality of experience. Native women may be particularly sensitive to these stereotypes of Native Americans as incompetent, not experiencing discrimination, and being part of a homogeneous group. No specific microaggressions were more upsetting than others were for Native men.

Analogous to Native men who were observed by Spaniards to take on men's roles, Native women were observed to take on masculine roles (Lang, 2016). This included fighting in wars and the shaman or healer role in tribes where healers were primarily men. As discussed previously, Europeans imposed and expected binary gender roles among Native Americans.

In some Native contexts, traditional gender roles are relatively binary. In a study of 493 Yu'pik Alaska Natives, spending time with family, doing chores, engaging in religious practices, and talking about personal issues with someone trusted were more frequent and more important for women than for men (Lardon, Wolsko, Trickett, Henry, & Hopkins, 2016). Men spent more time outside, connecting with nature, and engaging in subsistence activities (e.g., hunting, fishing). These activities that women and men separately engaged in are consistent with traditional Yu'pik gender roles.

Gender roles can change for Natives during their lifetimes. Tribes have specific names for alternate gender roles. For example, the Diné (Navajo) term for one whose gender role is constantly changing is *nádleeh*. One's occupational (e.g., woman involved in masculine activities) and sexual preferences (e.g., heterosexual woman) are also not consistently masculine or feminine. These flexible gender and sexual roles have resulted in acceptance of sexual minorities, such as Elizabeth described at the beginning of the chapter.

In some cultural contexts, current Native females may have more flexible gender roles than males do. In a study of 20 Arctic Alaska Native youth, girls discussed engaging in the masculine activities of caribou and seal hunting, and community leadership (Wexler, 2014). Meat obtained from hunting is the primary Arctic diet and girls' participation in hunting benefitted the whole community. Boys' roles were more narrowly focused on stoicism and strength, such as fighting back when bullied. Boys who did not fulfill these roles experienced stress. In contrast, there were community rituals to celebrate girls' hunting accomplishments.

Summary

Stereotypes of Native American females are similar to those of Native American males. Native American women and men experience similar types of discrimination and microaggressions. However, Native women may be particularly sensitive to these stereotypes of Native Americans as incompetent, not experiencing discrimination, and being part of a homogeneous group. Gender roles and sexual orientation for Native females are flexible and may change during a lifetime.

HISTORICAL TRAUMA

Historical trauma has been defined as "a collective complex trauma inflicted on a group of people who have a specific group identity or affiliation – ethnicity, nationality, and religious affiliation" (Warne & Lajimodiere, 2015, p. 569). As discussed in the first part of this chapter, Native American historical traumas include military conquest and genocide, loss of tribal land, reservation captivity, forced boarding school attendance, and loss of language, culture, and kinship patterns – all in their own homeland. These traumas have physical, emotional, psychological, and spiritual effects. Moreover, the effects of a community's coping responses to historical trauma are cumulative and intergenerational.

Native American historical trauma has been compared to the effects of the Jewish Holocaust and Japanese American internment during World War II (see Chapter 9). Similar to these historical traumas, Native American historical trauma was the result of exclusionary policies. However, unlike the other traumas, many of the effects of Native American historical trauma were unintentional, such as the spread of infectious disease, or ongoing, such as the inability to return to one's sacred homelands (Kirmayer, Gone, & Moses, 2014).

The concept of historical trauma was developed in the mid-1990s because of posttraumatic stress disorder (PTSD), which was viewed as insufficient to explain the complexity of Native American trauma (Gone, 2013b). Psychologist Eduardo Duran and social work professor Maria Yellow Horse Brave Heart adapted the framework of the Holocaust to applications with Native populations (Maxwell, 2014). Historical trauma can be mistaken for individual psychopathology, such as PTSD in response to a particular recent event (Peters et al., 2015). However, a focus on the individual may blame the victim for centuries of collective trauma (Hartmann & Gone, 2014).

Hartmann and Gone (2014) conceptualized Native historical trauma as involving the four Cs:

1   *Colonial injury* to Native peoples by European settlers
2   *Collective experience* of these injuries by entire Native communities whose identities and cultures were radically altered
3   *Cumulative effects* from these injuries via the historical consequences of subjugation, oppression, and marginalization, and
4   *Cross-generational impacts* until "healing" interrupts these processes.

Gone (2013a) has contended that a focus on historical trauma depicts Native Americans as victims of their circumstances rather than as resilient people involved in shaping their future. All Natives are not equally impacted by historical trauma. Moreover, viewing all Natives as traumatized may invoke pity among many non-Natives but may also serve to marginalize Natives as powerless victims.

The focus in many Native communities has been on healing of historical trauma. The healing process occurs at many levels, including the political (e.g., legislation toward political autonomy), community, and individual. A response to historical trauma in Native communities has been cultural revitalization (e.g., ceremonial participation) in an effort toward "decolonization" (Hartmann & Gone, 2014). Nevertheless, revitalizing a culture is complex. Access to suppressed cultural traditions may be limited and culture is constantly evolving in response to time and circumstances (Kirmayer et al., 2014).

Picture 11.3
Source: shutterstock.

Although revitalization of culture is a logical healing response to cultural oppression, there is some evidence that Native cultural identification is associated with *greater* distress. In a longitudinal study of over 500 adolescents from eight Native tribal groups in the United States and Canada, the effects of traditional spiritual activities on perceived racial discrimination, thoughts about historical loss, and psychological problems were examined (Walls, Whitbeck, & Armenta, 2016). Traditional spiritual activities included offering tobacco, participating in a sweat, ceremonial feasts, ceremonial dance, going to a traditional healer, seeking advice from a spiritual advisor, using traditional medicine, smudged/saged, attending a (traditional) ceremonial funeral, singing/participating in a drum group, being taught ceremonial songs, or experiencing puberty fast/feast. Thoughts about historical loss included thinking about "loss of our land," "loss of our language," and "loss of our family ties" because of boarding/residential schools. Psychological problems were depression, anxiety, and anger. Spiritual activities were associated with perceived racial discrimination and thoughts about historical loss, which in turn were associated with psychological problems. In other words, a person who is involved in spiritual activities is also more aware of racial discrimination and historical loss, and this awareness is associated with psychological problems.

A similar pattern was found with 123 Native college students from 21 different tribes (Tucker, Wingate, & O'Keefe, 2016). Ethnic identity was associated with thoughts of historical loss, which in turn were associated with depression. In contrast, assimilation into mainstream society (i.e., feeling comfortable in mainstream United States society) was associated with fewer thoughts of historical loss. Once again, identification with Native culture was indirectly associated with psychological problems.

The results of these two studies seem to suggest that less identification with Native culture is adaptive for Natives (Tucker et al., 2016; Walls et al., 2016). However, the psychological outcome measures in these studies were mainstream measures of depression, anxiety, and anger. So, less Native identification and greater assimilation is adaptive for adjustment to the mainstream. But neither study assessed adjustment to Native cultures. As discussed in Chapter 2, bicultural competence may be the optimal mode of functioning for a person whose life involves two cultures (LaFromboise et al., 1993). Moreover, historical loss is traumatic but it is an important part of Native history that should not be forgotten. In the words of philosopher George Santayana, those who cannot remember the past are condemned to repeat it.

Summary

Native American historical trauma involves colonial injury, collective experience of these injuries, cumulative effects of these injuries, and cross-generational impacts. Healing approaches to historical trauma have involved cultural revitalization. Although identification with Native culture may cause distress by focusing attention on historical trauma and discrimination, such attention is important in Native American health.

CONCLUSION

Native Americans have survived centuries of historical, cultural, spiritual, and psychological oppression. Nevertheless, their cultures remain diverse and vibrant. Native American gender roles and sexual orientation are flexible. However, stereotypes of Native males and females have influenced both Native and non-Native perceptions. Historical trauma has had cumulative and intergenerational effects on Native American health and mental health. Healing of historical trauma may involve Native cultural revitalization.

RESOURCES

Videos:
Changing the Way We See Native Americans – Matika Wilbur www.youtube.com/watch?v=GIzYzz3rEZU.
Native Americans Review "Indian" Sports Mascots www.youtube.com/watch?v=HTBT-_F6oYw.
Cultural Appropriation www.youtube.com/watch?v=KXejDhRGOuI.

REFERENCES

Abe-Kim, J., Takeuchi, D. T., Hong, S., Zane, N., Sue, S., Spencer, M. S., … Alegria, M. (2007). Use of mental health-related services among immigrant and U.S.-born Asian Americans: Results from the National Latino and Asian American study. *American Journal of Public Health, 97*, 91–98. doi: 10.2105/AJPH.2006.098541.

Abrams, J. A., Javier, S. J., Maxwell, M. L., Belgrave, F. Z., & Nguyen, A. B. (2016). Distant but relative: Similarities and differences in gender role beliefs among African American and Vietnamese American women. *Cultural Diversity and Ethnic Minority Psychology, 22*, 256–267. doi: 10.1037/cdp0000038.

Abrams, J. A., Maxwell, M., Pope, M., & Belgrave, F. Z. (2014). Carrying the world with the grace of a lady and the grit of a warrior: Deepening our understanding of the "strong Black woman" schema. *Psychology of Women Quarterly, 38*, 503–518. doi: 10.1177/0361684314541418.

Adamczyk, A., Boyd, K. A., & Hayes, B. E. (2016). Place matters: Contextualizing the roles of religion and race for understanding Americans' attitudes about homosexuality. *Social Science Research, 57*, 1–16. doi: 10.1016/j.ssresearch.2016.02.001.

Agbayani-Siewert, P., & Revilla, L. (1995). Filipino Americans. In P. G. Min (Ed.), *Asian Americans: Contemporary trends and issues* (pp. 134–168). Thousand Oaks, CA: Sage.

Alcantara, C., & Gone, J. P. (2014). Multicultural issues in the clinical interview and diagnostic process. In F. T. L. Leong, L. Comas-Díaz, G. C. N. Hall, V. C. McLoyd, & J. E. Trimble (Eds.), *APA handbook of multicultural psychology, Vol. 2: Applications and training* (pp. 153–163). Washington, DC: American Psychological Association. doi: 10.1037/14187-009.

Alcantara, C., Abelson, J. L., & Gone, J. P. (2012). Beyond anxious predisposition: Do *padecer de nervios* and *ataque de nervios* add incremental validity to prediction of current distress among Mexican mothers? *Depression and Anxiety, 29*, 23–31. doi: 10.1002/da.20855.

Alcantara, C., Casement, M. D., & Lewis-Fernandez, R. (2013). Conditional risk for PTSD among Latinos: A systematic review of racial/ethnic differences and sociocultural explanations. *Clinical Psychology Review, 33*, 107–119. doi: 10.1016/j.cpr.2012.10.005.

Alegria, M., Mulvaney-Day, N., Woo, M., Torres, M., Gao, S., & Oddo, V. (2007). Correlates of past-year mental health service use among Latinos: Results from the National Latino and Asian American Study. *American Journal of Public Health, 97*, 76–83. doi: 10.2105/AJPH.2006.087197.

Ali, M. M., Rizzo, J. A., & Heiland, F. W. (2013). Big and beautiful? Evidence of racial differences in the perceived attractiveness of obese females. *Journal of Adolescence, 36*, 539–549. doi: 10.1016/j.adolescence.2013.03.010.

Allport, G. W. (1954). *The nature of prejudice*. Reading, MA: Addison-Wesley.

Amer, M. M., & Awad, G. H. (Eds.). (2016). *Handbook of Arab American psychology*. New York: Routledge.

American Psychiatric Association (2013). *Diagnostic and statistical manual of mental disorders, fifth edition*. Arlington, VA: American Psychiatric Association.

American Psychological Association (2016). *Stress in America: The impact of discrimination*. Stress in America™ Survey. www.apa.org/news/press/releases/stress/2015/impact-of-discrimination.pdf.

Andreotti, C., Root, J. C., Ahles, T. A., McEwen, B. S., & Compas, B. E. (2015). Cancer, coping, and cognition: A model for the role of stress reactivity in cancer-related cognitive decline. *Psycho-Oncology, 24*, 617–623. doi: 10.1002/pon.3683.

Arciniega, G. M., Anderson, T. C., Tovar-Blank, Z. G., & Tracey, T. J. G. (2008). Toward a fuller conception of machismo: Development of a traditional machismo and caballerismo scale. *Journal of Counseling Psychology, 55*, 19–33. doi: 10.1037/0022-0167.55.1.19.

Arnett, J. J. (2008). The neglected 95%: Why American psychology needs to become less American. *American Psychologist, 63*, 602–614. doi: 10.1037/0003-066X.63.7.602.

Arnold, T., Braje, S. E., Kawahara, D., & Shuman, T. (2016). Ethnic socialization, perceived discrimination, and psychological adjustment among transracially adopted and nonadopted ethnic minority adults. *American Journal of Orthopsychiatry, 86*, 540–551. doi: 10.1037/ort0000172.

Aronson, J., Burgess, D., Phelan, S. M., & Juarez, L. (2013). Unhealthy interactions: The role of stereotype threat in health disparities. *American Journal of Public Health, 103*, 50–56. doi: 10.2105/AJPH.2012.300828.

Aronson, J., Quinn, D. M., & Spencer, S. J. (1998). Stereotype threat and the academic underperformance of minorities and women. In J. K. Swim & C. Stangor (Eds.), *Prejudice: The target's perspective* (pp. 83–103). San Diego, CA: Academic Press.

Asante, M. K. (1987). *The Afrocentric idea*. Philadelphia: Temple University Press.

Aud, S., Fox, M. A., & KewalRamani, A. (2010). *Status and trends in the education of racial and ethnic groups* (NCES 2010–015). Washington, DC: National Center for Education Statistics.

Balsam, K. F., Molina, Y., Blayney, J. A., Dillworth, T., Zimmerman, L., & Kaysen, D. (2015). Racial/ethnic differences in identity and mental health outcomes among young sexual minority women. *Cultural Diversity and Ethnic Minority Psychology, 21*, 380–390. doi: 10.1037/a0038680.

Barlow, F. K., Paolini, S., Pedersen, A., Hornsey, M. J., Radke, H. R., Harwood, J., … Sibley, C. G. (2012). The contact caveat: Negative contact predicts increased prejudice more than positive contact predicts reduced prejudice. *Personality and Social Psychology Bulletin, 38*, 1629–1643. doi: 10.1177/0146167212457953.

Baron, R. M., & Kenny, D. A. (1986). The moderator-mediator variable distinction in social psychological research: Conceptual, strategic, and statistical considerations. *Journal of Personality and Social Psychology, 52*, 1173–1182. doi: 10.1037/0022-3514.51.6.1173.

Barr, S. C., & Neville, H. A. (2008). Examination of the link between parental racial socialization messages and racial ideology among Black college students. *Journal of Black Psychology, 34*, 131–155. doi: 10.1177/0095798408314138.

Bauer, A. M., Chen, C., & Alegría, M. (2010). English language proficiency and mental health service use among Latino and Asian Americans with mental disorders. *Medical Care, 48*, 1097–1104. doi: 10.1097/MLR.0b013e3181f80749.

Beauvais, F. (1998). American Indians and alcohol. *Alcohol Health & Research World, 22*, 253–259.

Beck, A. T., & Haigh, E. A. P. (2014). Advances in cognitive theory and therapy: The generic cognitive model. *Annual Review of Clinical Psychology, 10*, 1–24. doi: 10.1146/annurev-clinpsy-032813-153734.

Belgrave, F. Z., & Abrams, J. A. (2016). Reducing disparities and achieving equity in African American women's health. *American Psychologist, 71*, 723–733. doi: 10.1037/amp0000081.

Benet-Martínez, V., & John, O. P. (1998). Los Cincos Grandes across cultures and ethnic groups: Multitrait-multimethod analyses of the Big Five in Spanish and English. *Journal of Personality and Social Psychology, 75*, 729–750. doi: 10.1037/0022-3514.75.3.729.

Benish, S. G., Quintana, S., & Wampold, B. E. (2011). Culturally adapted psychotherapy and the legitimacy of myth: A direct comparison meta-analysis. *Journal of Counseling Psychology, 58,* 279–289. doi: 10.1037/a0023626.

Berger, M., & Sarnyi, Z. (2015). "More than skin deep": Stress neurobiology and mental health consequences of racial discrimination. *Stress, 18,* 1–10. doi: 10.3109/10253890.2014.989204.

Bernal, G., & Enchautegui-de-Jesús, N. (1994). Latinos and Latinas in community psychology: A review of the literature. *American Journal of Community Psychology, 22,* 531–557. doi: 10.1007/bf02506892.

Bernal, G., & Shapiro, E. (1996). Cuban families. In M. McGoldrick, J. Giordano, & J. K. Pearce (Eds.), *Ethnicity and family therapy* (2nd ed., pp. 155–168). New York: Guilford.

Bernal, G., Cumba-Avilés, E., & Rodriguez-Quintana, N. (2014). Methodological challenges in research with ethnic, racial, and ethnocultural groups. In F. T. L. Leong, L. Comas-Díaz, G. C. N. Hall, V. C. McLoyd, & J. E. Trimble (Eds.), *APA handbook of multicultural psychology, Vol. 1: Theory and research* (pp. 105–123). Washington, DC: American Psychological Association. doi: 10.1037/14189-006.

Bernal, G., Jiménez-Chafey, M. I., & Domenech Rodríguez, M. M. (2009). Cultural adaptation of treatments: A resource for considering culture in evidence-based practice. *Professional Psychology: Research and Practice, 40,* 361–368. doi: 10.1037/a0016401.

Berry, J. W. (1974). Psychological aspects of cultural pluralism: Unity and identity reconsidered. *Topics in Cultural Learning, 2,* 17–22.

Berry, J. W. (2003). Conceptual approaches to acculturation. In K. M. Chun, P. B. Organista, & G. Marin (Eds.), *Acculturation: Advances in theory, measurement, and applied research* (pp. 17–37). Washington, DC: American Psychological Association. doi: 10.1037/10472-004.

Berry, J., Phinney, J., Sam, D., & Vedder, P. (2006). *Immigrant youth in cultural transition: Acculturation, identity, and adaptation across national contexts.* Mahwah, NJ: Erlbaum.

Berry, J. W., Poortinga, Y. H., Segall, M. H., & Dasen, P. R. (2002). *Cross-cultural psychology: Research and applications* (2nd ed.). New York: Cambridge University Press.

Betancourt, H., & López, S. R. (1993). The study of culture, ethnicity, and race in American psychology. *American Psychologist, 48,* 629–637. doi: 10.1037/0003-066X.48.6.629.

Bialystok, E. (2015). Bilingualism and the development of executive function: The role of attention. *Child Development Perspectives, 9,* 117–121. doi: 10.1111/cdep. 12116.

Birman, D., & Simon, C. D. (2014). Acculturation research: Challenges, complexities, and possibilities. In F. T. L. Leong, L. Comas-Díaz, G. C. N. Hall, V. C. McLoyd, & J. Trimble (Eds.), *APA handbook of multicultural psychology, Vol. 1: Theory and research* (pp. 207–230). Washington, DC: American Psychological Association. doi: 10.1037/14189-011.

Blashfield, R. K., Keeley, J. W., Flanagan, E. H., & Miles, S. R. (2014). The cycle of classification: DSM-I through DSM-5. *Annual Review of Clinical Psychology, 10,* 25–51. doi: 10.1146/annurev-clinpsy-032813-153639.

Bleich, S. N., Jarlenski, M. P., Bell, C. N., & LaVeist, T. A. (2012). Health inequalities: Trends, progress, and policy. *Annual Review of Public Health, 33,* 7–40. doi: 10.1146/annurev-publhealth-031811-124658.

Bodas, J., & Ollendick T. H. (2005). Test anxiety: A cross-cultural perspective. *Clinical Child and Family Psychology Review, 8,* 65–88. doi: 10.1007/s10567-005-2342-x.

Bombay, A., Matheson, K., & Anisman, H. (2013). Expectations among aboriginal peoples in Canada regarding the potential impacts of a government apology. *Political Psychology, 34,* 443–460. doi: 10.1111/pops.12029.

Bonham, V. L., Warshauer-Baker, E., & Collins, F. S. (2005). Race and ethnicity in the genome era: The complexity of the constructs. *American Psychologist, 60,* 9–15. doi: 10.1037/0003-066X.60.1.9.

Bowleg, L., English, D., del Rio-Gonzalez, A. M., Burkholder, G. J., Teti, M., & Tschann, J. M. (2016). Measuring the pros and cons of what it means to be a Black man: Development and validation of the Black Men's Experiences Scale (BMES). *Psychology of Men & Masculinity*, *17*, 177–188. doi: 10.1037/men0000026.

Brandon, D. T., Isaac, L. A., & LaVeist, T. A. (2013). The legacy of Tuskegee and trust in medical care: Is Tuskegee responsible for race differences in mistrust of medical care? In T. A. LaVeist & L. A. Isaac (Eds.), *Race, ethnicity, and health: A public health reader* (2nd ed., pp. 557–568). San Francisco: Jossey-Bass.

Bravo, M. (2003). Instrument development: Cultural adaptations for ethnic minority research. In G. Bernal, J. E. Trimble, A. K. Burlew, & F. T. L. Leong (Eds.), *Handbook of racial and ethnic minority psychology* (pp. 220–236). Thousand Oaks, CA: Sage.

Breland-Noble, A. M. (2013). The impact of skin color on mental and behavioral health in African American and Latina adolescent girls: A review of the literature. In R. E. Hall (Ed.), *The melanin millennium: Skin color as 21st century international discourse* (pp. 219–229). New York: Springer Science + Business Media.

Brennan, D. J., Souleymanov, R., George, C., Newman, P. A., Hart, T. A., Asakura, K., & Betancourt, G. (2015). Masculinity, muscularity, and HIV sexual risk among gay and bisexual men of color. *Psychology of Men & Masculinity*, *16*, 393–403. doi: 10.1037/a0038725.

Brewer, M. B. (1996). When contact is not enough: Social identity and intergroup cooperation. *International Journal of Intercultural Relations*, *20*, 291–303. doi: 10.1037/0022-3514.71.1.83.

Brody, G. H., Chen, Y., Murry, V. M., Ge, X., Simons, R. L., Gibbons, F. X., Gerrard, M., & Cutrona, C. E. (2006). Perceived discrimination and the adjustment of African American youths: A five-year longitudinal analysis with contextual moderation effects. *Child Development*, *77*, 1170–1189. doi: 10.1111/j.1467-8624.2006.00927.x.

Brody, G. H., Lei, M. K., Chae, D. H., Yu, T., Kogan, S. M., & Beach, S. R. (2014). Perceived discrimination among African American adolescents and allostatic load: A longitudinal analysis with buffering effects. *Child Development*, *85*, 989–1002. doi: 10.1111/cdev.12213.

Brown, C. A., & Weisman de Mamani, A. (2017). A comparison of psychiatric symptom severity in individuals assessed in their mother tongue versus an acquired language: A two-sample study of individuals with schizophrenia and a normative population. *Professional Psychology: Research and Practice*, *48*, 1–10. doi: 10.1037/pro0000125.

Brown, T. H., Richardson, L. J., Hargrove, T. W., & Thomas, C. S. (2016). Using multiple-hierarchy stratification and life course approaches to understand health inequalities: The intersecting consequences of race, gender, SES, and age. *Journal of Health and Social Behavior*, *57*, 200–222. doi: 10.1177/0022146516645165.

Brucker, P. S., & Perry, B. J. (1998). American Indians: Presenting concerns and considerations for family therapists. *American Journal of Family Therapy*, *26*, 307–319. doi: 10.1080/01926189808 251109.

Bujarski, S., Lau, A. S., Lee, S. S., & Ray, L. A. (2015). Genetic and environmental predictors of alcohol use in Asian American young adults. *Journal of Studies on Alcohol and Drugs*, *76*, 690–699. doi: 10.15288/jsad.2015.76.690.

Burlew, A. K. (2003). Research with ethnic minorities: Conceptual, methodological, and analytical issues. In G. Bernal, J. E. Trimble, A. K. Burlew, & F. T. L. Leong (Eds.), *Handbook of racial and ethnic minority psychology* (pp. 179–197). Thousand Oaks, CA: Sage.

Burrow, A. L., & Ong, A. D. (2010). Racial identity as a moderator of daily exposure and reactivity to racial discrimination. *Self and Identity*, *9*, 383–402. doi: 10.1080/15298860903192496.

Calzada, E. J., Huang, K. Y., Anicama, C., Fernandez, Y., & Brotman, L. M. (2012). Test of a cultural framework of parenting with Latino families of young children. *Cultural Diversity and Ethnic Minority Psychology*, *18*, 285–296. doi: 10.1037/a0028694.

Campos, B., Ullman, J. B., Aguilera, A., & Dunkel Schetter, C. (2014). Familism and psychological health: The intervening role of closeness and social support. *Cultural Diversity and Ethnic Minority Psychology*, *20*, 191–201. doi: 10.1037/a0034094.

Carlson, E. B. (1997). *Trauma assessments: A clinician's guide*. New York: Guilford Press.

Carson, D. K., & Hand, C. (1999). Dilemmas surrounding elder abuse and neglect in Native American communities. In T. Tatara (Ed.), *Understanding elder abuse in minority populations* (pp. 161–184). Philadelphia: Brunner/Mazel.

Carter, E. R., & Murphy, M. C. (2015). Group-based differences in perceptions of racism: What counts, to whom, and why?. *Social and Personality Psychology Compass, 9*, 269–280. doi: 10.1111/spc3.12181.

Casas, J. M., Turner, J. A., & Esparza, C. A. R. (2005). Machismo revisited in a time of crisis: Implications for understanding and counseling Hispanic men. In G. Good, & G. R. Brooks (Eds.), *The new handbook of psychotherapy and counseling with men: A comprehensive guide to settings, problems, and treatment approaches* (pp. 337–356). San Francisco: Jossey-Bass.

Casas, J. M., Wagenheim, B. R., Banchero, R., & Mendoza-Romero, J. (1994). Hispanic masculinity: Myth or psychological schema meriting clinical consideration. *Hispanic Journal of Behavioral Sciences, 16*, 315–331. doi: 10.1177/07399863940163009.

Cass, V. C. (1979). Homosexual identity formation: A theoretical model. *Journal of Homosexuality, 4*, 219–235. doi: 10.1300/J082v04n03_01.

Castro, F. G., Barrera, M., & Martinez, C. R. (2004). The cultural adaptation of prevention interventions: Resolving tensions between fidelity and fit. *Prevention Science, 5*, 41–45. doi: 10.1023/B:PREV.0000013980.12412.cd.

Castro, F. G., Proescholdbell, R. J., Abeita, L., & Rodriguez, D. (1999). Ethnic and cultural minority groups. In B. S. McCrady & E. E. Epstein (Eds.), *Addictions: A comprehensive guide* (pp. 499–526). New York: Oxford University Press.

Castro, F. G., Rios, R., & Montoya, H. (2006). Ethical community-based research with Hispanic or Latina(o) populations: Balancing research rigor and cultural responsiveness. In J. E. Trimble & C. B. Fisher (Eds.), *The handbook of ethical research with ethnocultural populations and communities* (pp. 137–153). Thousand Oaks, CA: Sage.

Caughy, M. O., O'Campo, P. J., Randolph, S. M., & Nickerson, K. (2002). The influence of racial socialization practices on the cognitive and behavioral competence of African American preschoolers. *Child Development, 73*, 1611–1625. doi: 10.1111/1467-8624.00493.

Caughy, M. O., Nettles, S. M., O'Campo, P. J., & Lohrfink, K. F. (2006). Neighborhood matters: Racial socialization of African American children. *Child Development, 77*, 1220–1236. doi: 10.1111/j.1467-8624.2006.00930.x.

Cavalli-Sforza, L. L., Menozzi, P., & Piazza, A. (1994). *The history and geography of human genes.* Princeton, NJ: Princeton University Press.

Ceballo, R., Kennedy, T. M., Bregman, A., & Epstein-Ngo, Q. (2012). Always aware (Siempre pendiente): Latina mothers' parenting in high-risk neighborhoods. *Journal of Family Psychology, 26*, 805–815. doi: 10.1037/a0029584.

Centers for Disease Control and Prevention. (2012). *HIV in the United States: The stages of care.* Atlanta, GA: U.S. Department of Health and Human Services.

Chambless, D. L., Sanderson, W. C., Shoham, V., Bennett Johnson, S., Pope, K. S., Crits-Christoph, P., … McCurry, S. (1996). An update on empirically validated therapies. *Clinical Psychologist, 49*, 5–18.

Chang, J., Chen, C. N., & Alegría, M. (2014). Contextualizing social support: Pathways to help seeking in Latinos, Asian Americans, and Whites. *Journal of Social and Clinical Psychology, 33*, 1–24. doi: 10.1521/jscp. 2014.33.1.1.

Chao, M. M., Chiu, C. Y., Chan, W., Mendoza-Denton, R., & Kwok, C. (2013). The model minority as a shared reality and its implication for interracial perceptions. *Asian American Journal of Psychology, 4*, 84–97. doi: 10.1037/a0028769.

Charmaraman, L., Woo, M., Quach, A., & Erkut, S. (2014). How have researchers studied multiracial populations? A content and methodological review of 20 years of research. *Cultural Diversity and Ethnic Minority Psychology, 20*, 336–352. doi: 10.1037/a0035437.

Chatters, L. M., Bullard, K. M., Taylor, R. J., Woodward, A. T., Neighbors, H. W., & Jackson, J. S. (2008). Religious participation and DSM-IV disorders among older African Americans: Findings from the national survey of American life. *The American Journal of Geriatric Psychiatry, 16,* 957–965. doi: 10.1097/JGP.0b013e3181898081.

Chavez-Dueñas, N. Y., Adames, H. Y., & Organista, K. C. (2014). Skin-color prejudice and within-group racial discrimination: Historical and current impact on Latino/a populations. *Hispanic Journal of Behavioral Sciences, 36,* 3–26. doi: 10.1177/0739986313511306.

Chen, S. H., Hua, M., Zhou, Q., Tao, A., Lee, E. H., Ly, J., & Main, A. (2014). Parent–child cultural orientations and child adjustment in Chinese American immigrant families. *Developmental Psychology, 50,* 189–201. doi: 10.1037/a0032473.

Chen, X., & Graham, S. (2015). Cross-ethnic friendships and intergroup attitudes among Asian American adolescents. *Child Development, 86,* 749–764. doi: 10.1111/cdev.12339.

Cheryan, S., & Bodenhausen, G. V. (2000). When positive stereotypes threaten intellectual performance: The psychological hazards of "model minority" status. *Psychological Science, 11,* 399–402. doi: 10.1111/1467-9280.00277.

Chiao, J. Y. (2015). Current emotion research in cultural neuroscience. *Emotion Review, 7,* 280–293. doi: 10.1177/1754073914546389.

Chiao, J. Y., & Blizinsky, K. D. (2010). Culture-gene coevolution of individualism–collectivism and the serotonin transporter gene (5-HTTLPR). *Proceedings of the Royal Society B: Biological Sciences, 277*(1681), 529–537. doi: 10.1098/rspb.2009.1650.

Choi, A. Y., & Israel, T. (2016). Centralizing the psychology of sexual minority Asian and Pacific Islander Americans. *Psychology of Sexual Orientation and Gender Diversity, 3,* 345–356. doi: 10.1037/sgd0000184.

Choi, N.-Y., & Miller, M. J. (2014). AAPI college students' willingness to seek counseling: The role of culture, stigma, and attitudes. *Journal of Counseling Psychology, 61,* 340–351. doi: 10.1037/cou0000027.

Choi, Y., Kim, Y. S., Kim, S. Y., & Park, I. J. (2013). Is Asian American parenting controlling and harsh? Empirical testing of relationships between Korean American and Western parenting measures. *Asian American Journal of Psychology, 4,* 19–29. doi: 10.1037/a0031220.

Chou, T., Asnaani, A., & Hofmann, S. G. (2012). Perception of racial discrimination and psychopathology across three U.S. ethnic minority groups. *Cultural Diversity and Ethnic Minority Psychology, 18,* 74–81. doi: 10.1037/a0025432.

Chun, K. M., Morera, O. F., Andal, J. D., & Skewes, M. C. (2007). Conducting research with diverse Asian American groups. In F. T. L. Leong, A. Ebreo, L. Kinoshita, A. G. Inman, & L. H. Yang (Eds.), *Handbook of Asian American psychology* (2nd ed., pp. 47–65). Thousand Oaks, CA: Sage.

Clark, K. B., & Clark, M. K. (1947). Racial identification and preference Negro children. In T. M. Newcomb & E. L. Hartley (Eds.), *Readings in social psychology* (pp. 169–178). New York: Holt.

Clark, R., Anderson, N. B., Clark, V. R., & Williams, D. R. (1999). Racism as a stressor for African Americans: A biosocial model. *American Psychologist, 54,* 805–816. doi: 10.1037/0003-066X.54.10.805.

CNN (2016, November 23). *Exit polls.* www.cnn.com/election/results/exit-polls.

Cole, E. R. (2009). Intersectionality and research in psychology. *American Psychologist, 64,* 170–180. doi: 10.1037/a0014564.

Cole, M. (1996). *Cultural psychology: A once and future discipline.* Cambridge, MA: Belknap Press.

Coleman, E. (1982). Developmental stages of the coming out process. *Journal of Homosexuality, 9,* 105–126. doi: 10.1300/J082v07n02_06.

Coley, R. L., Kull, M. A., & Carrano, J. (2014). Parental endorsement of spanking and children's internalizing and externalizing problems in African American and Hispanic families. *Journal of Family Psychology, 28,* 22–31. doi: 10.1037/a0035272.

Collins, P. H. (2000). *Black feminist thought: Knowledge, consciousness, and the politics of empowerment* (2nd ed.). New York: Routledge.

Comas-Díaz, L. (2001). Hispanics, Latinos, or Americanos: The evolution of identity. *Cultural Diversity and Ethnic Minority Psychology, 7,* 115–120. doi: 10.1037/1099-9809.7.2.115.

Comas-Díaz, L., Lykes, M. B., & Alarcón, R. D. (1998). Ethnic conflict and the psychology of liberation in Guatemala, Peru, and Puerto Rico. *American Psychologist, 53,* 778–792. doi: 10.1177/135910530000500312.

Commission on Wartime Relocation and Internment of Civilians (1982). *Personal justice denied.* Washington, DC: Government Printing Office.

Corneille, M., Fife, J. E., Belgrave, F. Z., & Sims, B. C. (2012). Ethnic identity, masculinity, and healthy sexual relationships among African American men. *Psychology of Men & Masculinity, 13,* 393–399. doi: 10.1037/a0026878.

Corona, R., Rodriguez, V. M., McDonald, S. E., Velazquez, E., Rodriguez, A., & Fuentes, V. E. (2017). Associations between cultural stressors, cultural values, and Latina/o college students' mental health. *Journal of Youth and Adolescence, 46,* 63–77. doi: 10.1007/s10964-016-0600-5.

Cosmides, L., Tooby, J., & Kurzban, R. (2003). Perceptions of race. *Trends in Cognitive Sciences, 7,* 173–179. doi: 10.1016/S1364-6613(03)00057-3.

Craig, M. A., & Richeson, J. A. (2014). On the precipice of a "majority-minority" America: Perceived status threat from the racial demographic shift affects White American's political ideology. *Psychological Science, 25,* 1189–1197. doi: 10.1177/0956797614527113.

Critcher, C. R., & Risen, J. L. (2014). If he can do it, so can they: Exposure to counterstereotypically successful exemplars prompts automatic inferences. *Journal of Personality and Social Psychology, 106,* 359–379. doi: 10.1037/a0035707.

Crosby, F. J., & Cordova, D. I. (1996). Words worth of wisdom: Toward an understanding of affirmative action. *Journal of Social Issues, 52,* 33–49. doi: 10.1111/j.1540-4560.1996.tb01847.x.

Cross, W. E. (1971). Negro-to-Black conversion experience. *Black World, 20,* 13–27.

Cross, W. E. (1991). *Shades of Black: Diversity in African American identity.* Philadelphia: Temple University Press.

Cross, W. E., & Vandiver, B. J. (2001). Nigrescence theory and measurement: Introducing the Cross Racial Identity Scale (CRIS). In J. G. Ponterotto, J. M. Casas, L. A. Suzuki, & C. M. Alexander (Eds.), *Handbook of multicultural counseling* (2nd ed., pp. 371–393). Thousand Oaks, CA: Sage.

Czopp, A. M., Mark, A. Y., & Walzer, A. S. (2014). Prejudice and racism. In F. T. L. Leong, L. Comas-Díaz, G. C. N. Hall, V. C. McLoyd, & J. Trimble (Eds.), *APA handbook of multicultural psychology: Vol. 1: Theory and research* (pp. 361–377). Washington, DC: American Psychological Association. doi: 10.1037/14189-019.

D'Andrea, M., Daniels, J., & Heck, R. (1991). Evaluating the impact of multicultural counseling training. *Journal of Counseling and Development, 70,* 143–150. doi: 10.1002/j.1556-6676.1991.tb01576.x.

Daboin, I., Peterson, J. L., & Parrott, D. J. (2015). Racial differences in sexual prejudice and its correlates among heterosexual men. *Cultural Diversity and Ethnic Minority Psychology, 21,* 258–267. doi: 10.1037/a0038444.

Dailey, A. B., Kasl, S. V., Holford, T. R., Lewis, T. T., & Jones, B. A. (2010). Neighborhood- and individual-level socioeconomic variation in perceptions of racial discrimination. *Ethnicity & Health, 15,* 145–163. doi: 10.1080/13557851003592561.

Dana, R. H. (1993). *Multicultural assessment perspectives for professional psychology.* Needham Heights, MA: Allyn & Bacon.

David, E. J. R., Okazaki, S., & Giroux, D. (2014). A set of guiding principles to advance multicultural psychology and its major concepts. In F. T. L. Leong, L. Comas-Díaz, G. C. N. Hall, V. C. McLoyd, & J. Trimble (Eds.), *APA handbook of multicultural psychology, Vol. 1: Theory and research* (pp. 85–104). Washington, DC: American Psychological Association. doi: 10.1037/14189-005.

Davis, D. E., Rice, K., Van Tongeren, D. R., Hook, J. N., DeBlaere, C., Worthington Jr., E. L., & Choe, E. (2016). The moral foundations hypothesis does not replicate well in Black samples. *Journal of Personality and Social Psychology, 110,* e23-e30. doi: 10.1037/pspp. 0000056.

Davis, I. R. (1993). Protest against the use of Native American mascots: A challenge to traditional American identity. *Journal of Sport and Social Issues, 17,* 9–22. doi: 10.1177/019372359301700103.

Davis, J. M., & Liang, C. T. H. (2015). A test of the mediating role of gender role conflict: Latino masculinities and help-seeking attitudes. *Psychology of Men & Masculinity, 16,* 23–32. doi: 10.1037/a0035320.

DeAnda, S., Poulin-Dubois, D., Zesiger, P., & Friend, M. (2016). Lexical processing and organization in bilingual first language acquisition: Guiding future research. *Psychological Bulletin, 142,* 655. doi: 10.1037/bul0000042.

Deater-Deckard, K., Dodge, K. A., Bates, J. E., & Pettit, G. S. (1996). Physical discipline among African American and European American mothers: Links to children's externalizing behaviors. *Developmental Psychology, 32,* 1065–1072. doi: 10.1037/0012-1649.32.6.1065.

Deater-Deckard, K., Lansford, J. E., Malone, P. S., Alampay, L. P., Sorbring, E., Bacchini, D., … Dodge, K. A. (2011). The association between parental warmth and control in thirteen cultural groups. *Journal of Family Psychology, 25,* 790–794. doi: 10.1037/a0025120.

DeLapp, R. C. T., Chapman, L. K., & Williams, M. T. (2016). Psychometric properties of a brief version of the Penn State Worry Questionnaire in African Americans and European Americans. *Psychological Assessment, 28,* 499–508. doi: 10.1037/pas0000208.

Deloria, V. (1998). Comfortable fictions and the struggle for turf: An essay review of "The invented Indian: Cultural fictions and government policies." In D. A. Mihesuah (Ed.), *Natives and academics: Researching and writing about American Indians* (pp. 65–93). Lincoln, NE: University of Nebraska Press.

Derntl, B., Habel, U., Robinson, S., Windischberger, C., Kryspin-Exner, I., Gur, R. C., & Moser, E. (2012). Culture but not gender modulates amygdala activation during explicit emotion recognition. *BMC Neuroscience, 13,* Article 54. doi: 10.1186/1471-2202-13-54.

Derose, K. P., Kanouse, D. E., Bogart, L. M., Griffin, B. A., Haas, A., Stucky, B. D., … Florez, K. R. (2016). Predictors of HIV-related stigmas among African American and Latino religious congregants. *Cultural Diversity and Ethnic Minority Psychology, 22,* 185–195. doi: 10.1037/cdp0000062.

Des Jarlais, D. C., McCarty, D., Vega, W. A., & Bramson, H. (2013). HIV infection among people who inject drugs: The challenge of racial/ethnic disparities. *American Psychologist, 68,* 274–285. doi: 10.1037/a0032745.

Devos, T. (2014). Stereotypes and intergroup attitudes. In F. T. L. Leong, L. Comas-Díaz, G. C. N. Hall, V. C. McLoyd, C. Vonnie, & J. E. Trimble (Eds.), *APA handbook of multicultural psychology, Vol. 1: Theory and research* (pp. 341–360). Washington, DC: American Psychological Association. doi: 10.1037/14189-018.

Devos, T., & Banaji, M. R. (2005). American = White? *Journal of Personality and Social Psychology, 88,* 447–466. doi: 10.1037/0022-3514.88.3.447.

Devos, T., & Mohamed, H. (2014). Shades of American identity: Implicit relations between ethnic and national identities. *Social and Personality Psychology Compass, 8,* 739–754. doi: 10.1111/spc3.12149.

Dickens, W. T., & Flynn, J. R. (2006). Black Americans reduce the racial IQ gap: Evidence from standardization samples. *Psychological Science, 17,* 913–920. doi: 10.1111/j.1467-9280.2006.01802.x.

Dolezsar, C. M., McGrath, J. J., Herzig, A. J. M., & Miller, S. B. (2014). Perceived racial discrimination and hypertension: A comprehensive systematic review. *Health Psychology, 33,* 20–34. doi: 10.1037/a0033718.

Domenech Rodríguez, M. M., Donovick, M. R., & Crowley, S. L. (2009). Parenting styles in cultural context: Observations of "protective parenting" in first-generation Latinos. *Family Process, 48,* 195–210. doi: 10.1111/j.1545-5300.2009.01277.x.

Dovidio, J. F., & Gaertner, S. L. (1996). Affirmative action, unintentional racial biases, and inter-group relations. *Journal of Social Issues, 52*, 51–75. doi: 10.1111/j.1540-4560.1996.tb01848.x.

Dovidio, J. F., & Gaertner, S. L. (2000). Aversive racism and selective decisions: 1989–1999. *Psychological Science, 11*, 315–319. doi: 10.1111/1467-9280.00262.

Dovidio, J. F., Gaertner, S. L., Kawakami, K., & Hodson, G. (2002). Why can't we all just get along? Interpersonal biases and interracial distrust. *Cultural Diversity and Ethnic Minority Psychology, 8*, 88–102. doi: 10.1037/1099-9809.8.2.88.

Doyle, O., Magan, I., Cryer-Coupet, Q. R., Goldston, D. B., & Estroff, S. E. (2016). "Don't wait for it to rain to buy an umbrella": The transmission of values from African American fathers to sons. *Psychology of Men and Masculinity, 17*, 309–319. doi: 10.1037/men0000028.

Dudley, N. M., McFarland, L. A., Goodman, S. A., Hunt, S. T., & Sydell, E. J. (2005). Racial differences in socially desirable responding in selection contexts: Magnitude and consequences. *Journal of Personality Assessment, 85*, 50–64. doi: 10.1207/s15327752jpa8501_05.

Dunbar, A. S., Perry, N. B., Cavanaugh, A. M., & Leerkes, E. M. (2015). African American parents' racial and emotion socialization profiles and young adults' emotional adaptation. *Cultural Diversity and Ethnic Minority Psychology, 21*, 409–419. doi: 10.1037/a0037546.

Duran, B. M., & Duran, E. F. (1999). Assessment, program planning, and evaluation in Indian country: Toward a postcolonial practice. In R. M. Huff, & M. V. Kline (Eds.), *Promoting health in multicultural populations: A handbook for practitioners* (pp. 291–311). Thousand Oaks, CA: Sage.

Duran, E., Duran, B., Brave Heart, M. Y. H., & Yellow Horse-Davis, S. (1998). Healing the American Indian soul wound. In Y. Danieli (Ed.), *International handbook of multigenerational legacies of trauma* (pp. 341–354). New York: Plenum.

Duster, T. (2015). A post-genomic surprise. The molecular reinscription of race in science, law and medicine. *The British Journal of Sociology, 66*, 1–27. doi: 10.1111/1468-4446.12118.

Eap, S., Degarmo, D. S., Kawakami, A., Hara, S. N., Hall, G. C. N., & Teten, A. L. (2008). Culture and personality among European American and Asian American men. *Journal of Cross-Cultural Psychology, 39*, 630–643. doi: 10.1177/0022022108321310.

Earnshaw, V. A., Bogart, L. M., Dovidio, J. F., & Williams, D. R. (2013). Stigma and racial/ethnic HIV disparities: Moving toward resilience. *American Psychologist, 68*, 225–236. doi: 10.1037/a0032705.

Edman, J. L., & Johnson, R. C. (1999). Filipino American and Caucasian American beliefs about the causes and treatment of mental problems. *Cultural Diversity and Ethnic Minority Psychology, 5*, 380–386. doi: 10.1037/1099-9809.5.4.380.

Ehlers, C. L., & Gizer, I. R. (2013). Evidence for a genetic component for substance dependence in Native Americans. *The American Journal of Psychiatry, 170*, 154–164. doi: 10.1176/appi.ajp.2012.12010113.

Ehrhart, K. H., Roesch, S. C., Ehrhart, M. G., & Kilian, B. (2008). A test of the factor structure equivalence of the 50-item IPIP five-factor model measure across gender and ethnic groups. *Journal of Personality Assessment, 90*, 507–516. doi: 10.1080/00223890802248869.

Elias, T., Jaisle, A., & Morton-Padovano, C. (2017). Ethnic identity as a predictor of microaggressions toward Blacks, Whites, and Hispanic LGBs by Blacks, Whites, and Hispanics. *Journal of Homosexuality, 64*, 1–31. doi: 10.1080/00918369.2016.1172888.

Elliott, D. S., & Mihalic, S. (2004). Issues in disseminating and replicating effective prevention programs. *Prevention Science, 5*, 47–53. doi: 10.1023/B:PREV.0000013981.28071.52.

Ellison, C. G., Musick, M. A., & Henderson, A. K. (2008). Balm in Gilead: Racism, religious involvement, and psychological distress among African-American adults. *Journal for the Scientific Study of Religion, 47*, 291–309. doi: 10.1111/j.1468-5906.2008.00408.x.

Else-Quest, N. M., & Hyde, J. S. (2016). Intersectionality in quantitative psychological research: I. Theoretical and epistemological issues. *Psychology of Women Quarterly, 40*, 155–170. doi: 10.1177/0361684316629797.

Erikson, E. H. (1968). *Identity: Youth and crisis.* New York: Norton Company.

Erol, R. Y., & Orth, R. (2011). Self-esteem development from age 14 to 30 years: A longitudinal study. *Journal of Personality and Social Psychology*, *101*, 607–619. doi: 10.1037/a0024299.

Essed, P. (1991). *Understanding everyday racism: An interdisciplinary theory*. Newbury Park, CA: Sage. doi: 10.4135/9781483345239.

Estrada, F., Rigali-Oiler, M., Arciniega, G. M., & Tracey, T. J. G. (2011). Machismo and Mexican American men: An empirical understanding using a gay sample. *Journal of Counseling Psychology*, *58*, 358–367. doi: 10.1037/a0023122.

Etzioni, A. (2007). Hispanic and Asian immigrants: America's last hope. In C. M. Swain (Ed.), *Debating immigration* (pp. 189–205). New York: Cambridge University Press. doi: 10.1017/CBO9780511804830.015.

Evans, J., Frank, B., Oliffe, J. L., & Gregory, D. (2011). Health, Illness, Men and Masculinities (HIMM): A theoretical framework for understanding men and their health. *Journal of Men's Health*, *8*, 7–15. doi: 10.1016/j.jomh.2010.09.22.

Falicov, C. J. (1998). *Latino families in therapy: A guide to multicultural practice*. New York: Guilford.

Fasula, A. M., Carry, M., & Miller, K. S. (2014). A multidimensional framework for the meanings of the sexual double standard and its application for the sexual health of young Black women in the U.S. *The Journal of Sex Research*, *51*, 170–183. doi: 10.1080/00224499.2012.716874.

Feighner, J. P., Robins, E., Guze, S. B., Woodruff, T. A., Winokur, G., & Munoz, R. (1972). Diagnostic criteria for use in psychiatric research. *Archives of General Psychiatry*, *26*, 57–63. doi: 10.1001/archpsyc.1972.01750190059011.

Ferguson, G. M., Costigan, C. L., Clarke, C. V., & Ge, J. S. (2016). Introducing remote enculturation: Learning your heritage culture from afar. *Child Development Perspectives*, *10*, 166–171. doi: 10.1111/cdep. 12181.

Fisher, C. B., Hoagwood, K., Boyce, C., Duster, T., Frank, D. A., Grisso, T., … Zayas, L. H. (2002). Research ethics for mental health science involving ethnic minority children and youths. *American Psychologist*, *57*, 1024–1040. doi: 10.1037/0003-066X.57.12.1024.

Fisher, P. A., & Ball, T. J. (2003). Tribal participatory research: Mechanisms of a collaborative model. *American Journal of Community Psychology*, *32*, 207–216. doi: 10.1023/B:AJCP.0000004742.39858.c5.

Fiske, S. T. (1998). Stereotyping, prejudice, and discrimination. In D. T. Gilbert, S. T. Fiske, & G. Lindzey (Eds.), *Handbook of social psychology* (4th ed., pp. 357–411). New York: McGraw Hill.

Fong, T. P. (1998). *The contemporary Asian American experience: Beyond the model minority*. Upper Saddle River, NJ: Prentice-Hall.

Fradkin, C., Wallander, J. L., Elliot, M. N., Tortelero, S., Cuccaro, P., & Schuster, M. A. (2015). Associations between socioeconomic status and obesity in diverse, young adolescents: Variation across race/ethnicity and gender. *Health Psychology*, *34*, 1–9. doi: 10.1037/hea0000099.

Franklin, A. J. (1999). Invisibility syndrome and racial identity development in psychotherapy and counseling African American men. *The Counseling Psychologist*, *27*, 761–793. doi: 10.1177/0011000099276002.

French, S. E., Seidman, E., Allen, L., & Aber, J. L. (2006). The development of ethnic identity during adolescence. *Developmental Psychology*, *42*, 1–10. doi: 10.1037/0012-1649.42.1.1.

Freng, S., & Willis-Esqueda, C. (2011). A question of honor: Chief Wahoo and American Indian stereotype activation among a university based sample. *The Journal of Social Psychology*, *151*, 577–591. doi: 10.1080/00224545.2010.507265.

Fryberg, S. A., Markus, H. R., Oyserman, D., & Stone, J. M. (2008). Of warrior chiefs and Indian princesses: The psychological consequences of American Indian mascots. *Basic and Applied Social Psychology*, *30*, 208–218. doi: 10.1080/01973530802375003.

Fu, A. S., & Markus, H. R. (2014). My mother and me: Why tiger mothers motivate Asian Americans but not European Americans. *Personality and Social Psychology Bulletin*, *40*, 739–749. doi: 10.1177/0146167214524992.

Fuligni, A. J., Witkow, M., & Garcia, C. (2005). Ethnic identity and the academic adjustment of adolescents from Mexican, Chinese, and European backgrounds. *Developmental Psychology*, *41*, 799–811. doi: 10.1037/0012-1649.41.5.799.

Fuller-Rowell, T. E., & Doan, S. N. (2010). The social costs of academic success across ethnic groups. *Child Development, 81,* 1696–1713. doi: 10.1111/j.1467-8624.2010.01504.x.

Galea, S., Ahern, J., Resnick, H., Kilpatrick, D., Bucuvalas, M., Gold, J., & Vlahov, D. (2002). Psychological sequelae of the September 11 terrorist attacks in New York City. *The New England Journal of Medicine, 346,* 982–987. doi: 10.1056/NEJMsa013404.

Gaertner, S. L., & Dovidio, J. F. (2000). *Reducing intergroup bias: The common ingroup identity model.* Philadelphia: Psychology Press.

Galinsky, A. D., Hall, E. V., & Cuddy, A. J. (2013). Gendered races implications for interracial marriage, leadership selection, and athletic participation. *Psychological Science, 24,* 498–506. doi: 10.1177/0956797612457783.

Garcia-Preto, N. (1996a). Latino families: An overview. In M. McGoldrick, J. Giordano, & J. K. Pearce (Eds.), *Ethnicity and family therapy* (2nd ed., pp. 141–154). New York: Guilford.

Garcia-Preto, N. (1996b). Puerto Rican families. In M. McGoldrick, J. Giordano, & J. K. Pearce (Eds.), *Ethnicity and family therapy* (2nd ed., pp. 183–199). New York: Guilford.

Garrett, M. T., & Pichette, E. F. (2000). Red as an apple: Native American acculturation and counseling with or without reservation. *Journal of Counseling and Development, 78,* 3–13. doi: 10.1002/j.1556-6676.2000.tb02554.x.

Geisinger, K. F. (1994). Cross-cultural normative assessment: Translation and adaptation issues influencing the normative interpretation of assessment instruments. *Psychological Assessment, 6,* 304–312. doi: 10.1037/1040-3590.6.4.304.

Gershoff, E. T., Lansford, J. E., Sexton, H. R., Davis-Kean, P., & Sameroff, A. J. (2012). Longitudinal links between spanking and children's externalizing behaviors in a national sample of White, Black, Hispanic, and Asian American families. *Child Development, 83,* 838–843. doi: 10.1111/j.1467-8624.2011.01732.x.

Ghavami, N., & Peplau, L. A. (2013). An intersectional analysis of gender and ethnic stereotypes. *Psychology of Women Quarterly, 37,* 113–127. doi: 10.1177/0361684312464203.

Gifford, R. (2011). The dragons of inaction: Psychological barriers that limit climate change mitigation and adaptation. *American Psychologist, 66,* 290–302. doi: 10.1037/a0023566.

Goedde, H. W., Agarwal, D. P., Fritze, G., Meier-Tackmann, D., Singh, S., Beckmann, G., … Czeizel, A. (1992). Distribution of ADH2 and ALDH2 genotypes in different populations. *Human Genetics, 88,* 344–346. doi: 10.1007/BF00197271.

Goldberg, W. A., Kelly, E., Matthews, N. L., Kang, H., Li, W., & Sumaroka, M. (2012). *Journal of Social Issues, 68,* 814–837. doi: 10.1111/j.1540-4560.2012.01777.x.

Gone, J. P. (2006). Research reservations: Response and responsibility in an American Indian community. *American Journal of Community Psychology, 37,* 333–340. doi: 10.1007/s10464-006-9047-2.

Gone, J. P. (2013a). Reconsidering American Indian historical trauma: Lessons from an early Gros Ventre war narrative. *Transcultural Psychiatry, 51,* 387–406. doi: 10.1177/1363461513489722.

Gone, J. P. (2013b). Redressing First Nations historical trauma: Theorizing mechanisms for indigenous culture as mental health treatment. *Transcultural Psychiatry, 50,* 683–706. doi: 10.1177/1363461513487669.

Gonzales, K. L., Noonan, C., Goins, R. T., Henderson, W. G., Beals, J., Manson, S. M., Acton, K. J., & Roubideaux, Y. (2016). Assessing the Everyday Discrimination Scale among American Indians and Alaska Natives. *Psychological Assessment, 28,* 51–58. doi: 10.1037/a0039337.

Gonzalez, J. (2000). *Harvest of empire: A history of Latinos in America.* New York: Viking.

Gonzalez, V. M., & Skewes, M. C. (2016). Association of the firewater myth with drinking behavior among American Indian and Alaska Native college students. *Psychology of Addictive Behaviors, 30,* 838–849. doi: 10.1037/adb0000226.

Gosling, S. D., Vazire, S., Srivastava, S., & John, O. P. (2004). Should we trust web-based studies? A comparative analysis of six preconceptions about Internet questionnaires. *American Psychologist, 59,* 93–104. doi: 10.1037/0003-066X.59.2.93.

Graham, S., Munniksma, A., & Juvonen, J. (2014). Psychosocial benefits of cross-ethnic friendships in urban middle schools. *Child Development, 85,* 469–483. doi: 10.1111/cdev.12159.

Gray-Little, B., & Hafdahl, A. R. (2000). Factors influencing racial comparisons of self-esteem: A quantitative review. *Psychological Bulletin, 126,* 26–54. doi: 10.1037/0033-2909.126.1.26.

Greene, M. L., Way, N., & Pahl, K. (2006). Trajectories of perceived adult and peer discrimination among Black, Hispanic, and Asian American adolescents: Patterns and psychological correlates. *Developmental Psychology, 42,* 218–238. doi: 10.1037/0012-1649.42.2.218.

Greenfield, P. M., & Quiroz, B. (2013). Context and culture in the socialization and development of personal achievement values: Comparing Latino immigrant families, European American families, and elementary school teachers. *Journal of Applied Developmental Psychology, 34,* 108–118. doi: 10.1016/j.appdev.2012.11.002.

Griffith, D. M., Gunter, K. G., & Watkins, D. C. (2012). Measuring masculinity in research on men of color: Findings and future directions. *American Journal of Public Health, 102,* 187–194. doi: 10.2105/AJPH.2012.300715.

Griner, D., & Smith, T. B. (2006). Culturally adapted mental health intervention: A meta-analytic review. *Psychotherapy: Theory, Research, Practice, Training, 43,* 531–548. doi: 10.1037/0033-3204.43.4.531.

Grollman, E. A. (2014). Multiple disadvantaged statuses and health: The role of multiple forms of discrimination. *Journal of Health and Social Behavior, 55,* 3–19. doi: 10.1177/0022146514521215.

Guarnaccia, P. J., Pincay, I. M., Alegría, M., Shrout, P. E., Lewis-Fernández, R., & Canino, G. J. (2007). Assessing diversity among Latinos: Results from the NLAAS. *Hispanic Journal of Behavioral Sciences, 29,* 510–534. doi: 10.1177/0739986307308110.

Gupta, A., Leong, F., Valentine, J. C., & Canada, D. D. (2013). A meta-analytic study: The relationship between acculturation and depression among Asian Americans. *American Journal of Orthopsychiatry, 83,* 372–385. doi: 10.1111/ajop.12018.

Hagelskamp, C., & Hughes, D. L. (2014). Workplace discrimination predicting racial/ethnic socialization across African American, Latino, and Chinese families. *Cultural Diversity and Ethnic Minority Psychology, 20,* 550–560. doi: 10.1037/a0035321.

Hall, A. V., Hall, E. V., & Perry, J. L. (2016). Black and blue: Exploring racial bias and law enforcement in the killings of unarmed Black male civilians. *American Psychologist, 71,* 175–186. Doi: 10.1037/a0040109.

Hall, E. V., Galinsky, A. D., & Phillips, K. W. (2015). Gender profiling: A gendered race perspective on person-position fit. *Personality and Social Psychology Bulletin, 41,* 853–868. doi: 10.1177/0146167215580779.

Hall, G. C. N. (2001). Psychotherapy research with ethnic minorities: Empirical, ethical, and conceptual issues. *Journal of Consulting and Clinical Psychology, 69,* 502–510. doi: 10.1037//0022-006X.69.3.502.

Hall, G. C. N. (2004). Editorial. *Cultural Diversity and Ethnic Minority Psychology, 10,* 3–4. doi: 10.1037/1099-9809.10.1.3.

Hall, G. C. N. (2010). *Multicultural psychology* (2nd ed.). Upper Saddle River, NJ: Prentice Hall.

Hall, G. C. N. (2014, July). *Toward a psychology of the future: Preparing for cultural climate change.* Invited paper presented at the 28th International Congress of Applied Psychology, Paris.

Hall, G. C. N., Bansal, A., & Lopez, I. R. (1999). Ethnicity and psychopathology: A meta-analytic review of 31 years of comparative MMPI/MMPI-2 research. *Psychological Assessment, 11,* 186–197. doi: 10.1037/1040-3590.11.2.186.

Hall, G. C. N., & Barongan, C. (1997). Prevention of sexual aggression: Sociocultural risk and protective factors. *American Psychologist, 52,* 5–14. doi: 10.1037/0003-066X.52.1.5.

Hall, G. C. N., & Barongan, C. (2002). *Multicultural Psychology.* Upper Saddle River, NJ: Prentice-Hall.

Hall, G. C. N., DeGarmo, D. S., Eap, S., Teten, A. L., & Sue, S. (2006). Initiation, desistance, and persistence of men's sexual coercion. *Journal of Consulting and Clinical Psychology, 74,* 732–742. doi: 10.1037/0022-006X.74.4.732.

Hall, G. C. N., & Eap, S. (2007). Empirically-supported therapies for Asian Americans. In F. T. L. Leong, A. Inman, A. Ebreo, L. Yang, L. Kinoshita, & M. Fu (Eds.), *Handbook of Asian American Psychology* (2nd ed., pp. 449–467). Thousand Oaks, CA: Sage.

Hall, G. C. N., Hong, J. J., Zane, N. W., & Meyer, O. L. (2011). Culturally competent treatments for Asian Americans: The relevance of mindfulness and acceptance-based psychotherapies. *Clinical Psychology: Science and Practice, 18*, 215–231. doi: 10.1111/j.1468-2850.2011.01253.x.

Hall, G. C. N., Ibaraki, A. Y., Huang, E. R., Marti, C. N., & Stice, E. (2016). A meta-analysis of cultural adaptations of psychological interventions. *Behavior Therapy, 47*, 993–1014. doi: 10.1016/j.beth.2016.09.005.

Hall, G. C. N., Lopez, I. R., & Bansal, A. (2001). Academic acculturation: Race, gender, and class issues. In D. Pope-Davis & H. Coleman (Eds.), *The intersection of race, gender, and class: Implications for counselor training* (pp. 171–188). Thousand Oaks, CA: Sage.

Hall, G. C. N., & Maramba, G. G. (2001). In search of cultural diversity: Recent literature in cross-cultural and ethnic minority psychology. *Cultural Diversity and Ethnic Minority Psychology, 7*, 12–26. doi: 10.1037/1099-9809.7.1.12.

Hall, G. C. N., Martinez, C. R., Tuan, M., McMahon, T. R., & Chain, J. (2011). Toward ethnocultural diversification of higher education. *Cultural Diversity and Ethnic Minority Psychology, 17*, 243–251. doi: 10.1037/a0024036.

Hall, G. C. N., Teten, A. L., DeGarmo, D. S., Sue, S., & Stephens, K. A. (2005). Ethnicity, culture, and sexual aggression: Risk and protective factors. *Journal of Consulting and Clinical Psychology, 73*, 830–840. doi: 10.1037/0022-006X.73.5.830.

Hall, G. C. N., & Yee, A. H. (2012). U.S. mental health policy: Addressing the neglect of Asian Americans. *Asian American Journal of Psychology, 3*, 181–193. doi: 10.1037/a0029950.

Hall, G. C. N., Yip, T., & Zárate, M. A. (2016). On becoming multicultural in a monocultural research world: A conceptual approach to studying ethnocultural diversity. *American Psychologist, 71*, 40–51. doi: 10.1037/a0039734.

Hamid, P. N., Lai, J. C. L., & Cheng, S. T. (2001). Response bias and public and private self-consciousness in Chinese. *Social Behavior and Personality, 29*, 733–742. doi: 10.2224/sbp.2001.29.8.733.

Han, W. (2012). Bilingualism and academic achievement. *Child Development, 83*, 300–321. doi: 10.1111/j.1467-8624.2011.01686.x.

Harding, J. F., Hughes, D. L., & Way, N. (2016). Racial/ethnic differences in mothers' socialization goals for their adolescents. *Cultural Diversity and Ethnic Minority Psychology, 23*, 281–290. doi: 10.1037/cdp0000116.

Harrell, S. P., & Bond, M. A. (2006). Listening to diversity stories: Principles for practice in community research and action. *American Journal of Community Psychology, 37*, 365–376. doi: 10.1007/s10464-006-9042-7.

Hartmann, W. E., & Gone, J. P. (2014). American Indian historical trauma: Community perspectives from two Great Plains medicine men. *American Journal of Community Psychology, 54*, 274–288. doi: 10.1007/s10464-014-9671-1.

Haslam, N. (2006). Dehumanization: An integrative review. *Personality and Social Psychology Review, 10*, 252–264. doi: 10.1207/s15327957pspr1003_4.

Haslam, N., & Loughnan, S. (2014). Dehumanization and infrahumanization. *Annual Review of Psychology, 65*, 399–423. doi: 10.1146/annurev-psych-010213-115045.

Haycox, S. (2002). *Alaska: An American colony*. Seattle: University of Washington Press.

Hayes, J. A., Owen, J., & Bieschke, K. J. (2015). Therapist differences in symptom change with racial/ethnic minority clients. *Psychotherapy, 52*, 308–314. doi: 10.1037/a0037957.

Hays, P. A. (2006). Cognitive-behavioral therapy with Alaska Native people. In P. A. Hays & G. Y. Iwamasa (Eds.), *Culturally responsive cognitive-behavioral therapy: Assessment, practice, and supervision* (pp. 47–71). Washington, DC: American Psychological Association. doi: 10.1037/11433-002.

Hehman, E., Gaertner, S. L., Dovidio, J. F., Mania, E. W., Guerra, R., Wilson, D. C., & Friel, B. M. (2012). Group status drives majority and minority integration preferences. *Psychological Science, 23*, 46–52. doi: 10.1177/0956797611423547.

Heine, S. J., & Norenzayan, A. (2006). Toward a psychological science for a cultural species. *Perspectives on Psychological Science, 1*, 251–269. doi: 10.1111/j.1745-6916.2006.00015.x.

Helms, J. E. (1990). *Black and White racial identity: Theory, research, and practice.* New York: Greenwood Press.

Helms, J. E. (2007). Some better practices for measuring racial and ethnic identity constructs. *Journal of Counseling Psychology, 54*, 235–246. doi: 10.1037/0022-0167.54.3.235.

Helms, J. E. (2015). An examination of the evidence in culturally adapted evidence-based or empirically supported interventions. *Transcultural Psychiatry, 52*, 174–197. doi: 10.1177/1363461514563642.

Helms, J. E., & Carter, R. T. (1990). Development of the White Racial Identity Inventory. In J. E. Helms (Ed.), *Black and White racial identity: Theory, research and practice* (pp. 67–80). Westport, CT: Greenwood Press.

Helms, J. E., Jernigan, M., & Mascher, J. (2005). The meaning of race in psychology and how to change it: A methodological perspective. *American Psychologist, 60*, 27–36. doi: 10.1037/0003-066X.60.1.27.

Hendershot, C. S., Neighbors, C., George, W. H., McCarthy, D. M., Wall, T. L., Liang, T., & Larimer, M. E. (2009). *ALDH2, ADH1B* and alcohol expectancies: Integrating genetic and learning perspectives. *Psychology of Addictive Behaviors, 23*, 452–463. doi: 10.1037/a0016629.

Herman, M. R., & Campbell, M. E. (2012). I wouldn't, but you can: Attitudes toward interracial relationships. *Social Science Research, 41*, 343–358. doi: 10.1016/j.ssresearch.2011.11.007.

Hernandez, M. (1996). Central American families. In M. McGoldrick, J. Giordano, & J. K. Pearce (Eds.), *Ethnicity and family therapy* (2nd ed., pp. 214–224). New York: Guilford.

Hernandez, M. M., Conger, R. D., Robins, R. W., Bacher, K. B., & Widaman, K. F. (2014). Cultural socialization and ethnic pride among Mexican-origin adolescents during the transition to middle school. *Child Development, 85*, 695–708. doi: 10.1111/cdev.12167.

Herrera, C. J., Owens, G. P., & Mallinckrodt, B. (2013). Traditional machismo and caballerismo as correlates of posttraumatic stress disorder, psychological distress, and relationship satisfaction in Hispanic veterans. *Journal of Multicultural Counseling and Development, 41*, 21–35. doi: 10.1002/j.2161-1912.2013.00024.x.

Herring, R. (1999). Helping Native American Indian and Alsaka Native male youth. In A. M. Horne & M. S. Kiselica (Eds.), *Handbook of counseling boys and adolescent males* (pp. 117–136). Thousand Oaks, CA: Sage.

Hill, C. E., Knox, S., Thompson, B. J., Williams, E. N., Hess, S. A., & Ladany, N. (2005). Consensual qualitative research: An update. *Journal of Counseling Psychology, 52*, 196–205. doi: 10.1037/0022-0167.52.2.196.

Hines, P. M., & Boyd-Franklin, N. (1996). African American families. In M. McGoldrick, J. Giordano, & J. K. Pearce (Eds.), *Ethnicity and family therapy* (2nd ed., pp. 66–84). New York: Guilford.

Hinton, D. E., & Lewis-Fernandez, R. (2011). The cross-cultural validity of posttraumatic stress disorder: Implications for DSM-5. *Depression and Anxiety, 28*, 783–801. doi: 10.1002/da.20753.

Hinton, D. E., Chhean, D., Pich, V., Safren, S. A., Hofmann, S. G., & Pollack, M. H. (2005). A randomized controlled trial of cognitive-behavior therapy for Cambodian refugees with treatment-resistant PTSD and panic attacks: A cross-over design. *Journal of Traumatic Stress, 18*, 617–629. doi: 10.1002/jts.20070.

Hirai, M., Winkel, M. H., & Popan, J. R. (2014). The role of machismo in prejudice toward lesbians and gay men: Personality traits as moderators. *Personality and Individual Differences, 70*, 105–110. doi: 10.1016/j.paid.2014.06.028.

Hodge, F. S., & Fredericks, L. (1999). American Indian and Alaska Native populations in the United States: An overview. In R. M. Huff & M. V. Kline (Eds.), *Promoting health in multicultural populations: A handbook for practitioners* (pp. 269–289). Thousand Oaks, CA: Sage.

Holliday, B. G. (2009). The history and visions of African American psychology: Multiple pathways to place, space, and authority. *Cultural Diversity and Ethnic Minority Psychology, 15,* 317–337. doi: 10.1037/a0016971.

Hornsey, M. J., & Hogg, M. A. (2000). Assimilation and diversity: An integrative model of subgroup relations. *Personality and Social Psychology Review, 4,* 143–156. doi: 10.1207/S153279 57PSPR0402_03.

Hough, R. L., Canino, G. J., Abueg, F. R., & Gusman, F. D. (1996). PTSD and related stress disorders among Hispanics. In A. J. Marsella, M. J. Friedman, E. T. Gerrity, & R. M. Scurfield (Eds.), *Ethnocultural aspects of posttraumatic stress disorder: Issues, research, and clinical applications* (pp. 301–338). Washington, DC: American Psychological Association. doi: 10.1037/10555-012.

Howard, J. T., & Sparks, P. J. (2016). The effects of allostatic load on racial/ethnic mortality differences in the United States. *Population Research and Public Policy Review, 35,* 421–443. doi: 10.1007/s11113-016-9382-4.

Hsin, A., & Xie, Y. (2014). Explaining Asian Americans' academic advantage over Whites. *Proceedings of the National Academy of Sciences, 111,* 8416–8421. doi: 10.1073/pnas.1406402111.

Hsu, K., & Iwamoto, D. K. (2014). Testing for measurement invariance in the Conformity to Masculine Norms-46 across White and Asian American college men: Development and validity of the CMNI-29. *Psychology of Men and Masculinity, 15,* 397–406. doi: 10.1037/a0034548.

Huddy, L., & Virtanen, S. (1995). Subgroup differentiation and subgroup bias among Latinos as a function of familiarity and positive distinctiveness. *Journal of Personality and Social Psychology, 68,* 97–108. doi: 10.1037/0022-3514.68.1.97.

Hughes, D., Rodriguez, J., Smith, E. P., Johnson, D. J., Stevenson, H. C., & Spicer, P. (2006). Parents' ethnic–racial socialization practices: A review of research and directions for future study. *Developmental Psychology, 42,* 747–770. doi: 10.1037/0012-1649.42.5.747.

Hunt, K., Lewars, H., Emslie, C., & Batty, G. D. (2007). Decreased risk of death from coronary heart disease amongst men with higher "femininity" scores: A general population cohort study. *International Journal of Epidemiology, 36,* 612–620. doi: 10.1093/ije/dym022.

Hunter, L. R., & Schmidt, N. B. (2010). Anxiety psychopathology in African American adults: Literature review and development of an empirically informed sociocultural model. *Psychological Bulletin, 136,* 211–235. doi: 10.1037/a0018133.

Hurley, R. J., Jensen, J. J., Weaver, A., & Dixon, T. (2015). Viewer ethnicity matters: Black crime in TV news and its impact on decisions regarding public policy. *Journal of Social Issues, 71,* 155–170. doi: 10.1111/josi.12102.

Hurtado, S. (2001). Linking diversity and educational purpose: How diversity affects the classroom environment and student development. In G. Orfield (Ed.), *Diversity challenged: Evidence on the impact of affirmative action* (pp. 187–203). Cambridge, MA: Harvard Education Publishing Group.

Huynh, V. W. (2012). Ethnic microaggressions and the depressive and somatic symptoms of Latino and Asian American adolescents. *Journal of Youth and Adolescence, 41,* 831–846. doi: 10.1007/s10964-012-9756-9.

Ibaraki, A. Y., & Hall, G. C. N. (2014). The components of cultural match in psychotherapy. *The Journal of Social and Clinical Psychology, 33,* 936–953. doi: 10.1521/jscp. 2014.33.10.936.

Ibaraki, A. Y., Hall, G. C. N., & Sabin, J. A. (2014). Asian American cancer disparities: The potential effects of model minority health stereotypes. *Asian American Journal of Psychology, 5,* 75–81. doi: 10.1037/a0036114.

Inclán, J. E., & Herron, D. G. (1998). Puerto Rican adolescents. In J. T. Gibbs & L. N. Huang (Eds.), *Children of color: Psychological interventions with culturally diverse youth* (2nd ed., pp. 240–263). San Francisco: Jossey Bass.

Insel, T., Cuthbert, B., Garvey, M., Heinssen, R., Pine, D. S., Quinn, K., ... Wang, P. (2010). Research domain criteria (RDoC): Toward a new classification framework for research on mental disorders. *American Journal of Psychiatry, 167*, 748–751. doi: 10.1176/appi.ajp. 2010.09091379.

Ito, A. T., & Bartholow, B. D. (2009). The neural correlates of race. *Trends in Cognitive Sciences, 13*, 524–531. doi: 10.1016/j.tics.2009.10.002.

Iwamasa, G. Y., & Sorocco, K. H. (2002). Aging and Asian Americans: Developing culturally appropriate research methodology. In G. C. N. Hall & S. Okazaki (Eds.), *Asian American psychology: The science of lives in context* (pp. 105–130). Washington, DC: American Psychological Association. doi: 10.1037/10473-004.

Iwamoto, D. K., & Kaya, A. (2016). Asian American men. In Y. J. Wong, & S. R. West (Eds.), *APA handbook of men and masculinities* (pp. 285–297). Washington, DC: American Psychological Association. doi: 10.1037/14594-013.

Iwamoto, D. K., & Liu, W. M. (2009). Asian American men and Asianized attribution: Intersections of masculinity, race, and sexuality. In D. K. Iwamoto & W. M. Liu (Eds.), *Asian American psychology: Current perspectives* (pp. 211–232). New York: Routledge.

Jabagchourian, J. J., Sorkhabi, N., Quach, W., & Strage, A. (2014). Parenting styles and practices of Latino parents and Latino fifth graders' academic, cognitive, social, and behavioral outcomes. *Hispanic Journal of Behavioral Sciences, 36*, 175–194. doi: 10.1177/0739986314523289.

Jackson, J. S., Neighbors, H. W., Torres, M., Martin, L. A., Williams, D. R., & Baser, R. (2007). Use of mental health services and subjective satisfaction with treatment among Black Caribbean immigrants: Results from the national survey of American life. *American Journal of Public Health, 97*, 60–67. doi: 10.2105/AJPH.2006.088500.

Jacobs, M. R. (2014). Race, place, and biography at play: Contextualizing American Indian viewpoints on Indian mascots. *Journal of Sport and Social Issues, 38*, 322–345. doi: 10.1177/0193723514530568.

Jacques, P. (2009). *Environmental skepticism: Ecology, power and public life*. Burlington, VT: Ashgate.

Jaffee, S. R., Caspi, A., Moffitt, T. E., & Taylor, A. (2004). Physical maltreatment victim to antisocial child: Evidence of an environmentally mediated process. *Journal of Abnormal Psychology, 113*, 44–55. doi: 10.1037/0021-843X.113.1.44.

Jamil, O. B., Harper, G. W., & Fernandez, M. I. (2009). Sexual and ethnic identity development among gay–bisexual–questioning (GBQ) male ethnic minority adolescents. *Cultural Diversity and Ethnic Minority Psychology, 15*, 203–214. doi: 10.1037/a0014795.

James, S., Hartnett, S. A., & Kalsbeek, W. D. (1983). John Henryism and blood pressure differences among Black men. *Journal of Behavioral Medicine, 6*, 259–278. doi: 10.1007/BF01315113.

Jenkins, M., Lambert, E. G., & Baker, D. N. (2009). The attitudes of Black and White college students toward gays and lesbians. *Journal of Black Studies, 39*, 589–613. doi: 10.1177/0021934707299638.

Jensen, J. M. (1988). *Passage from India: Asian Indian immigrants in North America*. New Haven, CT: Yale University Press.

Jonas, K. G., & Markon, K. E. (2014). A meta-analytic evaluation of the endophenotype hypothesis: Effects of measurement paradigm in the psychiatric genetics of impulsivity. *Journal of Abnormal Psychology, 12*, 660–675. doi: 10.1037/a0037094.

Jones, J. M. (1997). *Prejudice and racism* (2nd ed.). New York: McGraw-Hill.

Jones, J. M. (2003). TRIOS: A psychological theory of the African legacy in American culture. *Journal of Social Issues, 59*, 217–242. doi: 10.1111/1540-4560.t01-1-00014.

Jones, M. L., & Galliher, R. V. (2015). Daily racial microaggressions and ethnic identification among Native American young adults. *Cultural Diversity and Ethnic Minority Psychology, 21*, 1–9. doi: 10.1037/a0037537.

Jorde, L. B., & Wooding, S. P. (2004). Genetic variation, classification and "race." *Nature Genetics, 36*, 28–33. doi: 10.1038/ng1435.

Jost, J. T., & Hunyady, O. (2002). The psychology of system justification and the palliative function of ideology. *European Review of Social Psychology*, *13*, 111–153. doi: 10.1080/10463280 240000046.

Juang, L., & Syed, M. (2010). Family cultural socialization practices and ethnic identity in college-going emerging adults. *Journal of Adolescence*, *33*, 347–354. doi: 10.1016/j.adolescence.2009.11.008.

Kaiser, C. R., Major, B., Jurcevic, I., Dover, T. L., Brady, L. M., & Shapiro, J. R. (2013). Presumed fair: Ironic effects of organizational diversity structures. *Journal of Personality and Social Psychology*, *104*, 504–519. doi: 10.1037/a0030838.

Kao, G., & Vaquera, E. (2006). The salience of racial and ethnic identification in friendship choices among Hispanic adolescents. *Hispanic Journal of Behavioral Sciences*, *28*, 23–47. doi: 10.1177/0739986305284126.

Kapke, T. L., Grace, M. A., Gerdes, A. C., & Lawton, K. E. (2017). Latino early adolescent mental health: Examining the impact of family functioning, familism, and global self-worth. *Journal of Latina/o Psychology*, *5*, 27–44. doi: 10.1037/lat0000057.

Kaspar, V. (2014). The lifetime effect of residential school attendance on indigenous health status. *American Journal of Public Health*, *104*, 2184–2190. doi: 10.2105/AJPH.2013.301479.

Katigbak, M. S., Church, A. T., Guanzon-Lapena, M. A., Carlota, A. J., & del Pilar, G. H. (2002). Are indigenous personality dimensions culture specific? Philippine inventories and the five-factor model. *Journal of Personality and Social Psychology*, *82*, 89–101. doi: 10.1037//0022-3514.82.1.89.

Kaufman, C. E., Beals, J., Croy, C., Jiang, L., & Novins, D. K. (2013). Multilevel context of depression in two American Indian tribes. *Journal of Consulting and Clinical Psychology*, *81*, 1040–1051. doi: 10.1037/a0034342.

Kendler, K. S. (2005). "A gene for…": The nature of gene action in psychiatric disorders. *American Journal of Psychiatry*, *162*, 1243–1252. doi: 10.1176/appi.ajp. 162.7.1243.

Kessler, R. C., Berglund, P., Demler, O., Jin, R., Merikangas, K. R., & Walters, E. E. (2005). Lifetime prevalence and age-of-onset distributions of DSM-IV disorders in the National Comorbidity Survey Replication. *Archives of General Psychiatry*, *62*, 593–602. doi: 10.1001/archpsyc.62.6.593.

Kiesler, C. A. (1992). U.S. mental health policy: Doomed to fail. *American Psychologist*, *47*, 1077–1082. doi: 10.1037/0003-066X.47.9.1077.

Kim, C., & Sakamoto, A. (2010). Have Asian American men achieved labor market parity with White men? *American Sociological Review*, *75*, 934–957. doi: 10.1177/0003122410388501.

Kim, H. S. (2002). We talk, therefore we think? A cultural analysis of the effect of talking on thinking. *Journal of Personality and Social Psychology*, *83*, 828–842. doi: 10.1037/0022-3514.83.4.828.

Kim, H. S., & Sasaki, J. Y. (2014). Cultural neuroscience: Biology of the mind in cultural contexts. *Annual Review of Psychology*, *65*, 487–514. doi: 10.1146/annurev-psych-010213-115040.

Kim, H. S., & Sherman, D. K. (2007). "Express yourself": Culture and the effect of self-expression on choice. *Journal of Personality and Social Psychology*, *92*, 1–11. doi: 10.1037/0022-3514.92.1.1.

Kim, J. E., & Zane, N. (2016). Help-seeking intentions among Asian American and White American students in psychological distress: Application of the health belief model. *Cultural Diversity and Ethnic Minority Psychology*, *22*, 311–321. doi: 10.1037/cdp0000056.

Kim, S. Y., Hou, Y., & Gonzalez, Y. (2016). Language brokering and depressive symptoms in Mexican-American adolescents: Parent–child alienation and resilience as moderators. *Child Development*, *88*, 867–881. doi: 10.1111/cdev.12620.

Kim, S. Y., Wang, Y., Weaver, S. R., Shen, Y., Wu-Seibold, N., & Liu, C. H. (2014). Measurement equivalence of the language-brokering scale for Chinese American adolescents and their parents. *Journal of Family Psychology*, *28*, 180–192. doi: 10.1037/a0036030.

Kirmayer, L. J., Gone, J. P., & Moses, J. (2014). Rethinking historical trauma. *Transcultural Psychiatry*, *51*, 299–319. doi: 10.1177/1363461514536358.

Kitano, H. H. L., & Daniels, R. (1995). *Asian Americans: Emerging minorities*. Englewood Cliffs, NJ: Prentice Hall.

Kohout, J. L., Pate, W. E., & Maton, K. I. (2014). An updated profile of ethnic minority psychology: A pipeline perspective. In F. T. L. Leong, L. Comas-Díaz, G. C. N. Hall, V. C. McLoyd, C. Vonnie, & J. E. Trimble (Eds.), *APA handbook of multicultural psychology, Vol. 1: Theory and research* (pp. 19–42). Washington, DC: American Psychological Association. doi: 10.1037/14189-002.

Kraemer, H. C. (2014). The reliability of clinical diagnoses: State of the art. *Annual Review of Clinical Psychology, 10,* 111–130. doi: 10.1146/annurev-clinpsy-032813-153739.

Kressin, N. R., Chang, B., Hendricks, A., & Kazis, L. E. (2003). Agreement between administrative data and patients' self-reports of race/ethnicity. *American Journal of Public Health, 93,* 1734–1739. doi: 10.2105/AJPH.93.10.1734.

Kteily, N., & Bruneau, E. (2017). Backlash: The politics and real-world consequences of minority group dehumanization. *Personality and Social Psychology Bulletin, 43,* 87–104. doi: 10.1177/0146167216675334.

Kteily, N., Bruneau, E., Waytz, A., & Cotterill, S. (2015). The ascent of man: Theoretical and empirical evidence for blatant dehumanization. *Journal of Personality and Social Psychology, 109,* 901–931. doi: 10.1037/pspp. 0000048.

Kteily, N., Hodson, G., & Bruneau, E. (2016). They see us as less than human: Metadehumanization predicts intergroup conflict via reciprocal dehumanization. *Journal of Personality and Social Psychology, 110,* 343–370. doi: 10.1037/pspa0000044.

Kulkarni, V. S. (2015). Her earnings: Exploring variation in wives' earning contributions across six major Asian groups and Whites. *Social Science Research, 52,* 539–557. doi: 10.1016/j.ssresearch.2015.03.002.

Kurtz-Costes, B., Swinton, A. D., & Skinner, O. D. (2014). Racial and ethnic gaps in the school performance of Latino, African American, and White students. In F. T. L. Leong, L. Comas-Díaz, G. C. N. Hall, V. C. McLoyd, & J. E. Trimble (Eds.), *APA handbook of multicultural psychology, Vol. 1: Theory and research* (pp. 231–246). Washington, DC: American Psychological Association. doi: 10.1037/14189-012.

LaFromboise, T. D., Berman, J. S., & Sohi, B. K. (1994). American Indian women. In L. Comas-Díaz & B. Greene (Eds.), *Women of color: Integrating ethnic and gender identities in psychotherapy* (pp. 30–71). New York: Guilford.

LaFromboise, T. D., Coleman, H. L. K., & Gerton, J. (1993). Psychological impact of biculturalism: Evidence and theory. Psychological Bulletin, 114, 395–412. doi: 10.1037/0033-2909.114.3.395.

Lang, S. (2016). Native American men-women, lesbians, two-spirits: Contemporary and historical perspectives. *Journal of Lesbian Studies, 20,* 299–323. doi: 10.1080/10894160.2016.1148966.

Langford, I. H. (2002). An existential approach to risk perception. *Risk Analysis, 22,* 101–120. doi: 10.1111/0272-4332.t01-1-00009.

Lardon, C., Wolsko, C., Trickett, E., Henry, D., & Hopkins, S. (2016). Assessing health in an Alaska native cultural context: The Yup'ik wellness survey. *Cultural Diversity and Ethnic Minority Psychology, 22,* 126–136. doi: 10.1037/cdp0000044.

Lassiter, J. M. (2016). Religious participation and identity salience of Black men who have sex with men: Findings from a nationally recruited sample. *Psychology of Sexual Orientation and Gender Diversity, 3,* 304–312. doi: 10.1037/sgd0000176.

Le, H., Berenbaum, H., & Raghavan, C. (2002). Culture and alexithymia: Mean levels, correlates and the role of parental socialization of emotions. *Emotion, 2,* 341–360. doi: 10.1037/1528-3542.2.4.341.

Leavitt, P. A., Covarrubias, R., Perez, Y. A., & Fryberg, S. A. (2015). "Frozen in time": The impact of Native American media representations on identity and self-understanding. *Journal of Social Issues, 71,* 39–53. doi: 10.1111/josi.12095.

LeCuyer, E. A., & Swanson, D. P. (2017). A within-group analysis of African American mothers' authoritarian attitudes, limit-setting and children's self-regulation. *Journal of Child and Family Studies, 26,* 833–842. doi: 10.1007/s10826-016-0609-0.

Lee, B.-T., Paik, J.-W., Kang, R.-H., Chung, S.-Y., Kwon, H.-I., Khang, H.-S., … Ham, B.-J. (2009). The neural substrates of affective face recognition in patients with Hwa-Byung and healthy individuals in Korea. *World Journal of Biological Psychiatry*, *10*, 560–566. doi: 10.1080/15622970802087130.

Lee, D., & Ahn, S. (2011). Racial discrimination and Asian mental health: A meta-analysis. *The Counseling Psychologist*, *39*, 463–489. doi: 10.1177/0011000010381791.

Lee, D., & Ahn, S. (2012). Discrimination against Latina/os: A meta-analysis of individual-level resources and outcomes. *The Counseling Psychologist*, *40*, 28–65. doi: 10.1177/0011000011403326.

Lee, D., & Ahn, S. (2013). The relation of racial identity, ethnic identity, and racial socialization to discrimination–distress: A meta-analysis of Black Americans. *Journal of Counseling Psychology*, *60*, 1–14. doi: 10.1037/a0031275.

Lee, D., & Tracey, T. J. G. (2005). Incorporating idiographic approaches into multicultural counseling research and practice. *Journal of Multicultural Counseling and Development*, *33*, 66–80. doi: 10.1002/j.2161-1912.2005.tb00006.x.

Lee, E. (1997). Overview: The assessment and treatment of Asian American families. In E. Lee (Ed.), *Working with Asian Americans: A guide for clinicians* (pp. 3–36). New York: Guilford.

Lee, E. (2015). *The making of Asian America: A history*. New York: Simon & Schuster.

Lee, J. C., & Kye, S. (2016). Racialized assimilation of Asian Americans. *Annual Review of Sociology*, *42*, 253–273. doi: 10.1146/annurev-soc-081715-074310.

Lee, L. C. (1998). An overview. In L. C. Lee & N. W. S. Zane (Eds.), *Handbook of Asian American psychology* (pp. 1–20). Thousand Oaks, CA: Sage.

Leiserowitz, A., & Akerlof, K. (2010). *Race, ethnicity and public responses to climate change*. New Haven, CT: Yale Project on Climate Change.

Leong, F. T. L., & Okazaki, S. (2009). History of Asian American psychology. *Cultural Diversity and Ethnic Minority Psychology*, *15*, 352–362. doi: 10.1037/a0016443.

Leong, F. T. L., Okazaki, S., & Tak, J. (2003). Assessment of depression and anxiety in East Asia. *Psychological Assessment*, *15*, 290–305. doi: 10.1037/1040-3590.15.3.290.

Levy, D. J., Heissel, J. A., Richeson, J. A., & Adam, E. K. (2016). Psychological and biological responses to race-based social stress as pathways to disparities in educational outcomes. *American Psychologist*, *71*, 455–473. doi: 10.1037/a0040322.

Lewis, J. A., & Neville, H. A. (2015). Construction and initial validation of the Gendered Racial Microaggressions Scale for Black women. *Journal of Counseling Psychology*, *62*, 289–302. doi: 10.1037/cou0000062.

Lewis, N. A., & Sekaquaptewa, D. (2016). Beyond test performance: A broader view of stereotype threat. *Current Opinion in Psychology*, *11*, 40–43. doi: 10.1016/j.copsyc.2016.05.002.

Li, S. (2003). Biocultural orchestration of developmental plasticity across levels: The interplay of biology and culture in shaping the mind and behavior across the life span. *Psychological Bulletin*, *129*, 171–194. doi: 10.1037/0033-2909.129.2.171.

Liang, J., Matheson, B. E., & Douglas, J. M. (2016). Mental health diagnostic considerations in racial/ethnic minority youth. *Journal of Child and Family Studies*, *25*, 1926–1940. doi: 10.1007/s10826-015-0351-z.

Liao, K. Y. H., Weng, C. Y., & West, L. M. (2016). Social connectedness and intolerance of uncertainty as moderators between racial microaggressions and anxiety among Black individuals. *Journal of Counseling Psychology*, *63*, 240–246. doi: 10.1037/cou0000123.

Lickliter, R., & Honeycutt, H. (2003). Developmental dynamics: Toward a biologically plausible evolutionary psychology. *Psychological Bulletin*, *129*, 819–835. doi: 10.1037/0033-2909.129.6.819.

Lin, M. H., Kwan, V. S. Y., Cheung, A., & Fiske, S. T. (2005). Stereotype content model explains prejudice for an envied outgroup: Scale of Anti-Asian American stereotypes. *Personality and Social Psychology Bulletin*, *31*, 34–47. doi: 10.1177/0146167204271320.

Liu, H., Lieberman, L., Stevens, E. S., Auerbach, R. P., & Shankman, S. A. (2017). Using a cultural and RDoC framework to conceptualize anxiety in Asian Americans. *Journal of Anxiety Disorders*, *48*, 63–69. doi: 10.1016/j.janxdis.2016.09.006.

Livingston, R. W., Rosette, A. S., & Washington, E. F. (2012). Can an agentive Black woman get ahead? The impact of race and interpersonal dominance on perceptions of female leaders. *Psychological Science, 23*, 354–358. doi: 10.1177/0956797611428079.

Lommel, L. L., & Chen, J. L. (2016). The relationship between self-rated health and acculturation in Hispanic and Asian adult immigrants: A systematic review. *Journal of Immigrant and Minority Health, 18*, 468–478. doi: 10.1007/s10903-015-0208-y.

Lonner, W., & Ibrahim, F. (2002). Appraisal and assessment in cross-cultural counseling. In P. Pedersen, J. G. Draguns, W. J. Lonner, & J. E. Trimble (Eds.), *Counseling across cultures* (5th ed., pp. 355–379). Thousand Oaks, CA: Sage.

López, S. R., & Guarnaccia, P. J. J. (2000). Cultural psychopathology: Uncovering the social world of mental illness. *Annual Review of Psychology, 51*, 571–598. doi: 10.1146/annurev.psych.51.1.571.

Lorber, M. F., O'Leary, S. G., & Smith Slep, A. M. (2011). An initial evaluation of the role of emotion and impulsivity in explaining racial/ethnic differences in the use of corporal punishment. *Developmental Psychology, 47*, 1744–1749. doi: 10.1037/a0025344.

Louie, J. Y., Oh, B. J., & Lau, A. S. (2013). Cultural differences in the links between parental control and children's emotional expressivity. *Cultural Diversity and Ethnic Minority Psychology, 19*, 424–434. doi: 10.1037/a0032820.

Lowery, W. (2016, July 11). Aren't more White people than Black people killed by police? Yes, but no. *Washington Post.* www.washingtonpost.com/news/post-nation/wp/2016/07/11/arent-more-white-people-than-black-people-killed-by-police-yes-but-no/?utm_term=.40c157f76882.

Loya, R., Reddy, R., & Hinshaw, S. P. (2010). Mental illness stigma as a mediator of differences and South Asian college students' attitudes toward psychological counseling. *Journal of Counseling Psychology, 57*, 484–490. doi: 10.1037/a0021113.

Lu, A., & Wong, Y. J. (2013). Stressful experiences of masculinity among U.S.-born and immigrant Asian American men. *Gender & Society, 27*, 345–371. doi: 10.1177/0891243213479446.

Lu, W., Diep, C. S., & McKyer, L. J. (2015). Risk factors for childhood obesity among Asian Americans: A systematic review of literature and recommendations for health care research. *Journal of Health Care for the Poor and Underserved, 26*, 171–190. doi: 10.1353/hpu.2015.0056.

Luczak, S. E., Glatt, S. J., & Wall, T. J. (2006). Meta-analyses of *ALDH2* and *ADH1B* with alcohol dependence in Asians. *Psychological Bulletin, 132*, 607–621. doi: 10.1037/0033-2909.132.4.607.

Luczak, S. E., Yarnell, L. M., Prescott, C. A., Myers, M. G., Liang, T., & Wall, T. L. (2014). Effects of *ALDH2*2* on alcohol problem trajectories of Asian American college students. *Journal of Abnormal Psychology, 123*, 130–140. doi: 10.1037/a0035486.

Lui, P. P. (2015). Intergenerational cultural conflict, mental health, and educational outcomes among Asian and Latino/a Americans: Qualitative and meta-analytic review. *Psychological Bulletin, 141*, 404–446. doi: 10.1037/a0038449.

Ma, M., Malcolm, L. R., Díaz-Albertini, K., Klinoff, V. A., Leeder, E., Barrientos, S., & Kibler, J. L. (2014). Latino cultural values as protective factors against sexual risks among adolescents. *Journal of Adolescence, 37*, 1215–1225. doi: 10.1016/j.adolescence.2014.08.012.

MacInnis, C., & Page-Gould, E. (2015). How can intergroup interaction be bad if intergroup contact is good? Exploring and reconciling an apparent paradox in the science of intergroup relations. *Perspectives on Psychological Science, 10*, 307–327. doi: 10.1177/1745691614568482.

Maddux, W. W., Galinsky, A. D., Cuddy, A. J. C., & Polifroni, M. (2008). When being a model minority is good … and bad: Realistic threat explains negativity toward Asian Americans. *Personality and Social Psychology Bulletin, 34*, 74–89. doi: 10.1177/0146167207309195.

Mahalik, J. R., Locke, B. D., Ludlow, L. H., Diemer, M. A., Scott, R. P., Gottfried, M., & Freitas, G. (2003). Development of the Conformity to Masculine Norms Inventory. *Psychology of Men & Masculinity, 4*, 3–25. doi: 10.1037/1524-9220.4.1.3.

Maibach, E. W., Roser-Renouf, C., & Leiserowitz, A. (2008). Communication and marketing as climate change-intervention assets: A public health perspective. *American Journal of Preventive Medicine, 35*, 488–500. doi: 10.1016/j.amepre.2008.08.016.

Maiteny, P. T. (2002). Mind in the gap: Summary of research exploring "inner" influences on pro-sustainability learning and behaviour. *Environmental Education Research*, *8*, 299–306. doi: 10.1080/13504620220145447.

Major, B., Blodorn, A., & Blascovich, G. M. (2016). The threat of increasing diversity: Why many White Americans support Trump in the 2016 presidential election. *Group Processes & Intergroup Relations*. doi: 10.1177/1368430216677304.

Major, B., Gramzow, R., McCoy, S. K., Levin, S., Schmader, T., & Sidanius, J. (2002). Perceiving personal discrimination: The role of group status and status legitimizing ideology. *Journal of Personality and Social Psychology*, *80*, 782–796. doi: 10.1037/0022-3514.82.3.269.

Major, B., Kaiser, C. R., O'Brien, L. T., & McCoy, S. K. (2007). Perceived discrimination as worldview threat or worldview confirmation: Implications for self-esteem. *Journal of Personality and Social Psychology*, *92*, 1068–1086. doi: 10.1037/0022-3514.92.6.1068.

Majors, R., & Billson, J. M. (1992). *Cool pose: The dilemmas of African American manhood in America*. New York: Lexington.

Malcarne, V. L., Chavira, D. A. Fernandez, S., & Liu, P. (2006). The scale of ethnic experience: Development and psychometric properties. *Journal of Personality Assessment*, *86*, 150–161. doi: 10.1207/s15327752jpa8602_04.

Marcia, J. (1980). Identity in adolescence. In J. Adelson (Ed.), *Handbook of adolescent psychology* (pp. 159–187). New York: Wiley.

Marin, G., & Marin, B. V. (1991). *Research with Hispanic populations*. Newbury Park, CA: Sage.

Markowitz, J. (2016, October 14). There's such a thing as too much neuroscience. *New York Times*. www.nytimes.com/2016/10/15/opinion/theres-such-a-thing-as-too-much-neuroscience.html?mabReward=CTM&action=click&pgtype=Homepage&region=CColumn&module=Recommendation&src=rechp&WT.nav=RecEngine&_r=1.

Markus, H. R., & Hamedani, M. G. (2007). Sociocultural psychology: The dynamic interdependence among self systems and social systems. In S. Kitayama & D. Cohen (Eds.), *Handbook of cultural psychology* (pp. 3–39). New York: Guilford Press.

Markus, H., & Kitayama, S. (1991). Culture and the self: Implications for cognition, emotion, and motivation. *Psychological Review*, *98*, 224–253. doi: 10.1037/0033-295X.98.2.224.

Marsella, A. J., & Leong, F. T. L. (1995). Cross-cultural issues in personality and career assessment. *Journal of Career Assessment*, *3*, 202–218. doi: 10.1177/106907279500300207.

Martin, J. K., & Hall, G. C. N. (1992). Thinking Black, thinking internal, thinking feminist. *Journal of Counseling Psychology*, *39*, 509–514. doi: 10.1037/0022-0167.39.4.509.

Maruyama, G., & Moreno, J. (2000). University faculty views about the value of diversity on campus and in the classroom. In G. Maruyama, J. F. Moreno, R. H. Gudeman, & P. Marin (Eds.), *Does diversity make a difference?: Three research studies on diversity in college classrooms* (pp. 8–35). Washington, DC: American Council on Education and American Association of University Professors.

Masuoka, N. (2006). Together they become one: Examining the predictors of panethnic group consciousness among Asian Americans and Latinos. *Social Science Quarterly*, *87*, 993–1011. doi: 10.1111/j.1540-6237.2006.00412.x.

Mathur, V. A., Harada, T., & Chiao, J. Y. (2012). Racial identification modulates default network activity for same- and other-race faces. *Human Brain Mapping*, *33*, 1883–1893. doi: 10.1002/hbm.21330.

Matthews, D. D., Hammond, W. P., Nuru-Jeter, A., Yasmin, C. L., & Melvin, T. (2013). Racial discrimination and depressive symptoms among African-American men: The mediating and moderating roles of masculine self-reliance and John Henryism. *Psychology of Men & Masculinity*, *14*, 35–46. doi: 10.1037/a0028436.

Mattis, J. S., & Grayman-Simpson, N. (2013). Faith and the sacred in African American life. In K. I. Pargament, J. J. Exline, & J. W. Jones (Eds.), *APA handbook of psychology, religion, and spirituality: Vol. 2* (pp. 547–564). Washington, DC: American Psychological Association. doi: 10.1037/14045-030.

Maxwell, K. (2014). Historicizing historical trauma theory: Troubling the trans-generational transmission paradigm. *Transcultural Psychiatry, 51,* 407–435. doi: 10.1177/1363461514531317.

Mayhew, M. J., & Grunwald, H. E. (2006). Factors contributing to faculty incorporation of diversity-related course content. *The Journal of Higher Education, 77,* 148–168. doi: 10.1353/jhe.2006.0005.

Mays, V. M., Cochran, S. D., & Barnes, N. W. (2007). Race, race-based discrimination, and health outcomes among African Americans. *Annual Review of Psychology, 58,* 201–225. doi: 10.1146/annurev.psych.57.102904.190212.

McConahay, J. B. (1986). Modern racism, ambivalence, and the Modern Racism Scale. In J. F. Dovidio & S. L. Gaertner (Eds.), *Prejudice, discrimination and racism* (pp. 91–126). Orlando, FL: Academic Press.

McDonald, J. D., & Gonzalez, J. (2006). Cognitive-behavioral therapy with American Indians. In P. A. Hays & G. Y. Iwamasa (Eds.), *Culturally responsive cognitive-behavioral therapy: Assessment, practice, and supervision* (pp. 23–45). Washington, DC: American Psychological Association. doi: 10.1037/11433-001.

McKay, D., Chambless, D., Teachman, B., Mancusi, L., Holloway, E., Jursda, J., & Grossman, S. (2016, October). *Changing funding trends from the National Institute of Mental Health: 1997–2015.* Paper presented at the 50th Convention of the Association for Behavioral and Cognitive Therapies, New York.

Mendoza-Denton, R., Downey, G., Purdie, V. J., Davis, A., & Pietrzak, J. (2002). Sensitivity to status-based rejection: Implications for African American students' college experience. *Journal of Personality and Social Psychology, 83,* 896–918. doi: 10.1037/0022-3514.83.4.896.

Mertens, D. M. (2012). Ethics and social justice in ethnocultural qualitative research. In D. K. Nagata, L. Kohn-Wood, & L. A. Suzuki (Eds.), *Qualitative strategies for ethnocultural research* (pp. 61–84). Washington, DC: American Psychological Association. doi: 10.1037/13742-002.

Meyer, O. L., Zane, N., Cho, Y. I., & Takeuchi, D. T. (2009). Use of specialty mental health services by Asian Americans with psychiatric disorders. *Journal of Consulting and Clinical Psychology, 77,* 1000–1005. doi: 10.1037/a0017065.

Meyer, O., Zane, N., & Cho, Y. I. (2011). Understanding the psychological processes of the racial match effect in Asian Americans. *Journal of Counseling Psychology, 58,* 335–345. doi: 10.1037/a0023605.

Miller, G. A. (2010). Mistreating Psychology in the Decades of the Brain. *Perspectives on Psychological Science, 5,* 716–743. doi: 10.1177/1745691610388774.

Miller, S. J., & Stack, K. (2014). African-American lesbian and queer women respond to Christian-based homophobia. *Journal of GLBT Family Studies, 10,* 243–268. doi: 10.1080/1550428 X.2013.825219.

Miller-Cotto, D., & Byrnes, J. P. (2016). Ethnic/racial identity and academic achievement: A meta-analytic review. *Developmental Review, 41,* 51–70. doi: 10.1016/j.dr.2016.06.003.

Min, P. G. (1995). *Asian Americans: Contemporary trends and issues.* Thousand Oaks, CA: Sage.

Miranda, J., McGuire, T. G., Williams, D. R., & Wang, P. (2008). Mental health in the context of health disparities. *American Journal of Psychiatry, 165,* 1102–1108. doi: 10.1176/appi.ajp.2008.08030333.

Moreno, C. L. (2007). The relationship between culture, gender, structural factors, abuse, trauma, and HIV/AIDS for Latinas. *Qualitative Health Research, 17,* 340–352. doi: 10.1177/1049732306297387.

Morgan Consoli, M. L., & Llamas, J. D. (2013). The relationship between Mexican American cultural values and resilience among Mexican American college students: A mixed methods study. *Journal of Counseling Psychology, 60,* 617–624. doi: 10.1037/a0033998.

Moser, S. C. (2007). More bad news: The risk of neglecting emotional responses to climate change information. In S. C. Moser & L. Dilling (Eds.), *Creating a climate for change: Communicating climate change and facilitating social change* (pp. 64–80). New York: Cambridge University Press. doi: 10.1017/CBO9780511535871.006.

NAACP Legal Defense Fund (2014). *Brown at 60: The doll test.* www.naacpldf.org/brown-at-60-the-doll-test.

Nadal, K. L., & Corpus, M. J. H. (2013). "Tomboys" and "baklas": Experiences of lesbian and gay Filipino Americans. *Asian American Journal of Psychology, 4,* 166–175. doi: 10.1037/a0030168.

Nadal, K. L., Whitman, C. N., Davis, L. S., Erazo, T., & Davidoff, K. C. (2016). Microaggressions toward lesbian, gay, bisexual, transgender, queer, and genderqueer people: A review of the literature. *The Journal of Sex Research, 53,* 488–508. doi: 10.1080/00224499.2016.1142495.

Nadal, K. L., Wong, Y., Sriken, J., Griffin, K., & Fujii-Doe, W. (2015). Racial microaggressions and Asian Americans: An exploratory study on within-group differences and mental health. *Asian American Journal of Psychology, 6,* 136–144. doi: 10.1037/a0038058.

Nagata, D. K. (1998). The assessment and treatment of Japanese American children and adolescents. In J. T. Gibbs & L. N. Huang (Eds.), *Children of color: Psychological interventions with culturally diverse youth* (2nd ed., pp. 68–111). San Francisco: Jossey Bass.

Nagata, D. K., Kohn-Wood, L., & Suzuki, L. A. (2012). *Qualitative strategies for ethnocultural research.* Washington, DC: American Psychological Association. doi: 10.1037/13742-000.

Nagel, J. (1995). American Indian ethnic renewal: Politics and the resurgence of identity. *American Sociological Review, 60,* 947–965. doi: 10.2307/2096434.

Najdowski, C. J., Bottoms, B. L., & Goff, P. A. (2015). Stereotype threat and racial differences in citizens' experiences of police encounters. *Law and Human Behavior, 39,* 463–477. doi: 10.1037/lhb0000140.

Nakanishi, D. T. (1988). Seeking convergence in race relations research: Japanese-Americans and the resurrection of the internment. In P. A. Katz & D. A. Taylor (Eds.), *Eliminating racism: Profiles in controversy* (pp. 159–180). New York: Plenum.

Nanda, S. (2011). Multiple genders among North American Indians. In J. Z. Spae & G. Valentine (Eds.), *The kaleidoscope of gender: Prisms, patterns, and possibilities* (3rd ed., pp. 47–53). Washington, DC: Sage.

National Center for Health Statistics. (2011). *Health, United States, 2010: With special feature on death and dying.* Washington, DC: U.S. Government Printing Office.

National Commission for the Protection of Human Subjects of Biomedical and Behavioral Research (1979). *The Belmont Report: Ethical Principles and Guidelines for the Protection of Human Subjects of Research.* Washington, DC: U.S. Department of Health, Education, and Welfare.

National Women's History Museum (2007). *African American women and suffrage.* www.nwhm.org/online-exhibits/rightsforwomen/AfricanAmericanwomen.html.

Nelson, J. C., Adams, G., & Salter, P. S. (2012). The Marley hypothesis: Denial of racism reflects ignorance of history. *Psychological Science, 24,* 213–218. doi: 10.1177/0956797612451466.

Neville, H. A., Awad, G. H., Brooks, J. E., Flores, M. P., & Bluemel, J. (2013). Color-blind racial ideology: Theory, training, and measurement implications in psychology. *American Psychologist, 68,* 455–466. doi: 10.1037/a0033282.

Nguyen, A. B., Moser, R., & Chou, W. Y. (2014). Race and health profiles in the United States: An examination of the social gradient through the 2009 CHIS adult survey. *Public Health, 128,* 1076–1086. doi: 10.1016/j.puhe.2014.10.003.

Nguyen, A. D., & Benet-Martínez, V. (2013). Biculturalism and adjustment: A meta-analysis. *Journal of Cross-Cultural Psychology, 44,* 122–159. doi: 10.1177/0022022111435097.

Nisbett, R. E. (2005). Heredity, environment, and race differences in IQ: A commentary on Rushton and Jensen. *Psychology, Public Policy, and Law, 11,* 302–310. doi: 10.1037/1076-8971.11.2.302.

Nisbett, R. E., Aronson, J., Blair, C., Dickens, W., Flynn, J., Halpern, D. F., & Turkheimer, E. (2012). Intelligence: New findings and theoretical developments. *American Psychologist, 67,* 130–159. doi: 10.1037/a0026699.

Nishi, S. M. (1995). Japanese Americans. In P. G. Min (Ed.), *Asian Americans: Contemporary trends and issues* (pp. 95–133). Thousand Oaks, CA: Sage.

Nishio, K., & Bilmes, M. (1987). Psychotherapy with Southeast Asian American clients. *Professional Psychology: Research and Practice, 18*, 342–346. doi: 10.1037/0735-7028.18.4.342.

Norenzayan, A., & Heine, S. J. (2005). Psychological universals: What are they and how can we know? *Psychological Bulletin, 131*, 763–784. doi: 10.1037/0033-2909.131.5.763.

Norgaard, K. M. (2011). *Living in denial: Climate change, emotions, and everyday life.* Cambridge, MA: MIT Press.

Norton, I. M., & Manson, S. M. (1996). Research in American Indian and Alaska Native communities: Navigating the cultural universe of values and process. *Journal of Consulting and Clinical Psychology, 64*, 856–860. doi: 10.1037/0022-006X.64.5.856.

Nuñez, A., Gonzalez, P., Talavera, G. A., Sanchez-Johnsen, L., Roesch, S. C., Davis, S. M. ... Gallo, L. C. (2016). Machismo, marianismo, and negative cognitive-emotional factors: Findings from the Hispanic community health study/study of Latinos sociocultural ancillary study. *Journal of Latina/o Psychology, 4*, 202–217. doi: 10.1037/lat0000050.

Ogbu, J. U. (1986). The consequences of the American caste system. In U. Neisser (Ed.), *The school achievement of minority children: New perspectives* (pp. 19–56). Hillsdale, NJ: Erlbaum.

Ojeda, L., & Organista, K. C. (2016). Latino American men. In Y. J. Wong (Ed.), *APA handbook of men and masculinities* (299–318). Washington, DC: American Psychological Association. doi: 10.1037/14594-014.

Ojeda, L., & Piña-Watson, B. (2014). Caballerismo may protect against the role of machismo on Mexican day laborers' self-esteem. *Psychology of Men and Masculinity, 15*, 288–295. doi: 10.1037/a0033450.

Ojeda, L., Piña-Watson, B., & Gonzalez, G. (2016). The role of social class, ethnocultural adaptation, and masculinity ideology on Mexican American college men's well-being. *Psychology of Men and Masculinity, 17*, 373–379. doi: 10.1037/men0000023.

Okazaki, S. (2002). Beyond questionnaires: Conceptual and methodological innovations for Asian American psychology. In G. C. N. Hall & S. Okazaki (Eds.), *Asian American psychology: The science of lives in context* (pp. 13–39). Washington, DC: American Psychological Association. doi: 10.1037/10473-001.

Okazaki, S., & Sue, S. (1995). Methodological issues in assessment research with ethnic minorities. *Psychological Assessment, 7*, 367–375. doi: 10.1037/1040-3590.7.3.367.

Oney, C. N., Cole, E. R., & Sellers, R. M. (2011). Racial identity and gender as moderators of the relationship between body image and self-esteem for African Americans. *Sex Roles, 65*, 619–631. doi: 10.1007/s11199-011-9962-z.

Ong, A. D., Burrow, A. L., Fuller-Rowell, T. E., Ja, N. M., & Sue, D. W. (2013). Racial microaggressions and daily well-being among Asian Americans. *Journal of Counseling Psychology, 60*, 188–199. doi: 10.1037/a0031736.

Oparanozie, A., Sales, J. M., DiClemente, R. J., & Braxton, N. D. (2012). Racial identity and risky sexual behaviors among Black heterosexual men. *Journal of Black Psychology, 38*, 32–51. doi: 10.1177/0095798410397542.

Oyserman, D., Coon, H. M., & Kemmelmeier, M. (2002). Rethinking individualism and collectivism: Evaluation of theoretical assumptions and meta-analyses. *Psychological Bulletin, 128*, 3–72. doi: 10.1037/0033-2909.128.1.3.

Padilla, A. M., & Olmedo, E. (2009). Synopsis of key persons, events, and associations in the history of Latino psychology. *Cultural Diversity and Ethnic Minority Psychology, 15*, 363–373. doi: 10.1037/a0017557.

Page, J. (2003). *In the hands of the Great Spirit: The 20,000-year history of American Indians.* New York: Free Press.

Pardo, Y., Weisfeld, C., Hill, E., & Slatcher, R. B. (2013). Machismo and marital satisfaction in Mexican American couples. *Journal of Cross-Cultural Psychology, 44*, 299–315. doi: 10.1177/0022022112443854.

Parks, S. J., & Yoo, H. C. (2016). Does endorsement of the model minority myth relate to anti-Asian sentiments among White college student? The role of a color-blind racial attitude. *Asian American Journal of Psychology*, 7, 287–294. doi: 10.1037/aap0000056.

Pauker, K., Williams, A., & Steele, J. R. (2015). Children's racial categorization in context. *Child Development Perspectives*, *10*, 33–38. doi: 10.1111/cdep. 12155.

Paul, C., & Brookes, B. (2015). The rationalization of unethical research: Revisionist accounts of the Tuskegee Syphilis Study and the New Zealand "Unfortunate Experiment." *American Journal of Public Health*, *105*, e12–e19. doi: 10.2105/AJPH.2015.302720.

Peck, S. C., Brodish, A. B., Malanchuk, O., Banerjee, M., & Eccles, J. S. (2014). Racial/ethnic socialization and identity development in Black families: The role of parent and youth reports. *Developmental Psychology*, *50*, 1897–1909. doi: 10.1037/a0036800.

Peters, W. M. K., Straits, K. J. E., & Gauthier, P. E. (2015). Psychological practice with Native women. In C. Zerbe Enns, J. K. Rice, & R. L. Nutt (Eds.), *Psychological practice with women: Guidelines, diversity, empowerment* (pp. 191–224). Washington, DC: American Psychological Association. doi: 10.1037/14460-008.

Petersen, W. (1966, January 6). Success story: Japanese-American style. *New York Times Magazine*, pp. 20–21, 33, 36, 38, 40–43.

Pettigrew, T. F. (1998). Intergroup contact theory. *Annual Review of Psychology*, *49*, 65–85. doi: 10.1146/annurev.psych.49.1.65.

Pettigrew, T. F. (2004). Justice deferred a half century after Brown v. Board of Education. *American Psychologist*, *59*, 521–529. doi: 10.1037/0003-066X.59.6.521.

Pettigrew, T. F., & Tropp, L. R. (2006). A meta-analytic test of intergroup contact theory. *Journal of Personality and Social Psychology*, *90*, 751–783. doi: 10.1037/0022-3514.90.5.751.

Pettigrew, T. F., & Tropp, L. R. (2008). How does intergroup contact reduce prejudice? Meta-analytic tests of three mediators. *European Journal of Social Psychology*, *38*, 922–934. doi: 10.1002/ejsp.504.

Pew Internet & American Life Project (2007). *Demographics of Internet users*. www.pewinternet.org/trends/User_Demo_6.15.07.htm.

Pew Research Center (2012, July 19). *Asian Americans: A mosaic of faiths*. www.pewforum.org/2012/07/19/asian-americans-a-mosaic-of-faiths-overview/.

Pew Research Center (2015, May 12). *America's changing religious landscape*. www.pewforum.org/2015/05/12/americas-changing-religious-landscape/.

Phinney, J. S. (1989). Stages of ethnic identity development in minority group adolescents. *The Journal of Early Adolescence*, *9*, 34–49. doi: 10.1177/0272431689091004.

Phinney, J. S. (1992). The multigroup ethnic identity measure: A new scale for use with diverse groups. *Journal of Adolescent Research*, 7, 156–176. doi: 10.1177/074355489272003.

Phinney, J. S. (1993). A three-stage model of ethnic identity development in adolescence. In G. P. Knight & M. E. Bernal (Eds.), *Ethnic identity: Formation and transmission among Hispanics and other minorities* (pp. 61–79). Albany, NY: State University of New York Press.

Phinney, J. S. (1996). When we talk about American ethnic groups, what do we mean? *American Psychologist*, *51*, 918–927. doi: 10.1037/0003-066X.51.9.918.

Phinney, J. S., & Ong, A. D. (2007). Conceptualization and measurement of ethnic identity: Current status and future directions. *Journal of Counseling Psychology*, *54*, 271–281. doi: 10.1037/0022-0167.54.3.271.

Piaget, J. (1952). *The origins of intelligence in the child*. New York: Norton.

Piña-Watson, B., Lorenzo-Blanco, E. I., Dornhecker, M., Martinez, A. J., & Nagoshi, J. L. (2016). Moving away from a cultural deficit to a holistic perspective: Traditional gender role values, academic attitudes, and educational goals for Mexican descent adolescents. *Journal of Counseling Psychology*, *63*, 307–318. doi: 10.1037/cou0000133.

Plant, E. A., Goplen, J., & Kunstman, J. W. (2011). Selective responses to threat: The roles of race and gender in decisions to shoot. *Personality and Social Psychology Bulletin, 37*, 1274–1281. doi: 10.1177/0146167211408617.

Pleck, J. H. (1995). The gender role strain paradigm: An update. In R. F. Levant & W. S. Pollack (Eds.), *A new psychology of men* (pp. 11–32). New York: Basic Books.

Pomerville, A., Burrage, R. L., & Gone, J. P. (2016). Empirical findings from psychotherapy research with indigenous populations: A systematic review. *Journal of Consulting and Clinical Psychology, 84*, 1023–1038. doi: 10.1037/ccp0000150.

Ponterotto, J. G. (2013). Qualitative research in multicultural psychology: Philosophical underpinnings, popular approaches, and ethical considerations. *Qualitative Psychology, 1*, 19–32. doi: 10.1037/2326-3598.1.S.19.

Ponterotto, J. G., Utsey, S. O., & Pedersen, P. B. (2006). *Preventing prejudice: A guide for counselors, educators, and parents* (2nd ed.). Thousand Oaks, CA: Sage.

Poon, O., Squire, D., Kodama, C., Byrd, A., & Chan, J. (2016). A critical review of the model minority myth in selected literature on Asian Americans and Pacific Islanders in higher education. *Review of Educational Research, 86*, 469–502. doi: 10.3102/0034654315612205.

Portes, A., & Rumbaut, R. G. (1996). *Immigrant America: A portrait.* Berkeley: University of California Press.

Poston, W. S. C. (1990). The biracial identity development model: A needed addition. *Journal of Counseling and Development, 69*, 152–155. doi: 10.1002/j.1556-6676.1990.tb01477.x.

Powell, L. M., Wada, R., Krauss, R. C., & Wang, Y. (2012). Ethnic disparities in adolescent body mass index in the United States: The role of parental socioeconomic status and economic contextual factors. *Social Science & Medicine, 75*, 469–476. doi: 10.1016/j.socscimed.2012.03.019.

Quinn, K., & Dickson-Gomez, J. (2015). Homonegativity, religiosity, and the intersecting identities of young Black men who have sex with men. *Aids and Behavior, 20*, 51–64. doi: 10.1007/s10461-015-1200-1.

Ramirez, H. (2011). Masculinity in the workplace: The case of Mexican immigrant gardeners. *Men and Masculinities, 14*, 97–116. doi: 10.1177/1097184X10363993.

Ravenell, J. E., Johnson, W. E., & Whitaker, E. E. (2006). African American men's perceptions of health: A focus group study. *Journal of the National Medical Association, 98*, 544–550.

Reed, T. D., & Neville, H. A. (2014). The influence of religiosity and spirituality on psychological well-being among Black women. *Journal of Black Psychology, 40*, 384–401. doi: 10.1177/0095798413490956.

Regents of the University of California v. Bakke 438 U.S. 265 (1978).

Reser, J. P., & Swim, J. K. (2011). Adapting to and coping with the threat and impacts of climate change. *American Psychologist, 66*, 277–289. doi: 10.1037/a0023412.

Richardson, K. (1998). *The origins of human potential: Evolution, development, and psychology.* London: Routledge.

Richeson, J. A., & Nussbaum, R. J. (2004). The impact of multiculturalism versus color-blindness on racial bias. *Journal of Experimental Social Psychology, 40*, 417–423. doi: 10.1016/j.jesp. 2003.09.002.

Richeson, J. A., & Shelton, J. N. (2003). When prejudice does not pay: Effects of interracial contact on executive function. *Psychological Science, 14*, 287–290. doi: 10.1111/1467-9280.03437.

Richeson, J. A., & Shelton, J. N. (2007). Negotiating interracial interactions: Costs, consequences, and possibilities. *Current Directions in Psychological Science, 16*, 316–320. 10.1111/j.1467-8721.2007.00528.x.

Richeson, J. A., & Sommers, S. R. (2016). Toward a social psychology of race and race relations for the twenty-first century. *Annual Review of Psychology, 67*, 439–463. doi: 10.1146/annurev-psych-010213-115115.

Ritschel, L. A., Tone, E. B., Schoemann, A. M. & Lim, N. E. (2015). Psychometric properties of the Difficulties in Emotion Regulation Scale across demographic groups. *Psychological Assessment, 27*, 944–954. doi: 10.1037/pas0000099.

Rivas-Drake, D., Seaton, E. K., Markstrom, C., Quintana, S., Syed, M., Lee, R. M., … Ethnic and Racial Identity in the 21st Century Study Group. (2014). Ethnic and racial identity in adolescence: Implications for psychosocial, academic, and health outcomes. *Child Development, 85,* 40–57. doi: 10.1111/cdev.12200.

Ro, A., & Bostean, G. (2015). Duration of U.S. stay and body mass index among Latino and Asian immigrants: A test of theoretical pathways. *Social Science & Medicine, 144,* 39–47. doi: 10.1016/j.socscimed.2015.09.001.

Rodríguez, M. D., Davis, M. R., Rodríguez, J., & Bates, S. C. (2006). Observed parenting practices of first-generation Latino families. *Journal of Community Psychology, 34,* 133–148. doi: 10.1002/jcop. 20088.

Roediger, D. R. (1999). Is there a healthy White personality? *The Counseling Psychologist, 27,* 239–244. doi: 10.1177/0011000099272003.

Rogers, B. K., Sperry, H. A., & Levant, R. F. (2015). Masculinities among African American men: An intersectional perspective. *Psychology of Men & Masculinity, 16,* 416–425. doi: 10.1037/a0039082.

Rogers-Sirin, L. (2013). Segmented assimilation and attitudes toward psychotherapy: A moderated mediation analysis. *Journal of Counseling Psychology, 60,* 329–339. doi: 10.1037/a0032453.

Rosas, L. G., Sanchez-Vaznaugh, E. V., & Sanchez, B. N. (2015). Nativity, U.S. length of residence, and BMI among diverse Asian American ethnic groups. *Journal of Immigrant and Minority Health, 17,* 1496–1503. doi: 10.1007/s10903-014-0096-6.

Rose, T., Joe, S., Shields, J., & Caldwell, C. H. (2014). Social integration and the mental health of Black adolescents. *Child Development, 85,* 1003–1018. doi: 10.1111/cdev.12182.

Rosenbloom, S. R., & Way, N. (2004). Experiences of discrimination among African American, Asian American, and Latino adolescents in an urban high school. *Youth & Society, 35,* 420–451. doi: 10.1177/0044118X03261479.

Rosenthal, L., & Lobel, M. (2016). Stereotypes of Black American women related to sexuality and motherhood. *Psychology of Women Quarterly, 40,* 414–427. doi: 10.1177/0361684315627459.

Rosner, R. I. (2005). Psychotherapy research and the National Institute of Mental Health, 1948–1980. In W. E. Pickren & S. F. Schneider (Eds.), *Psychology and the National Institute of Mental Health: A historical analysis of science, practice, and policy* (pp. 113–150). Washington, DC: American Psychological Association. doi: 10.1037/10931-004.

Rouse, L. M. (2016). American Indians, Alaska Natives, and the psychology of men and masculinity. In Y. J. Wong & S. R. Wester (Eds.), *APA Handbook of Men and Masculinities,* (pp. 319–337). Washington, DC: American Psychological Association. doi: 10.1037/14594-015.

Rubin, K. H., & Chung, O. B. (Eds.). (2006). *Parenting beliefs, behaviors, and parent–child relations.* New York, NY: Psychology Press.

Rumbaut, R. G. (1995). Vietnamese, Laotian, and Cambodian Americans. In P. G. Min (Ed.), *Asian Americans: Contemporary trends and issues* (pp. 232–270). Thousand Oaks, CA: Sage.

Rushton, J. P. (1995a). *Race, evolution & behavior.* New Brunswick, NJ: Transaction.

Rushton, J. P. (1995b). *Race, evolution, and man.* Princeton, NJ: Princeton University Press.

Russell, S. L., Katz, R. V., Wang, M. Q., Lee, R., Green, B. L., Kressin, N. R., & Claudio, C. (2011). Belief in AIDS origin conspiracy theory and willingness to participate in biomedical research studies: Findings in Whites, Blacks and Hispanics in seven cities across two surveys. *HIV Clinical Trials, 12,* 37–47. doi: 10.1310/hct1201-37.

Ryan, C. L., & Bauman, K. (2016, March*). Educational attainment in the United States: 2015.* Washington, DC: U.S. Census Bureau. www.census.gov/content/dam/Census/library/publications/2016/demo/p20-578.pdf.

Ryder, A. G., Jian, Y., Zhu, X., Yao, S., Yi, J., Heine, S. J., & Bagby, M. R. (2008). The cultural shaping of depression: Somatic symptoms of China, psychological symptoms in North America. *Journal of Abnormal Psychology, 117,* 300–313. doi: 10.1037/0021-843X.117.2.300.

Sabogal, F., Marin, G., Otero-Sabogal, R., Marin, B. V., & Perez-Stable, E. J. (1987). Hispanic familism and acculturation: What changes and what doesn't? *Hispanic Journal of Behavioral Sciences*, *9*, 397–412. doi: 10.1177/07399863870094003.

Sack, W. H., & Clarke, G. N. (1996). Multiple forms of stress in Cambodian adolescent refugees. *Child Development*, *67*, 107–116. doi: 10.1111/j.1467-8624.1996.tb01722.x.

Salas-Wright, C., Vaughn, M. G., Todic, J., Cordova, D., & Perron, B. E. (2015). Trends in the disapproval and use of marijuana among adolescents and young adults in the United States: 2002–2013. *The American Journal of Drug and Alcohol Abuse*, *41*, 392–404. doi: 10.3109/00952 990.2015.1049493.

Sanchez, D., Whittaker, T. A., Hamilton, E., & Zayas, L. H. (2016). Perceived discrimination and sexual precursor behaviors in Mexican American preadolescent girls: The role of psychological distress, sexual attitudes, and marianismo believes. *Cultural Diversity and Ethnic Minority Psychology*, *22*, 395–407. doi: 10.1037/cdp0000066.

Sanchez-Hucles, J. V., & Davis, D. D. (2010). Women and women of color in leadership: Complexity, identity, and intersectionality. *American Psychologist*, *65*, 171–181. doi: 10.1037/a0017459.

Saxbe, D. E. (2008). A field (researcher's) guide to cortisol: Tracking HPA axis functioning in everyday life. *Health Psychology Review*, *3*, 163–190. doi: 10.1080/17437190802530812.

Schmader, T., & Johns, M. (2003). Converging evidence that stereotype threat reduces working memory capacity. *Journal of Personality and Social Psychology*, *85*, 440–452. doi: 10.1037/0022-3514.85.3.440.

Schmader, T., Block, K., & Lickel, B. (2015). Social identity threat in response to stereotypic film portrayals: Effects on self-conscious emotion and implicit ingroup attitudes. *Journal of Social Issues*, *71*, 54–72. doi: 10.1111/josi.12096.

Schug, J., Alt, N. P., & Klauer, K. C. (2015). Gendered race prototypes: Evidence for the non-prototypicality of Asian men and Black women. *Journal of Experimental Social Psychology*, *56*, 121–125. doi: 10.1016/j.jesp. 2014.09.012.

Schwartz, S. J., Lilienfeld, S. O., Meca, A., & Sauvigne, K. C. (2016). The role of neuroscience within psychology: A call for inclusiveness over exclusiveness. *American Psychologist*, *71*, 52–70. doi: 10.1037/a0039678.

Scollon, C. N., Diener, E., Oishi, S., & Biswas-Diener, R. (2004). Emotions across cultures and methods. *Journal of Cross-Cultural Psychology*, *35*, 304–326. doi: 10.1177/0022022104264124.

Sears, D. O. (1988). Symbolic racism. In P. A. Katz & D. A. Taylor (Eds.), *Eliminating racism: Profiles in controversy* (pp. 53–84). New York: Plenum.

Sellers, R. M., & Shelton, J. N. (2003). The role of racial identity in perceived racial discrimination. *Journal of Personality and Social Psychology*, *84*, 1079–1092. doi: 10.1037/0022-3514.84.5.1079.

Sellers, R. M., Rowley, S. A. J., Chavous, T. M., Shelton, J. N., & Smith, M. A. (1997). Multidimensional inventory of Black identity: A preliminary investigation of reliability and construct validity. *Journal of Personality and Social Psychology*, *73*, 805–815. doi: 10.1037/0022-3514.73.4.805.

Sellers, R. M., Smith, M. A., Shelton, J. N., Rowley, S. A. J., & Chavous, T. M. (1998). Multi-dimensional model of racial identity: A reconceptualization of African American racial identity. *Personality and Social Psychology Review*, *2*, 18–39. doi: 10.1207/s15327957pspr0201_2.

Severo, R. (May 2, 2005). Kenneth Clark, who fought segregation, dies. *New York Times*. www.nytimes.com/2005/05/02/nyregion/kenneth-clark-whofought-segregation-dies.html.

Shen, Y., Kim, S. Y., Wang, Y., & Chao, R. K. (2014). Language brokering and adjustment among Chinese and Korean American adolescents: A moderated mediation model of perceived maternal sacrifice, respect for the mother, and mother–child open communication. *Asian American Journal of Psychology*, *5*, 86–95. doi: 10.1037/a0035203.

Sheth, M. (1995). Asian Indian Americans. In P. G. Min (Ed.), *Asian Americans: Contemporary trends and issues* (pp. 169–198). Thousand Oaks, CA: Sage.

Shih, M., Ambady, N., Richeson, J. A., Fujita, K., & Gray, H. M. (2002). Stereotype perform-ance boosts: The impact of self-relevance and the manner of stereotype activation. *Journal of Personality and Social Psychology*, *83*, 638–647. doi: 10.1037/0022-3514.83.3.638.

Shih, M., Pittinsky, T. L., & Ambady, N. (1999). Stereotype susceptibility: Identity salience and shifts in quantitative performance. *Psychological Science*, *10*, 80–83. doi: 10.1111/1467-9280.00111.

Shih, M., Pittinsky, T. L., & Trahan, A. (2006). Domain-specific effects of stereotypes on per-formance. *Self and Identity*, *5*, 1–14. doi: 10.1080/15298860500338534.

Shweder, R. A. (1990). Cultural psychology: What is it? In J. W. Stigler, R. A. Shweder, & G. Herdt (Eds.), *Cultural psychology: Essays on comparative human development* (pp. 1–44). New York: Cambridge University Press. doi: 10.1017/CBO9781139173728.002.

Sidanius, J., & Pratto, F. (1999). *Social dominance: An intergroup theory of social hierarchy and oppres-sion*. Cambridge, UK: Cambridge University Press.

Simon, C. E., Crowther, M., & Higgerson, H. (2007). The stage-specific role of spirituality among African American Christian women throughout the breast cancer experience. *Cultural Diversity and Ethnic Minority Psychology*, *13*, 26–34. doi: 10.1037/1099-9809.13.1.26.

Simons, L. G., Simons, R. L., & Su, X. (2013). Consequences of corporal punishment among African Americans: The importance of context and outcome. *Journal of Youth and Adolescence*, *42*, 1273–1285. doi: 10.1007/s10964-012-9853-9.

Siy, J. O., & Cheryan, S. (2016). Prejudice masquerading as praise: The negative echo of positive ster-eotypes. *Personality and Social Psychology Bulletin*, *42*, 941–954. doi: 10.1177/0146167216649605.

Smalls, C., White, R., Chavous, T., & Sellers, R. (2007). Racial ideological beliefs and racial dis-crimination experiences as predictors of academic engagement among African American adoles-cents. *Journal of Black Psychology*, *33*, 299–330. doi: 10.1177/0095798407302541.

Smallwood, S. W., Spencer, S. M., Ingram, L. A., Thrasher, J. F., & Thompson-Robinson, M. V. (2017). Homonegativity among African American men who have sex with men in the deep south. *Journal of Homosexuality*, *64*, 45–60. doi: 10.1080/00918369.2016.1172869.

Smedley, A., & Smedley, B. D. (2005). Race as biology is fiction, racism as a social problem is real: Anthropological and historical perspectives on the social construction of race. *American Psychologist*, *60*, 16–26. doi: 10.1037/0003-066X.60.1.16.

Smith, S. J. (2015). Risky sexual behavior among young adult Latinas: are acculturation and religi-osity protective? *The Journal of Sex Research*, *52*, 43–54. doi: 10.1080/00224499.2013.821443.

Smith, T. B., & Trimble, J. E. (2016). *Foundations of multicultural psychology: Research to inform effective practice*. Washington, DC: American Psychological Association. doi: 10.1037/14733-000.

Spencer, S. J., Logel, C., & Davies, P. G. (2016). Stereotype threat. *Annual Review of Psychology*, *67*, 415–437. doi: 10.1146/annurev-psych-073115-103235.

Spickard, P. (2007). *Almost all aliens*. New York: Routledge.

Spillane, N. S., & Smith, G. T. (2007). A theory of reservation-dwelling American Indian alcohol use risk. *Psychological Bulletin*, *133*, 395–418. doi: 10.1037/0033-2909.133.3.395.

Spitzer, R. L., Endicott, J., & Robins, E. (1975). Clinical criteria for psychiatric diagnosis and DSM-III. *The American Journal of Psychiatry*, *132*, 1187–1192. doi: 10.1176/ajp. 132.11.1187.

Spitzer, R. L., Williams, J. B. W., Gibbon, M., & First, M. B. (1990). *Structured clinical interview for DSM-III-R – Patient edition*. Washington, DC: American Psychiatric Association.

Stafford, M., Newbold, B. K., & Ross, N. A. (2011). Psychological distress among immigrants and visible minorities in Canada: A contextual analysis. International *Journal of Social Psychiatry*, *57*, 428–441. doi: 10.1177/0020764010365407.

Steele, C. M. (1997). A threat in the air: How stereotypes shape the intellectual identities and per-formance of women and African Americans. *American Psychologist*, *52*, 613–629. doi: 10.1037/0003-066X.52.6.613.

Steele, C. M., & Aronson, J. (1995). Stereotype threat and the intellectual test performance of African Americans. *Journal of Personality and Social Psychology*, *69*, 797–811. doi: 10.1037/0022-3514.69.5.797.

Steidel, A. G. L., & Contreras, J. M. (2003). A new familism scale for use with Latino populations. *Hispanic Journal of Behavioral Sciences, 25*, 312–330. doi: 10.1177/0739986303256912.

Stein, G. L., Cupito, A. M., Mendez, J. L., Prandoni, J., Huq, N., & Westerberg, D. (2014). Familism through a developmental lens. *Journal of Latina/o Psychology, 2*, 224–250. doi: 10.1037/lat0000025.

Sternberg, R. J., Grigorenko, E. L., & Kidd, K. K. (2005). Intelligence, race, and genetics. *American Psychologist, 60*, 46–59. doi: 10.1037/0003-066x.60.1.46.

Stone, R. A. T., Whitbeck, L. B., Chen, X., Johnson, K., & Olson, D. M. (2006). Traditional practices, traditional spirituality, and alcohol cessation among American Indians. *Journal of Studies on Alcohol, 67*, 236–244. doi: 10.15288/jsa.2006.67.236.

Sue, D. W. (2001). Multidimensional facets of cultural competence. *The Counseling Psychologist, 29*, 790–821. doi: 10.1177/0011000001296002.

Sue, D. W. (2004). Whiteness and ethnocentric monoculturalism: Making the "invisible" visible. *American Psychologist, 59*, 761–769. doi: 10.1037/0003-066X.59.8.761.

Sue, D. W., Arredondo, P., & McDavis, R. J. (1992). Multicultural counseling competencies and standards: A call to the profession. *Journal of Counseling & Development, 70*, 477–486. doi: 10.1002/j.1556-6676.1992.tb01642.x.

Sue, D. W., Bingham, R. P., Porché-Burke, L., & Vasquez, M. (1999). The diversification of psychology: A multicultural revolution. *American Psychologist, 54*, 1061–1069. doi: 10.1037/0003-066X.54.12.1061.

Sue, D. W., Capodilupo, C. M., Torino, G. C., Bucceri, J. M., Holder, A. M. B., Nadal, K. L., & Esquilin, M. (2007). Racial microaggressions in everyday life: Implications for clinical practice. *American Psychologist, 62*, 271–286. doi: 10.1037/0003-066X.62.4.271.

Sue, S. (1977). Community mental health services to minority groups: Some optimism, some pessimism. *American Psychologist, 32*, 616–624. doi: 10.1037/0003-066X.32.8.616.

Sue, S. (1999). Science, ethnicity, and bias: Where have we gone wrong? *American Psychologist, 54*, 1070–1077. doi: 10.1037/0003-066X.54.12.1070.

Sue, S., & Okazaki, S. (1990). Asian-American educational achievements: A phenomenon in search of an explanation. *American Psychologist, 45*, 913–920. doi: 10.1037/0003-066X.45.8.913.

Sue, S., Cheng, J. K. Y., Saad, C. S., & Chu, J. P. (2012). Asian American mental health: A call to action. *American Psychologist, 67*, 532–544. doi: 10.1037/a0028900.

Sue, S., Fujino, D. C., Hu, L., Takeuchi, D. T., & Zane, N. W. S. (1991). Community mental health services for ethnic minority groups: A test of the cultural responsiveness hypothesis. *Journal of Consulting and Clinical Psychology, 59*, 533–540. doi: 10.1037/0022-006X.59.4.533.

Sun, S., Hoyt, W. T., Brockberg, D., Lam, J., & Tiwari, D. (2016). Acculturation and enculturation as predictors of psychological help-seeking attitudes (HSAs) among racial and ethnic minorities: A meta-analytic investigation. *Journal of Counseling Psychology, 63*, 617–632. doi: 10.1037/cou0000172.

Sutton, C. T., & Broken Nose, M. A. (2005). American Indian families: An overview. In M. McGoldrick, J. Giordano, & N. Garcia-Preto (Eds.), *Ethnicity and family therapy* (3rd ed., pp. 43–54). New York: Guilford.

Suzuki, B. H. (2002). Revisiting the model minority stereotype: Implications for student affairs practice and higher education. *New Directions for Student Services, 97*, 21–32. doi: 10.1002/ss.36.

Suzuki, L. A., & Quizon, C. (2012). Interdisciplinarity in qualitative research with ethnocultural populations. In D. K. Nagata, L. Kohn-Wood, & L. A. Suzuki (Eds.), *Qualitative strategies for ethnocultural research* (pp. 21–40). Washington, DC: American Psychological Association. doi: 10.1037/13742-002.

Tajfel, H. (1981). *Human groups and social categories: Studies in social psychology.* Cambridge, UK: Cambridge University Press.

Tajfel, H., & Turner, J. C. (1986). The social identity theory of inter-group behavior. In S. Worchel & L. W. Austin (Eds.), *Psychology of intergroup relations* (pp. 7–24.). Chicago: Nelson-Hall.

Takaki, R. (1993). *A different mirror: A history of multicultural America.* New York: Little, Brown.

Tao, K. W., Owen, J., Pace, B. T., & Imel, Z. E. (2015). A metaanalysis of multicultural competencies and psychotherapy process and outcome. *Journal of Counseling Psychology, 62,* 337–350. doi: 10.1037/cou0000086.

Taylor, G. J. (1984). Alexithymia: Concept, measurement, and implications for treatment. *American Journal of Psychiatry, 141,* 725–732. doi: 10.1176/ajp. 141.6.725.

Taylor, S. (2016). Disorder-specific genetic factors in obsessive-compulsive disorder: A comprehensive meta-analysis. *American Journal of Medical Genetics Part B: Neuropsychiatric Genetics, 171,* 325–332. doi: 10.1002/ajmg.b.32407.

Taylor, S. E., Sherman, D. K. Kim, H. S., Jarcho, J., Takagi, K., & Dunagan, M. S. (2004). Culture and social support: Who seeks it and why? *Journal of Personality and Social Psychology, 87,* 354–362. doi: 10.1037/0022-3514.87.3.354.

Telzer, E. H. (2010). Expanding the acculturation gap-distress model: An integrative review of research. *Human Development, 53,* 313–340. doi: 10.1159/000322476.

Telzer, E. H., Masten, C. L., Berkman, E. T., Lieberman, M. D., & Fuligni, A. J. (2010). Gaining while giving: An fMRI study of the rewards of family assistance among White and Latino youth. *Social Neuroscience, 5,* 508–518. doi: 10.1080/17470911003687913.

Telzer, E. H., Fuligni, A. J., Lieberman, M. D., & Galván, A. (2013). Meaningful family relationships: Neurocognitive buffers of adolescent risk taking. *Journal of Cognitive Neuroscience, 25,* 374–387. doi: 10.1162/jocn_a_00331.

Tenenbaum, H. R., & Ruck, M. D. (2007). Are teachers' expectations different for racial minority than for European American students? A meta-analysis. *Journal of educational psychology, 99,* 253–273. doi: 10.1037/0022-0663.99.2.253.

Thompson, N. L., Hare, D., Sempier, T. T., & Grace, C. (2008). The development of a curriculum toolkit with American Indian and Alaska Native communities. *Early Childhood Education Journal, 35,* 397–404. doi: 10.1007/s10643-007-0222-3.

Tong, Y. (2013). Acculturation, gender disparity, and the sexual behavior of Asian American youth. *Journal of Sex Research, 50,* 560–573. doi: 10.1080/00224499.2012.668976.

Torres, L., & Ong, A. D. (2010). A daily diary investigation of Latino ethnic identity, discrimination, and depression. *Cultural Diversity and Ethnic Minority Psychology, 16,* 561–568. doi: 10.1037/a0020652.

Torres, L., & Taknint, J. T. (2015). Ethnic microaggressions, traumatic stress symptoms, and Latino depression: A moderated mediational model. *Journal of Counseling Psychology, 62,* 393–401. doi: 10.1037/cou0000077.

Tran, A. G., Mintert, J. S., & Jew, G. B. (2016). Parental ethnic-racial socialization and social attitudes among ethnic-racial minority and White American emerging adults. *American Journal of Orthopsychiatry, 87,* 347–356. doi: 10.1037/ort0000204.

Tran, A. G., Miyake, E. R., Martinez-Morales, V., & Csizmadia, A. (2016). "What are you?" Multiracial individuals' responses to racial identification inquiries. *Cultural Diversity and Ethnic Minority Psychology, 22,* 26–37. doi: 10.1037/cdp0000031.

Trimble, J. E. (2007). Prolegomena for the connotation of construct use in the measurement of ethnic and racial identity. *Journal of Counseling Psychology, 54,* 247–258. doi: 10.1037/0022-0167.54.3.247.

Trimble, J. E., & Thurman, P. J. (2002). Ethnocultural considerations and strategies for providing counseling services to Native American Indians. In P. B. Pedersen, J. G. Draguns, W. J. Lonner, & J. E. Trimble (Eds.), *Counseling across cultures* (5th ed., pp. 53–91). Thousand Oaks, CA: Sage.

Trimble, J. E., Helms, J. E., & Root, M. P. P. (2003). Social and psychological perspectives on ethnic and racial identity. In G. Bernal, J. E. Trimble, A. K. Burlew, & F. T. L. Leong (Eds.), *Handbook of racial and ethnic minority psychology* (pp. 239–275). Thousand Oaks, CA: Sage.

Troiden, R. R. (1989). The formation of homosexual identities. *Journal of Homosexuality, 17,* 43–73. doi: 10.1300/J082v17n01_02.

Tropp, L. R., & Pettigrew, T. F. (2005). Relationships between intergroup contact and prejudice among minority and majority status groups. *Psychological Science*, *16*, 951–957. doi: 10.1111/j.1467-9280.2005.01643.x.

Trujillo, A. (2000). Psychotherapy with Native Americans: A view into the role of religion and spirituality. In P. S. Richards & A. E. Bergin (Eds.), *Handbook of psychotherapy and religious diversity* (pp. 445–466). Washington, DC: American Psychological Association. doi: 10.1037/10347-018.

Tsai, J. L., Chentsova-Dutton, Y., & Wong, Y. (2002). Why and how we should study ethnic identity, acculturation, and cultural orientation. In G. C. N. Hall & S. Okazaki (Eds.), *Asian American psychology: The science of lives in context* (pp. 41–65). Washington, DC: American Psychological Association. doi: 10.1037/10473-002.

Tsai, K. M., & Fuligni, A. J. (2012). Change in ethnic identity across the college transition. *Developmental Psychology*, *48*, 56–64. doi: 10.1037/a0025678.

Tuan, M. (1998). *Forever foreigners or honorary Whites?: The Asian ethnic experience today*. Piscataway, NJ: Rutgers University Press.

Tucker, R. P., Wingate, L. R., & O'Keefe, V. M. (2016). Historical loss thinking and symptoms of depression are influenced by ethnic experience in American Indian college students. *Cultural Diversity and Ethnic Minority Psychology*, *22*, 350–358. doi: 10.1037/cdp0000055.

Tukachinsky, R., Mastro, D., & Yarchi, M. (2015). Documenting portrayals of race/ethnicity on primetime television over a 20-year span and their association with national-level racial/ethnic attitudes. *Journal of Social Issues*, *71*, 17–38. doi: 10.1111/josi.12094.

Umaña-Taylor, A. J., Quintana, S. M., Lee, R. M., Cross, W. E., Rivas-Drake, D., Schwartz, S. J., … Seaton, E. (2014). Ethnic and racial identity during adolescence and into young adulthood: An integrated conceptualization. *Child Development*, *85*, 21–39. doi: 10.1111/cdev.12196.

Umaña-Taylor, A. J., Wong, J. J., Gonzales, N. A., & Dumka, L. E. (2012). Ethnic identity and gender as moderators of the association between discrimination and academic adjustment among Mexican-origin adolescents. *Journal of Adolescence*, *35*, 773–786. doi: 10.1016/j.adolescence.2011.11.003.

Unsworth, S. (2017). Quantity and quality of language input in bilingual language development. In E. Nicoladis & S. Montanari (Eds.), *Bilingualism across the lifespan: Factors moderating language proficiency* (pp. 103–121). Washington, DC: American Psychological Association. doi: 10.1037/14939-007.

Unzueta, M. M., & Binning, K. R. (2012). Diversity is in the eye of the beholder: How concern for the in-group affects perceptions of racial diversity. *Personality and Social Psychology Bulletin*, *38*, 26–38. doi: 10.1177/0146167211418528.

U.S. Bureau of the Census (2013, February). *Poverty rates for selected detailed race and Hispanic groups by state and place: 2007–2011*. www.census.gov/prod/2013pubs/acsbr11-17.pdf.

U.S. Bureau of the Census (2015, March 3). *New census bureau report analyzes U.S. population projections*. www.census.gov/newsroom/press-releases/2015/cb15-tps16.html.

U.S. Bureau of the Census (2016, October 12). *FFF: Hispanic Heritage Month 2016*. www.census.gov/newsroom/facts-for-features/2016/cb16-ff16.html.

U.S. Bureau of the Census (2016, November 2). *FFF: American Indian and Alaska Native Heritage Month: November 2016*. www.census.gov/newsroom/facts-for-features/2016/cb16-ff22.html.

U.S. Bureau of the Census (2017, January 10). *FFF: National African-American History Month: February 2017*. www.census.gov/newsroom/facts-for-features/2017/cb17-ff01.html.

U.S. Bureau of the Census (2017, March 14). *FFF: Asian-American and Pacific Islander Heritage Month: May 2017*. www.census.gov/newsroom/facts-for-features/2017/cb17-ff07.html.

U.S. Cancer Statistics Working Group. (2013). *United States cancer statistics: 1999–2010 incidence and mortality web-based report*. Atlanta, GA: U.S. Department of Health and Human Services, Centers for Disease Control and Prevention and National Cancer Institute. www.cdc.gov/uscs.

Van de Vijver, F. J. R., & Leung, K. (2000). Methodological issues in research on culture. *Journal of Cross-Cultural Psychology*, *31*, 33–51. doi: 10.1177/0022022100031001004.

van Widenfelt, B. M., Treffers, P. D. A., de Beurs, E., Siebelink, B. M., & Koudijs, E. (2005). Translation and cross-cultural adaptation of assessment instruments used in psychological research with children and families. *Clinical Child and Family Psychology Review, 8*, 135–147. doi: 10.1007/s10567-005-4752-1.

Velazquez, E., Corona, R., Easter, R., Barinas, J., Elshaer, L., & Halfond, R. W. (2017). Cultural values, mother–adolescent discussions about sex, and Latina/o adolescents' condom use attitudes and intentions. *Journal of Latina/o Psychology, 5*, 213–226. doi: 10.1037/lat0000075.

Vertovec, S. (1999). Conceiving and research transnationalism. *Ethnic and Racial Studies, 22*, 447–462. doi: 10.1080/0141998799329558.

Vorauer, J. D., & Sasaki, S. J. (2011). In the worst rather than the best of times: Effects of salient intergroup ideology in threatening intergroup interactions. *Journal of Personality and Social Psychology, 101*, 307–320. doi: 10.1037/a0023152.

Vygotsky, L. S. (1978). *Mind in society: The development of higher psychological processes.* Cambridge, MA: Harvard University Press.

Walker, J. J., & Longmire-Avital, B. (2013). The impact of religious faith and internalized homonegativity on resiliency for Black lesbian, gay, and bisexual emerging adults. *Developmental Psychology, 49*, 1723–1731. doi: 10.1037/a0031059.

Walker, J. N. J., Longmire-Avital, B., & Golub, S. (2015). Racial and sexual identities as potential buffers to risky sexual behavior for Black gay and bisexual emerging adult men. *Health Psychology, 34*, 841–846. doi: 10.1037/hea0000187.

Wall, T. L., Carr, L. G., & Ehlers, C. L. (2003). Protective association of genetic variation in alcohol dehydrogenase with alcohol dependence in Native American mission Indians. *The American Journal of Psychiatry, 160*, 41–46. doi: 10.1176/appi.ajp. 160.1.41.

Wallace, P. M., Pomery, E. A., Latimer, A. E., Martinez, J. L., & Salovey, P. (2010). A review of acculturation measures and their utility in studies promoting Latino health. *Hispanic Journal of Behavioral Sciences, 32*, 37–54. doi: 10.1177/0739986309352341.

Walls, M. L., Whitbeck, L., & Armenta, B. (2016). A cautionary tale: Examining the interplay of culturally specific risk and resilience factors in indigenous communities. *Clinical Psychological Science, 4*, 732–743. doi: 10.1177/2167702616645795.

Walton, G. M., & Cohen, G. L. (2007). A question of belonging: Race, social fit, and achievement. *Journal of Personality and Social Psychology, 92*, 82–96. doi: 10.1037/0022-3514.92.1.82.

Wang, V. O., & Sue, S. (2005). In the eye of the storm: Race and genomics in research and practice. *American Psychologist, 60*, 37–45. doi: 10.1037/0003-066X.60.1.37.

Warne, D., & Lajimodiere, D. (2015). American Indian health disparities: Psychosocial influences. *Social and Personality Psychology Compass, 9*, 567–579. doi: 10.1111/spc3.12198.

Waters, M. C., Kasinitz, P., & Asad, A. L. (2014). Immigrants and African Americans. *Annual Review of Sociology, 40*, 369–390. doi: 10.1146/annurev-soc-071811-145449.

Weber, E. U., & Stern, P. C. (2011). Public understanding of climate change in the United States. *American Psychologist, 66*, 315–328. doi: 10.1037/a0023253.

Wexler, L. (2014). Looking across three generations of Alaska Natives to explore how culture fosters indigenous resilience. *Transcultural Psychiatry, 51*, 73–92. doi: 10.1177/1363461513497417.

Whaley, A. L. (2001). Cultural mistrust and mental health services for African Americans: A review and meta-analysis. *The Counseling Psychologist, 29*, 513–531. doi: 10.1177/0011000001294003.

Whaley, A. L. (2003). Cognitive-cultural model of identity and violence prevention for African American youth. *Genetic, Social & General Psychology Monographs, 129*, 101–151.

Whitfield, K. E., & McClearn, G. (2005). Genes, environment, and race: Quantitative genetic approaches. *American Psychologist, 60*, 104–114. doi: 10.1037/0003-066X.60.1.104.

Wilkinson, C. (2005). *Blood struggle: The rise of modern Indian nations.* New York: Norton.

Williams, C. L., & Berry, J. W. (1991). Primary prevention of acculturative stress among refugees: Application of psychological theory and practice. *American Psychologist, 46*, 632–641. doi: 10.1037/0003-066X.46.6.632.

Williams, D. R. (1999). Race, socioeconomic status, and health: The added effects of racism and discrimination. In N. Adler & M. Marmot (Eds.), *Socioeconomic status and health in industrial nations: Social, psychological, and biological pathways: Annals of the New York Academy of Sciences* (Vol. 896, pp. 173–188). New York: New York Academy of Sciences.

Wittig, M. A. (1996). Taking affirmative action in education and employment. *Journal of Social Issues, 52,* 145–160. doi: 10.1111/j.1540-4560.1996.tb01855.x.

Wong, G., Derthick, A. O., David, E. J. R., Saw, A., & Okazaki, S. (2014). The what, the why, and the how: A review of racial microaggressions research in psychology. *Race and Social Problems, 6,* 181–200. doi: 10.1007/s12552-013-9107-9.

Wong, J., & Schwing, A. E. (2014). African American boys' and young men's experiences of racism-related stress. In K. C. Vaughans and W. Spielberg (Eds.), *The psychology of Black boys and adolescents* (pp. 107–121). Santa Barbara, CA: ABC-CLIO, LLC.

Wong, Y. J. Ho, M. H. R., Wang, S. Y, & Miller, I. S. K. (2017). Meta-analyses of the relationship between conformity to masculine norms and mental health-related outcomes. *Journal of Counseling Psychology, 64,* 80–93. doi: 10.1037/cou0000176.

Wong, Y. J., Kim, B. S. K., Nguyen, C. P., Cheng, J. K. Y., & Saw, A. (2014). The Interpersonal Shame Inventory for Asian Americans: Scale development and psychometric properties. *Journal of Counseling Psychology, 61,* 119–132. doi: 10.1037/a0034681.

Wong, Y. J., Nguyen, C. P., Wang, S., Chen, W., Steinfeldt, J. A., & Kim, B. S. K. (2012). A latent profile analysis of Asian American men's and women's adherence to cultural values. *Cultural Diversity and Ethnic Minority Psychology, 18,* 258–267. doi: 10.1037/a0028423.

Wong, Y. J., Owen, J., Tran, K. K., Collins, D. L., & Higgins, C. E. (2012). Asian American male college students' perceptions of people's stereotypes about Asian American men. *Psychology of Men and Masculinity, 13,* 75–88. doi: 10.1037/a0022800.

Wood, C. A., Helms, H. M., Supple, A. J., & Perlman, D. (2015). Gender-typed attributes and marital satisfaction among Mexican immigrant couples: A latent profile approach. *Journal of Family Psychology, 29,* 321–330. doi: 10.1037/fam0000077.

Woodcock, A., Hernandez, P. R., Estrada, M., & Schultz, P. (2012). The consequences of chronic stereotype threat: Domain disidentification and abandonment. *Journal of Personality and Social Psychology, 103,* 635–646. doi: 10.1037/a0029120.

Worsley, S. M. (2010). *Audience, agency and identity in Black popular culture.* New York: Routledge.

Wyer, N. A., Sherman, J. W., & Stroessner, S. J. (1998). The spontaneous suppression of racial stereotypes. *Social Cognition, 16,* 340–352. doi: 10.1521/soco.1998.16.3.340.

Yali, A. M., & Revenson, T. A. (2004). How changes in population demographics will impact health psychology: Incorporating a broader notion of cultural competence into the field. *Health Psychology, 23,* 147–155. doi: 10.1037/0278-6133.23.2.147.

Yan, H., Sgueglia, K., & Walker, K. (2016, December). "Make America White Again": Hate speech and crimes post-election. *CNN.* www.cnn.com/2016/11/10/us/post-election-hate-crimes-and-fears-trnd/.

Yanez, B., McGinty, H. L., Buitrago, D., Ramirez, A. G., & Penedo, F. J. (2016). Cancer outcomes in Hispanics/Latinos in the United States: An integrative review and conceptual model of determinants of health. *Journal of Latina/o Psychology, 2,* 114–129. doi: 10.1037/lat0000055.

Yeh, M., Viladrich, A., Bruning, N., & Roye C. (2009). Determinants of Latina obesity in the United States. *Journal of Transcultural Nursing, 20,* 105–115. doi: 10.1177/1043659608325846.

Yen, S., Robins, C. J, & Lin, N. (2000). A cross-cultural comparison of depressive symptom manifestation: China and the United States. *Journal of Consulting and Clinical Psychology, 68,* 993–999. doi: 10.1037/0022-006X.68.6.993.

Yip, T., Douglass, S., & Sellers, R. M. (2014). Ethnic and racial identity. In F. T. L. Leong, L. Comas-Díaz, G. C. N. Hall, V. C. McLoyd, & J. E. Trimble (Eds.), *APA handbook of multicultural psychology, Vol. 1: Theory and research* (pp. 179–205). Washington, DC: American Psychological Association. doi: 10.1037/14189-010.

Yip, T., Seaton, E. K., & Sellers, R. M. (2006). African American racial identity across the lifespan: Identity status, identity content, and depressive symptoms. *Child Development*, 77, 1504–1517. doi: 10.1111/j.1467-8624.2006.00950.x.

Yoo, H. C., Burrola, K. S., & Steger, M. F. (2010). A preliminary report on a new measure: Internalization of the model minority myth measure (IM-4) and its psychological correlates among Asian American college students. *Journal of Counseling Psychology*, 57, 114–127. doi: 10.1037/a0017871.

Yoon, E., Chang, C. T., Kim, S., Clawson, A., Cleary, S. E., Hansen, M., … Gomes, A. M. (2013). A meta-analysis of acculturation/enculturation and mental health. *Journal Counseling Psychology*, 60, 15–30. doi: 10.1037/a0030652.

Zane, N., & Mak, W. (2003). Major approaches to the measurement of acculturation among ethnic minority populations: A content analysis and an alternative empirical strategy. In K. M. Chun, P. B. Organista, & G. Marin (Eds.), *Acculturation: Advances in theory, measurement, and applied research* (pp. 39–60). Washington, DC: American Psychological Association. doi: 10.1037/10472-005.

Zárate, M. A., Quezada, S. A., Shenberger, J. M., & Lupo, A. K. (2014). Reducing racism and prejudice. In F. T. L. Leong, L. Comas-Díaz, G. C. N. Hall, V. C. McLoyd, & J. Trimble (Eds.), *APA handbook of multicultural psychology, Vol. 2: Applications and training* (pp. 593–606). Washington, DC: American Psychological Association. doi: 10.1037/14187-033.

Zeng, Z. (2011). The myth of the glass ceiling: Evidence from a stock-flow analysis of authority attainment. *Social Science Research*, 40, 312–325. doi: 10.1016/j.ssresearch.2010.06.012.

Zepeda, M., Castro, D. C., & Cronin, S. (2011). Preparing early childhood teachers to work with young dual language learners. *Child Development Perspectives*, 5, 10–14. doi: 10.1111/j.1750-8606.2010.00141.x.

Zheng, Y., Lin, K., Takeuchi, D., Kurasaki, K. S., Wang, Y., & Cheung, F. (1997). An epidemiological study of neurasthenia in Chinese-Americans in Los Angeles. *Comprehensive Psychiatry*, 38, 240–259. doi: 10.1016/s0010-440x(97)90056-0.

Zhou, M., & Kim, S. S. (2006). Community forces, social capital, and educational achievement: The case of supplementary education in the Chinese and Korean immigrant communities. *Harvard Educational Review*, 76, 1–29. doi: 10.17763/haer.76.1.u08t548554882477.

Zimmerman, L., Darnell, D. A., Rhew, I. C., Lee, C. M., & Kaysen, D. (2015). Resilience in community: A social ecological development model for young adult sexual minority women. *American Journal of Community Psychology*, 55, 179–190. doi: 10.1007/s10464-015-9702-6.

Zinn, H. (2003). *A people's history of the United States*. New York: Harper Perennial.

Zinn, H. (2005). *A people's history of the United States*. New York: Harper Perennial.

Zinn, H. (2015). *A people's history of the United States*. New York: Harper Perennial.

Author Index

Lu, A. 173
Lu, W. 78
Luczak, S. E. 71–2
Lui, P. P. 89, 90, 91, 92, 130, 201
Lupo, A. K. 114
Lykes, M. B. 189

Ma, M. 102
McCarty, D. 47
McClearn, G. 69
McConahay, J. B. 108
McCoy, S. K. 115
McDavis, R. J. 138
McDonald, J. D. 102, 211
McEwen, B. S. 80
McFarland, L. A. 53
McGinty, H. L. 80
McGrath, J. J. 79
McGuire, T. G. 125
MacInnis, C. 114
McKay, D. 125, 151
McKyer, L. J. 78
McMahon, T. R. 8
Maddux, W. W. 172
Magan, I. 154
Mahalik, J. R. 152
Maibach, E. W. 9, 12
Maiteny, P. T. 11
Major, B. 11, 115
Majors, R. 153
Mak, W. 19, 56, 180
Malcarne, V. L. 54
Mallinckrodt, B. 195
Manson, S. M. 212
Maramba, G. G. 17
Marcia, J. 32
Marin, B. V. 202
Marin, G. 202
Mark, A. Y. 119
Markon, K. E. 70
Markowitz, J. 76, 151
Markus, H. R. 15, 20, 21, 101
Marsella, A. J. 52
Marti, C. N. 136
Martin, J. K. 27
Martinez, A. J. 196
Martinez, C. R. 8, 9, 11, 135
Martinez, J. L. 56
Martinez-Morales, V. 110
Maruyama, G. 12
Mascher, J. 49
Masten, C. L. 74
Mastro, D. 116
Masuoka, N. 187
Matheson, B. E. 127
Matheson, K. 210
Mathur, V. A. 74
Maton, K. I. 14
Matthews, D. D. 154

Mattis, J. S. 159, 162
Maxwell, K. 219
Maxwell, M. L. 157, 178
Mayhew, M. J. 12
Mays, V. M. 105
Meca, A. 74
Melvin, T. 154
Mendoza-Denton, R. 113, 181
Mendoza-Romero, J. 194
Menozzi, P. 69
Merikangas, K. R.
Mertens, D. M. 60
Meyer, O. L. 132, 136, 139
Mihalic, S. 135
Miller, G. A. 151
Miller, I. S. K. 152
Miller, K. S. 152
Miller, M. J. 133
Miller, S. B. 79
Miller, S. J. 162
Miller-Cotto, D. 95
Min, P. G. 165, 167, 169, 170
Mintert, J. S. 94
Miranda, J. 125, 131
Miyake, E. R. 110
Moffitt, T. E. 69
Mohamed, H. 117
Montoya, H. 18
Moreno, C. L. 56
Moreno, J. 12
Morera, O. F. 47
Morgan Consoli, M. L. 201
Morton-Padovano, C. 199
Moser, R. 81
Moser, S. C. 11
Moses, J. 219
Munniksma, A. 98
Murphy, M. C. 106, 107, 108
Musick, M. A. 160

Nadal, K. L. 110, 176
Nagata, D. K. 60, 61
Nagel, J. 212, 213
Nagoshi, J. L. 196
Najdowski, C. J. 114
Nanda, S. 216
National Center for Health Statistics 80, 101
National Commission for the Protection of Human Subjects of Biomedical and Behavioral Research 47
National Women's History Museum 8
Nelson, J. C. 106
Nettles, S. M. 94
Neville, H. A. 9, 93, 94, 96, 108, 110, 156, 157, 160, 161
Newbold, B. K. 91
Nguyen, A. B. 81, 178
Nguyen, A. D. 5
Nguyen, C. P. 180

Subject Index

Page numbers in **bold** denote figures.